THIRD EDITION

Educational Evaluation

W. JAMES POPHAM
University of California, Los Angeles

ALLYN AND BACON
Boston   London   Toronto   Sydney   Tokyo   Singapore

Editor-in-Chief, Education: Nancy Forsyth
Series Editorial Assistant: Christine Nelson
Production Administrator: Annette Joseph
Production Coordinator: Holly Crawford
Editorial-Production Service: Lynda Griffiths/TKM Productions
Cover Administrator: Linda K. Dickinson
Cover Designer: Suzanne Harbison
Manufacturing Buyer: Megan Cochran

Library of Congress Cataloging-in-Publication Data

Popham, W. James.
    Educational evaluation / W. James Popham. — 3rd ed.
      p.   cm.
    Includes bibliographical references and index.
    ISBN 0-205-14217-6
    1. Educational evaluation. 2. Educational surveys.
  3. Educational consultants. I. Title.
LB2822.75.P66 1992
379.1'54—dc20   92-13806
                                      CIP

Printed in the United States of America

10 9 8 7 6 5 4 3 2 1   97 96 95 94 93 92

Cartoons: Joan Orme

Contents

Preface

This is the third rendition of an introductory textbook that was born in 1975 and given a solid reworking in 1988. In this third edition, an effort was made not only to update key concepts and procedures but also to add two chapters describing new tools to gather evaluative evidence regarding the quality of educational programs.

Chapter Eight describes several techniques that educational evaluators can employ to assess difficult-to-measure variables. When this textbook was first written in the mid-seventies, educational evaluators were concerned almost exclusively with gathering evidence about an educational program's impact on students' test scores (typically in reading and mathematics). Educational evaluators are still called on to gauge an instructional program's effects on traditional outcomes of education such as students' scores on tests. In addition, however, educational evaluators are now asked to measure the effects of far more varied instructional interventions such as a health education program's impact on the sexual behaviors that place students at risk of infection with the AIDS virus or students' use of illegal drugs. To get an accurate fix on such behaviors, assessment techniques other than true-false tests must be employed. Chapter Eight describes several such techniques.

Another information-gathering procedure that has come into its own since the first edition of *Educational Evaluation* was authored is the *focus group interview*. This useful technique is the topic of Chapter Nine. A sufficient introduction to the nuts and bolts of focus group interviews is provided so that readers can decide whether they wish to become more skilled on the design and conduct of focus group interviews.

Educational evaluation as a formal professional specialization is about 25 years old, having been jolted into existence chiefly by the enactment of the Elementary and Secondary Education Act of 1965. After a quarter of a century, a fair number of educational evaluators have paused to take stock of their relatively youthful specialization. An attempt has been made to incorporate a number of these recent observations into this new edition.

I would like to thank the reviewers of this manuscript for their helpful suggestions and comments: Robert B. Ingle, University of Wisconsin – Milwaukee; Catherine McCartney, Bemidji State University; R. David Mustian, North Carolina State University; and Vernon R. Utz, Western Oregon State College.

I hope readers will find this third edition of *Educational Evaluation* to be useful. The book describes an important set of procedures that, if employed judiciously, can help improve the quality of education—that's not such a bad aspiration.

W.J.P.

CHAPTER ONE

Educational Evaluation: A History without Mystery

Once upon a time there was a word. And the word was *evaluation*. And the word was good.

Teachers used the word in a particular way. Later on, other people used the word in a different way. After a while, nobody knew for sure what the word meant. But they all knew it was a good word. *Evaluation* was a thing to be cherished. But what kind of a good thing was it? More important, what kind of a good thing *is* it?

Looking Backward

Evaluation as Student Testing   For centuries the term *evaluation* has been used by classroom teachers, who thought of it only in relation to the grading of students. For most educators, indeed, the idea of evaluation was essentially equivalent to the idea of testing. A teacher might as readily say, "At the end of the term I shall *evaluate* my pupils," as say, "At the end of the term I shall *test* my pupils." To most teachers, evaluation *meant* testing.

Testing, of course, has been around almost as long as we have had recorded history. Over 4,000 years ago, for example, it was common practice in China to examine key officials every three years to determine their fitness for office.[1] Even before these Chinese civil service examinations, there were surely teachers who tried to find out the degree to which their students were learning. Future archaeologists will unquestionably unearth an artifact or two indicating that Neanderthal teachers of dinosaur dodging employed true-false tests (which, depending on the size of the dinosaur, may have been life-death tests).

Equating evaluation with student testing was the way that classroom *teachers* used the term *evaluation*. As we shall see, other people began to use the notion in a substantially different way.

Tyler's 1930s View of Evaluation   In 1932 Ralph W. Tyler, then a professor at Ohio State University, was designated to be the research director of the Eight Year Study, a formal appraisal of the college performance of students prepared in

1

progressive high schools versus the college performance of students prepared in more conventional high schools. During the conduct of the Eight Year Study, Tyler came to view evaluation not as the appraisal of *students* but rather as the appraisal of an educational *program's* quality. In the Eight Year Study, of course, that approach meant determining the quality of the educational programs represented by the progressive and conventional high schools that Tyler was studying.

Tyler's fundamental strategy was to determine the degree to which the objectives of an educational program had been attained. In essence, Tyler argued that a program should be judged positively to the extent that it promoted students' mastery of the objectives that the program's architects had established prior to the program's initiation. This objective-based (or goal-based) conception of evaluation, devised by Tyler in the 1930s, was destined to influence the view of subsequent generations of educators. (A more detailed description of the *Tylerian* approach is contained in Chapter Two.) Tyler's conception of educational evaluation stimulated a number of U.S. educators to view evaluation as something other than testing students for the purpose of giving grades.

A Beeping from Above   In October 1957 Americans were astonished to hear the "beep-beep" of a space satellite launched by the Soviet Union. Americans were not accustomed to being beaten to the punch in such matters. How, indeed, could another nation have exceeded the United States in scientific or technical matters? To many Americans, Sputnik, the first space satellite, was a substantial source of embarrassment. When embarrassed, of course, people often search for scapegoats. In the post-Sputnik soul searching of U.S. policymakers, the schools became splendid scapegoat candidates. After all, if U.S. schools had been doing their jobs more effectively, then American rather than Soviet scientists would have been boosting spheres into space. It was clearly time to spruce up America's public schooling!

As a consequence of such "let's catch up" analyses, substantial amounts of federal dollars were given to the development of new science and mathematics curriculum approaches. These federally funded curriculum development projects were not only supposed to result in more current conceptualizations of the subject areas under scrutiny (for example, "modern math" was born in one of these projects) but also supposed to lead to the development of instructional materials by which U.S. students could acquire updated conceptions of science and mathematics.

The professional staffs of these curriculum development projects, dominantly subject matter experts, found little virtue in the existing methods for determining whether their instructional materials worked. Such complaints led Lee J. Cronbach to author an important essay dealing with how educational evaluation might best be used in such curriculum development ventures. In a 1963 article entitled "Course Improvement Through Evaluation"[2] Cronbach argued that if educational evaluation were to be of assistance to curriculum developers, it had to be focused on the decisions faced by curriculum specialists during the process of their development efforts. Moreover, he argued that evaluation activities should deal less with comparisons between programs and more with the degree to which a given program promoted its desired consequences.

Although Cronbach's 1963 essay would later be viewed as a perceptive rethinking of evaluational matters, his views failed to attract much immediate interest beyond that of the individuals most directly involved in curriculum development projects. By and large, there was little interest on the part of U.S. educators in evaluation per se.

ESEA of 1965   In 1965 the U.S. Congress enacted a piece of precedent-setting legislation, the Elementary and Secondary Education Act (ESEA), which for the first time dished out federal dollars aplenty to local educational systems. As a consequence of ESEA, America's educational game was changed in a major way. Let's see why.

Education in the United States has historically been the responsibility of the individual states. Whereas many other nations have a federally directed educational system, educational enterprise in the United States is predicated on greater local autonomy. The financial support of schools, like their governance, has been drawn from state and local taxes rather than federal revenues. In the past few decades, however, that financial-support pattern has been shifted. Acting in part from a growing concern about the quality of the schools, federal lawmakers began to enact legislation in the 1950s and 1960s that provided financial support for schools throughout the nation. Such legislation emerged, in part, because of civil rights groups' concerns as to how the schools were serving minority students. The impact of these federal initiatives on education and, in particular, on educational evaluation has been enormous.

Many of the earliest federal education laws of the late 1950s provided modest funds for the support of research activities, particularly for specialized learner populations, such as mentally retarded or otherwise disadvantaged learners. But when Congress enacted the Elementary and Secondary Education Act of 1965, a comprehensive and heavily funded law providing for thousands of federal grants to local education agencies, the national government was clearly jumping into local education with both financial feet. In the debate preceding the passage of ESEA it was apparent that many federal legislators recognized the possibility that this considerable financial investment in the nation's educational system might be less effective than some were claiming. Senator Robert F. Kennedy and others contended that the new law must contain provisions for the mandatory evaluation of whether local agencies had used their federal grants properly. In the final version of the bill, two of its five titles (Title I and Title III) stipulated that each project conducted under support from those titles be evaluated and that such evaluations be reported to the federal government. Because of the magnitude of the funding, this stipulation meant that thousands of locally operated educational endeavors were now obligated to be evaluated. More precisely, local educators had to evaluate a given year's ESEA Title I and Title III projects if they wished to continue to receive the subsequent year's

Title I and Title III money. And money, as we know, represents an exceptionally powerful incentive for getting people to modify their behavior. With the passage of ESEA, educators suddenly shifted their evaluation activities from the realm of rhetoric to that of reality.

The federal requirements to conduct local education evaluations quite naturally resulted in the production of tons of evaluation reports that, for the most part, would have better served a school's paper drive than a nation's need to know whether its education laws were working. Educators untrained in educational evaluation simply foundered under the pressure to produce useful evaluation reports. Because the only substantial methodological training they had, if any, was in hypothesis-testing research, they tried to treat evaluation problems with a researcher's tools. More often, there was not even a misdirected effort to apply research techniques; there was merely a gathering of data, any data, so a number-laden report could be relayed to the federals. Appraisals of the resulting evaluation efforts, not surprisingly, were highly negative. Federal officials directing ESEA Title I and Title III programs as well as external reviewers[3] all concluded that the pool of evaluation expertise among the nation's educators resembled a puddle instead of an ocean.

However, this very situation, a scene in which educational evaluation was required but the would-be evaluators were nonexistent, provided the chief stimulus for what soon became a rapidly expanding field. Several outstanding educational scholars, trained in other specializations, turned their attention to the process of educational evaluation. Although there had been occasional references to evaluation in the literature of education, until the 1967 essays by Scriven[4] and Stake[5] few writers, other than Tyler and Cronbach, had addressed themselves seriously to the overall conceptual nature of educational evaluation. Prior to the 1967 publication of the papers by Scriven, a philosopher, and Stake, a psychometrician, barely legible copies of prepublication manuscripts were feverishly passed around the educational community. Interest in educational evaluation was intense. Any kind of writing on the topic was a treasured commodity.

Thus, during the last half of the 1960s, U.S. educators in large numbers were caught up with the conduct of educational evaluations. This attention to educational evaluation was not spurred by the unwavering professionalism of educators, nor by their latent desire to avoid the waste of taxpayers' dollars. Rather, educators were *forced* to evaluate their programs in a systematic manner in order to obtain governmental funds. The federal evaluation requirements of ESEA soon were emulated by state legislatures so that even state dollars for education were accompanied by evaluation requirements. U.S. educators evaluated their programs in the post-ESEA period not because they *wanted* to but because they *had* to.

An Era of Evaluative Optimism   Even though they had been initially forced to engage in educational evaluation, a good many educators became thoroughgoing converts to the virtues of systematic educational evaluation. In addition, state and national legislators began to look with favor on evaluation, for it appeared capable of indicating whether a particular legislatively supported program was worth the money the program cost. The late 1960s and early 1970s could be characterized as a period of profound optimism regarding the potential contributions of educational evaluation.

Not only was that 10-year span one of optimism, it was also an era of intense intellectual excitement regarding the nature and conduct of educational evaluation. A galaxy of conferences and workshops on evaluation were offered to educators. A spate of evaluation articles were raced into print. Many of these essays contained step-by-step "how-to" prescriptions for the conduct of educational evaluation. As will be seen in Chapter Two, whereas the enactment of 1965's ESEA found us with a dearth of formal educational evaluation models, by the early 1970s we were almost inundated by such models. Educational evaluation was in the air. It was viewed by many as the vehicle to transform shabby educational programs into shining ones. It was seen by more than a few as the long-awaited source of educational salvation.

To oversimplify a mite, many policymakers viewed evaluation as a definitive procedure for determining whether a particular program was worth its salt or, in the case of several competing programs, which program was saltiest. High-level policymakers, in particular, began to believe that formal evaluations could provide the information needed in order to determine whether a particular program should be scrapped or saved. Some newly legislated educational programs were accompanied by requirements that the programs be formally evaluated.

The educational evaluation community itself, although still fairly small in the early 1970s, began to take itself more than a little seriously. In retrospect, of course, we can dismiss the widespread enthusiasm for evaluation as the optimism engendered by recent converts. In the early 1970s, however, there was a pervasive belief that well-conducted educational evaluations could, *and should,* constitute the single most important factor in the rendering of educational decisions. Educational evaluators initiating a major project dreamed about that moment when educational policymakers, after diligently consulting the evaluator's report, would make decisions in essential accord with the report's findings. Such are the dreams of the inexperienced.

Disillusion Drops By   Pessimism often takes over the path trod by optimists. Such was the case with educational evaluation. The enthusiastic slogans of the early 1970s such as "Show us a decision that needs to be made, and we'll supply the evidence to make it" were replaced by more wary mottoes such as "Once in a while, if we're lucky, we might shed a bit of light on a decision."

Educational evaluators had learned a powerful lesson—the hard way—that the bulk of educational decisions are not made in a rational decision-arena in which the option best supported by credible data wins out. On the contrary, most educational decisions of importance are made in a patently political, interpersonal milieu wherein evidence plays a markedly minor role.

Educational decision makers, rather than breathlessly awaiting the evaluator's "definitive" report, typically made their choices without regard to the report's evidence of program effectiveness. Moreover, rarely did an educational evaluator's report unequivocally settle the issue of whether Program X was truly superior to Program Y. It is said that educational policymakers of the late 1970s yearned in earnest for one-armed educational evaluators, that is, evaluators not compelled to say "on the other hand."

Reasonable Aspirations   Thus, because it has been increasingly recognized that powerful interpersonal and political factors ordinarily account for most of the action in the rendering of educational decisions, and because educational evaluations rarely contain indisputable evidence, one might reasonably wonder why educational evaluators should even *try* to enhance educational decisions by studying the quality of educational programs. Educational evaluation may appear to be a fool's mission — a mission with powerful promise but paltry payoff. And yet it is precisely that modest amount of impact on decisions to which the evaluator must aspire.

If, as a consequence of an evaluator's efforts, an enterprise can be improved in effectiveness even a few percentage points, those modest and hard-won percentages represent benefits that otherwise would have been withheld from learners. Because most educational programs are aimed at children's well-being, is it not worth the effort to carry out activities that boost, ever so slightly, the quality of learning that children achieve?

In addition, because today's evaluators increasingly recognize the political nature of the decision-making process, they can carry out their activities with more political savvy and thus will be more apt to have impact on the political community that ultimately makes the final educational decisions. Cronbach[6] argues that educational evaluators rarely should fashion their efforts to satisfy a single decision maker. Rather, he contends, evaluators should focus their efforts on informing the "relevant political community." By and large, Cronbach believes, educational evaluations are not used by individual decision makers or unitary decision-making groups. "Evaluation," he asserts, "ordinarily speaks to diverse audiences through various channels, supplying each with political communication and with food for thought."

To the extent that today's educational evaluator accepts an obligation to illuminate the thinking of a more widespread political community, it is likely that future evaluation efforts will have more impact than the evaluations of a decade ago, when it was thought that all the evaluator had to do was present a final report and then sit back while decision makers rendered decisively improved decisions.

Educational evaluators now possess more than two decades worth of trial by fire. We have learned that a score of things we thought would work won't. We have, however, discovered a modest collection of things that do work. Today's evaluator must learn from the more than 20 years of intensive thinking and experience that followed 1965 ESEA's evaluation requirements. There is a large literature now available to the beginning evaluator. Errors of the past need not be recommitted. The naive delusions of power, widely held in the 1960s and early 1970s, need not be embraced by educational evaluators of the 1990s.

Educational evaluation in the last decade of the twentieth century will doubtlessly be a more mature specialization with markedly more modest aspirations. In the long run, that sort of orientation will surely be more useful in improving, ever so incrementally, the quality of education.

Defining Educational Evaluation

We have so far been employing the expression *educational evaluation* in a fairly relaxed fashion. The time has come to tighten up the conception of evaluation that we will use.

To evaluate something is to appraise its quality. We evaluate hundreds of things each day. Are our scrambled eggs too gooey to eat? Does that paperback book look interesting enough to buy? Is it too warm to wear a sweater? These everyday evaluations, no matter how informal, are efforts to appraise the quality of something.

In education, too, we encounter myriad instances of informal evaluations, ranging from a teacher's determination of whether a pencil is so dull that it must be sharpened, to a school superintendent's estimate of whether this year's leaders of the local teachers' organization are skillful.

But all the fuss in education about evaluation is not focused on these informal evaluative acts. The kind of educational evaluation that everyone is concerned with is formal or *systematic* educational evaluation. As we shall see, there are decisively different schools of thought regarding how to define evaluation as it applies to education, but for our purposes the definition that follows will prove most serviceable:

> Systematic educational evaluation consists of a formal appraisal of the quality of educational phenomena.

Let's look more carefully at this definition. By using the phrase *systematic educational evaluation,* we are clearly trying to divorce our focus from the informal, everyday evaluative acts referred to previously. For that reason, the definition asserts that systematic educational evaluation is *formal.* The heart of the definition involves an *appraisal of quality* or, in other words, a determination of worth. The educational phenomena that are to be appraised can include many things, such as the outcomes of an instructional endeavor, the instructional programs that produced those outcomes, educational products used in educational efforts, or the goals to which educational efforts are addressed.

A few illustrations of systematic educational evaluation may help illuminate the manner in which we have defined that operation.

> *Illustration No. 1:* A school superintendent gathers pretest and posttest data from schools using three different sets of self-instructional reading programs in order to determine the comparative effectiveness of each.

> *Illustration No. 2:* An evaluation consultant is hired by the parent advisory board of a newly instituted "alternative" school to see whether the school is good for their children. The evaluator gathers a wide variety of evidence, mostly from pupils, regarding

the impact of the new school. An evaluation report focusing on the worth of the new school in contrast to other available programs is then prepared for the parents.

Illustration No. 3: A number of citizens in a suburban school district that has experienced more than its share of school vandalism have instructed the district staff to reappraise the suitability of the educational goals the district's schools are pursuing. The curriculum staff prepares a document that delineates district educational goals clearly, then gathers estimates of each goal's worth from representatives of diverse clienteles, including pupils, teachers, parents, and various community leaders. A synthesis of these estimates is prepared for distribution throughout the district.

Illustration No. 4: A district social studies curriculum specialist supplies ongoing assistance to a high school's social studies faculty as they develop, as part of a three-month instructional unit, a series of simulation exercises designed to provide students with the ability to render more defensible decisions about the political process. The curriculum specialist attempts to supply pertinent evidence regarding the virtues of different development options available to the faculty as they create the exercises and design the procedures for their use.

In each of these examples there is an effort to appraise the quality of educational phenomena: different reading programs in the first illustration, an alternative school in the second, a set of goals in the third, and a series of en route decision options in the fourth. The objects to which educational evaluators attend are numerous — usually educational programs (including curriculum materials and other replicable instructional sequences) or goals (statements of educational intents). But there are other educationally relevant phenomena that evaluators might be asked to judge, such as the impact of testing programs or even the merits of evaluation programs themselves.

The four illustrations also involve formal attempts to gather information and to use that information in reaching judgments regarding quality. In the practice exercises at the close of this chapter the reader is given the opportunity to decide whether different types of evaluation activities are sufficiently formal to be subsumed under the rubric *systematic educational evaluation.* But, if for no other reason than to save ink and paper, from now on whenever the phrase *educational evaluation* appears in this book (unless otherwise indicated) it will refer to *systematic* educational evaluation. We shall restrict our attention to the kinds of formal quality appraisals depicted in the preceding illustrations.

A Terminology Jungle

For any youthful specialization, where there hasn't been enough time for people to become comfortable with the peculiar terms of that specialty, one should expect a certain amount of confused terminology. Educational evaluation is no exception. Many educators toss around evaluation-related expressions with cavalier imprecision. Because there is no single best definition for many of these terms, until the field of evaluation matures it would be prudent for educators to exchange terminology understandings before engaging in extended discourse. Let's examine a few of the terms some people use as synonyms for educational evaluation.

Measurement   Some educators mistakenly equate *measurement* with *evaluation*. For many years, particularly in the early decades of this century, U.S. educators expended considerable energy on the measurement of human ability; many people therefore think of this quantitatively oriented operation as evaluation. But measurement in education is merely the act of determining the degree to which an individual possesses a certain attribute. Typically, we try to assign some type of numerical index to a person's measured performance so that we can more precisely represent that individual's status with respect to the attribute of interest. For instance, we might say that Johnny obtained a score of 85 percent on a spelling test or that the average performance of a group of pupils on a mathematics test was 65.2 percent. Notice that we have not said how good or how bad those measured performances were. We are simply measuring. We are not appraising quality, that is, worth. Although evaluators often engage in measurement, these two operations are not equivalent. Measurement, at bottom, is *status appraisal.* Evaluation is *quality appraisal.*

Grading   Generations of teachers have referred to the act of *grading* their pupils as evaluation. Although there is no doubt that in order to assign a grade the teacher has to engage in a quality appraisal, and hopefully a formal one at that, grading is not equivalent to educational evaluation. The reason is that the focus of the quality appraisal is not on educational phenomena; it is on individual learners. That may seem like a fairly trivial distinction, but it really isn't. The only time educational evaluators focus on individual human beings is when these persons are serving as educational phenomena themselves (as would be the case when a *teacher* represents an instructional treatment).

Inasmuch as evaluators often use data from individual learners, that information should not be used to judge the individual child (and, by implication, that child's inherited genetic strengths and weaknesses). Instead, the appraisal of quality should be directed toward the educational phenomena we can (1) remedy if they are evaluated adversely or (2) emulate if they are evaluated positively.

Accountability   There is a continuing drive toward educational accountability in this country. Taxpayers want the schools to deliver evidence that they are giving the society its money's worth. Supplying this evidence characteristically requires educational evaluation. School boards have to be provided with evaluation reports that indicate how well the schools have been working. The state's citizens have to be supplied with evaluations of various aspects of the state's educational enterprise.

But whereas most accountability programs require educational evaluations, not all educational evaluations are carried out as part of an accountability program. For instance, without any kind of external coercion, classroom teachers might institute formal efforts to determine the quality of certain instructional schemes. Although this would qualify as an educational evaluation, it is certainly not the same thing as educational accountability, as no external decision makers are requiring the evidence regarding the quality of the teachers' programs. Educational accountability operations always involve the external imposition of demands for evaluative evidence. Educational evaluation may or may not spring from such accountability initiatives.

Assessment   Although for most educators the term *assessment* is used interchangeably with *measurement,* some people have begun to equate assessment and evaluation. One suspects that such people conceive of assessment as a euphemism for evaluation, believing it will be a less offensive term to some people. They believe that teachers will be less terrified if informed they are to be assessed rather than evaluated. Thus we find statewide evaluation projects, projects that are clearly formal efforts to appraise the quality of the state's educational programs, labeled as "assessment" operations. Although that kind of labeling is perfectly permissible, for there is no stone-tablet law that requires us to affix the term *evaluation* to all educational evaluations, it does illustrate how careful we must be in clarifying what we mean when we use expressions such as *educational assessment.* For when, without term clarification, two people use the term *assessment,* one meaning valueless measurement and one meaning systematic evaluation, a confused dialogue is sure to result.

Appraisal   Another term sometimes used as an equivalent for either evaluation or measurement is *appraisal.* Although most people seem to equate this term more readily with evaluation than with measurement, it is clear that we once more have to find out what people really mean when they use such an expression as *educational appraisal.* In this volume I shall sometimes use the term *appraisal* as a synonym for *evaluation.*

Educational Evaluation and Educational Research

Although terms such as *measuement, grading, accountability, assessment,* and *appraisal* are often used to describe educational evaluation or some related enterprise, the activity that is most often mistaken for educational evaluation is *educational research.* Because educational research and educational evaluation are so frequently confused, and because the distinctions between these two activities will prove useful in better understanding the nature of systematic educational evaluation, the differences between the two will be considered in some detail.

In the first place, there are many similarities between the activities of educational researchers and those of educational evaluators. They both engage in disciplined inquiry. They both use measurement devices. They both analyze their data systematically, often with the same analytic techniques. They both describe their endeavors in formal reports. They both rely on a technical set of tools. Indeed, if one could magically videotape brief segments of a researcher or evaluator in action, it would often be impossible to differentiate between them according to their activities.

If you watched them long enough, however, you could surely tell which was which, for there are substantial and significant differences between them. Delineating these differences, the profound and the petty, could be the focus of an extended monograph. In this discussion we shall attempt only to highlight the distinctions between educational research and evaluation. Just what are those differences?

Focus of the Inquiry   Both researchers and evaluators are attempting to secure additional knowledge, but the use to which they wish to put this knowledge differs. Researchers want to draw *conclusions*. Evaluators are more interested in *decisions*. Researchers are interested in understanding phenomena, often for no other purpose than that — to understand them better. Evaluators want to understand phenomena better in order to guide someone's actions.

Of course, there is a gradient of interest in either conclusions or decisions. We can think about basic research, which seems totally focused on producing conclusions, or about applied research, which deals more with information useful in reaching decisions. The dichotomies that will be used here to separate research from evaluation should be viewed as basic orientation differences. We may never encounter these distinctions in the real world quite as sharply as presented here. Rarely will one find a basic researcher who disdains information that might be used to make decisions. Rarely will one find an evaluator who isn't interested in understanding a phenomenon for its own sake. It is just that researchers tend to focus their inquiry on deriving conclusions, and evaluators tend to focus their inquiry on facilitating better decisions.

Generalizability of the Inquiry's Results   A pivotal difference between research and evaluation stems from the generalizability of the obtained results. An educational researcher is interested in discerning the nature of the relationships among educationally relevant variables. An ideal result of a research investigation would be findings that could be generalized to a wide variety of comparable situations. The more generality that a researcher's findings have, the better the researcher likes it. Evaluation, to the contrary, is typically focused on a particular educational program. There is no intention of generalizing results to other situations. The focus is on *this situation* and what decisions to make about it.

To illustrate, researchers may be interested in studying variables such as "knowledge of results" in an instructional context with the hope that their conclusions (dealing, for example, with the relationship between the immediacy of knowledge of results and the subsequent degree of student achievement) will hold for a variety of educational settings in which knowledge of results might be employed. Evaluators, however, are more concerned with a specific question such as, "Is the mathematical program in Hillsborough Elementary School in need of improvement?" No pretensions about generality of results are held by the evaluators. The job is particularistic, not general, in orientation.

There is a sense in which evaluators are interested in generalizing the results of a particular study to future renditions of a particular local program. To illustrate, an evaluator may be interested in a set of decisions to improve an instructional program in the Jefferson School District so that, in future years, refined versions of that program will work more effectively. Such "generalization" to future renditions of a program *are* of concern to an evaluator. By and large, however, educational evaluators are *not* interested in securing data so that they can generalize their findings to other sites in the nation, world, or galaxy. Those are the generalizability interests of educational researchers.

The Role of Valuing in the Inquiry   As was mentioned earlier, educational evaluation is concerned with quality appraisal. It is imperative for the evaluator to establish how worthwhile an educational phenomenon is in order to help make decisions regarding what should be done about it. Researchers, on the other hand, search for scientific truth without any desire to attach estimates of worth to their findings. When researchers detect a reliable relationship between two variables, they can legitimately cease their inquiry right there; there is no requirement that researchers attach an appraisal of quality to the discovered relationship. The researchers do not have to say whether it is a good or bad relationship. They do not have to compare the quality of one relationship with that of other relationships. Their job ends with the establishment of truths.

In an indirect way, of course, someone will subsequently attach quality appraisals to the researcher's findings, as when educators decide whether or not to build an instructional sequence that is, in part, based on the researcher's results. This, however, is not the responsibility of the researcher.

Because the evaluator is decision focused, however, the necessity to attach quality estimates to educational phenomena cannot be escaped. As we shall see later, these estimates are sometimes couched in comparative terms. Educational decisions, in a sense, always involve comparisons between alternative courses of action. But comparative or not, the evaluator's job is to value things. That value ingredient is not requisite in research.

Other Differences   A number of other distinctions might be drawn between educational research and educational evaluation. For instance, we could describe some differences in the investigative procedures used in the two approaches, such as the information-gathering designs used or the data-analysis techniques employed. However, one can become overwhelmed with minutia in these kinds of contrasts. The three distinctions in Table 1-1 should be sufficient to help the reader discriminate between the basic orientations inherent in educational research and educational evaluation.

By this time the reader should have a pretty fair idea of what systematic educational evaluation is all about. It is a formal effort to appraise the quality of things in education, such as programs, products, or goals. The reason we evaluate is to enable educators to make better decisions. Evaluation is an unashamedly practical undertaking. Evaluators want to improve education. Researchers are sometimes content to describe the world, but evaluators want to make it better.

There are, moreover, some other important characteristics of educational eval-

TABLE 1–1 • *Salient Differences between Educational Evaluation and Educational Research*

Inquiry Characteristics	*Educational Evaluation*	*Educational Research*
Focus:	Decisions	Conclusions
Generalizability:	Low	High
Value emphasis:	Worth	Truth

uation that must be understood more clearly. A consideration of one of the most important of these will better equip the reader to deal with this book more meaningfully.

Two Distinctive Roles of Evaluation

Although Cronbach's 1963 essay concentrated on improvement-focused evaluation, we must give credit to Michael Scriven for effectively labeling two basically different roles served by educational evaluation.[7] When Scriven, in his classic 1967 essay, distinguished between the *formative* and *summative* roles of educational evaluation, educational evaluators (and there were relatively few) instantly adopted the distinction. Rarely has a conceptual clarification been so quickly and so widely adopted by a specialization. In part, perhaps, the ready acceptance of Scriven's distinction can be attributed to the undernourished nature of evaluation technology: any clear-cut distinction would have been welcomed because so few existed. More important, however, Scriven cut through a confusing situation regarding evaluation's roles and set forth a useful way of conceptualizing it.

Formative Quality Appraisals   *Formative evaluation* refers to appraisals of quality focused on instructional programs that are still capable of being modified. The formative evaluator gathers information regarding the worth of aspects of an instructional sequence in order to make the sequence better. Examples of the kinds of still-malleable instructional sequences that formative evaluation might service would include (1) an early version of a set of self-instructional booklets or (2) a newly initiated "open" educational program where the faculty is still trying to devise effective components of the program. Formative evaluators attempt to appraise such programs in order to inform the program developers how to ameliorate deficiencies in their instruction. The heart of the formative evaluator's strategy is to gather empirical evidence regarding the efficacy of various components of the instructional sequence and then to consider this evidence in order to isolate deficits and suggest modifications.

Summative Quality Appraisals   *Summative evaluation* refers to appraisals of quality focused on completed instructional programs. The summative evaluator gathers information regarding the worth of an overall instructional sequence so that decisions can be made regarding whether to retain or adopt that sequence. Whereas the formative evaluator's audience consists of the designers and developers of an instructional program, the summative evaluator's audiences are the consumers of instructional programs or those charged with the consumers' well-being.

The summative evaluator would, for instance, gather evidence in order to help a school faculty decide which of three commercially distributed mathematics textbooks to adopt. There is no question about improving the math books. They come from the publisher, well bound in hard covers. They are to be bought and used as is. The summative evaluator's job is to help the teachers decide which of the completed books will do the best job.

In considering the distinction between these two evaluation roles, it should be apparent that the formative evaluator will function in a far more partisan role with respect to an educational sequence. Formative evaluators should do everything in their power to help an instructional program work better. They are not distant, aloof judges. They are usually members of a development team, trying to make the team's instruction work well. In contrast, summative evaluators should behave in a nonpartisan fashion, avoiding the tendency to be co-opted by those who have devised the instruction. In its most anxiety-inducing sense, summative evaluation should be equated with final judgment of an instructional endeavor.

It is possible, when playing either of these roles, for individuals to serve evaluation functions from within or from without a project. There are advantages in having *external* versus *internal* evaluators for some situations. In general, external evaluators are more apt to function in the summative context, whereas internal evaluators serve in a formative context. In some cases, however, individuals serving as internal-summative evaluators or external-formative evaluators can provide valuable inputs.

A Matter of Emphasis   It is fair to say that during the first decade of serious educational evaluation in the United States, say 1967–1977, there were more devotees of summative than formative evaluation. When most people wrote about educational evaluation, they drew the bulk of their illustrations from summative applications of educational evaluation, such as whether Instructional Program X really produced better results than Instructional Program Z. In the first edition of this book, for example, I suspect that I did most of my thinking about evaluation from a summative perspective. There is, after all, something so deliciously satisfying about rendering go/no-go decisions. Perhaps such thinking was stimulated by the competitive athletic atmosphere that surrounds our daily lives, an atmosphere in which there must be winners or losers—and ending up with a tie is like "kissing your sister/ brother."

In a sense, one supposes, part of the lure of summative evaluation is that it seems so much more important ("The program is to be terminated!") than merely improving a program ("Lesson A1 should come after Lesson A2, not before it"). Evaluators, like most people, want to feel important. Summative evaluation really reeks of importance.

Distressingly, at least for the ego needs of educational evaluators, summative educational evaluations during the past two decades have rarely yielded results so unequivocal that decision makers were compelled to act in accord with the summative evaluation's resounding results. More often than not, summative evaluations have resulted in only an additional political playing card that, depending on the political preferences of the decision-making community, is presented with audacity or timidity.

The majority of summatively oriented educational evaluations, at least those conducted during the past two decades, have proved to be far less influential than their architects had hoped. The quest for decisive yes/no or go/no-go decisions based on summative evaluations has, thus far, usually been frustrated. Rarely has an ongoing program truly been expunged on the basis of a summative evaluation's findings. Far more often, even a summative evaluation's negative findings have been translated into some form of improvement-oriented, formative advice to the program's staff.

Formatively oriented evaluators, in general, appear to have had a more beneficial impact on decision makers. In part, of course, this impact stems from the more congenial relationship between formative evaluators and their clients. The formative evaluator, after all, is seen as a member of the program's team. Summative evaluators are often viewed as program-threatening villains, whereas formative evaluators are viewed as the program staffs allies. In a good-guy versus bad-guy game, formative evaluators come across as the winners.

Formative evaluation's results, then, tend to be viewed with favor by the individuals whose day-by-day decisions regarding the program's nature can be influenced by the efforts of the formative evaluator. Summative evaluation's results, on the other hand, tend to be resisted unless they happen to coincide completely with the preferences of the decision makers.

In view of the foregoing considerations, it is not surprising that in recent years formative evaluation has been touted more vigorously than its summative counterpart. This situation represents a reversal of the prevalent view of a decade or so ago.

Nonetheless, Scriven argues in a recent essay that the attractiveness of formative evaluation should not disincline us to apply summative evaluation in those numerous settings where it is warranted: "Many programs are programs for the development of products, and all programs use personnel; it is inconceivable that program evaluation not be massively affected by the summative evaluation of those products and personnel. It may take time and politics may confuse the issue, but summative evaluation has staying power."[8]

In many ways, of course, it is difficult to draw decisive divisions between these two common roles of the educational evaluator. There are many assignments in which the two roles are merged, sometimes in a carefully considered fashion and sometimes unthinkingly. Most beginning educational evaluators will soon discover that they have their own preferences with regard to evaluation roles. You will personally determine, for example, whether you enjoy and are well suited for formative evaluation, summative evaluation, both, or neither.

Comparative Evaluation for Summative Evaluators   It has been previously asserted that the educational evaluator is concerned with decisions. Because of this action orientation, summative educational evaluators will find that their endeavors will most typically lead to comparative quality appraisals. Decisions characteristically involve choices among alternative courses of action. Should Textbook A or Textbook B be adopted? Of 15 possible educational goals, which 5 should be emphasized in this year's instructional program? Should a segment of an instructional sequence be replaced by a different segment? Should the history program or the art program be expanded? These are the kinds of decisions faced by educators, and these are the kinds of choices in which comparisons among competitors must be made.

Indeed, the ingenious summative evaluator will sometimes be obliged to create a competitive instructional alternative in order to discern whether the one under consideration is sufficiently meritorious to be recommended. For instance, suppose some evaluators were summatively evaluating a sophisticated and expensive multimedia approach to teaching youngsters about economics. It might be possible to produce an extremely inexpensive printed product that could be compared with the costly instructional scheme. If it turned out that the inexpensive version produced essentially the same kinds of results as the expensive version, then the evaluator would be in a better position to make recommendations than if no such comparative information were available.

Astute evaluators will always frame their inquiry in terms of the possible decision alternatives available, then gather information that permits the quality of these alternatives to be contrasted.

A Preoccupation with Programs

Although educational evaluators can deal with a variety of educational entities, such as appraising the quality of a set of educational objectives, most educational evaluators spend at least 90 percent of their time in formatively or summatively appraising educational *programs*. Therefore, it is imperative for novice evaluators to make sure that the program being evaluated is sufficiently well defined so that it is the program itself that is being evaluated, not a transitory cast of program staff members.

If you find yourself commissioned to appraise the quality of an educational program, make sure that the program's defining characteristics are sufficiently explicated so that an essentially similar program can be provided in subsequent years. After all, your task will be to help appraise the program this year in order for someone, or some group, to decide how (or whether) it should function next year. If the current program is heavily built around the largely unpredictable efforts of a half dozen excellent teachers, then you must be sure that it is the program rather than the half dozen teachers you're evaluating. To secure a *replicable* definition of the program, therefore, is a *sine qua non*.[9]

In a 1991 essay[10] regarding educational evaluation, Ralph Tyler observed that inadequate program definition was a shortcoming in many evaluations. Moreover, drawing on more than 60 years' worth of experience as an evaluator of educational and other social programs, he pointed out that inadequate implementation of a program often impedes effective evaluation. Tyler cited three impediments to the proper implementation of new educational programs: (1) great variability in local educational programs often demands idiosyncratic implementation of programs, (2) there is insufficient opportunity for the educators delivering a new program to acquire the skills and knowledge necessary to implement it, and (3) expectations are unrealistic regarding how long it takes to implement a major educational program. Tyler contends that it often takes six or seven years to implement a complex program.

Educational Evaluation as a Distinctive Specialization

If you are a graduate student who has already taken a fair number of research, measurement, or statistics courses, then a quick scanning of this text's table of contents will tell you that you're about to amble through some familiar territory. Yes, educational evaluators employ a good many procedures used by other types of educational specialists.

For the past 25 years I have taught at least one graduate course per year in the field of educational evaluation. Often, that course was the introductory class for which this book was written. I must confess that in the early part of that 25-year period I believed that there was a substantial body of content that was *unique* to the demands placed on educational evaluators. I realized that there was bound to be some borrowing from allied specialties such as measurement or research. Nonetheless, I was convinced that as more and more was learned about the content of evaluation, there would be an expanding core of procedures and constructs that were distinctive to the field of evaluation. I was wrong.

Time has shown me that the amount of content that is genuinely unique to the conduct of educational evaluation is mighty skimpy. As you journey through this text, I suspect you'll find that less than a fourth of the content you encounter will be distinctive to the field of educational evaluation. That's all right, though. A discipline doesn't have to be distinctive to be useful.

I've learned a few other things during those years. I have discovered that the incredibly particularistic nature of educational evaluation usually precludes pat approaches. I've learned that the truly effective evaluator is the one who can engage in incisive *ad hoc* analyses, that is, analyses of a highly particularistic nature regarding the program to be evaluated and the nature of the decision-making community that will ultimately decide what to do about the program. Skilled evaluators must be astute analysts and must be able to borrow as needed from a host of other disciplines. It will not be the unique body of content you will master that will transform you into a first-rate evaluator. Rather, if you are to become an outstanding educational evaluator, you need to be able to draw appropriately on a variety of specializations. You will need to know about data-gathering designs, and ways to create assessment devices, as well as ways to analyze the data you get from using those devices. You will need to know how to ferret out the interests of the people who really make the decisions so that you can address their needs. You'll need to know how to communicate information to those people so they will be influenced by your findings.

Educational evaluators exist in order to improve the caliber of education. In some instances, they will be aiding individuals or groups referred to as *decision makers* because those individuals will be obliged to make a particular decision, typically about an educational program. In other instances, educational evaluators will be aiding those who set policies that will automatically influence a set of decisions subsumed by those policies. Such policymakers can also be served by the skilled educational evaluator. But both decision makers and policymakers will be involved in the practical world of education. It is a world that can be improved by the efforts of effective educational evaluators.

A High-Stakes Game

There are some specializations in which, if the specialist errs, little harm is done. Gardeners who prune a bush improperly can be forgiven because the bush will grow again. Furnace repairers can, if they fail to correct a problem the first time, return to undertake additional repairs. Even a barber who, rather than subtly shaping, uses clippers like a lawn mower, can be forgiven. Hair grows back.

But educational evaluators are dealing with more easily damaged goods. Indeed, the harm that may be done to pupils as a consequence of inappropriate education may be as irreparable as the errors of a surgeon during an open-heart operation. The intellectual, emotional, and physical well-being of hundreds or thousands of learners can be influenced beneficially or adversely because of the actions of educational evaluators. With these kinds of stakes at issue, the educational evaluator must studiously master the procedures of the game. The rest of this book will deal with those procedures.

Discussion Questions

1. If you were asked to address the school board of a suburban school district to inform the members why there seems to have been so much concern about educational evaluation during the past two decades, what major points would you include in your presentation?

2. How would you distinguish everyday evaluation activities in education from *systematic* educational evaluation?

3. It was pointed out in the chapter that some evaluators, such as Scriven, believe that the bulk of educational evaluation should be *comparative* in nature. Not all evaluators—Cronbach, for example—agree with this proposition. Can you think of arguments in favor of, or opposed to, comparative educational evaluation?

4. If you were asked to explain to a group of citizens what the chief differences were between educational evaluation and educational research, how would you respond?

5. What differences, if any, might exist in the actual behaviors of those conducting summative evaluations versus those conducting formative evaluations?

Practice Exercises *

1. Decide whether each of the following activities should be characterized as educational evaluation. If not, indicate how the activity might be best described.
   a. A school superintendent wishes to establish the current status of district pupils with respect to certain reading skills and hence administers a series of achievement tests to all district students.
   b. A school principal compares the results of two different approaches to individualizing instruction in order to decide which should be adopted throughout the school.
   c. Mrs. Harris gathers a considerable amount of information regarding the performance of each pupil in her class in order to prepare defensible reports (for parents) on their progress at the close of the academic year.
   d. Pursuant to a newly enacted state law, each teacher in the state is judged every year in terms of the teacher's demonstrated effects on learners.
   e. Dr. Jason tests the relative efficacy of supplying learners with differential amounts of reinforcement in order to study the generalized nature of the relationship between the variable of *reinforcement magnitude* and the variable of pupils' *cognitive achievement.*

2. Indicate which of the following activities should be considered to represent *systematic educational evaluation.*
   a. A teacher's considered judgment regarding which clothes to wear at the fall orientation meeting.
   b. A school principal's personal appraisal of the intellectual integrity of each faculty member.
   c. A pretest-posttest study to see whether a new teaching intervention is preferable to an old one.
   d. An experienced teacher's intuitive sense of whether a new class of students will be "difficult to manage."
   e. Gathering data from different clienteles (e.g., students, parents, and teachers) to determine which educational goals are the most important.

3. Decide whether the following activities are more aptly characterized as *formative* or *summative.*
   a. Stella Smith tries to, in her words, "shape up" an early version of a set of materials to teach young children how to appreciate the arts more effectively. She gathers tryout data with respect to each component of the materials, then judges whether the component should be altered.
   b. An evaluator is trying to determine whether to adopt a newly distributed set of enrichment films in the field of biology. The films are tried out with a small group of district pupils to gauge their effectiveness.
   c. A curriculum development project staff tries out all its prototype instructional materials with a view to revising them substantially on the basis of their demonstrated effectiveness.
   d. A teacher annually evaluates the quality of pupil learning in order to make changes next year in the nature of the instruction.
   e. An evaluation consultant contrasts the relative worth of three commercially distributed textbooks dealing

---

*Answers to all practice exercises are given at the close of the practice exercises.

with sex education. Each book is tried out with a group of 30–50 learners, and then affective and cognitive measures of the students' reactions are made. An evaluation report is prepared in which one of the books is recommended.

Answers to Practice Exercises

1. *a.* No, this could best be described as measurement.
   b. Yes.
   c. No, this is best described as grading.
   d. Yes, this is an instance where individuals are evaluated, but the individuals in this instance, the teachers, are considered to represent instructional treatments.
   e. No, this is a clear case of educational research, not evaluation.
2. *a.* No; *b.* no; *c.* yes; *d.* no; *e.* yes.
3. *a.* Formative; *b.* summative; *c.* formative; *d.* formative; *e.* summative.

Notes

1. Philip H. Dubois, *A History of Psychological Testing* (Boston: Allyn and Bacon, 1970).

2. L. J. Cronbach, "Course Improvement Through Evaluation," *Teachers College Record,* 64 (1963), 672–83.

3. Egon G. Guba, "Evaluation and the Process of Change," in *Notes and Working Papers Concerning the Administration of Programs,* Title III, ESEA (Washington, DC: U.S. Senate, Committee on Labor and Public Welfare, Subcommittee on Education, 1967).

4. Michael Scriven, "The Methodology of Evaluation," in *Perspectives of Curriculum Evaluation,* ed. R. E. Stake. American Educational Research Association Monograph Series on Evaluation, no. 1 (Chicago: Rand McNally, 1967).

5. R. E. Stake, "The Countenance of Educational Evaluation," *Teachers College Record,* 68 (1967), 523–40.

6. L. J. Cronbach, *Designing Evaluations of Educational and Social Programs* (San Francisco: Jossey-Bass, 1982).

7. Scriven, "Methodology of Evaluation."

8. Michael Scriven, "Beyond Formative and Summative Evaluation," in *Evaluation and Education: At Quarter Century,* ed. M. W. McLaughlin and D. C. Phillips (Chicago: University of Chicago Press, 1991), pp. 19–64.

9. Having been obliged to complete two years of high school Latin and three years of college Latin, your congenial author will occasionally plunk in a Latin phrase or two. You, as the reader, may not be aided by this bit of Roman silliness. I, however, will feel that five years of *amo, amas,* and *amat* activities were less wasted.

10. Ralph W. Tyler, "General Statement on Program Evaluation," in *Evaluation and Education: At Quarter Century,* ed. M. W. McLaughlin and D. C. Phillips (Chicago: University of Chicago Press, 1991), pp. 3–17.

Selected References

Cronbach, L. J. "Course Improvement Through Evaluation." *Teachers College Record,* 64 (1963), 672–83.

———. *Designing Evaluations of Educational and Social Programs.* San Francisco: Jossey-Bass, 1982.

Cronbach, L. J. et al. *Toward Reform of Program Evaluation.* San Francisco: Jossey-Bass, 1980.

Ginsberg, Alan L. "Revitalizing Program Evaluation: The U.S. Department of Education Experience," *Evaluation Review* 13 (1989), 579–97.

Popham, W. J. (Ed.). *Evaluation in Education.* Berkeley, CA: McCutchan Publishing, 1974.

Raizen, S. A., and P. H. Rossi. *Program Evaluation in Education: When? How? To What Ends?* Washington, DC: National Academy Press, 1981.

Rossi, Peter H., and Howard E. Freeman. *Evaluation: A Systematic Approach* (4th ed.). Newbury Park, CA: Sage Publications, 1989.

Scriven, Michael. *Evaluation Thesaurus* (3rd ed.). Inverness, CA: Edgepress, 1981.

Stufflebeam, Daniel L. et al. *Educational Evaluation and Decision Making.* Itasca, IL: F. E. Peacock, 1971.

Tyler, Ralph W. *Basic Principles of Curriculum and Instruction.* Chicago: University of Chicago Press, 1950.

CHAPTER TWO

Alternative Approaches to Educational Evaluation

Although devout kitten lovers may be offended by the notion, there is substantial truth embodied in the adage that "there is more than one way to skin a cat." Similarly, there is more than one way to conduct a defensible educational evaluation. Skilled educational evaluators, like skilled cat skinners, must be aware of alternative options for carrying out their tasks. There are different evaluation strategies for different educational situations.

Although the next few paragraphs could be peppered with additional relevant aphorisms, the message to be bolstered by such succinct truth summations is a simple one: *There are different, defensible ways to carry out educational evaluations.* How should the educational evaluator deal with this unsurprising revelation that there are many roads to Mecca?

Dealing with Diversity

As we saw in Chapter One, a number of perceptive people have, through the years, conceptualized educational evaluation in different ways. How should one respond to these diverse recommendations regarding the conduct of educational evaluations?

There are those evaluators who contend that evaluators-in-training cannot or, more accurately, *should not*, enter the educational evaluation arena without being thoroughly grounded in the major alternative conceptualizations of educational evaluation. I can't be quite that enthusiastic about the virtues of comparative approaches to educational evaluation. Through the past two decades I have been influenced in my own thinking by a host of evaluation writers. Had I the patience to read more, I undoubtedly would have been influenced by more. Yet, snagging an idea here and a notion there, I have been able to adopt an approach to educational evaluation that seems to work well enough for me.

I do not recommend slavish adherence to Model X or Model Z. Rather, an unabashedly eclectic approach to alternative educational evaluation strategies is my recommendation. To make the point more generally, the dictionary[1] defines *eclectic* as "selecting what appears to be best in various doctrines, methods, or styles." This

seems a sensible way to respond to the various recommendations of evaluation writers regarding the "appropriate" way to play the evaluation game.

We shall consider here a number of approaches to the conduct of educational evaluations. If one or more of these approaches appeal to you, then by all means follow up on those of interest by pursuing the relevant source in the Selected References. A more thorough familiarity with any of these approaches will prove useful, particularly for those who wish to make educational evaluation a true field of specialization.

For most readers, however, the level of detail provided in this chapter should be sufficient to provide the general guidance needed for devising a reasonably defensible way to conduct educational evaluations.

In the actual practice of educational evaluation I have never encountered an evaluator who played out a particular evaluation "by the numbers," that is, by strict adherence to a specific model. In the real world, distressingly, textbook admonitions about evaluation requisites often crumble under the impact of the particulars in the situation at hand. Theoretical approaches to evaluation, while instructive, rarely can be employed in their pure form. Thus, pluck from the following evaluation approaches those pearls you think pertinent, and toss the rest back.

If you choose to delve further into any of the evaluation strategies described here, be wary of evaluation writers who push their own views to the exclusion of those put forward by others. Progenitors, as we know, often dote on their progeny. In more than a few treatises elaborating on Evaluation Model Z you will find such assertions as "This approach has power beyond that of any of its competitors." Take such self-interested statements for what they are, that is, statements of self-interest.

Overlapping Models

Over the years, particularly in the decade immediately following the enactment of the Elementary and Secondary Education Act of 1965, we have witnessed the emergence of evaluation models aplenty. For a time it appeared that an educational evaluation model was being generated by anyone who (1) could spell *educational evaluation* and (2) had access to an appropriate number of boxes and arrows. The building of educational evaluation models was, clearly, a fashionable activity of the late 1960s and early 1970s.

But, as is true with most cases of wheel reinvention, new inventors often build their own wheels by using other people's spokes. Thus, some of the later educational evaluation models incorporated chunks of previously presented models. Indeed, a detailed dissection of many evaluation models would reveal, as was true with Dr. Frankenstein's monster, that they were built from the remains of others.

Another difficulty with evaluation models is that they evade tidy classification. As we shall see, the approach recommended by Model Builder A is rarely so distinct from that recommended by Model Builder B that the two approaches can be comfortably placed in two mutually exclusive categories. Evaluation *models* are, as suggested in the dictionary, a "set of plans" or "an example for imitation or emulation."[2] Those who conjured up most of these models were doing their level best to lay out a course of action which, if followed, would lead to more effective evaluations. There was typically no thought given to the rendering of a new evaluation model that was truly *distinct* from its predecessors. As a consequence, when one is sorting out the numerous educational evaluation models now at hand, the sorting often gets sloppy. No matter what factors one chooses to employ in distinguishing among educational evaluation models, the resulting categories fail to satisfy those who would toss particular models into distinctive classification cells without overlap.

Alkin and Ellett[3] contend that prescriptive evaluation models, that is, those that indicate educational evaluation should be conducted in certain ways, can be categorized along three dimensions: *methodology, values,* and *uses.* These writers argue that by attending to methodology (the techniques used for description and evaluation), values (the focus on isolating the merit or worth of whatever is being evaluated), and uses (the purposes or functions of the evaluation), it is possible to make meaningful contrasts among alternative approaches to educational evaluation. Even by using these three rubrics, however, one must still note the *relative*, not exclusive, emphases that the architects of educational evaluation models give to methodology, values, and uses. As Alkin and Ellett observe, to get a fix on the essence of an educational evaluation model, the following question about the three explanatory dimensions must be posed: "When evaluators must make concessions, what do they most easily give up and what do they most tenaciously defend?"

An Imperfect Set of Categories

Although they are neither exhaustive nor mutually distinctive, we shall employ a five-category set of descriptors to dip into the more popular of the educational evaluation models currently available. These five categories are far from flawless. A given evaluation model may be classifiable primarily into one of the five categories, yet a strong counterargument could be mounted to place that model in another of the categories.

The purposes of devising a five-category descriptive framework were two. First, it is more convenient to deal with the diversity of extant evaluation models by lumping them into a modest number of reasonably cohesive categories. The aspiring evaluator can keep track of five categories more readily than five dozen different evaluation models. Second, there is heuristic virtue in isolating classificatory dimensions which, though not perfect, can be used to characterize most existing educational evaluation models and, more than likely, many new approaches that will emerge in the future.

Thus, with apologies to purists (who, in most instances, should actually be apologizing to us), the five classes of educational evaluation models to be considered in this chapter are the following:

- Goal-Attainment Models
- Judgmental Models Emphasizing Inputs

- Judgmental Models Emphasizing Outputs
- Decision-Facilitation Models
- Naturalistic Models

We shall consider these five general approaches to educational evaluation and provide illustrations of each. The references at the end of the chapter will provide readers who wish to engage in more advanced model meddling with requisite grist for their activities.

Goal-Attainment Models

A goal-attainment approach to educational evaluation conceives of evaluation chiefly as the determination of the degree to which an instructional program's goals were achieved. More ancient in its lineage than most evaluation models, the goal-attainment conception of educational evaluation is usually associated with the efforts of Ralph W. Tyler, whose approach to evaluation was reflected in the well-known Eight Year Study of the 1930s. During his extensive and illustrious career in education, Tyler often spoke and wrote on his view of an appropriate framework for planning and conducting educational evaluations.[4]

Tyler's general approach involves the careful formulation of educational goals according to an analysis of three goal-sources (the student, the society, and the subject matter) and two goal-screens (a psychology of learning and a philosophy of education). The resulting goals are then transformed into measurable (i.e., behavioral) objectives. At the conclusion of an instructional program, measurements of pupils are taken in order to see the degree to which the previously established goals were achieved. Unattained goals reflect inadequacies in the instructional program. Attained goals reflect a successful instructional program. It is for this reason, of course, that the Tylerian approach to educational evaluation can be considered, in essence, a goal-attainment model.

Tyler was one of the first proponents of behaviorally stated objectives, for he recognized that ill-defined statements of objectives were of little use in an evaluation approach that hinged on detecting the degree to which a program's objectives had been achieved. The Tylerian tradition of educational evaluation has had an enormous impact on the thinking of educators regarding the conduct of educational evaluations.

Even today, major evaluation projects are firmly rooted in Tyler's conception of educational evaluation. Tyler recognized, of course, that goals can be altered. Unattained goals, although permitting the inference that the instructional program was ineffectual, might also result from an inappropriate selection of goals in the first place. But educational goals and the degree to which they are achieved, without question, constitute the heart of Tyler's evaluation approach.

A more detailed variation of the goal-attainment model is that proposed by Hammond, who also conceives of evaluation in terms of whether an educational program is "really effective in achieving its expressed objectives."[5] The several steps in Hammond's model include (1) isolating that aspect of the current educational program to be evaluated, (2) defining the relevant institutional and instructional variables, (3) specifying objectives in behavioral terms, (4) assessing the behavior described in the objectives, and (5) analyzing goal-attainment results.

Hammond's model goes to greater length in attempting to spell out the nature of the institutional factors that might be relevant in considering the degree to which expressed objectives are achieved. The final step of his recommended sequence of operations involves analyzing the relationship between these instructional and institutional variables as they bear on measured learner behavior.

Another example of a goal-attainment model has been offered by Metfessel and Michael.[6] Their approach consists of eight steps:

1. Involve members of the total community.
2. Construct broad goals and specific objectives.
3. Translate specific objectives into forms that are communicable and that facilitate learning.
4. Develop measurement instrumentation.
5. Carry out periodic measurement.
6. Analyze measurement data.
7. Interpret analyzed data.
8. Formulate recommendations for program change or modified goals and objectives.

The most helpful part of the Metfessel and Michael approach is their effort to set forth different classes of criterion measures that might be employed to reflect the goal attainment of an educational program. Having recommended the use of multiple criterion measures, they provide a comprehensive list of diverse criterion measures that might be considered by evaluators.

In review, the main thrust of goal-attainment models is the degree to which prespecified instructional goals have been achieved. The quality of those goals is, obviously, of considerable import. In the next chapter we shall treat the topic of educational goals in more detail.

Judgmental Models Emphasizing Inputs

Another class of evaluation models includes those in which major attention is given to *professional judgment*. In these approaches the evaluator exercises considerable influence on the nature of the evaluation, inasmuch as it is that evaluator's judgment that determines how favorable or unfavorable the evaluation turns out to be. The particular focus of the evaluator's judgment permits us to subdivide this approach to evaluation further, depending on whether chief attention is given to *inputs* or *outputs*.

The distinction between inputs (sometimes referred to as *intrinsic criteria*) and outputs (sometimes referred to as *extrinsic criteria*) is rather straightforward. Suppose you are considering a number of electric drills with a view to purchasing one of them. You could judge them on the basis of such factors as their design, style, weight, and color. (Who wants an ugly electric drill?) These criteria are *intrinsic* to the object to be judged. You could also judge them on the basis of such factors as how fast or how neatly they drilled holes. (Who wants a glamorous drill that won't dent butter?) These criteria are *extrinsic* to the object to be judged. Outputs are associated with the *effects* of the object. For instance, we might judge a textbook on its input features, such as whether it is well illustrated and colorfully designed, or we could judge it on its outputs, such as how well students can learn something from it. Inputs are also referred to as *process criteria*. Outputs are also referred to as *product criteria*.

Judgmental approaches to educational evaluation in which the emphasis is on inputs are very common in education, but most are too haphazard to be properly classified as instances of systematic educational evaluation. An exception is the *accreditation* model. Accreditation approaches to evaluation of educational endeavors appear to be declining in popularity in some circles, yet there was a time when this approach represented perhaps the most prevalent form of systematic educational evaluation.

Accreditation evaluations are typically carried on by associations of schools, such as the well-known North Central Association. Representatives of the accrediting agency visit a school and, on the basis of previously determined evaluative criteria, judge the school's program. With few exceptions the dimensions of interest to accreditation teams have been input criteria, such as the number and quality of books in the school library, the degree of training of the school's faculty, and the physical plant.

Quite often, prior to the site visit, the accreditation agency directs the participating school to engage in an extended self-study in anticipation of the accreditation visit. Reports are prepared that are organized around the criteria supplied by the accreditation agency.[7] Participants often report that these anticipatory activities represent one of the most useful aspects of accreditation evaluations.

Although there is some intuitive support for the proposition that certain input factors are associated with the final outcomes of an instructional sequence, the scarcity of empirical evidence to confirm the relationship has created growing dissatisfaction with the accreditation approach among some educators. Although few evaluators would recommend that input criteria be discounted completely in judgmental models, for these factors can sometimes help clarify what is really operative in a given program, evaluation models that are dominated with a concern for inputs are not often recommended with fervor these days.

Judgmental Models Emphasizing Outputs

There are several recommended approaches to educational evaluation that can best be described as judgmental schemes in which primary attention is given to *outputs*. The most significant of these models are those developed by Michael Scriven, a philosopher by training, and Robert E. Stake, a psychometrician by training. Both men have contributed significantly to the understanding of the evaluation process as it applies to education.

Although Scriven's position has remained generally consistent with his early judgment-based approach to evaluation in which attention is given to outputs, Stake's views have changed considerably over the years. In this third category of educational evaluation approaches, however, Stake's early writings provide us with a lucid judgmentally oriented approach. Later we shall consider Stake's more recent views regarding educational evaluation.

Scriven's Recommendations

What Scriven has brought to educational evaluation is less a formal evaluative model, complete with diagrams, flowcharts, and the other regalia typically spawned by model builders, than a series of important insights and clarifications regarding various aspects of educational evaluation. Yet, by summing these distinctions and explanations we can arrive at a rather cohesive framework for the conduct of educational evaluations. Hence, it seems no major semantic distortion to deal with Scriven's recommendations in the context of a distinctive approach to educational evaluation.

The Formative-Summative Distinction   It has been previously noted that Scriven drew our attention to the distinction in roles served by evaluators who *formatively* try to improve a still-under-development instructional sequence and evaluators who *summatively* assess the merits of already completed instructional sequences. The differences in partisanship exercised by formative and summative evaluators, not to mention their use of different procedures (e.g., data-gathering designs and data-analysis techniques), have made this distinction a particularly influential one. Scriven's formative-summative distinction is widely used by educational evaluators, although in some cases with connotations somewhat different than those intended by Scriven.[8]

Attention to the Quality of Goals   Scriven conceives of evaluation as an assessment of merit. He is particularly dismayed with those who would equate educational evaluation merely with the degree to which goals are achieved. He stresses the necessity to assess the merit of the goals themselves. As he points out, "It is obvious that if the goals aren't worth achieving then it is uninteresting how well they are achieved."[9] His recommendation—namely, that evaluators bring considerable attention to appraising the quality of goals as well as whether the goals have been achieved—has alerted evaluators to the impropriety of passively accepting any goals proffered by program designers. For instance, if an autocratic school superintendent mandated a series of inhumane and antidemocratic goals, the evaluator should not meekly appraise the instructional program in terms of whether those reprehensible goals were achieved. Scriven would recommend a more rigorous evaluation and, in this case, repudiation of the goals themselves.

Payoff Evaluation   Scriven describes an evaluation approach that focuses on outputs (or the effects of a program) as *payoff evaluation*. He contrasts this with *intrinsic evaluation* which, as we have seen, attends more to the internal characteristics of an instructional program. Although Scriven tends to stress payoff evaluation rather than intrinsic evaluation (and it is for this reason that his approach is categorized here as a judgmental model emphasizing outputs), he is not disdainful of intrinsic evaluation. Indeed, he offers advice regarding how evaluators may engage in "hybrid evaluations," which combine attention to intrinsic and extrinsic criteria.[10] He even argues against the possibility of pure payoff evaluation, suggesting that attention to input factors is almost inescapable.

An Emphasis on Comparative Evaluation In his classic 1967 paper[11] on evaluation methodology, Scriven distinguishes between comparative and noncomparative evaluation, the latter having been proposed several years earlier by. Lee J. Cronbach in an essay[12] regarding how to improve instructional sequences via evaluation. Scriven opts for a comparative orientation to evaluation, pointing out that the decision focus of educational evaluation typically involves choices among competing alternatives, hence requiring comparisons of the competitors. Although conceding, as Cronbach contends, that comparative evaluations of educational programs often make it difficult to understand what accounts for the differences among the programs (because of the several ways in which the programs differ), Scriven observes that action decisions can be made without a complete understanding of why one program is better than another. If, on the basis of a comparison of two reading programs, the evaluator can show that one program produces effects markedly superior to the other, a recommendation can be reached to adopt the superior program even without one's completely comprehending the reasons it works better. It is the job of the educational researcher to ferret out the factors that lead to the more effective program's superiority. The educational evaluator can make action recommendations without that information. Scriven's strong advocacy of comparative evaluation has made many evaluators approach their task by searching for reasonable comparisons among the objects (e.g., goals or programs) they evaluate.

Goal-Free Evaluation In the late 1960s the federal government, sometimes because of legislative mandate and sometimes because of a drive for more effective management practice, attempted to monitor the manner in which major financial resources were being spent on education. Much of this federal money was being used to support the newly created research and development centers, located at major universities throughout the nation, and the regional laboratories for educational research and development. Several of these enterprises were heavily funded operations with annual budgets running as high as several million dollars per year. The typical scheme employed to evaluate these and similar agencies involved the appointment of a group of individuals who constituted an external review team for each agency. The review team typically spent several days conducting a site visit at the agency, visiting with staff members and examining the reports and products developed by the agency. At the conclusion of the site visit, the review team would prepare a report evaluating the agency's efforts, then submit the report to the appropriate federal funding organization.

Because of his increasing visibility as an evaluation theorist, Scriven was involved in a good many of these review teams. He detected an interesting phenomenon during the site visits which constituted the chief data-gathering phase of these evaluations. Without exception, the review team commenced their work by requesting information regarding the goals of the agency or of the various subprojects within the agency. Almost every subsequent interaction between review-team members and the staff of the research and development agency was influenced significantly by these initial revelations regarding the agency's aims. So influential, in fact, was the review team's awareness of project goals that Scriven opined such goal preoccupation might actually be interfering with the quality of the evaluators' work. He sensed that the evaluators' concern about the project's goals might, consciously or unconsciously, be leading to a form of tunnel vision in which the review team was actually inattentive to those outcomes of an agency program that, although not represented by the original intentions of the agency, were nonetheless real. To counteract these tendencies, Scriven proposed a technique he described as *goal-free evaluation*.[13]

In contrast to *goal-based evaluation*, in which the evaluator is attentive to not only the quality of an educational program's goals but also the degree to which those goals are achieved, goal-free evaluation focuses on the outcomes of a program, intended as well as unanticipated. The goal-free evaluator is not concerned with the *rhetoric* of the instructional designers regarding what they want to accomplish, but rather attends to the *results* accomplished by the designers' programs. Scriven did not recommend goal-free evaluation as a replacement for goal-based evaluation, but as a supplement to more goal-oriented frameworks.

How does goal-free evaluation work? In brief, it consists of assiduously avoiding any "contaminating" knowledge regarding project goals, while trying to discern what the total effects of the project are. This is a tricky job, since to figure out what a project's effects are without access to any information regarding its contents forces the evaluator to draw inferences about probable effects on the basis of inspecting the program's components. Once the evaluator has drawn such inferences, it is then the evaluator's job to devise measures, or borrow them from the project where available, and assess the program's effects. Scriven talks about the goal-free evaluator's "setting snares" to detect a program's consequences. These snares or measurement schemes would obviously have to be contrived so as to pick up the program consequences that, in the view of the goal-free evaluator, would be most likely to occur.

The chief advantage of goal-free evaluation is that it encourages the evaluator to be attentive to a wider range of program outcomes than might be the case with an evaluator who has been unduly influenced to look for project results consonant with project aims. Scriven conceives of goal-free evaluators functioning *internally* as well as *externally* to instructional projects. For instance, in a curriculum materials development project a goal free internal evaluator who was a member of the project staff might, either formatively or summatively, assess the worth of various project endeavors in terms of their results. Goal-free external evaluators, those who conducted their evaluations without being actual members of the instructional project's staff, could also prove useful in a summative or formative role.

Ideally, a well-designed evaluation would involve both goal-based and goal-free evaluators. If insufficient resources do not permit this luxury, then one must decide how to spend one's limited evaluation dollars. For instance, we might wish to utilize an internal goal-based evaluator whose focus was formative evaluation and an external goal-free evaluator whose focus was summative evaluation.

As can be seen, the thrust of Scriven's approach to educational evaluation is clearly oriented toward the program's outputs, whether or not intended. It is also a decisively judgmental approach, for Scriven would have evaluators render their own judgments regarding the virtues of a program. If the evaluator views the program as a disaster, then Scriven urges the evaluator to proffer that judgment in unequivocal language. Unlike some evaluative approaches, in which evaluators assiduously eschew judgmental pronouncements in fear that such judgments might inappropriately influence decision makers, Scriven's approach to evaluation calls for evaluators to render such judgments, attending chiefly to program outputs, in unequivocal terms.

Stake's Countenance Approach

Robert E. Stake proposed a system for conducting education evaluations in a 1967 article entitled "The Countenance of Education Evaluation."[14] Because of the title of that essay, Stake's approach to evaluation is often referred to as his *Countenance Approach*.

In a recent analysis, Stake suggested that it would be more appropriate to refer to his mid-sixties views as an evaluation "approach" or an evaluation "persuasion." As Stake put it, "The countenance paper was an overview of data available for an evaluation study. I advocated broader selection, especially more use of 'process data.' I was not offering a model for conducting a study."[15]

Stake's 1967 conception of evaluation emphasized two chief operations: description and judgment. He set forth a well-organized scheme for carrying out these two activities, drawing attention to several important considerations that should be heeded by those who would describe and judge.

One of the helpful aspects of the Countenance Approach is that it distinguishes between descriptive and judgmental acts of the evaluator according to three phases of an educational program: its *antecedent, transaction*, and *outcome* phases. Stake conceived of antecedents as conditions existing prior to instruction that may relate to outcomes. He viewed transactions as the "succession of engagements" that constitute the process of instruction. (It should be noted in passing that Stake's Countenance Approach is rarely used in the form that Stake originally devised it — even by Stake himself!) Outcomes were considered to be the effects of an instructional program. We shall illustrate each of these in a moment.

Stake then divided descriptive acts according to whether they refer to what was intended or what was really actually observed. He argued that both intentions and what actually took place must be fully described. He then divided judgmental acts according to whether they refer to the standards used in reaching judgments or to the actual judgments themselves. He assumed the existence of some kind of rationale guiding the design of an educational program.

Stake combined these several distinctions in a graphic representation of the statements and data needed to be gathered by an evaluator. This layout is presented in Figure 2-1. Notice that, apart from the rationale, the six cells at the left of the layout refer to descriptive operations, whereas the six cells at the right deal with judgmental operations.

We can illustrate the various dimensions of Stake's 1967 approach by the following fictitious example regarding a high school government teacher, Mr. Vine:

Rationale

Mr. Vine has decided to emphasize the distinctions between functions of local, state, and federal government because he believes that these distinctions are pivotal in one's understanding of citizenship responsibilities.

Intents

Antecedents: Mr. Vine knows that Chapter 9 has been assigned for Tuesday.
Transactions: He plans to have a lecture plus discussion on Tuesday.
Outcomes: He estimates what students will be able to do on a quiz Wednesday.

Observations

Antecedents: He observes that six students were absent on Tuesday.

Transactions: His lecture took so long that there was little time for discussion.

Outcomes: On Wednesday's quiz well over half the students answered an important question incorrectly.

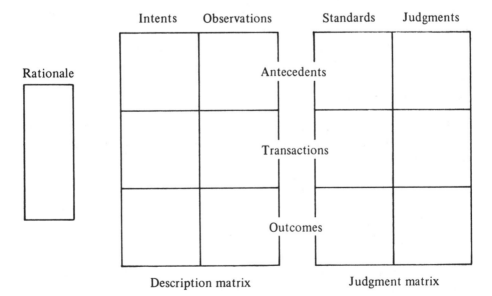

FIGURE 2-1 • *Stake's Depiction of the Statements and Data Needed by Educational Evaluators*

Standards

Antecedents: He expects a few absences on nonquiz days such as Tuesday.

Transactions: He believes his lectures are clear enough for 80 percent of the class to understand them.

Outcomes: His fellow government teachers believe three-fourths of their students should do well on these kinds of quizzes.

Judgments

Antecedents: Mr. Vine retrospectively judges the Chapter 9 reading assignment to be somewhat confusing.

Transactions: Several of his weaker students told him his lecture was unclear.

Outcomes: A teacher's aide assigned to grade the quiz papers said too many students performed poorly on the quiz.

Stake's data matrices help us to see how his approach inclines the evaluator to engage continually in description and judgment, *at the beginning, during,* and *at the end of* an educational program. His distinction between intents and observations reminds us that the aspirations of educators are often not realized in the antecedents, transactions, and outcomes that actually occur.

Stake's Countenance Approach also elaborated on the manner in which judgments are made by evaluators. He pointed out that when we judge an educational program we engage either in *relative comparisons* (one program versus another), *absolute comparisons* (one program versus standards of excellence not associated with any particular program), or both relative and absolute comparisons. Stake recommended that the judgmental criteria used in educational evaluations be explicated as clearly as possible prior to their being employed in actual judgments.

The real payoff in the Countenance Approach, of course, was the judged *outputs* of the program being evaluated. It is for this reason that Stake's 1967 approach can be placed in our third group of evaluation models.

Both Scriven's approach and Stake's 1967 approach are rooted in the belief that the capable evaluator will be able to make subtle judgments about various facets of an educational program. Although their emphasis is on judgment of outputs, it should be obvious that their models reflect considerable concern with a number of additional factors.

Decision-Facilitation Models

Several evaluation paradigms have been proposed that, although they involve the evaluator's use of judgment and determine whether goals are attained, can best be characterized as *decision-facilitation models*. The orientation of these models is so overwhelmingly toward servicing educational decision makers that some of their proponents conceive of the evaluator as the decision maker's handmaiden/handmister.

In a good many respects, one might argue, there is overlap between these decision-facilitation models and the three classes of evaluation models we have previously examined. However, there is an important difference. Decision-facilitation evaluators are less willing to assess personally the worth of educational phenomena. They will strive to collect and present the information needed by someone else, who will determine worth. Decision-facilitation evaluators view the final determination of a program's merit as the decision maker's province, not theirs.

Although it is obvious that decision-facilitation evaluators cannot completely avoid engaging in value-judging acts as they ply their trade, it is this overriding disinclination to engage in personal valuing, coupled with their mission to abet the decision maker's task, that renders them at least relatively distinct from the other evaluation approaches we have treated.

The CIPP Model

One of the best known of the decision-facilitation evaluation schemes is the CIIP Model (pronounced "sip" by its progenitors). CIPP is an acronym representing the four types of evaluation this model identifies, namely, *context* evaluation, *input* evaluation, *process* evaluation, and *product* evaluation. The CIPP Model was originated by Daniel Stufflebeam and Egon Guba. (Yes, Virginia, there is an Egon Guba.) The fact that it has become well known in spite of the fantasy-like names of its parents strongly suggests that the approach must possess some merit.[16] Because Stufflebeam has been more active in refining the CIPP Model during recent years, we shall use his writings as a chief source of our analysis. As we shall see, Guba has been particularly active in the refinement of *naturalistic* evaluation models.

The CIPP Definition of Evaluation   The CIPP approach to evaluation is rooted in its definition of evaluation:

> Evaluation is the process of delineating, obtaining, and providing useful information for judging decision alternatives.[17]

Stufflebeam elaborates on this definition by pointing out that "since evaluation is performed in the service of decision making," it should emphasize the provision of information useful to those who must make decisions. Because evaluation is a continuing and cyclic process, it must be implemented via a systematic program. Stufflebeam believes that of the three steps involved in this model — *delineating, obtaining,* and *providing information* — the delineating and providing operations are carried out collaboratively between evaluator and decision maker, whereas the obtaining of information is a technical activity carried out primarily by the evaluator.

These three major steps in the CIPP evaluation process are described as follows: (1) *delineating* refers to the focusing of informative requirements needed by decision makers through such operations specifying, defining, and explicating; (2) *obtaining* refers to the collection, organization, and analysis of information using such technical procedures as measurement and statistics; (3) *providing* refers to the synthesizing of information so that it will be optimally useful for purposes of the evaluation. Note that all three steps involve *information* and how it can best be isolated, gathered, and presented to those people who make educational decisions.

Decision Settings   The CIPP Model also distinguishes among different settings in which decisions are made. Decisions that involve maintenance of the normal balance of an educational system are described as *homeostatic*. Homeostatic decision making would involve such operations as determining faculty assignments or students' course schedules. Decisions that involve developmental activities aimed at the continuous improvement of a program are described as *incremental*. Incremental decision making would include such operations as the introduction of a model innovative program (e.g., the increased use of paraprofessional support personnel) that would not run the risk of a major expense or a major failure. Decisions that involve large innovative efforts to solve significant problems are described as *neomobilistic*. Neomobilistic decision making would include such activities as major governmentally subsidized efforts to develop instructional materials, such as those previously supported at several regional laboratories for educational research and development. Decisions that denote utopian activity designed to produce complete changes in an educational enterprise are described as *metamorphic*. The CIPP Model makers concede that a metamorphic decison setting is only of theoretical interest, as the possibilities of this type of dramatic system-modification is almost never encountered in the real world of education.

One clear contribution of the CIPP Model is that it augments the evaluator's vocabulary. Just think of how many school superintendents could be intimidated by an evaluator's assertion that "Your program is *utterly neomobilistic!*" Early users of the CIPP Model sometimes thought that neomobilism referred to that state of adolescence associated with the onset of driving privileges.

Types of Evaluation   The CIPP Model, in addition to identifying several decision settings, also distinguishes among four types of educational decisions. These are (1) planning decisions to determine objectives; (2) structuring decisions to design instructional procedures; (3) implementing decisions to use, monitor, and improve these procedures; and (4) recycling decisions to judge and react to the outcomes produced by those procedures. For each of these types of decisions, a corresponding type of evaluation is recommended: context, input, process, and product, respectively. These four forms of evaluation constitute the heart of the CIPP Model.

Context evaluation is, according to Stufflebeam, the most basic kind of evaluation. Its mission is to provide a rationale for the determination of educational objectives. A context evaluation attempts to isolate the problems or unmet needs in an educational setting. Consideration of such factors then leads to the identification of the general goals and specific objectives that should be the focus of an educational program. Context evaluation involves an analytic effort to conceptualize the relevant elements of an educational environment, as well as an effort to gather empirical data that help identify the problems, needs, and opportunities present in an educational context. The methods of context evaluation are chiefly descriptive and comparative. The context evaluator describes the status of an educational setting, then compares present, probable, and possible system outputs. The conclusion of context evaluation is characteristically the identification of a set of specific objectives for which an instructional program can be designed.

Input evaluation is supposed to provide information regarding how to employ resources to achieve program objectives. During input evaluation the task is to ascertain the nature of available capabilities of the instructional system and potential strategies for achieving the objectives identified as a consequence of context evaluation. The input evaluator secures information needed to appraise alternative strategies, whether they are based on the system's current capabilities or whether external resources need to be added to the system. Input evaluators help decision makers select and design the procedures deemed suitable for promoting attainment of program goals. For instance, if a set of program objectives had been selected that revolved around learner mastery of certain chemistry objectives, then the input evaluator's tasks would be to delineate, obtain, and provide information needed for decisions regarding which instructional resources to use and in what manner they should be employed in order to promote achievement of the objectives identified.

Process evaluation is required once the instruction program is up and running. The purpose of process evaluation is to identify any defects in the procedural design, particularly in the sense that planned elements of the instructional program are not being implemented as they were originally conceived. The process evaluator describes procedural events and activities so that any deficits in the instructional design can be discerned, or, in some cases, anticipated. The records made by the process evaluator are also useful in retrospective analyses of the instructional program in order to isolate any particular strengths or weaknesses. In essence, process evaluators monitor the actual instructional procedures in order to help the instructional decision makers anticipate and overcome procedural difficulties.

Product evaluation attempts to measure and interpret the attainments yielded by an instructional program not only at its conclusion but, as often as necessary, during the program itself. The methods of product evaluation are similar to those of the goal-attainment evaluator and the judgmental evaluator who emphasize extrinsic criteria, except that the CIPP product evaluator, as always, delineates, obtains, and provides information needed by those who must make decisions regarding the program. The emphasis in product evaluation, however, is clearly on the outcomes produced by the program. This outcome information is related to the objectives of the program; then comparisons are made between expectations and actual results. The product evaluator helps others decide whether to continue, terminate, modify, or refocus an instructional program.

These four types of evaluation, cast as they are in a decision-facilitation framework, constitute a fairly full-blown model, particularly when they are viewed in relationship to the types of decision settings previously examined. A number of years ago, shortly after the CIPP Model was conceived, diagrammatic flowcharts of the scheme, replete with its multiple destinations, inspired awe (if not understanding) on the part of many neophyte evaluators.

CIPP and the Formative-Summative Distinction Stufflebeam has attempted to relate the CIPP Model to Scriven's formative and summative evaluation.[18] In reconciling these constructs, Stufflebeam distinguishes between *evaluation for decision making* and *evaluation for accountability*. He believes that when evaluation serves a formative role it is *proactive* and is aimed at abetting decision makers. When, however, evaluation serves a summative role it is *retroactive* in nature and is aimed to serve as a basis for accountability.

Stufflebeam's reconciliation can be presented pictorially as in Figure 2–2, where it can be seen that the key distinction is based on whether the evaluation is *formative,* hence before-the-fact (proactive) and aimed at the needs of decision makers, or *summative*, after-the-fact (retroactive) and aimed at the needs of an accountability system.

The CIPP Model provided the first full-blown framework to guide those evaluators who saw their mission chiefly as one of helping those who must make educational decisions. Stufflebeam, Guba, and their colleagues reflect this bias succinctly in the introduction to a 1971 volume which describes their approach: "The purpose of evaluation is not to prove but to improve."[19]

The Discrepancy Model

Malcolm Provus, during his tenure as Director of Research for the Pittsburgh (Pennsylvania) public schools, devised another systematic approach to evaluation based on the premise that evaluation involves the comparison of *performance* with *standards*. Because Provus's model is particularly attentive to the discrepancies between posited standards and actual performance, it is generally referred to as the *Discrepancy Model* of educational evaluation.[20] More specifically, Provus offered the following definition of evaluation:

> *Program evaluation is the process of (1) defining program standards; (2) deteremining whether a discrepancy exists between some aspect of program performance and the*

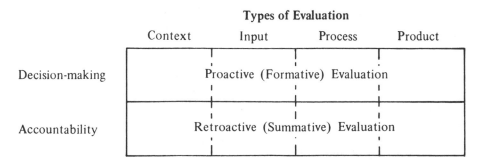

FIGURE 2–2 • *Stufflebeam's Framework for Relating the CIPP Model to the Formative and Summative Roles of Evaluation*

standards governing that aspect of the program; and (3) using discrepancy information either to change performance or to change program standards. [21]

The Discrepancy Model consists of five stages, the first four of which follow this general paradigm:

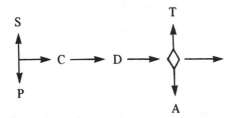

where S = standard
     P = program performance
     C = comparison of S with P
     D = discrepancy information resulting from C
     T = terminate
     A = alteration of P or S

As can be seen, after performance is compared with standards, the inspection of the resulting discrepancy information (which could, of course, reflect no discrepancy) leads to four alternatives. The program can be terminated, it can proceed unaltered, its performance can be altered, or its standards can be altered.

Design   The first state of the Discrepancy Model is the design stage. This operation is focused on documenting the nature of the program, including (1) the objectives of the program; (2) the students, staff, and other resources that must be present before program objectives can be realized; and (3) the instructional activities presumed to promote attainment of the objectives. In rough terms, the activities associated with this stage are comparable to those seen in the first two stages of the CIPP Model.

Installation   The second stage of the Discrepancy Model involves an effort to see whether an installed program is congruent with its installation plans. The program design emerging from stage 1 represents the standards (S) against which the program (P) is compared (C) to detect the presence or absence of discrepancies (D). The usual four choices of action are available to the program's decision makers: terminate, proceed, alter performance (in this case, the nature of the program), or alter standards (in this case, the design).

Process   In the third stage of the Discrepancy Model the evaluator attends to the question of whether "enabling objectives" are being achieved. The evaluator's role here is similar to that of Scriven's formative evaluator or CIPP's process evaluator. The usual Discrepancy Model paradigm is used involving comparison between standards and performance with resulting discrepancy information guiding decision makers.

Product   The fourth stage of the Discrepancy Model is focused on the question: "Has the program achieved its terminal objectives?" The standards (objectives) derived during stage 1 are contrasted with the actual postinstruction performance of learners to detect any discrepancies. This stage involves activities comparable to those employed during the final stage of the CIPP Model.

Program Comparison   The final stage of the Discrepancy Model, unlike the first four, which are developmental in nature, is concerned with a cost-benefit analysis of the now-completed program with other competing programs. Provus properly pointed out that unless there is a sufficient degree of replicability associated with the programs to be contrasted, such cost-benefit analyses are impossible.

As can be seen from a comparison of the Discrepancy Model with the CIPP approach, there is much similarity between those two evaluation frameworks. Because they both subscribe to the same general conception of evaluation's functions, this fact is not surprising. As Provus observed, "Those responsible for making decisions about one or more programs are the first and primary audience for evaluative information."[22]

Provus's untimely death not too long after he conceptualized the Discrepancy Model prevented his decision-facilitation approach from being refined further. In its most elementary form, however, it clearly constitutes an attempt to package information in such a way as to help decision makers make better choices among options.

Cronbach's View of the Evaluator as Teacher

Lee J. Cronbach has had an enormous influence on the field of educational evaluation. A long-time professor at Stanford University until his retirement in the early 1980s, Cronbach, through his seminal writings in the field of educational evaluation has influenced many subsequent commentators on the nature and conduct of educational evaluation.

A student of Ralph Tyler in the late 1930s, Cronbach soon established his own reputation as a preeminent applied psychologist.[23] He would, in time, often apply his substantial talent in the understanding and advancement of educational evaluation.

When in 1957 the USSR launched the first space satellite, it was widely held by U.S. policymakers that inadequacies in our nation's schooling system had permitted this ethnocentric calamity, namely, that the United States was not supreme in slinging satellites spaceward. As a response, the U.S. Congress poured massive amounts of federal dollars into sprucing up the nation's science curricula. The National Science Foundation sponsored major projects in physics, chemistry, and mathematics to (1) isolate more appropriate and up-to-date content for those fields and, once having isolated such content, (2) develop instructional materials that would help students master the new curricular content.

Those involved in such federally subsidized curriculum development projects attempted to employ the currently available approaches to evaluating their endeavors. Unfortunately, those federally supported curriculum developers found that on-the-shelf evaluation approaches provided little, if any, assistance. Sensing such shortcomings, Cronbach authored an influential 1963 essay, "Course Improvement Through Evaluation," published in the *Teachers College Record*. In that analysis he made several major points. First, he argued that if evaluation was to be of genuine utility to course developers, it had to focus on the decisions that those developers were obliged to make during the instructional development process. Second, he contended that an evaluation that would contribute to course developers' needs should deal more with a given course's effects rather than with a comparison between effects of the developers' course and the effects of other courses. Finally, he stressed the importance of evaluation to aid in the refinement of the course while it was still sufficiently "fluid" to make such changes. Clearly, Cronbach's 1963 essay was pushing for course-specific formative evaluation.

In 1974 Cronbach formed the Stanford Evaluation Consortium, a group of faculty and students concerned with evaluation, in an effort to infuse some fresh thinking into the field of evaluation. As Cronbach puts it, he and his colleagues were "uneasy" about what was then being written about evaluation and about the kinds of evaluations then being sponsored by governmental agencies. In 1980 Cronbach and seven other members of the Stanford Evaluation Consortium brought forward a major analysis of educational evaluation. That book, *Toward Reform of Program Evaluation*,[24] is, in my view, an essential volume for any serious student of educational evaluation. Shortly thereafter, in 1982, Cronbach provided the evaluation community with a singly authored text dealing with the design of evaluation studies.[25] Taken together, these two volumes provide an excellent view of Cronbach's thinking regarding the appropriate conduct of educational evaluations.

Cronbach's position regarding educational evaluation is categorized as decision-facilitative because he still contends that skillful evaluators should contribute to the making of better decisions. Unlike the prevalent view that there is "a decision maker" whose information needs must be serviced, Cronbach conceives of most evaluations as taking place in a politically lively setting in which the evaluation's results will be used by "a policy-shaping community" rather than "a lone decision maker or tight-knit group."[26] Indeed, Cronbach believes that most educational evaluations take place not in rational seminar rooms but rather in highly politicized situations. It is this conception of the political nature of the decision-making process, a process in which a broad political community influences the decisions to be made, that leads Cronbach to the view that an educational evaluator must be a *teacher*.

Cronbach does not believe that an evaluator should determine whether a program is worthwhile or decide what course of action should be taken. (Here, of course, he would differ sharply with those who encourage evaluators to render personal judgments about the merits of a program's inputs or outputs.) Cronbach believes that "the proper function of evaluation is to speed up the learning process by communicating what might otherwise be overlooked or wrongly perceived."[27] He argues that the evaluator's responsibility as teacher begins when the evaluator first probes the interests of the policy-shaping community. The evaluator's educative role continues throughout the project in every contact that the evaluator has with program participants or with other concerned audiences. The final report is only one vehicle to enable relevant audiences to understand the program. Indeed, as Cronbach puts it, teaching does far more than provide answers to the decision-shaping community's questions. The skilled evaluator helps clients ask better questions and determine what technical and political moves are appropriate for their purposes. The evaluator is a sensitizer, clarifier, and negotiator. To Cronbach, the talented evaluator is, in the finest sense of the term, an *educator*.

Clearly, then, although we may conceive of Cronbach's views as falling most directly in the category of decision-facilitation evaluation models, his is a far more politically sensitive conception of educational evaluation than other more apolitical approaches to educational evaluation.

Naturalistic Models

The fifth category of educational evaluation models we shall consider embraces those approaches generally referred to as *naturalistic*. Also described as *qualitative*, such evaluation models represent a substantial departure from most of the evaluation models we have considered thus far. A number of writers have advocated naturalistic approaches to educational evaluation. We shall consider several of these as illustrations, but first let's deal with what is meant by naturalistic evaluation.

Guba and Lincoln[28] have provided a useful way of contrasting "naturalistic" inquiry with "scientific" inquiry depending on the degree to which *constraints* are imposed on (1) antecedent variables and (2) possible outputs.

Antecedent variables are those factors that impinge on an evaluation at its outset. For instance, when two different instructional programs are contrasted, the differences between the two programs constitute an important antecedent variable, often referred to as the independent variable. Such independent variables are often manipulated. Other antecedent variables, such as pupil aptitudes, are controlled or randomized.

Outputs, of course, refer to the possible consequences emerging from the program(s) being evaluated. The evaluator may focus on some outputs and not others. Each choice made imposes a constraint on the inquiry.

In Figure 2–3 we see an adaptation of the Guba-Lincoln depiction of naturalistic and scientific inquiry. Note that to the extent that few or no constraints are imposed on either potential outputs or antecedents, the inquiry can be thought of as naturalistic. In other words, the fewer the constraints imposed on the evaluation, the more naturalistic the evaluation will be. As is seen in Figure 2–3, an "ideal" scien-

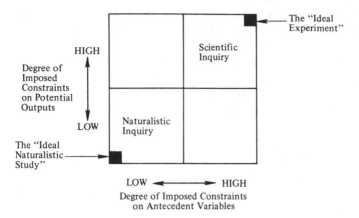

FIGURE 2–3 • *A Contrast between Naturalistic Inquiry and Scientific Inquiry According to the Imposed Constraints on Antecedent Variables and Potential Outputs (after Guba and Lincoln)*

tific inquiry would have substantial constraints imposed on both antecedents and outputs. A naturalistic educational evaluation, as is implied by the notion of "natural," would be just the opposite.

Stake's Responsive Evaluation

Robert Stake, the architect of the highly structured and judgmentally rooted Countenance Approach, later became increasingly disenchanted with the approach to evaluation embodied in his own 1967 Countenance Approach and similar models. Referring to such highly structured approaches as "preordinate" methods of evaluation, Stake turned from conventional evaluation methods in the early 1970s to endorse what he characterized as *responsive evaluation*. Stake became convinced that a major deficit of conventional approaches to evaluation was that they were not sufficiently attentive to the *concerns of the individuals for whom the evaluation was being conducted*.

Stake contended that, in order to be more responsive to the issues that were pivotal to those associated with the program, it would be preferable to decrease measurement precision. He argued that an educational evaluation would be responsive if it "orients more directly to program activities than to program intents; responds to audience requirements for information; and if the different value perspectives present are referred to in reporting the success and failure of the program."[29]

Stake's conception of responsive evaluation deals focally, therefore, with the issues that are perceived to be important by stakeholders, that is, the persons in and around the program such as program staff, program sponsors, taxpayers, students, parents, teachers, and administrators. Although the responsive evaluator may use whatever data-gathering schemes seem appropriate, most frequently those data-gathering schemes will be *human instruments*, that is, observers and judges. Once the data have been gathered, results are portrayed in as faithful a fashion as possible. Such faithful representations will often turn out to be case studies, videotapes, or artifacts, rather than merely a bound formal report.

Whereas Stake considers most conventional (preordinate) evaluations to be formal, preplanned, objective, and based on prespecified intentions, he views responsive evaluation to be informal, flexible, subjective, and based on evolving audience concerns. Whereas most conventional evaluation approaches are based, in Stake's views, on an experimental psychology paradigm of inquiry, responsive evaluation is based on anthropology, journalism, and even poetry.

Eisner's Connoisseurship Model

Elliott Eisner, drawing on his experience as an art educator, has devised a naturalistic approach to educational evaluation rooted in the domain of art criticism. Eisner's approach relies on the use of human judgment as the key data-gathering instrument. It is the human judge who appraises the quality of complex educational phenomena, just as it is the art critic who appraises a complex work of art.

Eisner's approach relies on two pivotal concepts: *educational connoisseurship* and *educational criticism*. Connoisseurship is the perceptive appreciation of complex entities. For instance, a wine connoisseur can discern subtle gradations in quality among varied wines. Similarly, an art connoisseur can make judgments of remarkable sophistication regarding divergent works of art. Connoisseurs, as a consequence of their background, are able to appreciate subtle qualities of phenomena with more sophistication than can other individuals. On the other hand, criticism is, in Eisner's words, "the art of disclosure."[30] The education critic strives not only to discern the qualities constituting an event or object, but also to render in verbal form what has been experienced, so that those who do not possess the critic's level of connoisseurship can understand what the critic has perceived.

Eisner's conception of educational evaluation is generally regarded as one of the first approaches to be based on a methodological rationale other than that associated with scientific inquiry. It offers, in Eisner's view, a "new window" through which educational phenomena can be viewed.

There is little doubt that perceptive observers can add to our insights regarding the conduct and consequences of instructional programs. Eisner's brand of naturalistic educational evaluation, of course, depends on the use of perceptive educational critics who, having observed a complex educational enterprise, can then derive and relay to others important insights about what was observed. Eisner and a number of his students are remarkably adept at these two key requirements of the connoisseurship approach, that is, both appreciating and communicating such appreciations. Because few operational guidelines have been provided for those who would implement a connoisseurship model of educational evaluation, the approach has been employed mostly by Eisner, his co-workers, and students.

Although Eisner maintains his support for an artistically oriented approach to evaluation, he recognizes that many evaluators will find this approach less acceptable than other forms of qualitative evaluation. In a recent essay, Eisner predicts that "acceptance of the diversity of scientifically oriented qualitative inquiry will precede acceptance of the artistic model. The former constitutes less of a break with tradition than the latter. Nevertheless, acceptance of the latter will occur."[31]

Ethnographic Evaluation

Ethnographies are detailed descriptions of intact situations in which the behaviors, beliefs, practices, artifacts, and knowledge of a group of people are depicted. In recent years, *ethnographic educational evaluation* has been proposed as a form of naturalistic evaluation which, because of its orientation and methods, can yield a more meaningful picture of educational undertakings than would be possible from a more traditional scientific paradigm.

Ethnographic educational evaluation calls for data-gathering strategies that permit the accurate representation of intact groups. Whereas ethnographies focus on merely understanding particular groups of people, ethnographic educational evaluations take the additional step of appraising that which has, through ethnographic methods, been understood.

Although there are specific investigative methods that are of substantial use to the ethnographic evaluator, proponents of ethnographic educational evaluation see it as more than merely the application of a collection of specific data-gathering schemes. Fetterman[32] argues that educational evaluators who would borrow the an-

thropolgist's tools should also embrace the anthropologist's values. Specifically, Fetterman contends that the following values of anthropology must be accepted by ethnographic evaluators:

- *Phenomenology.* The investigator must be guided by the viewpoints of those being studied.
- *Holism.* The investigator must be attentive to (1) the larger picture rather than details and (2) the interrelationship among elements in the group under analysis.
- *Nonjudgmentalism.* The investigator (1) avoids the rendering of judgments and, if possible, (2) makes biases explicit so that their effects can be reproduced.
- *Contextualization.* The investigator must place any acquired information in its own environment in order to provide a more accurate representation of such information.

Thus, ethnographic evaluators must attempt to adopt an anthropological orientation to their work and not merely rely on the anthropologist's data-gathering techniques. Nevertheless, we can consider the chief methods of collecting ethnographic data, for a review of these data-gathering ploys will provide a reasonable overview of the likely activities of ethnographic evaluators.

LeCompte and Geotz[33] categorize ethnographic data-collection techniques into *interactive methods*, that is, those involving an interaction between investigators and participants, and *noninteractive methods*, or those requiring little or no interaction between investigators and participants.

Interactive Methods of Collecting Ethographic Data

1. *Participant Observation.* Generally regarded as the primary ethnographic data-gathering technique, in this approach the investigator lives as much as possible with the individuals being investigated and takes part in their day-to-day activities. As soon as possible, the investigator records field notes to reconstruct the interactions and activities observed.
2. *Key Informant Interviewing.* Informants who possess special knowledge of status can be interviewed so the investigator can secure data otherwise unavailable.
3. *Career Histories.* Career histories, consisting of narrative accounts of people's professional lives, can supply ethnographic evaluators with insights regarding the responses of those people to particular occurrences, settings, or innovations.
4. *Surveys.* Typically, ethnographers employ surveys that are based on information initially gathered via less formal and less structured techniques such as those described above. Three forms of surveys are frequently used by ethnographers:
   - *Confirmation Surveys.* These are structured interviews or questionnaires aimed at verifying the applicability to the general population of key-informant data and other, similar data.
   - *Participant-Construct Instruments.* These surveys are designed to detect the "agreed upons," such as values and feelings, that constitute the world of the participants.
   - *Projective Devices.* Projective devices permit the investigator to draw inferences about participants' opinions and reactions based on their responses to such stimuli as photographs, games, or drawings.

Noninteractive Methods of Collecting Ethnographic Data

1. *Nonparticipant Observation.* If the observer is truly able to observe participants surreptitiously, as through a one-way mirror or by use of hidden cameras, participants can

be observed and their behaviors recorded. Three forms of such observations are common:

- *Stream-of-Behavior Chronicles*. Through the use of films, tapes, or by-hand recordings, a minute-by-minute narrative chronicle can be secured of what a participant says and does.
- *Proxemics and Kenetics*. Focusing, respectively, on (a) social uses of space and (b) bodily movement, these two approaches permit ethnographers to observe and then record participants' space use and bodily movements.
- *Interaction Analysis Protocols*. These nonparticipant observations range from informal, on-the-spot sociograms in which frequencies of interactions among particular people are recorded to elaborate standardized observation forms employed to identify verbal and/or nonverbal interactions.

2. *Archival and Demographic Collection*. This type of information includes the written and symbolic records kept by or on participants.
3. *Physical Trace Collection*. The erosion of natural objects (for example, wearing away of tiles in front of popular museum exhibits) or accretion of such objects (for example, the number of fingerprints and noseprints left on the viewing glass at zoo exhibits) can provide ethnographers with useful information regarding the behavior of participants that led to such physical traces.

The ethnographically inclined educational evaluator thus adopts the anthropologist's tool kit in attempting to understand educational phenomena. Then, through use of rich descriptive procedures, those understandings are relayed to the individuals concerned with appraising the quality of an educational program.

In review, we have considered three of the more popular approaches to naturalistic educational evaluation. Naturalistic methodology can be either *qualitative*, as when participant observers form judgments, or *quantitative*, as when evaluators note the frequency of physical traces. Clearly, there are meaningful differences among the three evaluative strategies reviewed here. Yet, recalling Guba and Lincoln's view of naturalistic evaluation models as being those relatively unfettered by imposed constraints (both of antecedents as well as potential outcomes), it is apparent that responsive evaluation, connoisseurship evaluation, and ethnographic evaluation are decisively more natural than the evaluation methods espoused earlier.

Final Thoughts on Evaluation Models

As was indicated earlier, any effort to dump a large number of evaluation models into a five-bin category system is bound to leave one feeling uneasy. A better classification job could surely be done if there were twice as many cells for classification purposes. Yet, in order not to overwhelm readers with endless sets of descriptive categories, only five were used here. Clearly, the evaluation-models cake could have been sliced in a different way. The purpose of this chapter, however, was to provide you with a reasonably useful set of descriptors to employ in thinking about currently available educational evaluation models.

Adversary Evaluation   Within these five general strategies there are also options to be considered. For instance, Wolf and other writers have proposed a form of educational evaluation, usually referred to as *adversary* or *judicial* evaluation, in which competing teams of educational evaluators take different sides of a proposition so that the two sets of conflicting views may clarify an appropriate course of action for decision makers. In some instances, adversary evaluations have been conducted in the form of an actual contest, complete with a determination of the "winning" and "losing" side of the argument. In other cases, the evaluation culminates in a "clarification hearing" in which no formal decision as to winners or losers is made.

Yet, adversary evaluation is more of a methodological wrinkle than a full-blown category of evaluation model, for it can be employed with any of the models we have been considering thus far. To illustrate, a meaningful adversary evaluation could be carried out in the context of a goal-attainment approach to evaluation, for example, "Did Program X or Program Y do a better job in promoting learner attainment of a specific set of goals?" Similarly, two adversary teams could tussle over the respective virtues of the input variables associated with different programs.

I have participated on two major applications of the adversary evaluation approach and am fairly skeptical of the virtues of this set of procedures. My negative appraisal of adversary evaluation schemes, however, is not universally shared.[34]

Illustrations of Models-in-Action   For readers who would like to see the actual differences resulting from the application of different educational evaluation models, Ronald Brandt of the Association for Supervision and Curriculum Development has edited a delightful volume in which proponents of different evaluation models describe how they would tackle an identical evaluative task.[35] The Brandt book shows rather vividly that goal-oriented evaluators fuss with goals, measurement-oriented evaluators mess with measurement, and naturalistic evaluators do what comes naturally. For those who would deal further with alternative evaluation approaches, Brandt's collection of essays is illuminating.

Model Merriment   The descriptions provided in this chapter of the most prominent contemporary conceptions of evaluation should accomplish several missions. For those who wish only an overview of the approaches currently espoused by different evaluators, these descriptions may be sufficient. For those readers whose appetites have been whetted for a more intensive pursuit of one or more of these approaches, the brief accounts may serve as introductions. One of the best collections of essays pertinent to these models is the book of readings compiled by Worthen and Sanders.[36] That volume also contains an excellent point-by-point comparison of several of the models described here.

Finally, for those who derive special raptures from engaging in model comparisons (at best, a mild form of masochism), the introductions supplied here will help circumscribe the different models' boundaries. It should be apparent, of course, that a builder of evaluation models has a difficult time subscribing to Polonius's admonition, "Neither a borrower nor a lender be." But although the effective evaluator will, it is hoped, avoid the perils of becoming preoccupied with model minutia, these diverse approaches to the task of educational evaluation are obviously instructive. To proceed without modest conversance with their major elements would be foolhardy.

Discussion Questions

1. If you were asked by a school district staff to describe, as briefly as possible, the five classes of evaluation models presented in this chapter, what major elements of each would you emphasize?

2. In surveying the five classes of evaluation models presented in the chapter, what do you think are the strengths and weaknesses of each?

3. How can theoretical models such as those treated here influence the actual behavior of practicing evaluators?

4. If you can think of other ways of classifying the various evaluation models described here, what classification categories would you employ?

Practice Exercises

Presented below are several descriptions of educational evaluation operations. After reading each description, decide to which of the following categories of evaluation models the evaluators are most closely adhering: (*a*) a goal-attainment model, (*b*) a judgmental model emphasizing inputs, (*c*) a judgmental model emphasizing outputs, (*d*) a decision-facilitation model, or (*e*) a naturalistic model. It is not necessary to identify the particular model (e.g., CIPP).

1. An evaluation consultant has been asked to appraise the worth of a new set of programmed self-instruction sound-filmstrips. The consultant personally completes each of the sound-filmstrip programs three times, then prepares an evaluation report that focuses on the number of practice opportunities students are allowed in relationship to program objectives. Although the evaluator concludes that enough practice has been provided in the program, a negative appraisal is rendered on the quality of the program's task analysis, that is, the manner in which the program's contents

and en-route objectives were sequenced.

2. Impressed by the possibility that unanticipated side effects of an instructional program may be more significant than the program's intended outcomes, this evaluator attends chiefly to program consequences irrespective of whether they are represented in the program's goals. Rather than providing information that others may employ for decision purposes, this evaluator reaches a personal decision regarding a program's merits and recommends appropriate courses of action regarding the program that was evaluated.

3. Having given great care to the explication of a clear and defensible set of measurable instructional objectives for their new program in early childhood education, this group of teachers wants to evaluate the program according to the degree to which those objectives were achieved.

4. An evaluation team approaches its tasks by attempting to understand the nature of an educational program

without disrupting that program as a consequence of the evaluation. In order to accomplish this goal, members of the team typically function as actual members of the project staff so that, as participant-observers, they can describe more meaningfully what takes place during the program's implementation.

5. An evaluation consultant firm has been hired to supply formative evaluation assistance for a newly approved curriculum development project in the field of economics. The instructional materials developers, all academically trained economists, want the evaluators to gather information to help them improve their instructional materials. A wide variety of data are assembled by the evaluation team for the economists' use, including field testing of early prototypes, student reactions, the reactions of other economists, and the like. The economists find that they can modify their curricular materials more effectively after inspecting the firm's formative evaluation reports.

6. This evaluator wants to look at both the planned and unplanned effects of a program, hence analyzes the degree to which goals were realized as well as the unanticipated side effects of an instructional program. A report describing the program's worth, as revealed by its consequences, is always the end product of this evaluator's efforts.

7. A highly analytic evaluator has agreed to provide a summative evaluation of two innovative programs to promote children's social studies skills. The evaluator extensively observes ongoing classroom activities carried out in the two programs. Then, calling on a refined awareness of classroom phenomena, the evaluator provides a rich narrative account of what seemed to be happening as a consequence of the two programs.

8. NCATE is an organization that accredits institutions engaged in teacher education. During their accreditation operations NCATE evaluation teams focus on the resources of a teacher-education program and the way those resources are employed.

9. A history teacher has set forth a number of explicit aims for each course taught and evaluates the success of a course on the basis of measurement data regarding whether those aims have been satisfactorily achieved.

10. Although this group of evaluators believes that the goals of a new civic education program are reprehensible, they conceive of their mission as providing information with which the program's staff can more successfully arrive at a scheme for achieving those goals. Thus they rarely articulate their distress with the basic direction of the project. Rather, they organize their evaluative efforts around the choice-points faced by the program staff.

Answers to Practice Exercises

1. (*b*); 2. (*c*); 3. (*a*); 4. (*e*); 5. (*d*);   6. (*c*); 7. (*e*); 8. (*b*); 9. (*a*); 10. (*d*)

Notes

1. *Webster's Ninth New Collegiate Dictionary* (Springfield, MA: Merriam-Webster, 1985).

2. Ibid.

3. M. C. Alkin and F. S. Ellett, "Evaluation Models: Development," in *International Encyclopedia of Education: Research and Studies,* pp. 1763–64 (Oxford, England: Pergamon Press, 1985).

4. For example, Ralph W. Tyler,

"General Statement on Evaluation," *Journal of Educational Research*, 35 (1942), 492–501.

5. Robert L. Hammond, "Evaluation at the Local Level." This essay is reproduced in B. R. Worthen and J. R. Sanders, *Educational Evaluation: Theory and Practice*. (Worthington, OH: Charles A. Jones, 1973), pp. 157–69.

6. Newton S. Metfessel and William B. Michael, "A Paradigm Involving Multiple Criterion Measures for the Evaluation of the Effectiveness of School Programs," *Educational and Psychological Measurement*, 27 (1967), 931–43.

7. See, for example, *Evaluative Criteria*, National Study of Secondary School Evaluation (Washington, DC, 1960).

8. For example, in their text on educational evaluation, Benjamin S. Bloom and colleagues use the notion of formative evaluation in a fashion quite different from that originated by Scriven. See Bloom et al., *Handbook on Formative and Summative Evaluation of Student Learning* (New York: McGrawHill, 1971).

9. Michael Scriven, "The Methodology of Evaluation," in *Curriculum Evaluation*, ed. R. E. Stake, American Educational Research Association Monograph Series on Evaluation, No. 1. (Chicago: Rand McNally, 1967).

10. Ibid.

11. Ibid.

12. Lee J. Cronbach, "Course Improvement Through Evaluation," *Teachers College Record*, 64 (1963), pp. 672–83.

13. Michael Scriven, "Prose and Cons About Goal-Free Evaluation," *Evaluation Comment*, 3:4 (December 1972), 1–4.

14. *Teachers College Record*, 68 (1967), 523–40.

15. Robert E. Stake, "Retrospective on 'The Countenance of Educational Evaluation,'" in *Evaluation and Education: At Quarter Century*, ed. M. W. McLaughlin and D. C. Phillips (Chicago: University of Chicago Press, 1991), pp. 67–88.

16. It is hoped that the reader will permit a bit of levity in the examination of some of these approaches. All these model designers are well known to the writer. They are all friends, unflustered by a little lightness. Indeed, it was Dan who once observed that in certain parts of the Midwest the CIPP Model was referred to as the "Gooblebeam Scheme."

17. Daniel L. Stufflebeam et al., *Educational Evaluation and Decision Making* (Itasca, IL: F. E. Peacock, 1971).

18. Daniel L. Stufflebeam, "Alternative Approaches to Educational Evaluation," in *Evaluation in Education: Current Applications* (Berkeley, CA: McCutchan Publishing, 1974).

19. Stufflebeam et al., *Educational Evaluation and Decision Making*.

20. Malcolm Provus, *Discrepancy Evaluation* (Berkeley, CA: McCutchan Publishing, 1971).

21. Ibid.

22. Ibid.

23. By the mid-1950s Cronbach was widely regarded as one of the most competent educational researchers in the land. The textbook used in my very first graduate course in educational psychology had been authored by him. That lucid text transformed me into a lifetime fan of Lee J. Cronbach. His subsequent works have only reinforced the wisdom of my early adulation.

24. L. J. Cronbach et al., *Toward Reform of Program Evaluation* (San Francisco: Jossey-Bass, 1980).

25. L. J. Cronbach, *Designing Evaluations of Educational and Social Programs* (San Francisco: Jossey-Bass, 1980).

26. Ibid., p. 6.

27. Ibid., p. 8.

28. E. G. Guba and Y. S. Lincoln, *Effective Evaluation: Improving the Usefulness of Evaluation Results Through Responsive and Naturalistic Approaches* (San Francisco: Jossey-Bass, 1981), pp. 28–81.

29. R. F. Stake, *Evaluating the Arts*

in Education: A Responsive Approach (Columbus, OH: Charles E. Merrill, 1975), p. 14.

30. E. W. Eisner, "The Perceptive Eye: Toward the Reformation of Educational Evaluation," *Occasional Papers of the Stanford Evaluation Consortium* (Stanford, CA: Stanford University, 1975).

31. Elliott W. Eisner, "Taking a Second Look: Educational Connoisseurship Revisited," in *Evaluation and Education: At Quarter Century*, ed. M. W. McLaughlin and D. C. Phillips (Chicago: University of Chicago Press, 1991), pp. 169–87.

32. D. M. Fetterman, "Ethnography in Educational Research: The Dynamics of Diffusion," *Educational Researcher*, 11:3 (1982), 17–22, 29.

33. M. D. LeCompte and J. P. Goetz, "Problems of Reliability and Validity in Ethnographic Research," *Review of Educational Research*, 52:1, 31–60.

34. On the negative side of the case are Popham, W. J. and Dale Carlson,

"Deep Dark Deficits of the Adversary Evaluation Model," *Educational Researcher* (June 1977), pp. 3–6, as well as Lipson, Leon, "Technical Issues and the Adversary Process," *Science*, 194 (1976), 890.

Proponents of adversary evaluation can derive succor from P. Thurston and E. R. House, "The NIE Adversary Hearing on American Competency Testing," *Phi Delta Kappan*, 63 (1981), 87–89, as well as K. C. Wood, S. E. Peterson, J. S. De Gracie, and J. K. Zaharis, "The Jury Is In: Use of a Modified Legal Model for School Program Evaluation," *Educational Evaluation and Policy Analysis*, 8:3 (Fall 1986), 309–315.

35. R. Brandt, *Applied Strategies for Curriculum Evaluation* (Alexandria, VA: Association for Supervision and Curriculum Development, 1981).

36. B. R. Worthen and J. R. Sanders, *Educational Evaluation: Theory and Practice* (Worthington, OH: Charles A. Jones Publishing, 1973).

Selected References

Alkin, Marvin C. *Debates on Evaluation.* Newbury Park, CA: Sage Publications, 1990.

Cronbach, L. J. "Course Improvement Through Evaluation." *Teachers College Record*, 64 (1963), 672–83.

Cronbach, L. J. "Functional Evaluation Design." In William R. Shadish, Jr., Thomas D. Cook, and Laura C. Leviton (Eds.), *Foundations of Program Evaluation: Theories of Practice.* Newbury Park, CA: Sage Publications, 1991, pp. 323–76.

Cronbach, L. J. et al. *Toward Reform of Program Evaluation: Aims, Methods, and Institutional Arrangements.* San Francisco: Jossey-Bass, 1980.

Eisner, E. W. "The Perceptive Eye: Toward the Reformation of Educational Evaluation." *Occasional Papers of the Stanford Evaluation Consortium.*

Stanford, CA: Stanford University, 1975.

Eisner, Elliot. *The Enlightened Eye: Qualitative Inquiry and the Enhancement of Educational Practice.* New York: Macmillan, 1991.

Eisner, Elliot, and Alan Peshkin (Eds.). *Qualitative Inquiry in Education.* New York: Teachers College Press, 1990.

Guba, E. G., and Y. S. Lincoln. *Effective Evaluation: Improving the Usefulness of Evaluation Results Through Responsive and Naturalistic Approaches.* San Francisco: Jossey-Bass, 1981.

House, E. R. "Assumptions Underlying Evaluation Models." *Educational Researcher*, 7:8 (1978), 4–12.

LaCompte, M. D., and J. P. Goetz. "Problems of Reliability and Validity in

Ethnographic Research." *Review of Educational Research*, 52:1 (1982), 31–60.

Lincoln, Yvonna S., and Egon G. Guba. *Naturalistic Inquiry.* Newbury Park, CA: Sage Publications, 1985.

Patton, Michael Quinn. *Qualitative Evaluation and Research Methods* (2nd ed.). Newbury Park, CA: Sage Publications, 1990.

Phillips, Denis C. "Validity in Qualitative Research: Why the Worry about Warrant Will Not Wane," *Education and Urban Society,* 20 (1987), 9–24.

Scriven, Michael. "Evaluation Perspectives and Procedures." In *Evaluation in Education: Current Applications.* Berkeley, CA: McCutchan Publishing, 1974.

_____. "The Methodology of Evaluation." In R. E. Stake (Ed.), *Curriculum Evaluation.* American Educational Research Association Monograph Series on Evaluation, No. 1. Chicago: Rand McNally, 1967.

Scriven, Michael S. "The Science of Valuing." In William R. Shadish, Jr., Thomas D. Cook, and Laura C. Leviton (Eds.), *Foundations of Program Evaluation: Theories of Practice.* Newbury Park, CA: Sage Publications, 1991, pp. 73–118.

Shadish, William R., Jr.; Cook, Thomas D.; and Leviton, Laura C. *Foundations of Program Evaluation: Theories of Practice.* Newbury Park, CA: Sage Publications, 1991.

Smith, J. K. "Quantitative versus Qualitative Research." *Educational Research*, 12:3 (1983), 6–13.

Stake, R. E. "The Countenance of Educational Evaluation." *Teachers College Record*, 68 (1967), 523–40.

Stake, Robert E. "Responsive Evaluation and Qualitative Methods." In William R. Shadish, Jr., Thomas D. Cook, and Laura C. Leviton (Eds.), *Foundations of Program Evaluation: Theories of Practice.* Newbury Park, CA: Sage Publications, 1991, pp. 270–314.

Stufflebeam, Daniel L. "Alternative Approaches to Educational Evaluation." In *Evaluation in Education: Current Applications.* Berkeley, CA: McCutchan Publishing, 1974.

Stufflebeam, Daniel L. et al. *Educational Evaluation and Decision Making.* Itasca, IL: F. E. Peacock, 1971.

Tyler, R. W. "General Statement on Evaluation." *Journal of Educational Research*, 35 (1942), 492–501.

Wholey, Joseph S. "Evaluation for Program Improvement." In William R. Shadish, Jr.; Thomas D. Cook; and Laura C. Leviton (Eds.), *Foundations of Program Evaluation: Theories of Practice.* Newbury Park, CA: Sage Publications, 1991, pp. 225–69.

Wolcott, H. F. "Mirrors, Models and Monitors: Educator Adaptations of the Ethnographic Innovation." In G. Spindler (Ed.), *Doing the Ethnography of Schooling: Educational Anthropology in Action.* New York: Holt, Rinehart and Winston, 1982.

Worthen, Blaine R., and James R. Sanders. "Alternative Views of Evaluation." *Educational Evaluation: Alternative Approaches and Guidelines.* White Plains, NY: Longman, 1987, pp. 43–61.

CHAPTER THREE

Educational Objectives and Educational Evaluation

During the early years of educational evaluation, considerable attention was given to the role of educational objectives. Indeed, in view of the mid-1960s preoccupation with both educational objectives and educational evaluation, one might reasonably assume that they had been whelped in the same litter. Such, however, was not the case.

This chapter will attempt to isolate the origins of educational objectives, describe the role of educational objectives during the early and later years of educational evaluation, and then identify a set of experience-derived guidelines regarding the uses of educational objectives by educational evaluators.

An Alternative Ancestry

American educators' attention to educational objectives was not triggered by mid-1960s federal education legislation. Quite apart from such federal initiatives, a series of developments in the field of instructional psychology resulted in the need for heightened attention to statements of instructional intent. It was the activity of instructional psychologists, not of educational evaluators, that first focused the attention of U.S. educators on the way in which statements of educational objectives were formulated.

More specifically, in the late 1950s B. F. Skinner[1] captured the attention of numerous educators as he proffered laboratory-derived principles for teaching children. Skinner's notions of carefully sequencing instructional materials in small steps, providing frequent positive reinforcement for learners, and allowing learners

Major segments of this chapter appeared in a paper by the author: *Instructional Objectives: Two Decades of Decadence* presented at the April 1986 annual meeting of the American Educational Research Association, San Francisco.

to move through such instructional materials at their own pace were, to many educators, both revolutionary and exciting. A key tenet of Skinner's approach involved the tryout and revision of instructional materials until they were demonstrably effective. Because Skinner believed that such "programmed instruction" could be effectively presented to learners via mechanical means, the prospect of "teaching machines" both captured the fancy of many laypeople and, predictably, aroused the apprehension of many educators.

Central to the strategy embodied in all of the early approaches to programmed instruction, including the small-step scheme espoused by Skinner, was the necessity to explicate, in terms as unambiguous as possible, the objective(s) of an instructional sequence. More precisely, early programmed instruction enthusiasts recognized that if an instructional sequence was to be tried out and revised until successful, it was necessary to have a solid criterion against which to judge the program's success. Hence, programmed instruction specialists universally urged that the effectiveness of instructional programs be judged according to their ability to achieve preset instructional objectives.

Without question, Robert Mager's 1962 primer on how to write instructional objectives served as the single most important force in familiarizing educators with measurable instructional objectives. Consistent with its roots, Mager's introduction to the topic of objectives was originally entitled *Preparing Objectives for Programmed Instruction*.[2] Later, as interest in the book burgeoned, it was given the more general title, *Preparing Instructional Objectives*. Organized as a branching program, which allowed readers to scurry through its contents rather rapidly, Mager's slender volume constituted a 45-minute trip from ignorance to expertise. During the mid-1960s, copies of Mager's cleverly written booklet found their way into the hands of numerous educators and, what was even more important, of influential federal education officials.

When, in the aftermath of 1965's ESEA enactment, federal officials attempted to guide U.S. educators toward defensible ESEA evaluation paradigms, they found an on-the-shelf evaluation approach best articulated by Ralph Tyler.[3] The Tyler strategy hinged on an evaluator's determining the extent to which the instructional program had promoted learner attainment of prespecified educational objectives. Such an objectives-attainment conception of educational evaluation, while destined to be replaced in future years by a number of alternative paradigms, seemed eminently sensible to many highly placed officials in the U.S. Office of Education. Both implicitly and explicitly, therefore, an objectives-attainment model of educational evaluation was soon being fostered by federal officials at the precise time that U.S. educators were becoming conversant with the sorts of measurable instructional objectives being touted by programmed instruction proponents.

In retrospect, it is far from surprising that a Tylerian conception of objectives-based educational evaluation became wedded to a Magerian approach to objectives formulation. That marriage occurred in such a way that many neophyte educational evaluators assumed the only bona fide way to evaluate an educational program was to see if its measurably stated educational objectives had been achieved.

The unthinking adoption of an objectives-attainment approach to educational evaluation led, in many instances, to the advocacy of evaluation models in which positive appraisals of an educational program were rendered if its objectives had been achieved — irrespective of the defensibility of the objectives. Not that Tyler had been oblivious of the quality of educational objectives, for in his writings he stressed the importance of selecting one's educational objectives only after systematic scrutiny of a range of potential objectives.

In his classic 1967 analytic essay, Scriven, having witnessed cavalier applications of objectives-attainment evaluations in the numerous national curriculum development projects then underway, attempted to distinguish between what he viewed as genuine evaluation and mere estimations of goal achievement.[4] In his subsequent observations regarding the role of educational objectives in evaluating educational programs, however, Scriven still came down solidly on the side of measurably stated objectives.[5]

As can be seen, then, although educational objectives trace their lineage more directly from instructional psychology than from educational evaluation, such objectives were widely accepted during the early years as an integral component of evaluation methodologies — particularly those based on objectives attainment.

The Behavioral Objectives Brouhaha

It was in the late 1960s and early 1970s that instructional objectives per se captured the attention of many educational evaluators. Many subscribed, at least rhetorically, to the form of measurable objectives set forth in the 1962 Mager booklet. Such instructional objectives had become known as *behavioral* objectives because, at bottom, they revolved around the postinstruction behavior of learners. Yet, although behavioral objectives were espoused by many,[6] a number of writers put forth heated criticisms of behaviorally stated objectives.[7]

Proponents of behavioral objectives argued that such objectives embodied a rational approach to evaluation because clearly explicated objectives helped clarify the nature of one's instructional aspirations. Critics countered that because the most important goals of education did not lend themselves readily to a behavioral formulation, the preoccupation with behavioral objectives would lead to instructional reductionism wherein the trivial was sought merely because it was measurable. Disagreements regarding the virtues of behavioral objectives were frequent at professional meetings of that era, some of those disputes finding their way into print.[8]

Although the academic dialogue regarding the virtues of behavioral objectives lingered until the early 1970s, most educational evaluators who made use of objectives tended to frame those objectives behaviorally. The bulk of professional opinion, whether or not warranted, seemed to support the merits of behaviorally stated objectives. And, because many educational evaluators believed it important to take cognizance of an educational program's instructional goals, behaviorally stated instructional objectives were encountered in many evaluation reports — and are to this day.

Perhaps the most serious shortcoming of behavioral objectives, however, was not widely recognized during the first decade of education evaluation. That short-coming stems from the common tendency to frame behavioral objectives so that they focus on increasingly smaller and more specific segments of learner postinstruction behavior. The net effect of such hyper-specificity is that the objectives formulator ends up with a plethora of picayune outcomes. Although early critics of behavioral objectives were wary of what they believed to be a tendency toward triviality in such objectives, no critic predicted what turned out to be the most profound problem with small-scope behavioral objectives. Putting it pragmatically, the typical set of nar-row-scope behavioral objectives were so numerous that decision makers would not attend to evidence of objective attainment. After all, if decision makers were liter-ally overwhelmed with lengthy lists of behavioral objectives, how could they mean-ingfully focus on whether such objectives had been achieved?

Simply stated, the most important lesson that educators should have learned about the use of behaviorally stated objectives for purposes of educational evaluation is that less is most definitely more. Too many objectives benumb the decision maker's mind. Too many objectives, because decision makers will not attend to them, are dysfunctional.

The experience-based discovery that too many behavioral objectives did not result in improved decision making need not, of course, force evaluators to retreat to an era when educational objectives were fashioned in the form of broad, vacuous generalities. (My favorite is the following, taken from a school district's language arts scope and sequence chart: "The student will learn to relish literature.")

There is a preferable alternative, namely, to coalesce small-scope behaviors under larger but still measurable behavioral rubrics. Thus, instead of focusing on 40 small-scope objectives, evaluators can present decision makers with only 5 or 6 broad-scope, measurable objectives.

To illustrate, a broad-scope objective might focus on a "student's ability to solve mathematical word problems requiring any two of the four basic operations, that is, addition, subtraction, multiplication, and division." Such an objective covers a good deal of mathematical terrain. A modest number of such broad-scope objec-tives will typically capture the bulk of a program's important intentions.

Taxonomic Travails

In 1956 Benjamin Bloom and his colleagues brought forth a taxonomy of educa-tional objectives in which they drew distinctions among objectives focusing on cog-nitive, affective, and psychomotor outcomes.[9] In their analysis, Bloom and his coauthors attended chiefly to the cognitive taxonomy, laying out six levels of what they argued were discernibly different types of hierarchically arranged cognitive op-erations. These cognitive operations, they argued, were needed by learners to sat-isfy different types of educational objectives. Eight years later David Krathwohl and his co-workers provided a second taxonomy focused on five levels of affective-domain objectives.[10] Although several taxonomies of psychomotor objectives were published shortly thereafter, none attracted the support of the initial two taxonomies dealing with cognitive and affective objectives.

Bloom's 1956 *Taxonomy of Educational Objectives: Handbook I, The Cognitive Domain* initially attracted scant attention. Sales of the book were modest for the first several years. However, when U.S. educators turned their attention to instructional objectives in the early 1960s, they found in their libraries an objectives-analysis scheme of considerable sophistication. Sales of the cognitive taxonomy became substantial and the six levels of the taxonomy, ranging from "knowledge" at the lowest level to "evaluation" at the highest level, became part of the lexicon employed by those who worked with educational objectives. Although the affective taxonomy never achieved the substantial popularity of the cognitive taxonomy, it too attracted its share of devotees. Though not prepared by Bloom, Krathwohl, or their colleagues, there were also a few psychomotor taxonomies of objectives published.

Now, what did educational evaluators actually do with these objectives-classification systems? Well, quite naturally, evaluators classified objectives. Much attention was given, for example, to the appropriate allocation of objectives to various taxonomic categories. Some evaluators would classify each of a program's objectives according to its proper taxonomic niche in the hope of bringing greater clarity to the objectives being sought.

Several authors even went to the trouble of identifying the action verbs in instructional objectives that would be indicative of particular levels of the taxonomies.[11] Thus, if an objective called for the student to "select from alternatives," this task was thought to represent a specific taxonomic level, whereas if the learner were

asked to "compose an essay," then a different taxonomic level was reflected. It is saddening to recall the large amounts of time that were devoted to teasing out the taxonomic distinctions among different objectives, for, in the main, this activity made no practical difference to anyone. (In fairness, it should be noted that some educators subscribe to the usefulness of the objectives taxonomies on the grounds that teachers are able to understand more clearly the nature of the intentions they pursue.)

One supposes, of course, that if certain educators derive personal satisfaction from doing taxonomic analyses, akin to the joys that some people derive from doing crossword puzzles, then such behavior should not be chided. However, extensive preoccupation with the classification potential of the objectives taxonomies seems to reflect time ill-spent. In fact, if there were a taxonomy of time-wasting activities, one might speculate that taxonomic analyses of educational objectives would be classified toward the top of the hierarchy.

For one thing, the taxonomies focus on *covert* processes of individuals, processes whose nature must be inferred from the *overt* behaviors we can witness. To illustrate, for the cognitive taxonomy, we present an assignment calling for students to write an essay in which discrete information is coalesced. We then infer that the "synthesis" level of the taxonomy has been achieved because the student whips out a requested essay. But what if the student is merely parroting an analysis heard at the dinner table earlier in the week? In that instance, memory rather than synthesizing ability has been displayed; hence a different level of the cognitive taxonomy is represented. Unless we have a solid fix on the relevant prior history of the learner, it is almost impossible to know whether a given type of cognitive learner response represents a higher- or lower-order intellectual process. Answering a challenging multiple-choice test item may represent the "application" level of the cognitive taxonomy—unless, of course, the correct answer to the question had been discussed and practiced during a previous class. There is, obviously, peril in attempting to infer the nature of the unobservable.

An even more substantial shortcoming with taxonomic analyses of educational objectives can be summed up with a succinct "So what?" Putting it another way, even if educational evaluators could categorize the taxonomy nuances of objectives with perfect accuracy, what is the meaningful yield from isolating these taxonomic levels? Are educational decision makers truly advantaged as a consequence of such classification forays? Is it, in fact, the case that higher-level objectives are more laudable than lower-level objectives? Or, more sensibly, must we not really determine the defensibility of an educational objective on its intrinsic merits rather than its taxonomic pigeonhole?

The taxonomies of educational objectives brought to educational evaluators a helpful heuristic when they are used as a broad-brush way of viewing a program's educational aspirations. It *is* useful to recognize that there are no affective objectives sought by the program or that the program's cognitive objectives deal predominantly with rote-recall knowledge. Beyond such general appraisals, however, fine-grained taxonomic analyses yield dividends of debatable utility.

During the first decade of serious attention to educational objectives, the taxonomies of educational objectives became new hammers for many educational evaluators who, consistent with the law of the hammer, discovered numerous things in need of hammering. For the taxonomies of educational objectives, hammering time has now ended.

However, after my having harped about the shortcomings of taxonomic analyses for several paragraphs, it would be unseemly not to provide the reader with at least a sketchy idea of the innards of these taxonomies. Accordingly, before bidding adieu to the taxonomies, a brief representation of the cognitive, affective, and psychomotor taxonomies is presented below.

The Cognitive Domain

The cognitive domain focuses on the ways an individual acquires and uses knowledge. In the volume on the cognitive taxonomy, Bloom and his associates attempt to define and categorize the ways in which information is used and, in the process, developed a scale ranging from simple, concrete behavior through complex, more abstract behavior. At the lowest level of the taxonomy is knowledge.

Knowledge   Knowledge basically consists of the recall of universals or specifics, of processes or methods, or of structures, patterns, and so forth. The essential attribute of this level of the taxonomy is *recall*. In other words, the knowledge level of the cognitive taxonomy describes learner activities that basically deal with memory or recollection. The knowledge level is further subdivided into 12 specific categories, such as knowledge of specifics and knowledge of terminology.

Comprehension   The second level of the cognitive taxonomy is comprehension, which represents the lowest nonrote form of understanding. At this level a learner knows what information is being communicated and is able to make use of it without necessarily seeing it in its fullest implications or relating it to other material. The comprehension level is subdivided into translation, interpretation, and extrapolation.

Application   At the application level of the cognitive taxonomy the learner uses abstractions in concrete or specific situations. Such abstractions might include general ideas, procedural rules, or generalized methods. The abstractions might also be technical principles or theories that must be recalled and applied. Bloom and his colleagues did not subdivide the application category, although they suggested that in writing measurement items to assess this cognitive level, the emphasis should be on devising situations that are new to the student.

Analysis   Behavior on the analysis level involves breaking down a communication into its constituent parts in such a way that the relationship of ideas is made clear, or, if a hierarchy of ideas is present, in a way that clarifies the hierarchy. Such analyses are intended to clarify communication by indicating how the communication is organized and the manner in which it conveys its effect. The analysis category is subdivided into analysis of elements, analysis of relationships, and analysis of organizational principles.

Synthesis   Synthesis involves blending elements and parts in order to form a whole. This essentially involves working with parts, pieces, and elements and reorganizing them in such a way as to constitute a structural pattern that was not previously present. The synthesis category is subdivided into production of a unique communication, production of a plan, and derivation of a set of abstract relations.

Evaluation   At the highest level of the cognitive taxonomy is evaluation. Evaluation involves judgments made about the value of methods and materials for particular purposes. Qualitative and quantitative judgments are made about the extent to which certain phenomena satisfy given criteria. The criteria applied may be determined by the learner or given by someone else. The evaluation category is subdivided into judgments in terms of internal evidence and judgments in terms of external criteria.

The Affective Domain

Affective objectives deal chiefly with learners' interests, attitudes, and values. The affective domain devised by Krathwohl and his associates assumes that the pattern involved in acquiring values moves from a very low level of awareness toward the highest level of internalization. At the lowest level of the affective taxonomy, we find receiving.

Receiving (Attending)   The initial level of the affective taxonomy is concerned with the learner's sensitivity to the existence of certain stimuli and the willingness to receive or attend to them. Krathwohl and his associates identified this as the first crucial step if a learner is to acquire other skills intended by the teacher. This category is subdivided into awareness, willingness to receive, and controlled or selected attention.

Responding   At the second level of the affective taxonomy we are concerned with responses that go beyond merely attending to phenomena. Students are sufficiently concerned with the stimuli that they are not simply willing to attend but are actively attending. Many teachers employ this level of the affective taxonomy to describe interest objectives. We frequently use the term *interest* to describe the attitude of an individual who has become sufficiently involved with a subject or activity to seek it out. The responding level is subdivided into acquiescence in responding, willingness to respond, and satisfaction in response.

Valuing   The third level of the affective taxonomy employs a descriptive term that is in common use by many educators. It is employed in its ordinary sense, namely, to indicate that a thing, phenomenon, or behavior has worth to someone. This category describes many objectives that use such terms as *attitude* and *values*. The valuing category is subdivided into acceptance of a value, preference for a value, and commitment.

Organization   When learners internalize values, they encounter instances in which more than one value pertains. This situation requires the individual to reorganize such values into some kind of cohesive system. As the organized value system emerges, it becomes necessary both to conceptualize the values and to establish their hierarchical relationship. Accordingly, the organizational category is subdivided into conceptualization of a value and organization of a value system.

Characterization   At the highest level of the affective taxonomy we find individuals acting consistently in accordance with values they have previously accepted. The influence of these organized values is so pervasive that it is possible to characterize an individual in relationship to these values. For example, we might think of individuals who are so ardently liberal in their values that we can really describe them as liberals in most realms of activity. The characterization level of the affective taxonomy is subdivided into generalized set and characterization.

The Psychomotor Domain

The psychomotor domain is concerned with the development and use of the muscles and the body's ability to coordinate its movements. *The Classification of Educational Objectives: Psychomotor Domain* by E. J. Simpson is a frequently cited taxonomy dealing with this type of behavior.[12] The major elements of the Simpson taxonomy are presented here.

Perception   The first step in performing a motor act is the process of becoming aware of objects, qualities, or relations through the sense organs. It is the main portion of the situation-interpretation-action chain leading to motor activity.

Set   Set is a preparatory adjustment for a particular kind of action or experience. Three distinct aspects of set have been identified—mental, physical, and emotional.

Guided Response   This is an early step in the development of a motor skill. The emphasis is on the abilities that are components of the more complex skill. Guided response is the overt behavioral act of an individual under the guidance of another individual.

Mechanism   At this level the learner has achieved a certain confidence and degree of skill in the performance of an act. The habitual act is a part of the learner's repertoire of possible responses to stimuli and the demands of situations where the response is appropriate.

Complex Overt Response   At this level the individual can perform a motor act that is considered complex because of the movement pattern required. The act can be carried out efficiently and smoothly, that is, with minimum expenditure of energy and time.

There are other available taxonomies that might be used in categorizing educational objectives. An illustration of one of these schemes follows. The educational evaluator should be attentive to the introduction of new categorization schemes that can be used to describe better, hence understand, instructional goals.

Gagné's Classification of Objectives by Types of Learning

Robert Gagné, one of America's premier instructional psychologists, has identified six types of objectives appropriate for describing intellectual skills to be produced in learners.[13] Each type of objective is associated with a different kind of learning. This scheme is helpful in appraising the quality of instructional objectives under consideration for an instructional sequence.

In Gagné's six-category system, the *major verb* is the key descriptor because it identifies the kind of intellectual operation being carried out by the learner. The learner can display the requisite skill by any number of overt behaviors, which are described by a variety of *minor verbs*. For example, an objective might be stated as follows:

> The learner will be able to *reinstate* [major verb] the names of the current Justices of the Supreme Court by *writing* [minor verb] them without prompts.

The minor verb in this objective could also have been *saying* the names, *listing* the names, or any other "ing" verb that would suggest an appropriate way for students to demonstrate that they possess the skill called for in the objective.

Reinstating   The learner reinstates a verbal or motor stimulus, such as reciting a memorized poem or performing the basic operations involved in tying a shoelace. This kind of learning is called *chain learning*. In such learning, the student becomes able to reel off a sequence of individual responses, either motor or verbal. For example, the motions required for buttoning a button or for printing the letter *K* constitute motor chains. Memorized word sequences, such as "Two heads are better than one," are also verbal chains.

Discriminating   The learner discriminates between two or more stimulus objects, usually objects that resemble each other to some extent. The type of learning involved is *discrimination learning:* the learner is able to discern the difference between two or more objects—that is, to tell whether two things are alike or different.

Identifying   Gagné's third category of objectives requires the student to identify a concept, such as an object quality like *green* or *rectangular*, by its appearance. The type of learning involved here is *concrete concept learning*. In such learning, a child would be able to distinguish between the letters *b* and *d* after having identified them in given words.

Classifying Gagné's fourth category of objectives requires the learner to classify, which should be understood to mean "classify by using a definition." Most of the concepts learned in school fall into this category, and the type of learning involved is called *defined concept learning*. Concepts, such as *society* or *culture*, have to defined and cannot be denoted by simply pointing to them. This type of objective obliges the learner to use a definition rather than simply to recall (reinstate) information.

Demonstrating Learners demonstrate that they know a given rule. For instance, if the rule under consideration is "water flows downhill," then learners must somehow show that they know what the rule means. The kind of learning involved is called *rule learning*. Although there is not much difference between defined concepts and rules, definitions are one class of rules—that is, a rule that has the purpose of identifying a class of objects. An example of a suitable objective for this class of learning behavior might be, "Given a pair of dissimilar fractions, demonstrate the rule for their multiplication."

Generating The final class of objectives provided by Gagné uses the verb *generate*. It is associated with *higher-order rule learning*. Such rules consist of two or more simpler rules and are not simply applied or demonstrated, but in a sense, are invented by the learner. The learner solves problems in novel situations. For instance, if we present to a child a brand-new problem of explaining why shadows cast at noon are shorter than those cast in the afternoon, then the learner has to put together several simple rules in order to discover a higher-order rule.

Selecting versus Generating Objectives

During the 1960s the writer spent a fair chunk of his professional life extolling the virtues of well-stated instructional objectives. Although I did not view them as panacean, I certainly thought that the use of measurable objectives could significantly improve the quality of instructional efforts. The use of explicit instructional objectives had helped my own teaching, and I was convinced they could help other instructors.

Thus I did everything I could to teach educators how to state their objectives in behavioral terms. I wrote journal articles. I gave speeches. I developed filmstrip-tape programs about objectives. I taught regular classes and short institutes in which the use of behavioral objectives was emphasized. I even had bumper stickers printed and distributed to my UCLA classes, which read: "Help Stamp Out Nonbehavioral Objectives!" There was no doubt about it, I was an ardent proponent of measurable goals. Michael Scriven even described me as "the licensed midwife to the birth of behavioral objectives."

Although I was able to reach a good many educators regarding the raptures of behavioral objectives, and even instructed them regarding how to write such objectives, I had an uneasiness that my instructional zeal was misdirected. This nagging feeling was confirmed in unequivocal terms during a mid-1960s trip to Ethiopia.

At that time UCLA participated in a number of Peace Corps training programs, particularly for prospective Peace Corps teachers in various parts of Africa. I was contacted by a Peace Corps official in Washington, DC, who asked me if I would be interested in visiting Ethiopia for a few weeks to talk with a group of Peace Corps volunteers we had trained at UCLA eight months earlier. The Peace Corps officials were concerned about whether the training given volunteers in Los Angeles was, in fact, relevant to their Ethiopian instructional responsibilities. Without hesitation, I accepted the invitation. After all, how often does one get to go to an empire?

While in Ethiopia I traveled around a good bit, spending a day or two with volunteers on teaching assignments in various parts of the country. During my third week there I was scheduled to visit a small town south of the capital, Addis Ababa. A volunteer there was teaching sixth-grade Ethiopian children. We flew in on an Ethiopian Air Lines charter plane, *literally* landing in a cow pasture (unoccupied by cows at that instant). I set out immediately to locate the volunteer. Now, remember that these volunteers hadn't seen me for over eight months and that during their three-month stay at UCLA they had no idea that I would be following them over to Ethiopia. Thus, when I finally spotted the volunteer and greeted him, he could only sputter "Doctor . . ." (It was apparent he couldn't remember my name.) "Doctor . . ." And then, with a gleam of recognition, "Doctor . . . *objectives!*"

I was pleased, for at least he remembered my main message. He invited me to return with him to his hovel for lunch. (It was fashionable for Peace Corps volunteers in Africa to live in hovels.) When we arrived, I asked him whether he remembered what he'd been taught about objectives at UCLA. He responded with enthusiasm, "Oh yes, I recall it all, cognitive, affective, psychomotor, the whole bit!" "Great," I replied, then asked expectantly whether he found objectives useful in his work. "Hell, no," he snapped, "I'm too damned busy teaching!"

That was a very sobering experience for me. On the flight home I kept thinking about the hundreds of teachers who knew how to write objectives, indeed who even wanted to write objectives but, as my Peace Corps friend had reminded me, were "too damned busy teaching," I had probably been making an unrealistic request of teachers, namely, to sit down at the end of an exhausting day and produce sparkling behavioral objectives. Faced with flocks of children and multiple preparations, they're lucky to make it home for dinner. Most teachers don't have the energy and some don't have the skill to generate a raft of high-level instructional objectives. But because they don't have the time to generate their own objectives doesn't mean that educators cannot employ objectives in their work. Surgeons don't have to fashion their own scalpels at the end of a day; scalpels, just like prepared sets of objectives, represent *resources* that can be used by professionals.

Thus, if educational evaluators find themselves working with educational decision makers who wish to employ educational objectives in the evaluative enterprise, it is not necessary to force those educators to articulate their own objectives. Rather, the skilled educational evaluator can provide a menu of possible alternative objectives (preferably a manageable number of broad-scope objectives) from which the decision makers can make selections and/or modifications. Wheel reinvention need not take place when educators decide upon objectives. It's easier and more efficient to have decision makers choose objectives rather than churning them out from scratch.

Measurement and Objectives

Any educational evaluator who seriously believes that objectives achievement ought to be a key element in the evaluation of educational programs must reckon with a major task: determining whether objectives have, in fact, been achieved. It is because of this requirement that we must consider the evolving manner in which educational evaluators have employed measuring devices to discern whether educational objectives have been achieved.

There are some educational objectives, of course, that require little or nothing in the way of assessment devices to indicate whether they have been accomplished. For instance, if the chief objective of a "make-school-interesting" campaign is to reduce absenteeism, then the verification of that objective's attainment hinges on a clerk's counting absence records. If the nature of the educational objective is such that it does not require the use of formal assessment devices such as tests or inventories, then objectives can be employed without much attention to assessment considerations.

Yet, because program objectives in the field of education often focus on improving the status of students' knowledge, attitudes, or skills, determination that educational objectives have been achieved usually hinges on the use of some type of formal assessment device. During the past two decades educational evaluators have learned some important lessons about how to use such assessment devices.

For one thing, it is now generally accepted that criterion-referenced tests are to be strongly preferred over their norm-referenced counterparts. The distinction between traditional norm-referenced tests and the newer criterion-referenced tests was initially drawn by Robert Glaser in 1963.[14] Glaser characterized norm-referenced measures as instruments yielding *relative* interpretations, such as the percentage of examinees in a normative group whose performance had been exceeded by a given examinee's performance. In constrast, criterion-referenced measures were seen to yield *absolute* interpretations, such as whether or not an examinee could master a well-defined set of criterion behaviors. Although the utility of this distinction was generally accepted, precious little attention was given to criterion-referenced testing by educational measurement specialists until the 1970s.

It was during the 1970s, indeed, that increasing numbers of educational evaluators began to recognize a continuing pattern of "no significant differences" whenever norm-referenced achievement tests were employed as indicators of an educational objective's achievement. We shall consider some of the reasons for that situation in the next chapter.

Although almost all educational evaluators recognized that norm-referenced tests were better than nothing, the 1970s were marked by growing dissatisfaction with norm-referenced achievement tests. Yet, it was soon discovered that not every test being paraded by its creators as a "criterion-referenced" assessment device was, in fact, a meaningful improvement over its norm-referenced predecessors. Many of the so-called criterion-referenced tests of that decade were so shoddy that they were better suited for the paper shredder than for use in educational evaluations.

This discussion of the relationship between educational objectives and measures leads naturally into a choice-point for evaluators. Should educational evaluators focus on program objectives initially, then move toward measurement, or should they leap directly toward measurement and dispense with objectives altogether?

Although it is true that objectives without assessment often represent only a planner's rhetoric, it is difficult to deny that framing one's intentions clearly can aid in both program design and the subsequent formative and/or summative evaluation of the program. There seems to be virtue, however, in first determining what the range of available assessment options actually is, then framing one's objectives in such a way that those objectives are linked to available assessment instrumentation. To formulate educational objectives while remaining oblivious of assessment possibilities is folly.

Performance Standards as Separable

When Mager[15] offered his conception of an acceptable instructional objective, he argued that such an objective would (1) identify and name the student behavior sought, (2) define any important conditions under which the behavior was to occur, and (3) define a level of acceptable performance. Thus, an example of an acceptable Magerian objective might be this:

> The student must be able, in 10 minutes or less, to name correctly the items depicted in 18 of 20 previously unencountered blueprints.

Note that the student behavior, "to name," must occur under two conditions: the carrying out of the naming "in 10 minutes or less," plus the blueprints being "previously unencountered." In addition, the objective establishes the performance level as 18 of 20 correct. Yes, in 1962 Bob Mager would have smiled a happy smile when viewing such an instructional objective.

But since 1962 we have learned that the behavior identified in the objective and the performance level sought from that behavior are decisively separable. Indeed, there is substantial virtue in keeping an objective's behavior and performance standards distinct. If evaluators are forced to attach a performance standard to educational objectives in advance of a program's implementation, the standard will almost always be arbitrary and indefensible. In most settings it makes far more sense to await the program's impact, then render an experience-informed judgment regarding acceptable levels of performance.

During the past decade considerable attention has been directed toward the establishment of defensible performance standards.[16] Most of this work has been linked to competency testing programs and the need to establish acceptable performance on competency tests for, say, awarding of high school diplomas. There is no reason that educational evaluators cannot profit from this standard-setting literature and apply it to judgments regarding hoped-for program effectiveness. The isolation of the student behaviors to be sought is, however, a different task than the determination of *how well* those behaviors must be displayed. Mixing behavioral aspirations and performance standards in educational objectives adds not clarity but confusion.

Needs Assessment

The really difficult task for any educator is not to learn how instructional objectives should be stated in a precise form; there are a number of instructional materials that can demonstrably promote one's competence in the techniques of specifying objectives. The real obstacle is deciding on which objectives should be pursued. Evaluators are often called on to help assess the merits of competing instructional goals.

There are several schemes that have been proposed by curriculum specialists for deciding on instructional goals;[17] however, most of these approaches are more intuitive than systematic. A model recommended by some evaluators for coping with the goal-determination dilemma is known as *educational needs assessment*. The needs-assessment approach to the isolation of educational objectives was used more frequently in the early days of educational evaluation than in recent years. However, because some evaluators still believe in the efficacy of this approach to objectives isolation, it will be described here.

In brief, an educational needs assessment involves an attempt to identify educational needs so that instructional goals can be selected to ameliorate those needs. An educational need is assumed to consist of:

Desired		Current		An
Status of	minus	Status of	equals	Educational
Learners		Learners		Need

The most popular needs-assessment models emphasize the accumulation of a considerable amount of *preference* data, typically from a variety of *different* educational clienteles, such as pupils, teachers, and parents. This preference information deals with which educational goals various groups would most like to see a given instructional system achieve. At the same time, information regarding the current status of learners is assembled so that contrasts can be made between what should be and what is, in order to identify the needs toward which an educational system can be directed.

One common procedure for carrying out a needs assessment starts with assembling a pool of existing objectives, then submitting these objectives to representatives from various groups, such as classroom teachers, university academic specialists, parents, and pupils. Sometimes a specially constituted panel of "futurists" appraises possible objectives from a perspective of the twenty-first century, not just the present. Other panels, for example, internationalists or traditionalists, might be constituted in order to represent distinctive points of view that might otherwise be overlooked.

These groups could then be given a set of possible objectives to be ranked or rated in terms of importance. Opportunities should be provided for groups to augment the set of objectives if serious omissions are noted. The advantage of having individuals rate objectives, for instance on a 5-point scale, is that by using a rating rather than ranking system we can sample more effectively. Such samples could be carried out by giving different individuals less than the total set of objectives to rate, then combining the ratings of all the people sampled for all the objectives. Using a ranking approach, such as identifying the most- to least-preferred objectives, makes such sampling difficult to implement.

The groups could be given some straightforward directions, such as these:

> For purposes of helping determine which educational objectives our schools should be pursuing, please read then rate each of the objectives presented below according to its importance. Use a 5-point scale where 5 = very important, 4 = important, 3 = average, 2 = unimportant, and 1 = very unimportant.

Each respondent could be given such directions along with a manageable number of objectives to rate, say 20 to 30. If there are more objectives to be rated, they can be divided into manageable sets so that different representatives of the same group can rate them. We need not have each individual rate all the objectives, because we will be looking for group estimates anyway. The ratings resulting from this preference-gathering operation can then be averaged for each group and presented in a table such as that seen in Table 3–1.

TABLE 3–1 • *Illustrative Average Preference Ratings of Instructional Objectives by Various Groups*

	Average Preference Ratings[a]			
Objectives	*35 Pupils*	*32 Parents*	*27 Teachers*	*8 Futurists*
1	4.2	4.1	3.7	2.6
2	2.1	2.0	3.1	2.4
3	4.7	4.6	4.5	4.2
4	3.8	4.2	2.9	3.0
5	4.3	4.6	4.2	4.1
6	3.1	2.7	1.6	1.9

[a]5 = very important, 1 = very unimportant.

When decision makers have access to data such as these, they should be in a more defensible position to choose certain objectives over others. For instance, note the consistently high ratings received by objectives 3 and 5. Note also the generally low ratings received by objectives 2 and 6. Such consistency of perceptions on the part of the several rater groups is significant. More often than not, of course, the picture will not be so clear. In such cases as objectives 1 and 4 the information leads to no simple interpretation.

It is not necessary, incidentally, to weight all rater groups equally in this type of analysis. For example, the group of decision makers for whom a needs assessment is being conducted (such as a district school board) might decide that student input was more important than the reactions of other groups. Accordingly, they might decide on the following weighting scheme:

Pupils	.40
Parents	.20
Teachers	.20
Futurists	.20

These weightings could be used to multiply each group's average rating, then all of these (now weighted) averages could be combined into a single numerical index reflecting the several groups' overall preferences.

It is further possible to gather recommended performance standards from various clienteles, for example, parents, teachers, and pupils, and then combine the summary preference and performance standard data indicators, such as seen in Table 3–2. The figures in this illustrative set of data have been rounded off for ease of interpretation.

But if we stopped our needs-assessment operation at this point (and some evaluators do) we do not have a needs assessment, we only have a *preference assessment*. We know better what the preferences of various groups are with respect to certain objectives as well as desired levels of learner proficiency. What we don't know yet is what the status of the learners actually is. And unless we isolate the gap

TABLE 3–2 • *Illustrative Summary Preference Ratings and Desired Performance Standard Estimates for a Set of Instructional Objectives*

Objectives	*Pooled and Weighted Preference Ratings*	*Pooled and Weighted Performance Standard Estimate*
1	3.9	90–70[a]
2	2.4	80–80
3	2.7	100–80
4	3.8	60–60
5	4.1	90–90

[a]90–70 should be interpreted as 90 percent or more of the students will socre 70 percent or better on the objective.

between what we wish of learners and where those learners currently are, we cannot identify needs. Thus, the next step in a needs-assessment operation is to determine student status on measures related to each objective, then report such information in a form comparable to that seen in Table 3-3. It must be emphasized that unless the measures employed are congruent with the objectives used in the earlier phases of the needs-assessment undertaking, no meaningful comparisons can be made. More details on how to construct such instruments will be provided in later chapters.

Note that in Table 3-3, for ease of comparing performance data with performance standard estimates, identical student minimal levels have been used. For example, with the first objective the pooled performance estimates resulted in an 80–90 level, that is, at least 80 percent of the learners were to be able to perform with at least 90 percent proficiency. The actual performance data based on averaged learner performance are reported according to what percentage of the student population can currently exceed that 90 percent proficiency level.

Now an inspection of data such as those seen in Table 3-3 can be most helpful in deciding which objectives should be pursued. We see, for instance, that objective 3 has already been mastered by a larger proportion of the pupil group than had been anticipated. Such an objective would not be chosen as the focus of an instructional program. Objective 5, on the other hand, represents the kind of situation that would make an evaluator's work fool's play. (Having recently seen some particularly pitiful examples of educational evaluations, the writer wonders if the descriptor *fool's play* is not too literal.) Objective 5 is highly valued by the pooled rater groups, yet it is one for which estimated performance standards far exceed actual pupil performance. Objective 5 would certainly be included in those objectives selected.

Other objectives present a more perplexing puzzle, after putting the evaluator directly into a situation where a conflict resolution is requisite. Note that for objective 1 there is a high preference rating but only a modest discrepancy between desired and actual performance. Then observe that for objective 2 there is a lower preference rating but a substantial discrepancy between desired and actual performance. The problem is clear. Should preference data or performance discrepancies be considered more heavily in deciding upon a set of objectives to pursue?

Once more this decision can be made rationally and quantitatively. Those

TABLE 3-3 • *Illustrative Data Reflecting Pooled Preference Ratings, Pooled Performance Standard Estimates, and Average Pupil Performance*

Objectives	Pooled Preference Ratings	Pooled Performance Standard Estimates	Current Pupil Performance Averages
1	4.2	80–90	70–90
2	3.1	70–80	20–80
3	3.8	70–90	90–90
4	3.9	60–70	40–70
5	4.4	100–100	50–100

commissioned with the responsibility to make the ultimate decisions will have to decide whether these two factors should be weighted equally or unequally. For example, if it were decided that preference data should be given twice the significance of discrepancy data, then we might rank the contending objectives according to the pooled preference ratings, then rank them on the discrepancy data, and combine the rankings into composite rankings after giving the discrepancy rankings only a 50 percent weighting.

Now all these machinations with data and numbers in order to decide what goals to choose may seem too ponderous for the typical evaluator. Whether the effort exceeds the problem obviously depends on the significance of the problem. A classroom teacher deciding what objectives to emphasize in next semester's algebra class would be foolish to indulge in such an elaborate needs-assessment operation. A state superintendent of schools who has to make major resource allocations, however, might make better allocations after getting the result of a statewide needs assessment of this sort.

The procedural illustrations presented here are only that — illustrations — and should not be interpreted as representing the best way to carry out needs-assessment schemes. There are, however, a couple of points that should be noted in connection with the conduct of needs-assessment operations of this general nature.

First, although there were numerous numbers flying around, the reliance on quantification does not excuse someone from making a personal judgment as to the worth of the objectives under consideration. All that a needs assessment is designed to do is to gather a reasonable number of judgmental inputs from different concerned groups, then coalesce these inputs so they can be meaningfully interpreted. Decision makers having access to such information ought to be able to make more enlightened judgments as to the worth of various educational objectives. Those decision makers should not abdicate their responsibilities to a numbers game. The final, difficult decisions are still theirs to make.

A second theme running through such a needs-assessment scheme is that the key decision operations are made as visible as possible. For example, if it is decided to discount the preference data supplied by any group (young pupils, for example), this decision is reflected openly in the weighting system employed to pool preference ratings. If there are those who wish to quarrel with any of these open decision rules, then they may do so. If poor judgments have been rendered by the decision makers, the openness of the process permits those concerned to register disagreement and to try to alter the nature of the needs-assessment procedure. The openness of such systems seems far more consonant with the premises of a democratic society than would be the case if educational goals were selected behind closed doors at a school board meeting or in a superintendent's private office.

Guideline Time

In review, a number of experience-derived observations have been offered regarding the evolution of the use of educational objectives by evaluators during recent years.

These observations lead naturally to a series of guidelines for those evaluators who would employ educational objectives in their work today.

Before we turn to the five guidelines recommended, perhaps it would be fair to report that in current educational evaluations, the role of educational objectives is typically modest. Whereas yesteryear's educational evaluators were frequently caught up in the importance of objectives, today's evaluators typically focus on evidence of program effects irrespective of whether those effects were ensconced in prespecified objectives. Although objectives are regarded as useful mechanisms for inducing clarity of intent, they are not considered the *sine qua non* of sensible evaluations.

Guideline 1: Educational evaluators should formulate or recommend educational objectives so that the degree to which an objective has been achieved can be accurately determined.

Comment: Hindsight informed us that the early advocates of behaviorally stated instructional objectives chose the wrong label, namely, "behavioral" objectives. Not only did that descriptor result in acrimonious repercussions in the 1960s, it still arouses the ire of critics.[18] However, whether characterized as a "behavioral," "measurable," or "performance" objective, an objective that doesn't permit us to judge reliably when it has been attained is of limited utility. Elsewhere it has been argued that, for purposes of curricular design, a modest proportion of objectives targeted at the ineffable may be of value.[19] Yet for educational evaluators who must communicate with decision makers, the ineffable has its limitations. Thus, if an objective is stated nonbehaviorally, it should be accompanied by an indication of how the objective's attainment will be established.

Guideline 2: Educational evaluators should eschew numerous narrow-scope educational objectives and instead focus on a manageable number of broad-scope objectives.

Comment: Educational evaluation is a decision-oriented endeavor. Decision makers need to have access to information that will increase the wisdom of their decisions. Decision makers who are inundated with oodles of trifling objectives will pay heed to none. Too much information befuddles the prospective user of that information. Educational evaluators must encourage program personnel to coalesce narrow-scope objectives under broader rubrics so that decision makers need contemplate only a comprehensible amount of data. Evaluators who countenance a gaggle of narrow-scope objectives do a disservice to both program personnel and decision makers. Less is truly more.

Guideline 3: Educational evaluators should employ the Taxonomies of Educational Objectives only as gross heuristics, not fine-grained analytic tools.

Comment: When evaluators use the taxonomies to remind themselves and program personnel that there are, in truth, affective, psychomotor, and cognitive objectives—and that most cognitive objectives articulated by today's educators demand only the recall of information—they have discovered the mother lode of taxonomic treasure. More detailed use of the taxonomies typically results in our analyzing with a microscope an objective that was fashioned with a sledgehammer.

Guideline 4: If measurement devices are required to ascertain an educational objective's attainment, educational evaluators should employ criterion-referenced rather than norm-referenced measures.

Comment: This guideline assumes the existence of properly constructed criterion-referenced tests. Such an assumption requires sufficient sophistication on the part of the evaluator to distinguish between criterion-referenced tests that are dowdy and those that are dandy. It was also suggested in this analysis that, whenever possible, educational evaluators should encourage program personnel to formulate their objectives so that they are operationally linked to acceptable measuring devices. (We shall consider the notion of criterion-referenced tests carefully in Chapter Seven.)

Guideline 5: Educational evaluators should keep the behavioral focus of educational objectives separate from the performance levels expected of students.

Comment: Above all, educational objectives should bring with them a degree of clarification that elevates the rigor of rational decision making. Embodiment of standard setting in the objective itself typically adds confusion, not clarity, to statements of instructional intent. Moreover, the premature setting of performance standards often leads to indefensible and arbitrary performance expectations.

An Experience-Derived View

As one looks back at the role that educational objectives have played since the early days of educational evaluation, it is clear that interest in objectives per se has abated. For a while, behavioral objectives were like new toys—and it seemed almost every educational evaluator wanted to play.

Experience has shown us that there are other evaluation games worth playing. Test results these days capture far more of the decision maker's attention than assertions about how many objectives were or were not achieved.

As has been stressed throughout this chapter, statements of instructional intent can accomplish much good. When we clarify our educational aspirations in precise form, it is both easier to fashion programs to achieve those aspirations and easier to mold evaluation endeavors that help us see to what extent our objectives were achieved.

Clearly stated educational objectives can help an evaluator if their import is not overemphasized. *Judiciously* employed, educational objectives can contribute to more defensible evaluations.

Discussion Questions

1. What would you say, *from an evalua-tor's perspective*, are the major divi-dends associated with using broad-scope educational objectives? What are the major deficits associated with their use?
2. If you were given the task of devising guidelines for the production of educa-tional objectives with a consistent level of generality, what approaches to this problem would you suggest?

3. What arguments against measurable educational objectives can you iden-tify? Are there any defenses against such criticisms? 1f so, what are they?
4. How do you think that performance standards for educational objectives can be set most defensibly?
5. What is your personal opinion of the five guidelines regarding objectives presented in the chapter?

Practice Exercises

1. Decide which of the following objec-tives are *measurable*, as opposed to *nonmeasurable*.
   a. At the close of the instructional program the learners will be more positively disposed toward individ-uals from ethnic groups other than their own.
   b. Presented with any previously unencountered complex or com-pound sentence, the learner will be able to circle the clauses constitut-ing those sentences.
   c. The student will be able to deal meaningfully with previously un-seen algebra problems.
   d. At least 80 percent of the class will tend to display more positive values regarding U.S. participation in international ventures.
   e. Students will manifest an interest in theater by volitionally attending one or more of the free plays offered by the school drama group during the academic year.
2. Examine the following objectives, then decide whether each is primarily *cog-nitive, affective*, or *psychomotor*.
   a. All students in the typing class should be able to type at least 50 words per minute, without errors.
   b. At least two-thirds of the students

who complete anonymous self-report questionnaires should supply more positive than negative answers regarding the quality of the school's program and their interest in it.
   c. Students will be able to solve new puzzles based on the geometric theorems treated in class.
   d. Given new instances of plant rem-nants to classify, the students in a biology class can properly catego-rize them according to the classifi-cation schemes encountered during the course.
   e. Pupils will display a positive inter-est in mathematics by enrolling in the nonrequired eleventh- and twelfth-grade mathematics classes.
3. Even though some of the objectives given in Practice Exercise 1 were stated somewhat loosely, it should be possible for you to identify whether they are *primarily* cognitive, affective, or psychomotor. Reread them and decide which domain they represent.
4. Consider the following educational objectives, then indicate whether each is a broad-scope objective or a narrow-scope objective.
   a. Given any previously unencountered play from the 38 authors whose works were studied in class, the

student will be able to identify the play's author from stylistic and plot-structure clues.

b. The learner will be able to explain how the following chemical compounds can be formed: H_2O, H_2SO_4, NaCl.

c. The student will be able to recite the Gettysburg Address from memory while alternately imitating the appearance of Abraham Lincoln, Charles DeGaulle, and Winston Churchill.

d. From a set of 200 possible problems, the student will be able to develop satisfactory geometric proofs for any 5 selected at random.

e. The student will be able to incorporate any previously unencountered French adjective into a syntactically correct oral sentence in French.

Answers to Practice Exercises

1. *b* and *e* are measurable.
2. *a.* Psychomotor; *b.* affective; *c.* cognitive; *d.* cognitive; *e.* affective.
3. *a.* Affective; *b.* cognitive; *c.* cognitive; *d.* affective; *e.* affective.
4. *a.* Broad scope; *b.* narrow scope; *c.* narrow scope; *d.* broad scope; *e.* broad scope.

Notes

1. B. F. Skinner, "Teaching Machines," *Science,* 128 (October 1958), 969–77.

2. R. F. Mager, *Preparing Objectives for Programmed Instruction* (San Francisco: Fearon Press, 1962).

3. R. W. Tyler, *Basic Principles of Curriculum and Instruction* (Chicago: University of Chicago Press, 1950).

4. M. Scriven, *Evaluation Skills,* American Educational Research Association, Washington, DC, Series B. Training Tape, 1971.

5. Ibid.

6. R. Glaser, *Teaching Machines and Programmed Learning, II: Data and Directions* (Washington, DC: Department of Audio Visual Instruction, NEA, 1965). W. J. Popham, *The Teacher Empiricist* (Los Angeles: Aegus Press, 1965).

7. D. G. Arnstine, "The Language and Values of Programmed Instruction: Part 2," *The Educational Forum,* 28 (1968), 337–45; E. W. Eisner, "Educational Objectives: Help or Hindrance?" *The School Review,* 75 (1967), 250–60.

8. W. J. Popham, E. W. Eisner, H. J. Sullivan, and L. L. Tyler, AERA monograph series on curriculum evaluation: *Instructional Objectives* (Chicago: Rand McNally, 1969).

9. B. S. Bloom et al., *Taxonomy of Educational Objectives: Handbook I: The Cognitive Domain* (New York: David McKay, 1956).

10. D. R. Krathwohl, B. S. Bloom, and B. B. Masia, *Taxonomy of Educational Objectives: Handbook II: Affective Domain* (New York: David McKay, 1964).

11. Norman E. Gronlund, *Measurement and Evaluation in Teaching* (New York: Macmillan, 1971); N. M. Sanders, *Classroom Questions: What Kinds?* (New York: Harper and Row, 1966).

12. Elizabeth J. Simpson, *The Classification of Educational Objectives: Psychomotor Domain* (Urbana, IL: University of Illinois, 1965–1966).

13. Robert M. Gagné, *Defining Objectives for Six Types of Learning* (Washington, DC: American Educational Research Association, 1971). Adapted with the author's permission from a research training tape prepared for AERA.

14. Glaser, *Teaching Machines and Programmed Learning, II.*

15. Mager, *Preparing Objectives for Programmed Instruction.*

16. M. J. Zieky and S. A. Livingston, *Manual for Setting Standards on the Basic Skill Assessment Tests* (Princeton, NJ: Educational Testing Service, 1977).

17. For example, Ralph W. Tyler, *Basic Principles of Curriculum and Instruc-* *tion* (Chicago: University of Chicago Press, 1950).

18. A. J. Wesson, "Behaviorally Defined Objectives: A Critique," *The Vocational Aspect of Education*, 35:100.91 (August 1963), 51–58.

19. W. J. Popham, "Must All Objectives Be Behavioral?" *Educational Leadership*, 29:7 (April 1972), 605–608.

Selected References

Atkin, J. M. "Behavioral Objectives in Curriculum Design: A Cautionary Note." *The Science Teacher*, 35, (1968): 27–30.

Bloom, B. S., M. D. Engelhart, E. J. Furst, W. H. Hill, and D. R. Krathwohl. *Taxonomy of Educational Objectives: Handbook I: The Cognitive Domain*. New York: David McKay, 1956.

DeLandsheere, V. "On Defining Educational Objectives." *Evaluation in Education*, 1, (1977): 73–150.

Eisner, E. W. "Educational Objectives: Help or Hindrance?" *The School Review*, 75, (1967): 250–60.

Furst, E. J. "Bloom's Taxonomy of Educational Objectives for the Cognitive Domain: Philosophical and Educational Issues." *Review of Educational Research*, 51, (1981): 441–53.

Gronlund, Norman E., and Robert L. Linn. "Preparing Instructional Objectives." In *Measurement and Evaluation in Teaching* (6th ed.). New York: Macmillan, 1990, pp. 23–46.

Krathwohl, D. R., B. S. Bloom, and B. B. Masia. *Taxonomy of Educational Objectives: Handbook II: Affective Domain*. New York: David McKay, 1964.

Lewenstein, M. "In Defense of Behavioral Objectives." *Social Education*, 40, (1976): 560, 564–65.

Mager, R. F. *Preparing Instructional Objectives*. Palo Alto, CA: Fearon Press, 1962.

_____. *Preparing Objectives for Programmed Instruction*. San Francisco: Fearon Press, 1962.

_____. *Goal Analysis*. Belmont, CA: Fearon Press, 1972.

Popham, W. J. "Objectives and Instruction." In W. J. Popham, E. W. Eisner, H. J. Sullivan, and L. L. Tyler, *Instructional Objectives*. AERA Monograph Series on Curriculum Evaluation, No. 3. Chicago: Rand McNally, 1969.

_____. *The Uses of Instructional Objectives: A Personal Perspective*. Belmont, CA: Fearon Press, 1973.

Popham, W. James, Elliot W. Eisner, Howard J. Sullivan, and Louise L. Tyler. *Instructional Objectives*. American Educational Research Association Monograph Series on Curriculum Evaluation. Chicago: Rand McNally, 1969.

Scriven, Michael. "Pros and Cons About Goal-Free Evaluation." *Evaluation Comment*, 3:4 (December 1972).

Simpson, E. J. *The Classification of Educational Objectives, Psychomotor Domain*. Urbana, IL: University of Illinois, 1965–1966.

Worthen, Blaine R., and James R. Sanders, "Objectives-Oriented Evaluation Approaches." *Educational Evaluation: Alternative Approaches and Guidelines*. White Plains, NY: Longman, 1987, pp. 62–76.

CHAPTER FOUR

A Wealth of Assessment Alternatives

We measure to understand. An archaeologist who uses radiocarbon-dating techniques to measure the age of an unearthed artifact wants to understand more about the origins of the relic. A baseball coach who has his players weigh themselves at the beginning of spring practice typically wants to understand how much overweight or underweight they are. It is difficult to imagine anyone engaging in the act of measuring something who didn't want to know more about what was measured.

The purposes to which people wish to put their measurement-derived knowledge are almost as varied as the objects they measure. Yet, it is possible to draw one rather basic distinction that can help us comprehend why individuals engage in measuring things. Some people measure a phenomenon simply to understand it more completely, with little interest in having the measurement-derived knowledge influence their future behavior. The archaeologist, for example, may want to understand more about the unearthed relic only because of an intrinsic interest in the relic itself. On the other hand, many persons engage in measurement activities to illuminate alternative courses of action. The baseball coach, for instance, wants to secure information about the weight of his ballplayers in order to decide what kinds of diets or exercise routines to assign to them during spring practice.

A Matter of Orientation

We can conveniently distinguish between these two classes of measurement purposes on the basis of whether we are engaged in *conclusion-oriented* or *decision-oriented measurement*. Measurement that is conclusion oriented will be directed toward securing information about phenomena largely for its own sake. The scholar often wants to measure an object in order to reach a conclusion regarding the object itself, or perhaps a conclusion regarding how the object is related to other objects. We often use the expression *basic research* to describe the work of scientists who are engaged in trying to understand the world around them for no other purpose than to augment the knowledge base. Measurement activities in such a context would typically be conclusion oriented.

A decision-oriented measurement activity, on the other hand, has a focus on choosing among action alternatives. We examine the gasoline gauge on our auto's dashboard to decide whether it is time to get more gasoline at the next service station or if we can drive farther without refueling. A physician measures the congeala- bility of a hemophiliac's blood in order to decide which of a wide variety of medications to prescribe. In all such situations we find a common element: There is a decision to be made. Measurement activity undertaken in such contexts can be aptly described, therefore, as decision oriented.

It should be clear, of course, that even though basic research is concerned with the isolation of conclusions, such conclusions can be useful to decision makers. Knowledge generated for its own sake can, in many instances, be helpful in reaching decisions. But educational evaluators cannot play a "gather data and hope" game. Their measurement endeavors must be more sharply focused.

The field of measurement offers many useful tools to the educational evalua- tor. The purpose of this chapter is to broaden the reader's awareness of the measure- ment alternatives open to those who would evaluate educational programs.

A Decision Orientation

In the field of education we have individuals who display either a conclusion orien- tation or a decision orientation. We do find some educators, typically educational researchers, engaged in inquiry merely for the sake of better understanding the rela- tionships among educationally relevant variables. More commonly, however, we en- counter teachers, administrators, and other educators who display a decision orientation in their endeavors. Such is certainly the case with respect to educational evaluation.

Most of the activities of educational evaluators are focused directly on helping decision makers select more defensible courses of action. In fact—although this states it a mite too strongly—because all educational evaluation should be decision oriented, all measurement carried out in an educational evaluation context should be *decision oriented*.

Now why is this an important point? Well, we have experienced many decades of systematic educational research and, until the last decade or two, little that could be classified as systematic educational evaluation. To the extent that educational re- search is organized in a conclusion-oriented manner, we may find those associated with it adopting the dispositions of a conclusion-oriented researcher. Such disposi- tions, in some cases, may be totally unacceptable for the decision-oriented efforts of the educational evaluator. A few illustrations may be of some help.

There are many situations faced by an educator using a conclusion-oriented measurement approach where it is not clear exactly what measurements should be made in order for one to understand a particular situation better. For instance, sup- pose an educational sociologist is attempting to uncover relationships between the quality of high school students' peer-group affiliations and the variables that may impinge on those relationships. The sociologist is operating in a conclusion-oriented manner because there is only a quest for understanding. There are no decision alternatives to be nurtured with evidence. In such situations it is often sensible to measure as many variables as possible—for example, parental income, sex, ethnicity, educational history, personality factors, and so on. The more measurements the better, because some of those measurements might just help isolate variables that bear a strong relationship to peer-group affiliation. Although the conclusion-oriented educational researcher's resources are obviously not unlimited, there are many instances when it makes sense to go after as much data as can possibly be obtained (or processed).

The educational evaluator, however, must be a decision-oriented professional. The luxury of gathering a galaxy of measurement data is often counterproductive. Educational decision makers are human beings—and human beings can make sense out of only so much information. Instead of gathering an overwhelming array of data, evaluators should adopt a *lean* measurement strategy, obtaining only those data essential to a decision. Indeed, before securing any measurements, the evaluator should consider exactly how an educational decision might be influenced by the data. If there is no decision to be serviced, then the measurement should not be made—at least not for purposes of educational evaluation. By trying to gather too much information, an evaluator can obscure the pivotal data that should influence a decision.

There are other instances in which the decision orientation of an educational evaluator will markedly influence the evaluator's measurement operations. For example, the evaluator must constantly consider the question, "What difference will this information make?" when deciding whether to gather data. If the only response to this question is, "Well, it would be nice to know," then evaluators had best turn their attention elsewhere. In fact, because there is a special, prestigious allure associated with the more basic inquiry stance of the conclusion-oriented researcher, evaluators often must remind themselves to retain their decision-oriented assessment stance.

More than Numbers

Most often we find people seeking measurements in *quantitative* terms. We are, indeed, surrounded by the results of quantitatively oriented measurement activities—the days of the month on a wall calendar, the number of dollars earned each payday, the ounces of applesauce in a jar, and so on. But there are also instances when we engage in measurement activities leading to *qualitative* knowledge. For instance, when we are asked to recommend the better of two films that we have recently seen, we often consider several criteria as they pertain to each film, then render the judgment that Film X was superior to Film GP. The judges who must appraise the performances of gymnasts are typically more concerned with measuring the qualitative nuances of a performance than the quantifiable attributes. Thus, although we are prone to conjure up measurement images exclusively in quantitative forms, merely because of the predominance of quantitative measurements in the world around us, measurement can also focus on qualitative assessments.

We have to remember that easily quantified data will be simpler to measure, and thus we will often gravitate toward such measurement approaches. It is far more taxing to devise an assessment scheme to detect subtle qualitative differences. Yet the importance of these qualitative variables often warrants the evaluator's efforts to measure them accurately.

Indeed, since many of the most important decisions in education revolve around qualitative considerations such as which educational goals are most praiseworthy, the competent educational evaluator will be particularly attentive to the acquisition of measurement competencies that can be used to deal with the qualitative aspects of education.

A Measurement Tradition

During this century Western Hemisphere educators have established a truly rich measurement tradition and a rather full-blown technology to accompany it. Even though the focus of educational measurement has been the admittedly elusive behavior of human beings, some rather sophisticated techniques have been devised for measuring a host of variables relevant to education.

For example, we have developed numerous ways to assess the reliability of a test. We could undoubtedly fill a small book with the formulas and computational procedures used in the many reliability indices now available. Similarly, many techniques have been devised for improving the quality of tests via empirically based revision strategies. Major test-development firms have devoted millions of dollars to sharpening their capabilities for producing high-quality testing instruments.

Much of this interest in educational measurement was initiated around the time of World War I, when the United States was faced with a variety of selection decisions for the military — for example, which young men would make the most effective officers. Thus in the United States one finds a measurement tradition abetted by well over a half century of rather intense technological refinement.

Most recipients of graduate degrees in education have, by way of a required course in educational tests and measurements, become acquainted with the main features of this educational measurement tradition. Unfortunately, such educators assume that the measurement insights they picked up in such courses will service their educational *evaluation* requirements. Such is not necessarily the case, for a good deal of the traditional measurement technology available to educators is not appropriate in situations requiring educational evaluation.

The target of traditional educational measurement has been the *individual*, and the chief purpose of measuring an individual has been to make decisions about that person. Often these have been selection decisions, such as which students should be selected for more advanced (or remedial) educational opportunities. The bulk of the analyses regarding the validation of tests, for instance, has centered on how we can validly predict from a learner's performance on a test (e.g., an IQ test) whether that learner will succeed in a subsequent educational situation (e.g., college).

The decisions that our educational measurement operations were helping to service were almost always individual decisions about particular persons. If, for instance, we could validly predict a student's subsequent academic performance by using some type of aptitude test, then by using the predictor test early in that individual's educational career we could better decide what educational decisions to make about that student. The focus was on learners and how to deal with them; it was not on the educational program itself. We were not trying to shape up our educational sequences by measuring the effects of those sequences on learners. Instead, we were trying to adjust the learner to a largely unappraised educational enterprise.

It is for this reason that almost all our measurement technology has been fashioned in a norm-referenced mode, where the effort has been to see how an individual learner compares with a norm group, so we could make a better decision regarding the learner. But this is not what educational evaluation is all about. As a consequence, much of that finely honed traditional measurement technology won't work in educational evaluation settings. Evaluators who unthinkingly try to impose that traditional measurement technology on educational evaluation problems will typically be doing a disservice to the decision makers they are attempting to aid.

Number Magic

We live in an evidence-conscious society. People like to have facts before reaching judgments. In particular, the public schools have been subjected in recent years to increasing public scrutiny regarding the quality of their performance. It is not surprising that evidence-prone people usually warm up to numerically displayed data. There is something terribly reassuring about numbers. We tend to ascribe to numerically represented measurement data the precision of finely calibrated physical science measures.

It is because of this human proclivity to display excessive reverence for numerically displayed measurement results that the educational evaluator must be particularly cautious in the use of measurement procedures. There are too many examples of policymakers deriving totally unwarranted inferences from social science measurement data that, though numerically portrayed, just didn't tap the proper performance.

There are, for example, classic examples of policymakers who draw erroneous conclusions regarding the quality of educational *programs* from measurement data based on tests designed only to measure how *individuals* compare with each other. Often, the very kinds of items that people assume constitute certain educational tests have, because of traditional test-improvement procedures, been totally eliminated from the instruments. Although we tend to rely on summary indicators, such as total test scores, there is no substitute for inspecting the actual items that constitute an educational test. This point will be treated at greater length in subsequent chapters.

Educational evaluators must realize that by presenting a few means, standard deviations, or percentages they can dramatically influence the nature of educational decisions that will affect many human beings. This is a heavy responsibility. Being sensitive to the tendency of educators to ascribe almost magical significance to measurement results should incline evaluators not only to advise caution to the users of measurement data but to exercise such caution themselves.

Making a Difference

Perhaps more than any other set of technical tools available to the educational evaluator, those associated with educational measurement will be of particular value. For a variety of evaluation situations, the more conversance that the evaluator has with different measurement techniques, the more astutely the evaluator can gather data pertinent to the decisions at hand.

The nation's schools have been more than amply nurtured on a tests-and-measurements diet since the early twentieth century. Indeed, for most adults, the acts of being tested or of testing someone else are so routine that we almost automatically assume such endeavors are worthwhile. But, as is true with many traditional practices, there are occasions when the enterprise of gathering measurement data is more ritualistic than rewarding. We often go through the motions of administering and scoring tests only to discover that the resulting data have scant influence on our subsequent behavior. In view of the current clamor for evidence of educational effectiveness, we can be certain that the numerous educational assessment schemes established at local and state levels will not soon disappear. We must make sure that these measurement systems are operated so that they make clear contributions to the quality of the educational endeavors with which they are associated.

A measurement system that doesn't make a difference is possibly worse than none at all, for not only does such a data-gathering scheme consume educational resources that could be used better elsewhere, it lulls us into the complacency of misplaced confidence. And complacent educators do little to improve the quality of the instructional interventions they direct. Evaluators must employ assessment approaches that contribute directly to improved decision making.

Expanding Our Measurement Options

For most educators the term *measurement* is synonymous with *test*—and a paper-and-pencil test at that. Educational evaluators, however, must realize that there are myriad measurement possibilities open to them, only a small portion of which are represented by paper-and-pencil assessment devices.

Inasmuch as educational evaluation is typically concerned with the impact of educational programs on human beings, most evaluative measurements are naturally designed for people. And, as we know, people are a puzzling lot. A physician dealing with the physical side of people problems would find diagnosis difficult if the only available measuring device were a thermometer. Even with a host of measurement tools, it is tough enough for physicians to get an accurate fix on a patient's maladies. For those who must measure the intellectual and affective dimensions of human behaviors, the problems are even more baffling. Educational evaluators need to possess the largest possible arsenal of measurement tactics in order to deal with the subtle and elusive problems they will continually encounter. Even using the best available measurement technology, the educational evaluator will find it difficult to gauge the true effects of an instructional program on learners. Without bringing the full range of relevant measurement devices to bear on an educational evaluation problem, the evaluator will often end up with superficial evidence and, as a result, spurious conclusions.

Although few of us have ever operationally tested the ancient admonition regarding the perils of placing one's total egg supply in a single basket, we generally accept the common sense of the rule, because it aptly captures the potential dangers of jostling the basket too vigorously, thereby leading to shell shock. Those securing educational evaluations should be equally wary of pinning their faith on a single criterion measure. There are several reasons, in fact, why evaluators should rely only on results secured by multiple measuring devices.

For one thing, most of the factors to be measured are sufficiently complex that a single measuring instrument can rarely portray an accurate picture. For example, educators are often interested in detecting learners' attitudes toward school. It is unlikely that any one measuring device could provide a satisfactory portrayal of such attitudes. Those attitudes are so multidimensional and elusive that it would typically take several measures to assess properly the ways students really feel about their school.

Another reason for employing multiple rather than single measures is that many measuring devices are far less than perfect. By using only one measuring procedure, we may secure a false impression.

Thus, when considering the range of potential measuring devices, evaluators should characteristically not opt for *the* measure. The array of data resulting from multiple measures will typically be more defensible and will lead to better evaluative judgments.

Helpful Heuristics

Heuristics serve to guide, discover, or reveal. There are several heuristic schemes that can assist the evaluator who is disposed to look for diverse ways of securing valid educational measurement data. We shall consider a few.

The Cognitive-Affective-Psychomotor Taxonomies

Some measurement specialists have found the widely used taxonomies of educational objectives helpful in considering alternative types of test items.[1] At a gross level, the basic distinctions among learner behaviors that are primarily *affective, cognitive*, or *psychomotor* have surely led to the development of types of measuring instruments more diverse than would have been the case had no such tripartite classification scheme been employed. In pre-taxonomy days, for example, we would usually find all measuring instruments focusing on the cognitive (intellectual) behavior of learners rather than, for instance, their affective dispositions.

In each of the taxonomies devised by Bloom,[2] Krathwohl,[3] and their associates, there are subdivisions that represent an attempt to categorize each domain even more precisely. For example, in the cognitive domain we find such subdivisions as *analysis, synthesis*, and *application*. Some evaluators find these subdivisions helpful in generating different types of assessment devices within particular domains.

Although there are some basic conceptual difficulties associated with these taxonomies because of their heavy reliance on the nature of *inferred* learner behaviors (such as the inference that a student is *synthesizing* rather than *analyzing*), novice educational evaluators might wish to become more familiar with the taxonomies as devices to stimulate the generation of more diverse measures.

A Product versus Behavior Dimension

Most educational measurements are based on some type of artifact produced by the learner. For instance, we often encounter test papers or answer sheets the learner has been obliged to complete. Any physical artifact that is produced or modified by learners constitutes a *product* that can subsequently be appraised. Other examples of products that can be measured for purposes of educational evaluation are the following:

Product	*Evaluation Focus*
A bronze tray made in metal shop class	To reflect the effects of instruction aimed at promoting specific metal-shaping skills
Defaced school desks	To index one's respect for the property of others as one element in gauging the quality of school morale
Monthly tonnage of litter collected on school playground	To indicate the effectiveness of a schoolwide environmental education program

The real advantage of learner-generated products is that, once they have been produced, the evaluator can leisurely judge them in a variety of ways. For instance, once a group of high school English students have produced a batch of early-in-course and late-in-course essays, the evaluator can scrutinize the essays in a variety of ways (such as looking for syntax deficiencies, vocabulary level, organization, and spelling). Evaluators ought to search more diligently for learner products that could reveal pertinent things about the impact of an educational program. Try to generate a list of 10 or so such products. The more divergently you can approach such an exercise, the more likely you will be to identify uncommon but potentially meaningful products to measure.

Besides learner products, evaluators only really look at one other thing, namely, learner *behavior*. The behavior of learners differs from our previous product designation, because in the case of products we see that the learner's activity (behavior) results in a product. With respect to learner behaviors, however, no such product results. Indeed, if the learner's behavior is not recorded in some way, it quite literally is gone forever. For example, when a student presents an extemporaneous speech in an English class, this is the kind of learner behavior that could usefully be measured for purposes of educational evaluation. Obviously, if the student gave the speech in an empty room, without any kind of recording—even a teacher's rating—then the behavior could not be used for evaluative purposes.

Here are some other examples of learner behaviors and the sorts of evaluation focus to which they might be relevant:

Behavior	*Evaluation Focus*
Exercises by gymnast on parallel bars	To indicate the effectiveness of special muscle control exercises
Normal conversation by students during lunch hour	To reflect the degree to which desirable usage patterns have been incorporated in uncued oral discourse
Seat-selection patterns by student ethnic groups during schoolwide assemblies	To reveal the degree of students' ethnocentrism after a special program to promote acceptance of those from other ethnic groups

As is true with products, use of a wide range of learner behaviors offers the educational evaluator a potentially valuable source of data for measuring important kinds of educational effects. In particular, measures of learner behavior often reveal some particularly important insights regarding what learners will really do in situations where they are free to behave more naturally. Normal oral discourse often provides insights regarding individuals' true values, feelings, and dispositions. Almost any kind of oral learner utterance falls within the category of learner behavior. Obviously, there are many situations in which we are most interested in such behavior, such as in group discussion settings.

As with the other heuristic distinctions drawn in this chapter, the evaluator will find the product/behavior distinction helpful in identifying possible assessment devices that could be used for purposes of educational evaluation.

Natural versus Controlled Stimulus Situations

Whether product or behavior, the learner's responses are always made to some specific stimulus or, more generally, to some configuration of stimuli. Another dimension that might be considered when one ponders possible measurement techniques is whether the stimulus situation to which the learner reacts is *natural* or *controlled*. By natural, we mean situations that would normally occur without intervention from the evaluator. When a controlled stimulus situation is present, we know that the evaluator has deliberately modified the situation for purposes of measurement. Some illustrations will help clarify this distinction.

Suppose we were observing the behavior of students during lunch periods to see whether they displayed basic courtesy toward cafeteria service personnel. We might be interested, for example, in whether students treated courteously the cafeteria employees who were from ethnic groups other than their own. If the evaluator simply observed what was going on in the cafeteria, without modifying the situation in any respect, we would have a *natural stimulus situation*. Now, obviously, someone has influenced the stimulus conditions. For example, the cafeteria manager clearly has arranged for work schedules, menus, and the like. But we are focusing on whether the evaluator has modified the stimulus situation specifically *in order to secure measurement data*.

In this cafeteria example, imagine that an evaluator wants to see whether the courteous behaviors of students toward cafeteria employees is affected when prices are raised dramatically. The evaluator might arrange to display temporary price increases of 50 percent, then study how the students treat cafeteria employees under such aversive circumstances. This would be a clear instance of the evaluator's controlling the stimulus conditions in order to secure learner response data to the contrived stimulation.

More routinely, the evaluator will select or construct a paper-and-pencil test. Such tests, when administered to students, represent clear instances of controlled stimulus conditions; without the test booklet and its accompanying answer sheet, why would any sane student spend time circling a series of *As, Bs, Cs,* or *Ds*? When a teacher directs a student to deliver an impromptu address for a final examination in the speech class, we have another instance of controlled stimulus conditions. What normal pupil would, without insistence from a teacher, burst into a five-minute oration about "My Summer Vacation"?

There are times when evaluators should be most concerned with learner behavior occurring under natural stimulus conditions. The English teacher who has engaged in a classroom crusade to expunge from human discourse the expression "he don't" should be more than casually interested in whether students succumb to this usage in their normal discourse. If, by some means of recording or reporting, the teacher could get a frequency count on the use of "he don't" in students' routine conversations, then valuable measurement data would have been acquired.

Here are a few examples of the kinds of measurement data that might be obtained under the two different types of stimulus conditions:

Natural Stimulus Conditions	*Controlled Stimulus Conditions*
Student tardiness or attendance data	Student performance on history achievement test
Effectiveness of routine school-picnic cleanup activities	A pupil's final violin recital in a music class
Student care of textbooks or other classroom supplies	Observed pupil response to reactionary political materials deliberately posted by evaluators for that purpose

The trouble with most beginning evaluators is that they fail to recognize the importance of this stimulus-situation distinction in considering measurement possibilities. Too often they routinely gravitate toward typical testing practices and, therefore, the all-too-customary controlled stimulus situation. Rarely do they realize how many rich opportunities exist in natural settings for measuring important kinds of learner behaviors (or the products emerging from such behaviors). Even when natural stimulus situations are employed, few evaluators see the chances for securing meaningful data by subtly altering the natural environment so that ever more significant sorts of learner responses will emerge.

The natural versus controlled stimulus situation distinction reflects a dimension well worth mastering for the evaluator who wishes to become facile in the use of measurement tactics.

Selected versus Constructed Responses

A final heuristic distinction that has been used for many years by measurement experts, not to mention those teachers who are creative test constructors, is the difference between *selected* and *constructed* learner responses. Sometimes this distinction is couched in terms of recognition (selected responses) versus recall (constructed responses). Regardless of the descriptors, it is a useful distinction, particularly with respect to certain kinds of cognitive and affective learner responses.

The learner makes a selected response when making choices among competing alternatives. The most common example would be selecting an alternative in a multiple-choice achievement test or in a multiple-choice attitude inventory. If the learner is obliged to create an entire response, as in short-answer or essay tests, then we have an instance of a constructed learner response. There is considerable agreement in measurement circles that, in certain instances, the evaluator can really get at different things by using one or the other of these two approaches. In some other cases, it probably makes little difference whether the learner selects or constructs a response, for the correlation between the two techniques is so high.

It is generally known that, in the case of cognitive achievement tests, many selected-response devices are easier than comparable constructed-response devices. Because pupil performance on selected-response tests is often superior, even after correction for guessing,[4] it cannot be asserted that the only reason for such superior performance is the possibility of answering correctly by chance. But sometimes it is impossible to devise parallel tests of these two varieties, for they will be parallel only in the sense that the content is comparable. Basically different kinds of intellectual responses are called for in the two tests. For example, if the evaluator is trying to assess a student's ability to compose an original essay, a selected-response assessment approach just won't do.

Whether affective or cognitive (it is difficult to conceive of a selected psychomotor response), the evaluator should carefully consider whether there is any substantial reason to opt for constructed over selected responses. If the answer is yes, then by all means go to the trouble of securing constructed responses. Even though there typically are problems of securing constructed-response data (both time consumption and reliability of scoring), there are instances when the only defensible measure must be a constructed response. If, on the other hand, the evaluator can find no compelling reason to opt for a constructed-response measure, then the selected-response tests are characteristically much easier and far more reliable to score.

General Measurement Strategies

Although it is beyond the scope of this text to undertake an elaborate consideration of the various measurement strategies available to educational evaluators, it may prove useful at least to isolate and briefly discuss the general measurement approaches most frequently employed in educational settings. The reader interested in studying these measurement strategies in more detail is urged to consult one or more of the excellent educational-measurement textbooks in the Selected References cited at the close of the chapter.

Classifying Measurement Strategies

There are as many ways of slicing up the field of measurement as there are of dividing a 10-tier wedding cake. For instance, Cronbach[5] draws a basic distinction between tests that seek to measure *maximum* performance (i.e., how individuals perform when they are trying to do their best) and tests that seek to determine *typical* performance (i.e., what individuals are likely to do in a routine situation). Others distinguish between teacher-made *classroom* tests and *standardized* tests, using such subdivisions of classroom tests as objectively or subjectively scorable, and such subdivisions of standardized tests as achievement and aptitude.[6] Indeed, measurement experts have devised nearly as many schemes for classifying measures as there are measures themselves. Obviously, no one categorization system is ideal, and no such claim will be made for the one employed here. The chief purpose of examining differing overall approaches to educational measurement, as was the case with the previously considered heuristic dimensions, is to increase the range of measurement approaches with which you are familiar. The Law of the Hammer asserts that those who possess only a single tool will find a number of ways to use it— rightly or wrongly. Can you imagine how easily misled an educational evaluator would be who tried to gather all pertinent data by using only variations of a true-false test?

The football coach who devises an effective offense knows that a variety of options typically leads to more success than do a few oft-repeated plays. Similarly, the skilled evaluator will have access to a considerable repertoire of measurement approaches, thereby increasing the likelihood that appropriate ones will be employed.

Paper-and-Pencil Tests of Ability

Without question, the most common measurement device used throughout the world is the paper-and-pencil test of ability. Sometimes the test consists of professionally printed test items. Sometimes it will have been copied via one of today's increasingly inexpensive photocopying machines. Typically, students respond with marks or written answers made with pencils, pens, or even crayons. Few of us have not, during our lives, been obliged to complete hundreds of such tests.

The two major types of paper-and-pencil tests of ability attempt to measure either *achievement* or *aptitude*. For the assessment of achievement, we are interested in such questions as "How much does the learner know about European history?" or "How well can the learner solve certain types of mathematical problems?" When we focus on aptitude we are really interested in the student's ability *potential* and want answers to such questions as "How well is this pupil apt to perform in subsequent instructional situations?" The most common types of aptitude measures are those often referred to as "intelligence" or IQ tests.

As we shall see in Chapter Six, the real trick in devising paper-and-pencil achievement tests is to define adequately the domain of learner behaviors being measured so that we truly understand what is being assessed. Clearly, the critical ingredient in a paper-and-pencil test is the nature of the questions themselves. Merely deciding on a paper-and-pencil test format is an important decision, however, and it is often made for purposes of economy. Many individuals can be tested at low cost, because of the relative inexpensiveness of the testing materials and scoring operations.

The range of paper-and-pencil tests is limited only by the test constructor's creativity. Evaluators with sufficient imagination will discover, for example, that it is possible to devise verbal simulations of reality such that the learner is faced with stimuli closely approximating the world. There is much more to paper-and-pencil test construction than the creation of conventional true-false, multiple-choice, or essay items.

Paper-and-pencil tests of aptitude are of less interest to the evaluator, although there are instances when it may be important to secure an estimate of the intellectual capabilities of certain learners in order to understand better the impact of a particular instructional treatment. Most tests of aptitude follow the general schemes derived by French physician Alfred Binet over 70 years ago for the measurement of intelligence. The most important ingredient of aptitude tests, intellectual or otherwise, is that they permit one to make reasonably accurate predictions regarding how well an individual will perform at some future time. This being the case, almost any kind of test item that helps make that prediction is used, regardless of whether (on logical grounds) we might think it to be a good predictor.

Paper-and-Pencil Self-Report Devices

In contrast to paper-and-pencil tests of ability, which Cronbach would refer to as tests of maximum performance, educators also have devised hundreds of paper-

and-pencil interest inventories, attitude scales, and questionnaires. These instruments, which Cronbach would describe as tests of typical performance, can be conveniently thought of as *paper-and-pencil self-report devices*. The key difference between self-report devices and tests of ability is that in a very real sense the self-report instrument is not a test. A test of ability is just that — a genuine assessment of how well the test taker can perform. Everyone knows it, including the person administering the test and certainly the person completing it. Ability testing is testing with a capital *T*. With self-report devices, however, the person completing the form (an interest inventory, for example) is usually not responding in terms of *best possible performance*. Instead, the responses we want generally get closer to revealing how the person usually feels about a given phenomenon. Evaluators want to know what interests or attitudes students have, and the more *truthful* their responses are, the more accurately we can draw inferences about such affective dispositions.

Now most of the paper-and-pencil self-report devices that people have encountered during the years have been rather straightforward. For example, most of us have received questionnaires that ask us to rank or rate the importance or worth of various phenomena. If we can think back to our earlier years in school, there were usually a few attitude or interest scales to complete as part of some districtwide test battery. Often these instruments required us to choose among groups of avocational activities, job descriptions, and the like. It didn't take much sophistication to figure out what these devices were intended to measure.

There are, however, more sophisticated self-report devices available to us. Sometimes these instruments might be used as is, or with slight modifications. Sometimes they might provide format models for us to parallel. We can look at a few of these to get some idea of the multiplicity of extant self-report devices available.

Most educators have at least heard about, if not experienced, *projective techniques*. The most widely known of these is the *Rorschach* test, devised by Hermann Rorschach, a Swiss psychiatrist. First published in 1921, the test consists of a series of irregular inkblots whose form permits an almost infinite number of interpretations. Persons taking the test are asked to tell what they see in the inkblots. Although the reported images the test taker "projects" into the inkblots are based on an intellectual response, emotional patterns are often revealed.

The *Thematic Apperception Test* (TAT), devised in the mid-1930s by H. A. Murray and his associates, is a widely known projective technique that requires one to interpret a picture by telling a story about it. The individual taking the test is typically given 20 pictures and is asked to describe what is happening, what led up to the scene, and what will be the outcome. In essence, the test taker is projected into the scene vicariously, with responses allegedly reflecting any defeatist attitudes, preoccupation with sex, and so on.

Although projective techniques such as the Rorschach and the TAT can tap data unavailable from more simple self-report devices, the scoring of a subject's response obviously requires considerable sophistication. Although evaluators may find instances when, by presenting ambiguous stimuli to learners, they may ferret out important "projected" responses, such measurement techniques should be used with considerable caution.

   Although most projective tests have been designed to elicit oral responses, typically to be interpreted by a trained clinician, the general idea of having individuals respond to ambiguous stimuli could obviously be transferred to a paper-and-pencil format.

   Another paper-and-pencil self-report device that has received considerable attention from educators through the years is the *Semantic Differential*, devised by Charles E. Osgood. This technique uses indirect connotations of words to reveal one's sentiments regarding specific objects of interest. Subjects are asked to respond to a series of objects on a series of seven-point scales such as the following, in which "justice" and "school" are the objects of interest:

Justice

deep	____:____:____:____:____:____:____	shallow
thick	____:____:____:____:____:____:____	thin
truthful	____:____:____:____:____:____:____	untruthful
soft	____:____:____:____:____:____:____	hard

School

deep	____:____:____:____:____:____:____	shallow
thick	____:____:____:____:____:____:____	thin
truthful	____:____:____:____:____:____:____	untruthful
soft	____:____:____:____:____:____:____	hard

The person completing the scales is asked to do so rapidly, recording first impressions. Because it is difficult to know what the "socially acceptable" answer is when "justice" is to be judged on a truthful-untruthful scale, the device is considered to be less fakeable than other, more direct approaches. For example, in the illustration given, for the stimulus "school" we might secure a series of student responses that, albeit oblique, would reflect student sentiments regarding school. Scoring methods for the Semantic Differential are fairly complicated, and the reader who wishes to explore this technique further is urged to consult a detailed treatment by Osgood and his associates.[7]

   Another self-report approach of some interest is the *Q-sort* technique devised by William Stephenson in the early 1950s. The Q-sort procedure requires individuals to rate a series of descriptive phrases according to which are most or least accurate depictions of an individual, institution, or object. For example, an evaluator might generate the following series of statements, which a student would be obliged to rate according to the degree to which they described the student's perception of "school":

Being there gives me a pain.

The people who run it are first rate.

There are few other places I'd rather be.

A place where dull things go on.

   The descriptive phrases are presented on separate cards and the person supplying the ratings is directed to place the cards in piles with the most descriptive statements on the left and the least descriptive statements on the right. Although the number of cards and number of piles can vary, the subject is ordinarily restricted with respect to the number of cards that can be placed in each pile. For instance, if there are 100 statements to be Q-sorted into 11 piles, the subject might be required to place them in this sort of distribution:

| | *Most* | | | | | | | | | *Least* | |
	Descriptive									*Descriptive*	
Pile	1	2	3	4	5	6	7	8	9	10	11
No. of cards	2	4	8	11	16	18	16	11	8	4	2

Because raters can shift cards back and forth, the Q-sort approach has some advantages over typical self-report devices, where one's responses to items during the early part of a form are often difficult to retrieve, and sentiments may shift during the completion of an instrument. This approach also requires the respondent to make distinctions that, in less-detailed rating schemes, might be masked. Obvious applications in educational evaluation settings would include having students supply Q-sort ratings of their classes, their government, instructional materials, and so on. There are both simple and complex ways of scoring Q-sort data. Stephenson describes several that should be considered.[8] Others have criticized the more elaborate Q-sort scoring techniques.[9] These cautions should be noted by the evaluator contemplating use of the Q-sort approach.

These few illustrations obviously fail to exhaust the diversity of paper-and-pencil self-report devices available to evaluators, but they do suggest some of the possibilities for this general measurement strategy.

Ratings

There are innumerable things in education that must be judged. One common technique for rendering these judgments in a relatively systematic fashion is to employ *ratings*. Evaluators may be interested in securing ratings of pupil performance (either products or behaviors), teacher effectiveness, quality of staff morale, and the like. Rating forms are particularly useful in reducing judgmental impressions to a manageable form. Ratings can be supplied by teachers, administrators, parents, and others. The use of self-ratings is also possible and sometimes quite profitable. There are difficulties associated with ratings, however, and the astute evaluator will wish to become familiar with some of the more prominent of these problems.

Commonly Used Rating Scales   Although there are various types of rating scales, the three most commonly used are *numerical* rating scales, *graphic* rating scales, and *rankings*. Each of these three types of scales will be briefly described.

Numerical rating scales are probably the type most frequently encountered in education. Because of the ease with which such scales can be constructed, not to mention the apparent precision of the quantitative indices that they yield, numerical rating scales are particularly attractive. Box 4–1 presents a typical numerical rating form in which the rater is supposed to render a numerical rating on each of several specified dimensions of a teacher's instructional techniques.

One of the most serious shortcomings of numerical rating scales is that there are insufficient descriptions provided regarding both the dimensions to be rated and the meanings of the numerical ratings themselves. For example, in Box 4–1 there is substantial ambiguity associated with the dimensions being rated. What, for instance, is actually meant by "Maintenance of Classroom Order"? Moreover, even the guidance regarding the meaning of the five rating options is skimpy. Is "outstanding," for example, the actual opposite of "poor"?

Such deficits are all too common in the types of numerical rating scales one encounters in education. It is almost as though the numerical basis of such scales renders them, in the eyes of their creators, quantitative enough to be above criticism. After all, such devotees of numerical rating scales would argue, if one has 10 dimensions, each of which is to be rated on a 1 to 5 scale, the resulting ratings will necessarily fall between 10 and 50. The sense of confidence and precision that springs from such thinking should be avoided by astute evaluators. Unfortunately, with ambiguous descriptions of the dimensions to be rated, as well as of the possible response options, numerical rating scales used by different raters can yield identical numbers that nonetheless signify dramatically different appraisals.

The creation of high-quality numerical rating scales requires time, careful analysis of the scale's directions and dimensions, tryout, revision, and so on. Creating decent numerical rating scales, just like creating any truly defensible assessment instrument, requires care.

Beyond the instrument itself, there is the matter of training those who will use the instrument. If different raters are to be used, it is necessary to make sure they are using the numerical rating scale in the manner its architects intended. Formal training of raters, therefore, is highly desirable. There must be opportunities for raters to practice using a scale and for clarifications to be provided regarding the scale's components. Then, if possible, raters should be given an opportunity to demonstrate

---

BOX 4–1 • *An Excerpt from a Numerical Rating Form*

Directions: For each of the techniques presented below under *Instructional Dimensions*, circle the appropriate number according to the following scheme: 1 = Outstanding, 2 = Above Average, 3 = Average, 4 = Below Average, 5 = Poor

Instructional Dimensions	*Rating*
I. Question-Asking Skills	1 2 3 4 5
II. Provision of Student Feedback	1 2 3 4 5
III. Maintenance of Classroom Order	1 2 3 4 5
IV. Clarity of Explanations	1 2 3 4 5

their competence by displaying their rating skill in some sort of rater-certification exercise.

Clearly, such rater-training and rater-certification activities can be time consuming and costly, yet shortcuts at this point may yield data of limited values. However, with numerical rating scales the limitations of the data are often not seen because the scale yields a *number*. As with most numerically oriented assessment schemes, educational evaluators should not place unwarranted confidence in the results of such scales merely because they yield numbers. After all, numbers can be generated at random by computers or inept mathematics students. Any evaluator who puts excessive confidence in numbers merely because they are quantitative is naive.

Graphic rating scales are a second type of rating scale that evaluators may wish to employ. A graphic rating scale capitalizes on the capabilities of individuals to use visual displays as ways of rendering judgments about qualitative differences among attributes to be rated. Note that in the example given in Box 4–2, the rater is to place an X along a line representing a gradient in quality.

Graphic rating scales can be designed so that the rating options are identical for all characteristics to be rated. Such unmodified responses options are used in a *constant-alternatives* rating scale. If it is desirable to alter the nature of the rating options for different characteristics, this can be done so that a *changing-alternatives* rating scale is created. With changing-alternative scales, of course, it is imperative to remind raters that they must be alert to the particular response dimension that is to be used for rating each characteristic.

To use graphic rating scales effectively, educational evaluators must employ the same care as was described for numerical rating scales. The scale itself must be carefully developed so that its characteristics to be rated and its rating options are well described. The form should be tried out in actual or simulated situations to make sure that it will work properly and, if it does not, to discern what changes in the form must be made. Also, as with numerical rating forms, those destined to use the form must be trained and, if possible, certified as to their proficiency in using the scale properly.

BOX 4–2 • *An Excerpt from a Graphic Rating Form*

Directions: Indicate the extent to which a school principal engages in staff-development activities for the school's faculty by placing an X at the appropriate point on the line below each item.

1. Provides staff-development workshops for faculty

   _____

   Always　　Frequently　　Occasionally　　Seldom　　Never

2. Encourages faculty to attend formal staff-development courses

   _____

   Always　　Frequently　　Occasionally　　Seldom　　Never

Rankings, the third type of rating form to be considered here is, in fact, not really a rating at all. Note in the example given in Box 4–3 that on the left we have *rated* the academic capabilities of the five students, but on the right we have *ranked* the academic capabilities of those students.

When we rank, we make judgments about qualitative gradations among individuals or objects on the basis of those ranked highest, next highest, next highest, and so on. One of the virtues of a ranking procedure is that it obliges the individual doing the ranking to make fine-grained discriminations among individuals that are lacking in a rating procedure. For instance, if a teacher is asked to *rate* 10 pupils on a five-point scale which has "Excellent" as the highest rating, the teacher may dole out "Excellent" ratings to the top 8 pupils. As far as the evaluator is concerned, there is no difference among those 8 pupils; they are, it appears, all "excellent." However, if the teacher is asked to *rank* the 10 pupils, then there will, of necessity, be a first ranked, a second ranked, and so on. This increase in discrimination among the individuals or objects being ranked can sometimes prove invaluable, because if ratings rather than rankings are employed, some raters can at times rate everyone too positively (or too negatively). We shall see later in this chapter that school administrators are notorious for rating their teachers too positively. If asked to *rank* the same teachers, however, such across-the-board positive appraisals cannot be as easily rendered.

When many objects or individuals must be ranked, the task becomes onerous. Even with a small class of students, for instance, it is difficult to keep track of whether Johnny should really be ranked ahead of Jane or whether Jill is ever-so-slightly better than both of them. Subtle distinctions in rank are difficult to render when so many rankings are required.

Even more time consuming is a special application of ranking referred to as the *paired-comparison* method, in which pairs of objects (or individuals) are compared. Paired-comparison rankings are carried out in order that all possible comparisons can be made in a one-on-one context. If there are many individuals to be ranked, such paired-comparison methods can prove genuinely exhausting. The comparison permutations are unbelievably numerous. Unless one has but a relatively few paired comparisons to make, this approach should be reserved for those who wish to rank their way into eternity.

BOX 4–3 • *An Example of Ratings versus Rankings*

Student	Academic Ratings	Academic Rankings
Joe	Excellent	First
Jill	Excellent	Second
Bill	Good	Third
Raul	Fair	Fourth
Sally	Weak	Fifth
Tom	Weak	Sixth

Sources of Error in the Rating Process One deficiency in ratings is that judges will display *constant errors* or biases. For example, some judges consistently are too stringent in their ratings. Such biases can often be detected by having two or more judges complete the same rating scale for the individual or object being rated. A particularly common constant error is the tendency for raters to be too lenient, that is, to commit a *generosity error*. Most school administrators, for example, if asked to rate the effectiveness of their school's teachers will tend to rate the entire group as better than average. Indeed, given categories ranging from "poor" to "outstanding," a teacher who receives an "average" rating may be at the bottom of the scale, since the principal never uses the "poor" or "below average" segments of the scale. At the other extreme, some raters display a *severity error* in which they tend to undervalue the phenomenon being rated.

Another difficulty with ratings is *ambiguity*. Often the rating scales used possess descriptive dimensions that can be interpreted in far too many ways. In a case where different judges are asked to supply a single, overall rating of a teacher's competence, some will think well of a teacher who plays a fairly authoritarian role whereas others will praise the nondirective teacher. In addition to ambiguity associated with the more comprehensive dimensions on which the ratings are desired, there are instances when the rating form's subcategories are ambiguous. For instance, on one rating scale in use by a school district, teachers were asked to rate a variety of pupil attributes, such as "curiosity," on a scale from 0 to 100. The fact that nobody was able to interpret the meaning of a curiosity rating of 75 failed to distress the teachers, who, with obvious dedication, struggled to increase students' mean curiosity ratings from 65 to 70, whatever that meant. Rating categories such as "excellent" or "inferior" are equally vague. If possible, they should be replaced with more specific descriptions, such as, "among the top 5 percent of students with respect to this category."

Another source of error in rating scales is that novice developers of rating scales try to capture every dimension that appears to them to be even mildly meritorious. Such scale developers end up with a plethora of dimensions to be rated, dimensions so numerous as to preclude meaningful responses from raters. Imagine, for example, that you were asked to rate a parent's child-rearing skills on 60 separate dimensions. You doubtlessly would become so overwhelmed by the magnitude of the task that you would not give sufficient care to any of the ratings you supplied. A rater overwhelmed is a rater rendered ineffectual. Skilled educational evaluators will keep at an intellectually manageable level the number of dimensions to be rated. "Less," as has often been observed, almost always turns out to be "more."

Another problem with ratings is *limited information*; some raters have access to far less data than others when asked to rate individuals. It makes sense to choose as raters those who have the most experience with the individual to be rated. For example, would a teacher's pupils or principal have access to a greater experiential base regarding the teacher's performance? Quite obviously, the teacher's students have more opportunity to see the teacher in action, and for this reason some teacher evaluators rely quite heavily on student input rather than a principal's occasional visit. It has been suggested that, when evaluating instructors, we discard "snapshot" data (based on the principal's infrequent visits) and prefer, instead, "motion picture" information (based on the pupils' ratings).

Evaluators should also be attentive to the problem of *halo effect*, whereby a judge who is positively (or negatively) impressed with one aspect of an individual lets this impression influence ratings of all aspects of the individual. The result is an unwarrantedly high intercorrelation among the many dimensions rated. When halo effect is operative, a single overall rating typically does the job just as well as a multidimensional rating form.

However, as has been suggested earlier, it is possible to improve ratings so that they are far more effective. In the first place, the selection of raters is critical. Securing raters who are really conversant with the phenomena to be judged is imperative. Training raters, that is, giving them opportunities to rate identical phenomena, then comparing ratings and discussing differences, is helpful. The certification of raters' skills is also a useful ploy. The categories on which ratings must be supplied should be spelled out as carefully as possible. In general, 5- to 7-point rating scales are better than on-off, binary-choice scales. Some measurement specialists prefer even numbers of rating categories so that a neutral middle point is not available. Rating scales can also be devised that include such categories as "insufficient opportunity to observe," thereby releasing the rater from the responsibility of guessing on some rating categories. Also, to reduce halo on multiscale rating forms, the rater should rate all individuals on one scale at a time, rather than rating one individual at a time on all scales. Combining impressions of several raters is particularly effective, as the reliability coefficient of one judge's ratings (e.g., .45) can almost double (e.g., .80) when five judges' ratings are pooled.

A considerable number of educators, incidentally, are critical of any measuring devices that involve *subjective* judgments. Some of these critics go so far as to suggest that all subjective measures, such as ratings, be considered essentially worthless because of their obvious subjectivity. Subjectivity can have two meanings, however. In a pejorative sense, subjectivity reflects a haphazard and indefensibly idiosyncratic personal stance. In another sense, subjectivity reflects an opinion based on personal experience. It is the latter sense of the term that evaluators use when employing rating approaches. No physician should dismiss a patient's complaint of pain because it is based on personal experience, an experience base that cannot be *objectively* confirmed. Evaluators cannot cavalierly dismiss all subjective measurements, because sometimes the very phenomena we have the most difficulty measuring objectively will be those most worth measuring. The dilemma is clear: Is it better to measure well something trivial or to measure less well something significant? Evaluators will have to consider this question seriously.

By using some of the improvement techniques suggested here, and by consulting more advanced treatments regarding the methodology of constructing and employing rating scales, evaluators will be able to add this effective procedure to their measurement tools. Because many times the evaluator will be searching for qualitative judgments, mastery of rating approaches is imperative.

Systematic Observations

Ratings are generally employed to supply answers to the question, "How acceptable is a given product or behavior?" When we are interested only in the question, "Did a given behavior *occur*?" we must turn to the use of systematic observations. Systematic observations of behavior differ quite substantially from ratings, although many people use the two phrases as though they were identical. One difference between ratings and observations is that ratings are typically based on a more or less haphazard composite of observations, because the rater has not seen an individual in all pertinent situations and, even if so, selectively recalls such situations when the rating is made. Systematic observations, on the other hand, are based on more careful planning and scrutiny of ongoing behavior. Characteristically, the objectivity of systematic observations will be higher than the objectivity of ratings, that is, interobserver agreement tends to exceed interjudge agreement. In addition, ratings can be used with both learner behavior and learner products; observations are used only with behaviors.

There are two distinctive types of systematic observation situations. In one case we observe a representative sample of behavior in situations that really occur in life. Such actual situations vary considerably for different individuals. In the second case we make observations in a standardized situation that is, insofar as possible, identical for all individuals. There are advantages and disadvantages in each of these approaches, of course. For instance, the standardized observation system controls for the possibility that (unaccounted for) situational variables will contaminate the nature of the observed behavior. On the other side of the case, an individual's behavior is typically less natural in a contrived situation than a routine one.

In the 1960s and 1970s we saw the birth of innumerable scales for observing teachers, students, supervisors, and so on. Many of these scales were developed with the proprietary care of the gold prospector who is certain that "this time he'll hit it." Although the literature abounds with observation scales, it seems every recent arrival on a particular educational scene is compelled to fashion a new observation scale that is "just right" for the problem. Of course, a good many of these scales are next to worthless, conceptually unclear, and surely conducive to unreliable observations. The educational evaluator in need of observation scales would be wise to examine available scales prior to engaging in a scale-development escapade. It is often easier to modify existing scales than to create a fresh measurement monster.

A choice facing those who attempt to employ careful observation systems involves whether to record merely *if* a given behavior occurs or whether to record *the number of times* a behavior occurs. These two approaches result in the creation of substantially different types of observation forms (often referred to as observational schedules).

Some observation forms are structured around specified time periods, for example, 12 *five-minute* segments distributed across a one-hour observation period. To illustrate, such an observation form might be used to observe a 60-minute segment of an elementary teacher's classroom instruction. Let's imagine that the observer is attempting to see whether a teacher uses any of several nondirective

Nondirective Procedure	FIVE-MINUTE SEGMENT				
	1	2	3	4	etc.
A	✓	✓	✓		
B		✓	✓		
C			✓		
D		✓		✓	
etc.					

teaching procedures. An observation form might be structured along the lines of the example provided here, in which checkmarks are entered to indicate that the teacher used a particular procedure *at least once* during a *specified* time segment.

Note that the key to this approach is identifying whether a behavior of interest occurred one or more times during the specified time intervals. Even if a particular teacher used procedure B 15 times during the second time period, there would be only one checkmark registered for that segment. This approach is particularly attentive to the spread of behaviors over an extended span of time.

Another observation approach is based on the *frequency* with which a behavior of interest occurs. Suppose we were looking for the same nondirective teaching procedures over a 60-minute period but merely observed the number of times those behaviors occurred during the period. We might employ an observation form such as the following, in which there are no 5-minute units, only tally marks to indicate how many times a specific nondirective procedure was employed by the teacher.

Nondirective Procedure	Frequency
A	‖‖‖ ‖‖‖ ‖
B	‖‖‖
C	‖ ‖
D	‖‖‖ ‖‖‖
etc.	

In this approach, of course, a teacher might use a specific procedure many times but all in a short burst of activity during, say, the first few moments of the class period. Using only a frequency-of-behavior scale, there is no way to determine when a set of recorded behaviors actually occurred.

Each of these two approaches has its virtues and vices. The selection of one observation strategy over the other will depend on the importance of, for instance, getting an accurate fix on frequency versus the time that behaviors occurred. Some observation schedules attempt to capture both dimensions by requiring observers to record the frequencies of observed behaviors *within* small segments of time. Completing such forms can be quite taxing for observers, however, particularly if there are many behaviors to observe.

The observers themselves are the pivotal people in our observation extravaganza. Careless observers produce worthless data. Conscientious observers, *with proper training*, can yield excellent evidence for the evaluator. Proper training of observers, complete with specific directions, practice sessions, and interobserver disagreement resolution, is imperative. Carrying out one or more shakedown observation tryouts, with subsequent correction sessions anticipated, is the way to initiate a systematic observation effort.

It is widely believed that observational approaches yield excellent data, for one will often hear cited the results of observation-based investigations in which high levels of interobserver agreement are reported and the resulting observation-based data are seen as highly useful. In almost all of these cases, however, the investigators have employed sophisticated observation schedules and well-trained observers (so well trained, in fact, that in some investigations the observers even must pass an observer-accuracy certification test). If aspiring educational evaluators believe that they can easily achieve the rigor of such sophisticated observational investigations, they are due for a disappointment. It is difficult, costly, and time consuming to gather defensible data via observations. Evaluators, therefore, ought not embark on an observation-based effort unless they have the expertise and the resources to carry out the observations properly.

Anecdotal Records   A departure from the customary observation operations with their time samples and multidimensional checklists, is the *anecdotal record*. Anecdotal records are descriptions of observed events, in a classroom discussion, for example. The observer is free to note any behavior that appears important and is not required to focus on the same traits for all subjects. The observer records in a few descriptive paragraphs exactly what was observed, attempting to keep facts and interpretations separate. Such records are usually made as soon after an incident as possible in order to reduce recall errors. When gathered periodically over some segment of time, such accumulated anecdotal observations sometimes offer a more striking depiction of behavior than would have been yielded by other more routine techniques. Used judiciously, anecdotal records can provide a rich and welcome change of pace from the bland qnantitative orientation of most observation procedures.

High and Low Inference   With both ratings and systematic observation, particularly observations, the evaluator should be aware of a distinction between operations that require the persons gathering the measurements to engage in *low-* or *high-inference* operations. This distinction can be most readily illustrated in the case of observations where we might ask the observer to record how many times during a class period selected students:

1. Engage in aggressive behavior (high inference)
2. Strike a neighboring child (low inference)

Low-inference observation categories or rating dimensions require few inferential leaps on the part of the observer or rater. A child either strikes another child or doesn't. An observer can readily detect such an act. The only person more certain than the rater that a child has been hit is the one who has been clobbered. High-inference categories, however, demand that the observer or rater draw inferences regarding what a child's behavior represents. In a rater's deciding how many times the child engages in "aggressive behavior," inferences will have to be made with respect to what it is that constitutes aggressive acts.

The higher the required inference, the less reliable the measurement. On the other hand, lower-inference measurement categories may tend to focus on less-important behaviors and rating categories. Again, the choice is between measuring less significant factors more effectively or more significant factors less effectively. These kinds of trade-offs will be most apparent to evaluators who consider the degrees of inference necessitated by their measurement devices.

Interviews

Use of the personally conducted interview is roughly akin to the live administration of a questionnaire. The advantages of interviews over their paper-and-pencil self-report brethren are several. For one thing, an interviewer can often put a subject at ease, thereby securing more candid responses. In addition, a skilled interviewer can often follow up responses of the interviewee in a manner obviously not possible with written questionnaires. In essence, the interviewer can be more responsive to the interviewee than the questionnaire designer can be to an unseen self-report respondent. Interviews can be conducted in a face-to-face setting or, in an often overlooked data-gathering variation, by telephone.

The difficulty with gathering data via interviews is that the procedure is much more expensive than questionnaire administration. The personnel costs for interviewers, in person or by telephone, not to mention their training requirements, represent the chief expense of this approach. Selectively used, on a scale consonant with one's budget, interview data can prove most illuminating.

Performance Tests

Another general measurement strategy, often overlooked or avoided because of its complexities, is the *performance test*. Performance tests generally refer to nonverbal performance, unless the test has been specifically designed to have the subject display a particular verbal behavior. Examples of performance tests include presenting the examinee with a malfunctioning electrical system and then measuring how long it takes to identify the malfunction. In medical training situations recent advances have permitted the development of human-like dummies that can be programmed to display realistic symptoms of disease. The would-be physician is then obliged to diagnose the possible illness underlying such symptoms.

Some years ago graduate archaeology students at Harvard University were presented with a performance test consisting of a specially constituted chamber simulating an archaeologcal excavation site. The student was obliged to sift through the various earth strata, identifying any relics encountered, then prepare a report describing the archaeological inferences warranted by the data. The only problem with this ingenious performance test was that, inasmuch as previous graduate students were less than complete in their unearthing of all planted artifacts, the aspirant archaeologist might simultaneously encounter, in the midst of a simulated Egyptian excavation, relics from Scandinavia, South America, and Mongolia. Making sense out of such diversity would represent a performance indeed.

Because performance tests often approximate reality more closely than do paper-and-pencil simulations, they can be of much use to the evaluator who is willing to go to the trouble of developing them. The creating, monitoring, and scoring of such performance tests are clearly expensive undertakings. Nevertheless, the advantages stemming from the verisimilitude they provide can be most advantageous for evaluators.

Early in the 1990s considerable enthusiasm was generated in support of *authentic assessment*, that is, a form of performance testing in which examinees were obliged to display their abilities on performance tasks that more closely resembled the sorts of things that people have to do on a day-to-day basis. The major deterrent to more wide-scale applications of authentic assessment is its substantial costs.

In general, authentic assessment approaches call for constructed responses rather than selected responses from examinees, and the costs of scoring large numbers of such constructed responses has frequently disinclined educators to embark on large-scale applications of authentic assessment.

Recapitulating

In this chapter an effort has been made to consider the decision-versus-conclusion orientation of educational measurement and then to provide the reader with two general frameworks for thinking about alternative measurement approaches that may be suitable for educational evaluation. First, classification dimensions were presented that might be used in either generating or selecting measurement schemes. The reader is encouraged to complete the practice exercises at the close of the chapter in order to become more familiar with these heuristic dimensions. Second, several conventional measurement strategies were briefly described, along with a few comments regarding special strengths or difficulties associated with each. Clearly, the complexities of any of these approaches are such that more thorough consideration of each is advisable. Fortunately, because these measurement strategies have been in common use for many years, they have been well treated in a number of standard educational or psychological measurement texts. The Selected References cited at the close of the chapter provide excellent starting places for the evaluator who wishes to become facile in the use of such strategies.

Throughout the chapter the emphasis has been on getting the reader to think more divergently about measuring approaches, so that the best assessment approach can be selected for the task at hand. The converse of this advice is equally compelling, that is, the effective evaluator will possess sufficient knowledge about various techniques so that proper decisions can be made regarding when *not* to use a given procedure. Almost all the approaches described in the chapter possess some special advantages. All possess some limitations. Only the evaluator who is conversant with both the strengths and weaknesses of a wide range of measuring devices will be in a position to decide which assessment techniques to employ.

Discussion Questions

1. Why should a competent educational evaluator be skilled in using a wide array of measurement devices?
2. How do the general measurement strategies described in the latter part of the chapter relate to the heuristic categories described earlier in the chapter?
3. In the chapter a distinction was drawn between effectively measuring less significant phenomena and measuring more significant phenomena less effec-

tively. What do you think should be an evaluator's stance with respect to this issue?
4. What are the comparative strengths and weaknesses of ratings versus systematic observations?
5. Can you think of any educational measurement activities that epitomize a conclusion orientation? Any that epitomize a decision orientation?

Practice Exercises

1. Decide whether the following measurement activities are chiefly *decision oriented* or *conclusion oriented.*
   a. To provide a picture of how today's youth view higher education, a group of researchers gathers a series of questionnaire responses from college students across the nation.
   b. In the hope of identifying the schools in a district that need additional staff resources to aid their reading programs, the reading proficiencies of a sample of stu-

dents from each school are measured.
   c. Because he is interested in the nature of the relationships among variables potentially pertinent to physical endurance, Professor Schmidt measures a variety of factors that might be relevant.
   d. Mrs. Johnson wants to know whether to revise her instructional sequences, hence always measures pupils' preinstruction and postinstruction knowledge.
   e. In order to allocate state educational

funds to "educationally disadvantaged" schools, the state superintendent of public instruction has initiated an annual end-of-year assessment of each sixth-grade child's educational achievement in reading and mathematics.

2. Indicate whether the following measurement approaches are *primarily* cognitive, affective, or psychomotor.
   a. Assessing a student's typing proficiency via a timed typing test.
   b. A teacher-made test of pupil's knowledge of physics principles.
   c. An essay test in which the student is directed to display specific composition techniques.
   d. A forced-choice inventory in which the student must choose between pairs of possible vocations and avocations.
   e. An index of subject-matter preference derived from volitionally selected upper-division courses.

3. Which of the following measures are best described as learner *behaviors* and which are best described as learner *products*?
   a. A member of the swimming team's performance in the 100-yard freestyle event.
   b. A class discussion.

   c. A written essay examination response.
   d. Tardiness.
   e. A pupil-produced bookend from the woodshop course.

4. Decide whether the following circumstances best reflect *natural* or *controlled* stimuli.
   a. Observing pupil "sportsmanship" behaviors during intramural basketball games.
   b. Administering a naturally standardized group intelligence test.
   c. Unobstrusively tape-recording the classroom discussion of a U.S. government class.
   d. Having a group of students present a symposium to reflect their group-interaction skills.
   e. Recording the breakage and other misuses of gymnasium equipment.

5. Indicate whether the following instances better reflect *selected* or *constructed* student response.
   a. Student autobiographical essays.
   b. A small-scale radio transmitter built in the electronics class.
   c. Scores on a true-false test.
   d. An extemporaneous speech.
   e. Performance on a multiple-choice exam.

Answers to Practice Exercises

1. Although with these brief examples it is sometimes difficult to ferret out the actual purpose of the individual engaged in the measurement operation, the following answers seem preferable: *a.* conclusion oriented; *b.* decision oriented; *c.* conclusion oriented; *d.* decision oriented; *e.* decision oriented.

2. *a.* Psychomotor; *b.* cognitive; *c.* cognitive; *d.* affective; *e.* affective.
3. *a.* Behavior; *b.* behavior; *c.* product; *d.* behavior; *e.* product.
4. *a.* Natural; *b.* controlled; *c.* natural; *d.* controlled; *e.* natural.
5. *a.* Constructed; *b.* constructed; *c.* selected; *d.* constructed; *e.* selected.

Notes

1. See Norris M. Sanders, *Classroom Questions: What Kinds?* (New York: Harper and Row, 1966).

2. B. S. Bloom et al., *Taxonomy of Educational Objectives: Handbook I: Cog-*

nitive Domain (New York: David McKay, 1956).

3. D. R. Krathwohl et al., *Taxonomy of Educational Objectives: Handbook II: Affective Domain* (New York: David McKay, 1964).

4. R. C. Anderson and D. L. Myrow, "Retroactive Inhibition of Meaningful Discourse," *Journal of Educational Psychology Monograph*, 62 (1971), 81–94.

5. Lee J. Cronbach, *Essentials of Psychological Testing* (New York: Harper and Row, 1984).

6. Norman E. Gronlund, *Measurement and Evaluation in Teaching*, 5th ed. (New York: Macmillan, 1985).

7. Charles E. Osgood, George J. Suci, and Percy H. Tannenbaum, *The Measurement of Meaning* (Urbana, IL: University of Illinois Press, 1957).

8. William Stephenson, *The Study of Behavior* (Chicago: University of Chicago Press, 1953).

9. Lee J. Cronbach and Goldine C. Gleser, Review of *The Study of Behavior, Psychometrika*, 19 (1954), 327–33.

Selected References

Bock, R.D., R. Mislevy, and C. Woodson. "The Next Stage in Educational Assessment." *Educational Researcher*, 11:3 (1982): 4–11, 16.

Chelimsky, Eleanor. "Program Evaluation and the Use of Extant Data." In Leigh Burstein, Howard E. Freeman, and Peter H. Rossi (Eds.), *Collecting Evaluation Data: Problems and Solutions*. Beverly Hills, CA: Sage Publications, 1985.

Gronlund, Norman E., and Robert L. Linn. *Measurement and Evaluation in Teaching* (6th ed.). New York: Macmillan, 1990.

Linn, Robert L. (Ed.). *Educational Measurement*. New York: American Council on Education, 1989.

Messick, S. "Potential Uses of Noncognitive Measurement in Education." *Journal of Educational Psychology*, 71 (1979): 281–92.

Metfessel, N. S., and W. B. Michael. "A Paradigm Involving Multiple Criterion Measures for the Evaluation of Effectiveness of School Programs." *Educational and Psychological Measurement*, 27 (1967): 931–43.

Quellmalz, Edys S. "Designing Writing Assessments: Balancing Fairness, Utility, and Cost." *Educational Evaluation and Policy Analysis*, 6:1 (Spring 1984): 63–72.

Sax, Gilbert. *Principles of Educational and Psychological Measurement and Evaluation* (3rd ed.). Belmont, CA: Wadsworth, 1989.

Simon, A., and E. G. Boyer (Eds.). *Mirrors for Behavior: An Anthology of Classroom Observation Instruments*. Philadelphia: Research for Better Schools, 1968.

Stiggins, R. J., and N. J. Bridgeford. *The Use of Performance Assessment in the Classroom*. Portland, OR: Northwest Regional Educational Laboratory, 1984.

Wiersma, William, and Stephen G. Jurs. *Educational Measurement and Testing*. Boston: Allyn and Bacon, 1985.

Wolf, Dennie, Janet Bixby, John Glenn III, and Howard Gardner. "To Use Their Minds Well: Investigating New Forms of Student Assessment." In Gerald Grant (Ed.), *Review of Research in Education*. Washington, DC: American Educational Research Association, 1991, pp. 31–74.

CHAPTER FIVE

Classical Measurement Considerations

There are basic ideas in measurement with which educational evaluators should be conversant. Important concepts such as reliability and validity, for example, pop up all the time in discussion of evaluation operations. Most of these measurement concepts have been developed as a result of the endeavors of those working with traditional measurement procedures since the turn of the century. As we shall see, certain of these classical measurement concepts must be reconsidered when used in connection with educational evaluation endeavors. But before rethinking any of the more traditional measurement concepts, the evaluator should be well acquainted with these notions as they apply to classical measurement operations.

The topics to be treated in this chapter will be drawn from those normally encountered in a typical course in educational or psychological tests and measurement. Thus the reader who is well versed in such topics need not deal with this chapter at all. Although space limitations preclude an extensive treatment of any of these topics, the topics to be considered in the chapter will be these: norm-referenced measurement, types of measurement scales, graphic and statistical methods of describing data, reliability, validity, and test usability. If the reader needs a brief review or an introduction to these concepts, the once-over-lightly treatment that follows may be of some value.

Norm-Referenced Measurement

The basic purpose of almost all educational measurement activities conducted during the twentieth century has been to assess the performance of an individual so that such performance can be interpreted according to the performance of other individuals who have completed the same measuring device. Because, in order to make much sense out of an individual's performance, it was necessary to reference the performance to that of a normative group of individuals, the phrase *norm-referenced measurement* has been aptly applied to typical tests of achievement, aptitude, attitudes, and the like. When such norm-referenced measures are employed, one is typically anxious to discover such things as whether Billy scores at the 20th, 50th, 70th, or 90th percentile in relationship to the performance of the norm group. Now the normative group to which the student's performance is referenced is nothing more than a large (and, it is hoped, representative) sample of individuals who have previously completed the test. Major test-development agencies usually renorm their most popular instruments every 5 to 10 years in order to keep the normative group's performance relatively current.

One of the overriding characteristics of norm-referenced tests is that in order to fulfill their chief function, namely, to permit comparisons between an individual's performance and that of a norm group, such tests must yield considerable *response variance*. If there is only modest variance in the performance of the individuals completing a test, then it is exceedingly difficult to make those comparisons without which norm-referenced measures would be ineffectual. To illustrate, suppose an achievement test were devised which proved so easy that everyone scored almost perfectly on it. Because most students were obtaining the same or similar scores, there would be no possibility of making meaningful comparisons among them. Indeed, it is for this reason that most norm-referenced test developers strive to detect the underlying variability that they believe to be present in most human performance. That is, norm-referenced test developers wish to produce a wide range of performance on an instrument and thus make fine-grained comparisons possible.

As was indicated previously, the bulk of the rather sophisticated educational measurement technology that has been devised during this century has been addressed to the problem of improving the caliber of norm-referenced tests. Many of these measurement refinements will be useful to evaluators, but many will not. Let's examine a typical operation in the construction and refinement of a norm-referenced achievement test to see why some of these difficulties arise.

Because response variance is the *sine qua non* of a satisfactory norm-referenced test, those individuals who originally construct the test items for such tests are very conscious of the need to devise items that will contribute to the production of variations in examinees' performances. Even though norm-referenced test developers may initially map out the important content or concepts to be covered in the test, if it appears to them that an item that taps one of these key concepts may not contribute sufficiently to response variance because it seems too easy or too hard, the item writers may (deliberately or perhaps subconsciously) lean toward other items. Sometimes, with an achievement item that appears to be too easy, a bit of ambiguity will be injected in order to render the item a mite more difficult.

The drive toward tests that yield sufficient response variance is even more manifest as we observe the activities of those who must improve norm-referenced tests on the basis of empirical field tryouts. One of the most common techniques for improving the quality of these tests is to compute an *item discrimination index* for each test item in the instrument. Although there are some differences in the specifics of how these itemdiscrimination indices are computed, the general idea is to see how performance on an individual test item is related to performance on the total test. The first thing needed is to have a number of individuals complete the test. Typically, those who score well on the total test and those who score badly are separated into two groups. For statistical reasons, the upper and lower 27 percent of subjects are often used, although other procedures call for different, though equal upper and lower proportions of the distribution. Then each test item is analyzed to see what proportions of the two groups (the high scorers and the low scorers) answered the item correctly. Ideally, a larger percentage of the high scorers would have answered the item correctly, and a larger proportion of the low scorers would have missed the item. This results in a *positive item discrimination index*. If the reverse is true, that is, if more low scorers than high scorers answer the item correctly, a *negative item discrimination index* results. This usually signifies that there is some defect in the item causing those pupils who know most about the subject (as reflected by their high total test scores) to miss it while their less knowledgeable brethren are getting correct answers. Such items are typically modified or eliminated altogether.

But while the refiners of norm-referenced tests rhapsodize over positive discrimination indices and despair over negative discrimination indices, they are not indifferent to items that yield no substantial discrimination in either direction. Such often occurs when an item is too hard or too easy, because if everyone is either missing an item or answering it correctly, the resulting item discrimination index will hover around zero. It is for this reason that the ideal difficulty level on test item is .50, that is, 50 percent of the subjects answering correctly and 50 percent answering incorrectly. These nondiscriminating items, particularly if response variance on the total test is deemed inadequate, will also be modified or jettisoned. As we shall see, doing this leads to several difficulties when norm-referenced tests are used for purposes of educational evaluation.

Deficiencies of Norm-Referenced Measures for Educational Evaluation

Norm-referenced measures have been produced and sharpened through the years chiefly to permit comparisons between individuals and a norm group. They are most appropriate, therefore, when decisions are to be made about *individuals*. For example, if an educator must determine which of several youngsters is best suited for a specialized enrichment program, then a test that yields data regarding individual learners will clearly provide useful information. In *fixed-quota* situations, where selections must be made and there are more applicants than openings, norm-referenced tests are doubtlessly the best measures available. However, educational evaluation is not a game where the goal is to make decisions about individuals. Rather, because the evaluator's function is to help decision makers select among such alternatives as different instructional treatment, the focus is on the effects of such treatments with *groups* of learners. Measures designed to provide information for making decisions about individuals sometimes display serious defects when applied to group appraisals.

Whether the test is norm-referenced or otherwise, the evaluator must be attentive to the possibilities that *cultural bias* in a measuring instrument renders it inappropriate for the evaluation application at hand. Too many tests of achievement, aptitude, and even affective dispositions have been constructed, tried out, and normed using mostly middle-class, white children. Only in the past decade or two have test developers become sensitive to the fact that this sort of ethnocentric test development results in serious disadvantages for individuals from divergent ethnic or cultural backgrounds. Educational evaluators should be attentive to discovering the specifics of how any test was developed, the vocabulary employed in the items, the types of individuals involved in the review of test items, the tryout of items, and the constitution of the normative group. Too many youngsters from ethnic minorities have been irreparably harmed as a consequence of educational decisions made on the basis of culturally biased tests that were inappropriate for those youngsters. Cultural bias must be guarded against when any kind of educational test is used.

Cultural bias can be found in any type of test, but there are some distinctive problems associated with norm-referenced measures that must be identified. For one thing, the technical procedures for appraising the adequacy of norm-referenced testing instruments are often inappropriate for treating tests devised principally to serve evaluation functions. This topic will be discussed later.

One major defect in the use of norm-referenced measures for purposes of educational evaluation is that *unrecognized mismatches will occur between testing and teaching* — that is, mismatches between what the test measures and what is stressed in a local curriculum. Let's see why this is so. Most widely used norm-referenced achievement tests are distributed by commercial testing firms who must design their tests to service an entire nation. However, the curricular preferences in Iowa, New York, Mississippi, and Oregon often vary substantially. Test publishers are faced with a nontrivial problem in this regard, because if they were to spell out just what it is that their tests measure, a good many educators in locally controlled, hence curricularly diverse, school systems would reject the tests as not matching the emphases of their instructional programs. Many test publishers have escaped this dilemma by describing their tests in general terms, thereby picking up the Rorschach dividend that when local educators encounter a general descriptor such as "quantitative competence" they will read into it what they wish. The problem is, however, that there may still be a considerable mismatch between what a norm-referenced achievement test actually measures and what a local instructional program emphasizes. A mismatch between curriculum and measurement typically yields misleading data and spurious conclusions. Because of test publishers' needs to produce tests for an entire nation, and the resulting probability that such norm-referenced tests will not suitably mesh with local curricular predilections, evaluators should be wary of using norm-referenced achievement tests unless satisfactory congruence has been established between the measure and the instructional program.

A second deficit of norm-referenced tests for purposes of educational evaluation is also derivative from the level of generality that commercial test publishers must employ in describing their tests in order to sell the tests widely. Put simply, *the opaqueness with which a norm-referenced test's contents are described reduces the likelihood of providing effective formative evaluation guidance* for instructional personnel. Focusing on achievement tests, for example, the degree of descriptiveness regarding what a norm-referenced test actually measures is typically quite weak. Because a major task of educational evaluators is to supply the kind of clear information that can aid instructional personnel formatively, any ambiguity in a test's instructional targets reduces the clarity and cogency of the information that the evaluator can supply. It is extremely difficult for the evaluator to offer on-target assistance even when the instructional targets *are* well known. To prescribe on-target assistance for murky targets is next to impossible.

A final, and perhaps even more insidious, weakness of norm-referenced tests for evaluative purposes stems from their previously noted need to produce a reasonable degree of response variance. In essence, this deficit deals with the likelihood that norm-referenced *technical procedures tend to eliminate test items covering key content.*

As was pointed out earlier, test items that do not produce sufficient variation among those taking the test are typically chucked out during early field trials or in test-revision efforts. This will definitely happen to test items that are answered correctly by most students. Indeed, as the proportion of students answering an item correctly approaches 100 percent, the discriminating efficiency of the item will drop accordingly. And what items will most students perform well on? They will be the very items that deal with concepts most teachers judge to be important and hence stress in their classroom instruction. This means that even with many recently developed norm-referenced achievement tests, but certainly with oft-revised norm-referenced tests, these items will have been discarded because of their inadequate

contributions to response variance. Items will be left in that deal with less significant aspects of content. What results is an "achievement" test that functions more like an intelligence test. The curricular significance of the instrument will often have been dissipated.

But isn't that why many evaluators are there in the first place? Aren't educational evaluators often trying to help improve instructional sequences so that more students will achieve mastery of key knowledge and skills? Of course, the answer is *yes*. And for this reason the evaluator who espouses use of norm-referenced measures for evaluation purposes and, at the same time, attempts to improve the effectiveness of instruction has adopted two conflicting positions.

Because of these three basic problems with norm-referenced tests — (1) their curricular incongruence, (2) their descriptive vagueness, and (3) their built-in tendency to systematically eliminate items on which most students succeed — these instruments are relatively *insensitive to instruction*. Thus, because of such tests' decreased likelihood of detecting the effects of an instructional program, even an effective instructional program, educators who use such measures to help evaluate innovative instructional programs are making a serious error. When it is tough enough to design an educational system that will produce improved results, why reduce your chances of detecting improved results?

The reader is reminded that this critique of norm-referenced tests has been directed toward their applications in educational evaluation settings. For the purpose for which they were originally designed and have been perfected during many decades, norm-referenced devices are quite serviceable — but that purpose was not educational evaluation.

Measurement Scales

There are a number of frequently used measurement and statistical concepts associated with traditional measurement devices. One of these concerns the properties of the scores produced by such tests. The most widely used system for classifying educational measurement data is that described by S. S. Stevens, who distinguished many years ago between *nominal, ordinal, interval,* and *ratio* scales.[1] The differences between these scales sometimes becomes important for purposes of statistical analysis of measurement data. The evaluator should have a rudimentary understanding of the differences among the four types of scales, because the scalar qualities of evaluation data will often dictate using particular statistical analysis procedures.

Nominal Scales

At the lowest level of measurement, a *nominal* scale simply assigns different names (from the Latin, *nomen* = name) to categories representing some variable or dimension of interest. For example, we might be concerned with marital status and employ a scale that has the following categories: *married, single, divorced, other*. (With society's current shifting value patterns, the category "other" includes a rapidly expanding variety of alternatives.) There is no notion of order among the categories of a nominal scale. One category is not necessarily "better than" or "bigger than" another. Even though, for analysis purposes, evaluators sometimes assign numbers to nominal scale data, such as when a computer analyst assigns the symbol "0" to rural residents and "1" to urban residents, these numbers do not possess any of the characteristics (such as order, distance, origin) we usually attribute to real number series.

Ordinal Scales

An *ordinal* scale contains categories that reflect order but not equidistance (between themselves). For instance, we might rank-order 10 pupils according to who is best in spelling. We realize that the difference in spelling ability is not necessarily the same between the first- versus second-ranked pupils and the ninth- versus tenth-ranked pupils. In ordinal scales, therefore, magnitude is indicated only in a somewhat gross fashion. A typical ordinal scale used in educational measurement would be a 3-point rating scale composed of Good – Average – Poor. Some years ago several statisticians argued very compellingly that if one were working with ordinal data the use of certain widely employed techniques was not warranted.[2] Instead, they recommended the use of a set of statistical procedures specifically designed to treat data representing nominal and ordinal measurement scales. These statistical procedures are referred to as *nonparametric* techniques. Many statisticians still advise the use of nonparametric techniques for use with ordinal data. For nominal data, nonparametric techniques are often the only alternatives available. The evaluator may wish to become familiar with some of the more prominent of these nonparametric approaches.[3]

Interval Scales

An *interval* scale possesses all the characteristics of an ordinal scale and, in addition, is composed of units that are equal. For instance, the distance between test scores of 30 and 40 is considered as large as the distance between test scores of 60 and 70. Most measurement specialists believe that the bulk of educational measurement data can be treated as though they constitute an interval scale.

Ratio Scales

If an interval scale has an actual zero point it is said to be a *ratio* scale. We can thus give meaning to the ratios between scores. A person who is six feet tall is twice as tall as a person three feet tall because the measurement of zero height actually means *no height*. Another example of a ratio scale would involve the measurement of weight: As with height, there is a true zero. Even though we occasionally assign scores of zero to pupils, as on an arithmetic test, for instance, we do not mean they have *no* arithmetic ability whatsoever. Ratio scales, therefore, are rarely encountered by educational evaluators.

Describing Measurement Data

The evaluator will find that without adequate techniques for describing the results of a series of measurement operations, it would have been wise never to have taken the measurements, for no one will be able to make much sense out of them. In the next few pages we shall examine some of the more common procedures for reducing a set of data to a form interpretable by humans. It should be apparent that data-reduction techniques are requisite whenever we work with many bits of information. If, for instance, Mrs. Lee were trying to describe the performance of 6 of her senior high school students on an academic aptitude test, it would be possible for her to cite the scores of all 6 students. However, if Mrs. Hale were attempting to describe the post-instruction performance of 600 sixth-grade pupils who used special math enrichment materials, then citing each of the 600 scores would obviously be silly. More economical data-representation techniques would have to be employed.

Graphs

One of the best procedures for displaying data in a form readily interpretable to decision makers is to employ graphic presentation schemes. In Figures 5–1 and 5–2, for example, are *histograms* (also called *bar graphs*) that can effectively communicate to most people.

The nice thing about bar graphs is that many individuals have been obliged to interpret such devices at one time or another, hence such graphs intimidate few people. The evaluator has to be careful, of course, to set up the graph as clearly as possible, often trying out several alternative presentation and labeling schemes to see which offers the most clarity.

Another graphic method often used by evaluators is the *frequency polygon*,

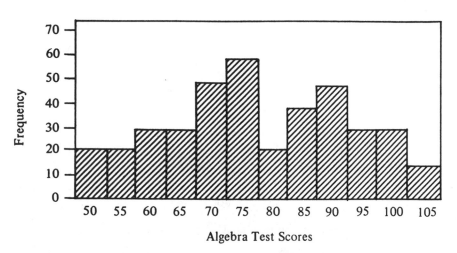

FIGURE 5–1 • *Histogram of Algebra Test Scores*

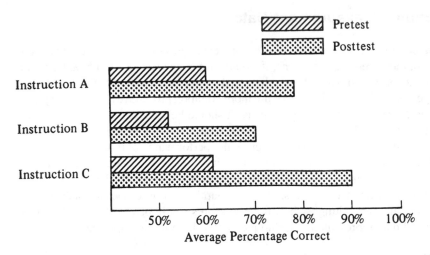

FIGURE 5-2 • *A Bar Graph Indicating Relative Pretest and Posttest Performance of Groups Receiving Three Different Instructional Treatments*

sometimes with two or more results of competing instructional treatments being represented. Such a scheme is illustrated in Figure 5–3. The astute evaluator should be particularly attentive to the sophistication level of the audience for whom the evaluation results are intended. In general, err in the direction of more simple rather than more exotic data-description techniques. You'll communicate with more people that way.

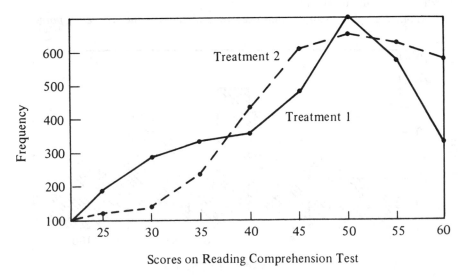

FIGURE 5-3 • *Frequency Polygons Representing Reading Comprehension Test Scores for Two Treatment Groups*

Indices of Central Tendency

If we were to plot a set of scores in a fashion similar to that seen in Figure 5–4, where each X represents one student's score on a 10-item test, we could use several statistical indices to describe the central tendency of that set (distribution) of scores—because we are often anxious to convey *by a single numerical index* how well the total group of students performed.

The Mean   The most commonly used indicator of central tendency is the *mean*. The mean is nothing more than the arithmetic average of the scores in a distribution, calculated by adding the scores and dividing by the number of scores in the distribution. Thus, the formula for calculating the mean looks like this:

$$\text{Mean} = \frac{\text{Summed values of a set of scores}}{\text{Number of scores}}$$

In the case of the test data in Figure 5–4, we would calculate the mean by summing all the score values (140), then dividing by the number of scores (26). The result is a group mean of 5.4.

The Median   Another common index of central tendency is the *median*, that is, the *midpoint* of a distribution of scores. In the case of the data in Figure 5–4, we could count from the lowest score until half of the 26 scores were counted. The median is the point between the two halves of the set of scores. In this case the median would be 5.5 because there are precisely 13 scores at 5 and below as well as 13 scores at 6 and above. The midpoint between 5 and 6 is 5.5, hence in this instance the median is slightly higher than the previously calculated mean.

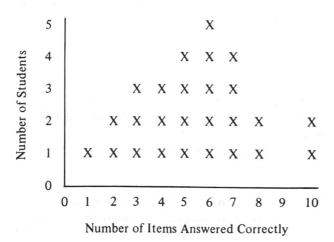

FIGURE 5–4 • *Test Data*

The Mode   The most frequently occurring score in a distribution is referred to as the *mode*. In our fictitious distribution the most frequently occurring score is 6. Thus in this case the mode is higher than either the median or the mean.

Which Average Is Best?   In Figure 5–2, each bar is said to represent an "average" percentage correct. Which average? All three of the indices we have seen here (mean, median, and mode) can legitimately be referred to as averages, yet it is apparent that each can represent the central tendency of a distribution in sometimes dramatically different ways.

In general, the mean is the only one of the three indices that uses all the data in a distribution, since every score in a set of scores is used in calculating the mean. Less information is needed to compute the median and the mode. The mean is generally preferred over the other two measures.

In some cases, however, the median is a preferable choice, particularly if a few extreme scores will unrealistically distort the value of the mean. For instance, if an evaluator were computing the mean annual income of parents for children in different schools, the knowledge that there were several millionaires with children in one school should incline the evaluator to choose the median rather than the mean, for the few enormous incomes would artificially inflate the general parental income level in that school. The median parental income would give the millionaires only as much weight as a comparable number of low-income parents.

Because it is easily located, the mode provides a handy index of central tendency. In a few cases, the mode is the only sensible type of index to employ. For instance, if a manufacturer of school athletic equipment is deciding on what shoe sizes to emphasize in a new production operation, the manufacturer's best bet is to go with those shoes that most people can wear, not some arithmetically derived average. The mode would be preferred in this instance. Generally, applied statisticians encourage people to compute all three indices, and if they're substantially different, to comment about such differences.

Indices of Variability

To provide additional meaning when describing a set of test-score results, in addition to one or more measures of central tendency we often need an index of the *variation* present within the distribution. In other words, besides wanting to know what the center of a distribution is, we want to know how spread out the scores in that distribution are. Measures of *variability*, or *dispersion* as it is sometimes called, provide us with such estimates.

The Range   One simple index that gives us a rough notion of the variability of a set of scores in the *range*. The range is computed by simply subtracting the lowest score in a distribution from the highest score. Thus, if the top score in a set of scores were 78 and the lowest score were 16, the range would be 52. But because the range is determined only by the two extreme scores in a distribution, other methods are needed.

The Standard Deviation   Statisticians have devised a clever index of variability known as the *standard deviation*, which is nothing more than an average of the differences (deviations) between the scores of a distribution and its mean. The standard deviation computation is straightforward, with one twist. First, the mean of the distribution is calculated and then it is subtracted from the value of each score, thus yielding a series of *deviation* scores. To illustrate, if the mean of a distribution were 10, that number would be subtracted from all scores in the distribution; for example 12 − 10 = 2; 16 − 10 = 6. But, of course, there will be scores *lower* than the mean; for example, 8 − 10 = −2; 7 − 10 = −3. Subtracting the mean from these scores yields *minus* deviation scores. If we were simply to sum all these deviation scores, they would add up to zero. So before trying to compute an average of these deviations, we first *square* each deviation because that operation gets rid of the minus signs. (A minus number times itself yields a positive product: −5 × −5 = +25.) These squared deviations are then added, and divided by the number of scores in the distribution, just as is done in computing the mean. Finally, to get things back to the number size we were working with originally, we take the square root of the summed squared deviations.

The computation procedure for the standard deviation can thus be represented as follows:

$$\text{Standard deviation} = \sqrt{\frac{\text{Sum of squared deviation scores}}{\text{Number of scores in the distribution}}}$$

If you will think for a moment about the procedure involved in computing the standard deviation, you will realize that the more distant the scores of a distribution are from its mean (i.e., the more spread out they are), the *larger* will be the standard deviation. Thus, in describing two sets of pupil scores on the same test, if we indicated that the standard deviation of Group X was 10.4 and the standard deviation of Group Z was 6.7, we would know that the scores in Group X were much more variable (i.e., spread out from the mean) than scores in Group Z. Used in combination with the mean, the standard deviation is an extremely useful way of reflecting group variability. It is undoubtedly the most widely employed index of variability that will be encountered by evaluators.

Indices of Relationship

In addition to knowing the central tendency and variability of a group of scores, occasions arise when we need to represent the way in which the performance of individuals on two different measures (or the same measure administered at two different times) is *related*. There are several indicators of relationship that might be employed, but the most frequently used are the *product-moment correlation coeffi-*

cient and the *rank-order correlation coefficient*. Any standard statistical text will provide formulas for these two measures of relationship. The reader wishing to learn how to compute them is urged to consult such references. For our purposes, it will suffice if the reader is able to make meaningful, intuitive interpretations of the coefficients derived from these two procedures.

Interpreting Correlation Coefficients

The product-moment correlation coefficient is designed to be used with data representing an interval or ratio scale. Because it is assumed that there is equidistance between points on the measurement scale involved, mathematical operations such as multiplying and dividing are considered legitimate when one is computing the product-moment correlation coefficient. The rank-order correlation coefficient requires only ordinal data and does not treat the data quite as precisely as is required by the product-moment correlation. Nonetheless, if the same sets of data were to be analyzed by these two methods, the resulting correlation coefficient would most often be strikingly similar. Hence, for purposes of this discussion, we shall simply refer to a *correlation coefficient*, leaving aside the question of which technique was used to produce it.

What we are interested in when we compute a correlation coefficient is the degree and nature of the relationship between the same individuals' performances on two different measurement occasions. For instance, to help counsel students, an instructor might want to know whether those students who scored well (or poorly) on a midterm exam also scored well (or poorly) on the final exam. A correlation coefficient could be computed to reflect the degree of relationship between the students' performances on the two examinations. Let's use a few fictitious examples to help explain how to interpret correlation coefficients.

Suppose every student in the class obtained precisely the same scores on the two different exams. In other words, all students would retain identical relative positions in the class. Mary Jones would be the top scorer on both the midterm and final exams, scoring 17 points above the mean in each instance. Billy Hill would be the second highest scorer, two points behind Mary, and so on. The correlation between students' performance on the two exams would be a *perfect positive* relationship and would be represented by a correlation coefficient (r) of $+1.00$. If the relationship had been slightly less than perfect, for instance, if everyone except Mary and Billy had retained their identical positions on the two exams but Mary and Billy had reversed positions, then the correlation coefficient would be positive but less than perfect, say, $r = .96$.

Let's imagine a weird situation in which there was a complete flip-flop between performances on the two exams—Mary scoring highest on the midterm but lowest on the final, Billy scoring second highest on the midterm but second lowest on the final. Aside from raising substantial questions about the teacher's instructional prowess during the second half of the term, these data would result in a *perfect negative* relationship, with $r = -1.00$.

If pupil performances on the two exams were so mixed up that there were literally no relationship present, that is, given a person's score on one exam we were totally unable to say where the individual would tend to score on the second exam, then the correlation coefficient would be zero.

In review, then, correlation coefficients reflect not only the direction (positive or negative), but also the strength of the relationship between two variables. The three main reference points to recall in order to interpret this numerical index of relationship are these:

> 1.00 = Perfect positive relationship
> .00 = No relationship
> −1.00 = Perfect negative relationship

We shall find many occasions to employ the correlation coefficient in describing measurement data. The reader is urged to consult the statistical references cited at the close of the chapter to learn more about the computation and interpretation of this useful statistical tool.

Malleable Psychometric Standards

We now turn our attention to two pivotal concepts in the field of measurement: *reliability* and *validity*. It is sometimes thought by novice educational evaluators that these two concepts are uniformly understood, time honored, and more or less immutable notions. Such is not the case.

Although most seasoned educational researchers and measurement specialists have reasonably similar ideas of the *general* meanings of reliability and validity, there are still substantial differences among those individuals regarding certain aspects of the two concepts. When we consider the knowledge base of typical, run-of-the-classroom educators regarding reliability and validity, then we encounter enormous variations regarding the meanings of these two key measurement concepts.

Although reliability and validity have been major concerns of measurement wizards for decades, it is inaccurate to assume that this attention over the years has resulted in the evolution of unchangeable concepts. As recently as 1985, for example, the publication of the revised *Standards for Educational and Psychological Testing*[4] (a joint project of the American Educational Research Association, the American Psychological Association, and the National Council on Measurement in Education) led to a number of minor, yet meaningful modifications in the *Standards*-sanctioned delineations of reliability and validity. Because of the general acceptance of the *Standards*, not only by educational measurement specialists but also by courts of law, the skilled educational evaluator will doubtlessly need to become familiar with the 1985 *Standards* and, of course, any subsequent revisions of those standards. The treatment of reliability and validity provided in the following pages is consonant with the guidelines provided in the 1985 *Standards*.

Reliability

One of the most time-honored constructs of the classical measurement tradition is that of *reliability*. Reliability refers to the *consistency* with which a measure assesses whatever it is measuring. In contrast to validity, which focuses on whether a test yields scores from which valid inferences can be drawn, reliability merely reflects the consistency of the measuring device. In other words, irrespective of what the test is measuring, does it perform its measurement function consistently?

Another way of thinking about reliability is to regard it as "the degree to which test scores are free from errors of measurement."[5] Errors of measurement refer to differences between scores from one testing occasion or one test form to another. Such measurement errors, in reducing the consistency of measurement, reduce the generalizability of measurement as well. It is well known, of course, that an individual's score on two testing occasions will not ordinarily be identical. After all, the test taker may be more anxious, fatigued, or motivated on one occasion than on another. Similarly, even the most meticulous matching of test content and item difficulties will rarely produce two different test forms on which an examinee will perform *exactly* the same. Such measures of error, of course, reduce the consistency, that is, the reliability, with which a test measures whatever it measures.

Reliability is a necessary but not sufficient condition for a test's validity. The existence of a reliable test makes valid score interpretations possible, but reliability does not *guarantee* the validity of score-based inferences. For example, you could devise a simple test that consisted of nothing more than asking a friend, on separate occasions, to supply you with the maiden name of this friend's mother. Assuming you would get the same response consistently, you would have been using a *reliable* test. But if you tried to make predictions, on the basis of such a test, regarding your friend's ability to succeed in law school, you would obviously have a test with serious validity problems. A test of this sort, clearly, could be reliable without permitting valid score-based inferences. On the other hand, a test having rotten reliability, in other words, a test that does not yield consistent measurements, cannot yield valid inferences under any circumstances. There is simply no situation in which an unreliable test can yield scores from which valid inferences can be drawn. Thus, tests that permit valid score-based inferences must be reliable, but tests that are reliable may or may not yield valid inferences. Because of their import, therefore, reliability questions have occupied the attention of measurement specialists for a good many years. There are three general procedures used to supply estimates of test reliability; we shall consider each of these briefly.

Stability

One way of looking at reliability is to focus on the *stability* of examinee performance over a period of time. The typical technique for computing a stability index is to administer a test on two separate occasions, calculating a correlation coefficient to reflect the relationship between subjects' performances on the two occasions. Frequently, this technique is referred to as a *test-retest* estimate of reliability. Obviously, the designers of a test would like it to yield essentially comparable measures for examinees on two separate occasions, assuming no major intervention has occurred between those assessment occasions. Because the interval between the two test administrations is clearly important, this should always be reported when describing stability indices. For properly developed norm-referenced tests, test-retest correlation coefficients (which can be referred to as *reliability coefficients*) often range between .80 and .95. It should be noted that coefficients for traditional norm-referenced tests are typically based on tests containing 50 to 100 test items.

Alternate Form

The *alternate form* method of estimating reliability (sometimes referred to as an *equivalent form reliability*) typically involves giving two forms of a test (with identical content, means, and standard deviations) to the same group of persons on the same day, then correlating the results. Using such a procedure, we can conclude how an examinee would perform if given other similar but different test items. Alternate form reliability coefficients for reasonably long tests also often exceed .80.

Sometimes alternate forms of a test are administered to the same group of individuals with a time interval between administrations (as in the test-retest method). This procedure involves a simultaneous effort to establish the degree of a measure's consistency with respect to both *equivalence and stability*. The resulting reliability coefficient associated with such an approach is usually much lower than is true with either the stability or alternate form methods used separately.

Internal Consistency

The two previously described methods of estimating reliability require data from two testing sessions. There are several *internal consistency* methods of calculating reliability, which can be used with data from only a single test administration. Internal consistency methods of determining reliability focus on the degree to which a test's items function homogeneously. Such methods should not be used with "speeded" tests.

Split-Half   The split-half technique involves dividing a test into two equal halves, ordinarily by treating the odd, then the even items, as though they constituted separate tests. The total test is administered to a group of individuals, then their two subscores (derived from the odd and the even items) are correlated. The resulting correlation coefficient is considered an estimate of the degree to which the two halves of the test are performing their functions consistently. Because *longer tests are more reliable than shorter tests*, it is possible to apply the Spearman-Brown prophecy formula, which, using the correlation between the two half-tests, estimates what the reliability would be on the full-length test, that is, including both odd and even items. The procedure works as follows:

$$\text{Reliability on full test} = \frac{2 \times \text{reliability on half-test}}{1 + \text{reliability on half-test}}$$

The ease with which the Spearman-Brown formula can be used is illustrated in the following equation, where the half-test correlation coefficient is .60:

$$\text{Reliability on full test} = \frac{2 \times .60}{1 + .60} = \frac{1.20}{1.60} = .75$$

As can be seen, use of the Spearman-Brown formula will increase the magnitude of the reliability estimate (unless the half-test $r = 0$).

Kuder-Richardson Approaches   An often-used index of the homogeneity of a set of test items is the Kuder-Richardson method, particularly their formulas 20 (K-R20) and 21 (K-R21). The K-R21 formula is somewhat less accurate than the K-R20 formula, but it is so simple to compute that it is probably the most frequently employed estimate of internal consistency. One version of the K-R21 formula is the following:

$$\text{K-R21 reliability coefficient} = \frac{K}{K-1}\left(1 - \frac{M(K-M)}{Ks^2}\right)$$

where K = number of items in the test
M = mean of the set of test scores
s = standard deviation of the set of test scores

Like other internal consistency approaches to reliability, the Kuder-Richardson method focuses on the degree to which the items in the test are functioning in a homogeneous fashion.

Coefficient alpha,[6] developed by Lee J. Cronbach, is a more generalizable estimate of the internal consistency form of reliability.

Indeed, because of this diversity of reliability-determination approaches, it is unacceptable to assert that "the reliability of Test Z is .85." The following type of statement does the job better: "Based on the correlation between alternate test Forms I and II administered on the same day to a sample of 250 seventh-grade pupils drawn from a middle-class suburban public school system in Florida, the reliability coefficient was estimated to be .85." It is also possible to calculate a range of accuracy, that is, a *confidence interval* around the .85 reliability coefficient. For example, we could compute a 95 percent confidence interval around the .85 of, say, .78–.92. This interval of .14 indicates that if we were to replicate the gathering of data 100 times, 95 of those times the reliability coefficient would fall between .78 and .92. Such confidence intervals, of course, provide a more realistic estimate of the "true" size of the reliability coefficient.

Consistency Comes in All Flavors

It should be apparent from the foregoing discussion of techniques for estimating reliability that in classical measurement theory there is no such thing as a single way of calculating a test's reliability. It is important, therefore, to discern which of these several methods have been employed when evaluators appraise testing devices.

Validity

Test *validity* refers to the defensibility of inferences made from test scores. It is, in fact, not the validity of the test with which we should be concerned but the validity of the score-based inference we make after having administered the test. Thus, it is inappropriate to talk about "the validity of Test X," for the test itself possesses no inherent validity. For example, if a sophisticated verbal aptitude test designed for American adults were used with Norwegian preschoolers, any inferences about verbal aptitude based on the children's scores would be meaningless. It is the *validity of the score-based inference*, not the validity of the test, that should be our concern.

There are three traditional methods of gathering validity evidence. These approaches are referred to as *content-related, criterion-related*, and *construct-related evidence of validity*. Although these evidence categories are convenient, their use should not imply that there are three truly distinctive categories of validity evidence. For instance, validity evidence identified as criterion related or content related can also be regarded as a meaningful form of construct-related evidence of validity. Nor should one think that for each specific type of test use or inference there is one preferred evidence-gathering category. Ideally, evidence of validity should encompass all three of the traditional categories. Other things being equal, more sources of validity evidence are better than fewer sources of evidence.

Content-Related Evidence

When one seeks *content-related* evidence of validity, an attempt is made to judge the degree to which a test is consonant with the content, skills, or objectives it is supposed to measure. Another way of looking at content validity is to think of it as a way of estimating whether the content of the test adequately samples the behavior or content domain about which inferences are to be made. Because content-related evidence validity involves someone's inspecting the items and deciding whether they are sufficiently consonant with the content or learner behaviors that are to be measured, there is obviously a heavy reliance on human judgment in using this approach.

The expression *face validity* was often used some years ago as a way of describing whether a test appeared (on the basis of visual inspection) to measure what it was supposed to. Face validity simply describes a relatively superficial technique for using a content-validity approach. Because face validity is not an approach to validity endorsed in the *standards*, its use should be avoided.

Although the concept of content validity has been around for a good many years, there have been few exemplary applications of the approach. More often than not, this approach, because it does not lend itself readily to quantification, has been employed in a somewhat haphazard fashion. As we shall see later when discussing *criterion-referenced testing*, there are preferable techniques for determining this sort of validity.[7]

Criterion-Related Evidence

When we attempt to secure *criterion-related* evidence of validity, we typically correlate performance on a measure (the one we are hoping to validate) with an independent external criterion. For instance, if a verbal aptitude test is designed to predict how well elementary-school students will succeed in a secondary school, then the correlation between a group of students' scores on the aptitude test and those same students' high school grade-point averages (the external criterion) would provide us with criterion-related evidence of validity. A distinction is often drawn between two different forms of this approach because of the presence or absence of a temporal delay between the administration of the test and the gathering of the criterion data. If the test and the criterion were measured without any intervening time, for instance, as when one administers an IQ test to students and correlates the test performance with their *current* grade-point averages, this is referred to as the *concurrent* form of criterion-related validity evidence. If an interval occurred between the test administration and the gathering of the criterion data, as in the previous example of predicting secondary-school grade performance from a test administered much earlier in elementary school, we refer to this as the *predictive* form of criterion-validity evidence. However, concurrent and predictive approaches are both commonly grouped under the single rubric of criterion-related evidence of validity.

In the gathering of criterion-related evidence of validity, the most important ingredient is the quality of the criterion. There have been many unfortunate examples of measurement people's gathering mounds of correlational data relating test performance to a criterion variable that, under close scrutiny, was seriously flawed.

Construct-Related Evidence

A quite different approach to validity is represented when one sets out to gather *construct-related evidence* of validity. For this type of evidence we assemble a series of different sorts of evidence bearing on the validity of score-based inferences. There is no single, "once-and-for-all-time" type of evidence that definitively clinches the case for construct-related validity. Rather, one must carry out a series of studies so that a *network* of evidence allows us, finally, to assert that a test aimed at assessing a hypothetical construct such as "self-esteem" yields scores from which accurate inferences regarding self-esteem can be drawn.

Although many measurement specialists employ construct validation approaches only to deal with such patently hypothetical constructs as "anxiety" or "confidence," the logic of construct validation can be applied with equal force to the assessment of such prosaic attributes as the examinee's spelling ability. After all, one's "spelling ability" is just as covert as one's "self-esteem." We are simply more familiar with such capabilities as one's reading or mathematics skills, hence devote less effort to verifying the existence of these equally unseeable attributes.

Typically, there are three steps involved in a construct-validation approach: (1) a hypothetical construct presumed to account for test performance is identified, (2) one or more hypotheses regarding test performance are derived from the theory underlying the construct, and (3) the hypotheses are tested by both logical and empirical methods.

Let's illustrate the approach with a simple example. Suppose we are trying to measure a tendency in certain pupils to "choke" under test conditions and to perform less well than they ordinarily would. Let's say we refer to the covert factor underlying this tendency as Test Terror (TT). Now if we were to prepare some kind of paper-and-pencil self-report device that purported to measure TT, we could use a construct-validity approach as follows: First, we would derive a hypothesis regarding test performance on the basis of our knowledge of TT. For example, we might hypothesize that, for most persons afflicted with the malady, Test Terror is most intense when significant (as opposed to unimportant) examinations are completed. Our hypothesis might be that if pupils are identified who perform *relatively* worse on high-stakes versus low-stakes exams, they will display higher scores on our new TT Test.

Suppose we locate a group of pupils, sort out those who score the same or differently on high-stakes and low-stakes exams, then administer our TT Test to all of them. We could then support or negate our prediction on the basis of the empirical data. We could see if, as predicted, those performing worse on high-stakes exams received high scores on the TT Test.

If things work out as we anticipated, that is, if the hypothesis is confirmed, then both our theory regarding the existence of a Test Terror construct is supported and relevant construct-related evidence of validity has been assembled. If, however, the hypothesis is not supported, either a deficiency in the theory or the test *or both* is evidenced. In a construct-validity approach, evidence is being gathered regarding both the construct theory and potential inference to be based on test scores.

The most common methods of obtaining evidence in using a construct-validation approach are (1) comparisons of scores before and after a particular treatment, such as predicting that after instruction from a humanistically oriented teacher-educator, pupils' scores on a newly devised Neohumanism Inventory should rise; (2) comparisons of scores of known groups, such as predicting dramatic differences between senior citizens and adolescents on a newly developed Puberty Preoccupation Inventory; and (3) correlations with other tests, such as correlating a new test of intellectual aptitude with an already validated test of intellectual aptitude. Note that this last situation is a rather weak form of construct validity, not an instance of criterion-related validity. The established test is not an external criterion but, rather, another test assumed to be validly doing the same kind of job as our new test. Correlations between like-purposed tests should obviously be higher than between tests with dissimilar missions.

To review, a construct-validation approach requires us to identify one or more hypothetical constructs, that is, ways of conceptualizing an unobservable quality of individuals such as their "courage" or "honesty." Then, on the basis of our knowledge of how that hypothetical construct ought to operate, for example, how it might influence one's behavior or how it might be influenced by certain events, we formulate one or more hypotheses involving the test to be validated. Finally, we gather empirical evidence, one element of which will always involve performance on the test to be validated. If the evidence confirms our hypothesis, we have evidence supporting both the existence of the hypothetical construct and our test's ability to measure it. If the evidence fails to support the hypothesis, there may be something wrong with (1) the way we conceptualized the hypothetical construct, (2) our test, or (3) both the theory and the test.

As we shall see, evidence of construct-related validity is particularly suitable for dealing with affective dimensions of interest to educational evaluators. For that matter, construct-related evidence of validity is pertinent information for assessing the quality of a measure designed to assess any elusive attribute.

Usability

In addition to the more esoteric considerations associated with classical measurement operations, a number of practical issues can be considered under the general heading of *usability*. Evaluators must be sensitive to the ease with which the tests can be administered. How long will they take to administer? How readily can tests be scored? How easily can test results be interpreted? How expensive are the tests? Are there equivalent forms available for pretesting, posttesting, and so forth? Is there evidence that the test is suitable for all the ethnic groups with whom it will be used?

If the evaluator overlooks one of these key questions, the whole measurement operation can collapse. Theory is lovely, but practical payoff is often more dependent on such considerations as whether or not test results can be processed with the financial resources available for that task. And who can deny that the most resplendently reliable tests, even those accompanied by a treasure trove of validity evidence, will do a school administrator little good if they cost twice as much as the school district can afford. Usability considerations are obviously important.

Reprise

In this chapter we have encountered most of the key notions permeating classical measurement technology for the past half-century. That the constructs are important should be apparent. No less apparent should be the fact that the fleeting treatment given those key concepts in this brief chapter is far from adequate for anyone who would truly master them. As a review for the reader who has previously studied these topics, the chapter may have been useful. For those less acquainted with traditional measurement methods, one hopes the chapter accomplished its largely introductory mission.

Discussion Questions

1. What were the three major deficiencies noted with respect to using norm-referenced measures for purposes of educational evaluation? How might these deficiencies be remedied in the creation of measuring devices better suited for evaluation purposes?
2. Which one of the four kinds of measurement scales treated in the chapter (nominal, ordinal, interval, and ratio) is *least* often found in the field of educational measurement? Can you think of any examples of each of the four scales that might be encountered by educational evaluators?
3. Think of different kinds of educational decision makers, and then decide whether educational measurement results would be most effectively presented to these individuals via graphic techniques, such as histograms or frequency polygons, or statistical measures of central tendency and variability, such as means and standard deviations. Why?
4. Which type (or types) of reliability estimates will be more apt to be employed in educational evaluation settings? Why?
5. Can you describe, in a single sentence, each of the following types of validity evidence: content related, criterion related, and construct related?

Practice Exercises

1. Decide whether the following measurement data are most appropriately classified as *nominal, ordinal*, or *interval* scales.
   a. History teachers, physics teachers, and mathematics teachers.
   b. Scores on a well-standardized norm-referenced achievement test.
   c. Pupils ranked according to most cooperative, next most cooperative, and so on.
   d. Judging pupil essays as unacceptable, acceptable, or superior.
2. Decide which of the following descriptions or operations is most closely associated with these concepts: *mean, median, mode, range, standard deviation*, and *correlation coefficient*. (Not all concepts will be needed for the descriptions.)
   a. This index represents a distribution's central tendency by constituting the exact center, that is, the midpoint of the distribution.
   b. Often used in the quantitative estimation of reliability and validity, this statistic can range in magnitude from 1.00 to −1.00.
   c. An average of dispersion, that is, the distance between the mean and other scores in the distribution.
   d. The most stable index of central tendency.
3. Indicate whether the following estimates of test consistency are most reflective of the *stability, alternate forms*, or *internal consistency* form of reliability.
   a. An estimate is derived of the degree to which the items on a test are performing in a homogeneous manner.
   b. A new achievement test is given to a group of learners, then readministered one week later so a correlation can be computed between the two sets of scores.
   c. Two forms of a test have been constituted by dividing a large pool of test items into two content-parallel versions, which have identical means and standard deviations. The

two forms are administered to learners on the same day and a correlation coefficient is computed
between the two sets of scores.

d. A test is divided into odd and even
item subscores. The two parts are
correlated, then a Spearman-Brown
formula is used to increase the size
of the correlation derived between
the two half-tests.

4. Indicate which of the following types
of validity evidence is being gathered:
*content-related evidence, criterion-
related evidence*, or *construct-related
evidence*.

a. Subject-matter experts have been
summoned to rate the consonance
of a test's items with the objectives
the test is supposed to measure.

b. A correlation is computed between
a new test of student self-esteem
and a previously validated and
widely used test of student self-
esteem.

c. Scores on a screening test (used to
assign college sophomores to standard or enriched English classes)
are correlated with English competence of college juniors (as reflected
by grades assigned at the close of
junior-year English classes).

d. Scores on a government test designed to assess "good citizenship"
during the twelfth grade are correlated with subsequent citizenship
ratings of students during their
college careers.

Answers to Practice Exercises

1. *a*. Nominal; *b*. interval; *c*. ordinal; *d*.
ordinal.
2. *a*. Median; *b*. correlation coefficient;
c. standard deviation; *d*. mean.
3. *a*. Internal consistency; *b*. stability; *c*.

alternate form; *d*. internal consistency.
4. *a*. Content related; *b*. construct related; *c*. criterion related; *d*. criterion
related.

Notes

1. S. S. Stevens, "On the Theory of
Scales of Measurement," *Science* 103
(1946), 677–80.

2. Such as analysis of variance,
product-moment correlation coefficients,
and *t* tests.

3. See, for example, W. James
Popham and Kenneth A. Sirotnik, *Educational Statistics: Use and Interpretation*,
2nd ed. (New York: Harper & Row, 1973),
Chapters 19 and 20.

4. American Psychological Association, *Standards for Educational and Psychological Testing*, Washington, DC, 1985.

5. Ibid.

6. Lee J. Cronbach. "Coefficient
Alpha and the Internal Structure of Tests,"
Psychometrika 16 (1951), 297–334.

7. Because content-related evidence
of validity does not directly support a

particular score-based inference, some
writers have argued that this type of evidence, although it constitutes important
information about a test, is not a bona fide
form of validity evidence at all. (See Samuel Missick, "Evidence and Ethics in the
Evaluation of Tests," *Educational Researcher* [November 1981], 9–20.) A
colleague and I have responded, however,
that content-related evidence of validity
does, in fact, represent a meaningful form
of validation evidence. (See E. S. Yalow
and W. J. Popham, "Content Validity at the
Crossroads," *Educational Researcher* [Octo-
ber 1983], 10–21.) This disagreement illustrates that such concepts as validity are far
from moribund. Rather, they represent
important, *evolving* psychometric constructs.

Selected References

Cunningham, George K. *Educational and Psychological Measurement*. New York: Macmillan, 1986.

Hambleton, Ronald K. (Review Ed.). "Standards for Educational and Psychological Testing: Six Reviews." *Journal of Educational Measurement*, 23:1 (Spring 1986): 83–98.

Mehrens, William A. and Irvin J. Lehmann. *Measurement and Evaluation in Education and Psychology* (3rd ed.). New York: Holt, Rinehart and Winston, 1984.

Messick, S. "Testing Validity and the Ethics of Assessment." *American Psychologist*, 35, (1980): 1012–28.

Popham, W. James. *Modern Educational Measurement*. Englewood Cliffs, NJ: Prentice-Hall, 1981.

Shepard, Lorrie A., Gregory Camilli, and David M. Williams. "Validity of Approximation Techniques for Detecting Item Bias." *Journal of Educational Measurement*, 22:2 (Summer 1985): 77–105.

Stiggins, Richard J., and Nancy J. Bridgeford. "The Ecology of Classroom Assessment." *Journal of Educational Measurement*, 22:4 (Winter 1985): 271–86.

CHAPTER SIX

Criterion-Referenced Measurement

There are a number of reasons why traditional norm-referenced tests are not ideal assessment tools for purposes of educational evaluation. Fortunately, a different approach to measurement has evolved during the past two decades, one far more compatible with the requirements of educational evaluation. This assessment approach is referred to as *criterion-referenced measurement.*

Before we turn to a consideration of the nature of criterion-referenced measurement and to the ways in which its technical procedures differ from those of norm-referenced measurement, an analysis of the events that led to the creation of criterion-referenced measurement devices may prove helpful.

Background

We have had over a half-century of experience in using formal, systematically developed educational tests (as opposed to tests churned out by the teacher on the way to class). Because current conceptions of the role of educational tests are sometimes not consonant with earlier views of how such test were to be used, let's try to go back to the 1940s or 1950s and get inside the head of an educator who used commercially produced, standardized educational tests. Such an educator tended to view tests largely as devices to identify differences among learners with respect to their aptitudes, achievements, and so on. Though it was conceded that the educational enterprise contributed to the student's increased subject-matter knowledge, it was generally thought that what a student *brought* to the instructional situation was chiefly responsible for what the student *left* the instructional situation with. When achievement test results were portrayed graphically and they resembled the normal distribution seen in Figure 6–1, few educators threatened to take early retirement. A normal distribution of postinstruction attainments was pretty much the way things were expected to turn out. It was assumed that there should be some high achievers, some low achievers, and most middlish achievers. Test developers wrote test items to distinguish between high total-test scorers and low total-test scorers; it was only natural for some people to answer a test item incorrectly. After all, most educators assumed that the shape of any distribution of learner test scores, including "genetically determined" *aptitude* as well as instructionally influenced *achievement* test scores, would be splattered out in a fairly normal shape. The job of the test constructor was to identify the differences among people, then represent those differences according to pupils' percentile scores, stanine scores,[1] or some other indicators of *relative* student standing. Test-item writers congratulated themselves if they could write an item that, on the basis of field-test results, turned out to have a difficulty level of .50, that is, an item that only 50 percent of the examinees answered correctly. An item that approximately half the examinees answered correctly (and, therefore, half answered incorrectly) was optimal for producing the spread of scores that was so necessary for effectively functioning norm-referenced tests.

It is difficult to document, but one has the definite impression that American measurement specialists of the first half of this century had an uncommonly low opinion of the potency of conventional instruction. These measurement folks thought that, by and large, students entered an educational situation with normally distributed skills and, after instruction was finished, left that educational situation with a comparable distribution of skills. Public education, they thought, did little to alter the relative abilities of students.

Such a low opinion regarding the effectiveness of education seems prevalent in the approach of many early educators to measurement, with respect to both the way tests were originally built and the way those tests were subsequently revised. For instance, the most pervasive statistical index used in calculating test reliability and validity is the correlation coefficient. But correlational methods, in order to be fully effective, require a reasonably large response variance (that is, spread of scores) in the examinee scores under consideration. In other words, if the scores on one or both measures involved in the correlation computation have small standard deviations, it will be next to impossible to secure a strong correlation, because of what is known technically as *range restriction*. But few self-respecting measurement people of the 1940s or 1950s were ever truly worried about range restriction. It was assumed that, just as we once viewed our energy reserves as potentially unlimited,

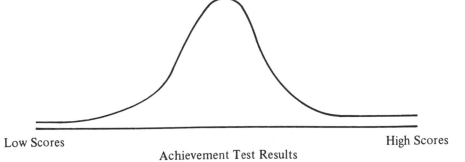

Low Scores   High Scores

Achievement Test Results

FIGURE 6–1 • *Fictitious Achievement Test Results (the Area Beneath the Curve Represents Frequency of Student Performance)*

there would always be enough student variability to go around. The task of the measurement expert was merely to determine who scored better than whom – and by how much.

Near the close of the 1950s, however, a group of educational psychologists became fascinated by the possibilities of an approach to teaching known as *programmed instruction*. These psychologists were influenced most heavily by B. F. Skinner's attempts to apply laboratory-derived learning principles to classroom instructional schemes – best reflected in his pioneering work with teaching machines. Because these programmed-instruction enthusiasts were careful to follow research-derived instructional principles, and because they tried out their instructional schemes with students, and then revised an instructional sequence until it worked, they began to develop greatly increased respect for the potency of properly conceived instruction. Indeed, in the early 1960s one was obliged to view with unbridled skepticism the outlandish claims of programmed-instruction zealots who offered such claims as "with programmed instructional sequences, every child can reach 100 percent mastery of any objective in 50 percent of the time required by conventional instruction."

One particularly outrageous teaching-machine advertisement that appeared in those days showed a picture of a kitchen in which a mother was happily washing dishes (surely, prior to the women's liberation movement) while her young son joyfully worked with his very own "Brand X" teaching machine. The son was obviously intent on his work. This intensity was reflected by his anxiously poised pencil and the fact that his tongue was extended ever so slightly from the corner of his mouth. Below this heartwarming picture the advertisement pointed out that by using the Brand X teaching machine for only *15 minutes per day*, any child could keep up with classmates. By using the Brand X teaching machine for *30 minutes per day*, one's classmates could be easily outdistanced. In view of this device's apparent effectiveness, it was surprising that the advertisement did not push the more-time-per-day principle to its logical limit and promise, to those who devoted *several hours daily* to the Brand X machine, a prepubescent Ph.D.

These excesses were, fortunately, the exception rather than the rule, but they did reflect the general view held by a growing number of instructional specialists during the early 1960s that well-devised, empirically revised instructional sequences could help most learners achieve mastery of desired instructional objectives. Unlike many previous educators who tended to put the blame for an ineffectual instructional sequence on the students, these programmed-instruction specialists took personal responsibility for instructional sequences that failed. Happily, there were some startlingly successful applications of programmed instruction. Cases were reported where 100 percent of the students did indeed master the desired program goals. Small wonder that programmed-instruction people began to believe in the power of their procedures.

Yet, as instructional programmers began to measure the effects of their increasingly powerful instructional interventions, they encountered anomalies with respect to measuring the effects of those interventions. It began to dawn on instructional experts that the available standardized achievement tests didn't work very well in gauging the efficacy of their instructional programs. The tests were too general. In addition, the traditional norm-referenced techniques for designing and improving educational tests, techniques that most programmed-instruction people had been reared on, just didn't work.

A personal experience may illustrate the point. Upon joining the faculty at UCLA in 1962 I devoted considerable attention to teaching a course in instructional methodology for preservice teachers. I not only tried to make the course increasingly effective but also attempted to sharpen the quality of the examinations that I used in the course. After each midterm and final exam, I would diligently transport my exam data to the campus computing center, which was inhabited by well-wired machines that had been taught to provide internal consistency estimates of test reliability. During my first couple of terms at UCLA, computer analyses of my examinations led to my considerable elation, for my reliability coefficients were around .85. A reliability coefficient of .85 for a teacher-made test is very good; for a professor-made test, it is awe inspiring. I took special glee in informing my colleagues of the resplendent reliability coefficients I was getting. (After all, I was eager to secure tenure.) But, as a consequence of my improvement efforts, the course became more effective and, instead of the students' exam performances being nicely spread out in a normal distribution, almost everyone started to do well. The response variance on my exams dropped dramatically, as did my exams' reliability coefficients. In four successive terms my reliability coefficients dropped from .85 to .60 to .40 to .25. The reduced coefficients stemmed chiefly from range restriction and its depressing effect on the possible size of a correlation coefficient. Then came the term that I received my first *negative* reliability coefficient! I no longer displayed my reliability coefficients to colleagues with pride. Rather, I darted from the computing center to my office, hoping fervently that no one would ask about the printouts under my arm. It was clearly time to relate theory to practice. The traditional measurement procedures that I had been employing were not compatible with an improvement-oriented approach to instruction.

The person who called the attention of educators and psychologists to the inappropriateness of applying traditional measurement notions to situations involving newer instructional techniques was Robert Glaser of the University of Pittsburgh. Glaser had been heavily involved in the early programmed-instruction movement, and the title of his classic 1963 article, "Instructional Technology and the Measurement of Learning Outcomes: Some Questions," accurately reflected his concerns.[2] Glaser's article stimulated many people, particularly those involved in applications of instructional technology, to realize ever more keenly that classical measurement approaches were often inappropriate for improvement-focused instructional purposes. Glaser drew the basic distinction between norm-referenced measurement, which he conceived of as focusing on the determination of a student's relative standing (in relationship to that of other students), and criterion-referenced measurement, which he said focused on "an absolute standard of quality."

As we shall see, certain language used by Glaser in his 1963 paper led to some confusion with respect to the meaning of *criterion* when used in connection with criterion-referenced measurement. Nevertheless, although others[3] had previously drawn the distinction that Glaser described, it was his article that catalyzed interest in this measurement issue. He raised a number of pivotal questions regarding the difficulty of having test items simultaneously serve in the isolation of examinees' relative status (as in norm-referenced applications) and examinees' absolute status (as in criterion-referenced applications).

With respect to what the "criterion" is in the phrase *criterion-referenced measurement*, Glaser seemed to be stressing the importance of a well-described domain of learner behaviors when he asserted that "a student's score on a criterion-referenced measure provides explicit information as to what the individual can and cannot do." This is probably what he meant even when he asserted that "criterion-referenced measures depend on an absolute standard of quality." Unfortunately, some writers who did not consider the full context of Glaser's remarks reached the conclusion that his notion of criterion focused on the *standard*, using standard or criterion in the same way that traditional measurement specialists used it, that is, as a *level* of performance. Some confusion, as a consequence, resulted.

The Nature of a Criterion-Referenced Test

As was pointed out in the previous chapter, tests traditionally used in education have been designed to permit comparisons among examinees in relationship to the performance of other examinees. More specifically, to interpret an examinee's score, it was determined how that score stacked up in comparison to the scores of a group of examinees (known as the *norm group*) who had previously completed the examination. In other words, when interpreting an examinee's score on a traditional educational test, such as a nationally standardized achievement or aptitude test, we *reference* the examinee's performance to that of the norm group. Because the interpretive framework for making sense out of such test scores is provided by the norm group's performance, we can aptly characterize such assessment tests as *norm-referenced tests*.

Criterion-referenced tests, on the other hand, are used to ascertain an individual's status with respect to a defined behavioral domain. A properly constructed criterion-referenced test will provide a sufficiently clear description of the behavioral domain being assessed so that the examinees' test score can be *referenced* to that domain of behaviors. Thus the interpretive framework for a criterion-referenced test is the domain of tasks or behaviors to which an examinee's test score is referenced.

Nitko argues that a criterion-referenced test's behavioral "domain is *well defined* if it is clear which categories of performance or which kinds of tasks are or are not potential test items."[4] It should be clear that the nub of criterion-referenced testing is the "domain" of behaviors according to which the examinee's test score is interpreted. A brief consideration of such domains is therefore in order.

Careful reading of Glaser's influential 1963 essay on criterion-referenced testing will reveal that he was introducing a novel way of thinking about testing, in which we interpret examinees' results according to what those examinees can or cannot do — more precisely, what examinees can or cannot do with respect to defined set of *criterion behaviors*. Recalling that Glaser and his colleagues were heavily involved in the programmed-instruction movement, it is clear that such instructional specialists wished learners to master specified criterion behaviors, such as the ability to solve simultaneous equations. Thus, programmed-instruction experts naturally conceived of instructional targets as criterion behaviors or, in some instances, as *domains* of criterion behaviors. It is to such criterion domains that the examinees' behavior is referenced in a criterion-referenced test.

These behavioral domains might include the following:

1. The ability, when examinees are presented with specific types of reading selections, to select from alternative statements the one that best represents a selection's main idea
2. The skill of identifying errors in written mechanics when examinees are presented with compositions in which errors in spelling, punctuation, and/or capitalization have been made
3. The ability to name the artist of previously unseen oil paintings on the basis of an analysis of the artist's technical and stylistic idiosyncrasies

For each of these sorts of domains, a set of detailed rules for test-item generation would be prepared. These item-generation rules, in a very real sense, *operationalize* the behavioral domain. By setting forth a behavioral domain's key item-generation rules, the criterion-referenced test developer clarifies the domain to which the examinee's performance is to be referenced.

Not a Criterion Level Some writers, and more than a few educators, have been confused about the meaning of the word *criterion* in the phrase *criterion-referenced test*. To them, the criterion was the cut-off score (that is, passing standard) established on a test to distinguish between those examinees who passed and those who didn't. Such an interpretation is rooted in the time-honored use of "criterion" as a desired *level* of examinee proficiency. However, as criterion-referenced testing is viewed these days, the criterion refers to a *domain* of criterion behaviors, *not* a cut-off level.

After all, a cut-off level can be set for any type of test, norm referenced or criterion referenced. Yet, if we set a cut-off score of 75 percent correct on a widely used norm-referenced aptitude test, would that instantly transform the test into a criterion-referenced assessment device? Of course not.

The heart of a criterion-referenced test is the defined behavioral domain to which examinees' performances are referenced. A criterion-referenced test may or may not have a cut-off score (or *criterion level*) attached to it.

Absolute versus Relative Interpretations

As we shall see later in the chapter, there are differences in the way that criterion- and norm-referenced tests are constructed. A chief difference between the two hinges on the interpretation of a test score. Typically, when using a norm-referenced test, we make a *relative* interpretation by determining that the examinee's score represents a particular percentile based on the norm group's performance. We might say, for example, that "Eva scored at the 87th percentile on the mathematics achievements test.

When using a criterion-referenced test, however, we are more apt to make an *absolute* interpretation of the test score by determining the proportion of the task in the criterion domain that the examinee can master. Putting it another way, if we conceived of a large number of test items that could be generated to assess a particular behavior domain, what percent of those items would the examinee be apt to answer correctly? Hence, we might make an interpretive statement such as "Mary's score on the test indicated that she could define only 35 percent of the 300 words contained in the Nurse's Professional Terminology Vocabulary." Whereas norm-referenced interpretations typically focus on *percentiles*, criterion-referenced interpretations typically focus on *percentage* correct.

Theoretically, we could make a norm-referenced or criterion-referenced interpretations about any test score. For example, even for a criterion-referenced test it is possible to assemble normative data and hence make a percentile-based *relative* interpretation of an examinee's score. However, for almost all norm-referenced tests there is little descriptive rigor regarding what is actually being measured; hence it is extremely difficult to make meaningful *absolute* interpretations of an examinee's score. After all, what good does it do to say that the "examinee's score represented 92 percent mastery of the test's contents" if we're really unclear about what those contents are?

Tyler has recently noted the educational shortcomings of widely used norm-referenced schemes for reporting test performances: "It should be clear . . . that the abstract numbers now commonly used in reporting test results are not appropriate for educational purposes. To report that a student is at the 66th percentile on a standard test does not tell what she or he has learned and what she or he has yet to learn. . . . So far as possible, test results should be reported in terms that those involved can understand and be helped in their roles in improving education in our society."[5]

It should be noted that in the most recent revision (1985) of the *Standards for Educational and Psychological Testing*[6] the position is taken that in some instances "norm-referenced tests can be interpreted in criterion-referenced ways and vice versa." As we pointed out, although the vice versa may well be true, that is, norm-referenced interpretations can be made from criterion-referenced tests, in most practical situations there is little hope of making criterion-referenced interpretations from a typical norm-referenced test in which the domain of behavior being measured is only loosely defined. I have never encountered a norm-referenced test descriptive of sufficient rigor to permit a meaningful criterion-referenced interpretation. Until I do, I'm obliged to disagree with the authors of the 1985 *Standards* regarding the likelihood of making criterion-referenced interpretations from results of norm-referenced tests.

The Advantages of Criterion-Referenced Tests for Educational Evaluation

Educational evaluators assemble information so that educational decision makers can arrive at more defensible decisions. It is in this connection that the singular advantage of criterion-referenced tests should be apparent. Criterion-referenced test scores lead to clearer, that is, more understandable interpretations. Because clarity normally contributes to more defensible decisions, criterion-referenced testing devices should be employed whenever possible by educational evaluators. Such tests simply yield more meaningfully interpretable data and hence will be of more utility to decision makers.

The foregoing recommendation should not be interpreted as an across-the-board discounting of norm-referenced tests. There are a number of purposes for which such tests are ideal. For instance, in "fixed-quota" settings where there are more applicants than openings, a norm-referenced test will do the best job of sorting out applicants according to their relative abilities.

There are also situations in which educational evaluators may be faced with a choice between (1) test data and (2) no data at all. Clearly, choice number one wins. Some data, though less than perfect, are usually preferable to no data whatsoever.

Nonetheless, because results on criterion-referenced tests will usually contribute more crisply to the decision maker's intellectual grasp of a program's effects, such test results should be sought by educational evaluators. The dividends in clarity attained from such tests, and the resultant increase in the decision maker's rational analyses, will generally lead to better educational decisions.

Translating this recommendation into action, what are the implications for educational evaluators? Well, quite clearly, skilled educational evaluators need to become thoroughly conversant with the innards of criterion-referenced assessment. This means going well beyond the introductory treatment supplied in this chapter. There are several volumes, notably one edited by Berk,[7] that provide a good deal of information regarding the nuts and bolts of criterion-referenced measurement.

If you aspire to be a truly skilled educational evaluator, then it is imperative that you become able to (1) determine whether a criterion-referenced test is properly constructed and, if possible, (2) construct a defensible criterion-referenced test yourself. Although the remainder of this chapter will introduce you to the content needed for both those tasks, you will clearly need to do a good deal of additional reading or coursework regarding the nature and nurture of criterion-referenced tests.

Describing the Criterion Behavior

As has been indicated, the heart of a properly constructed criterion-referenced test is the description of the domain of criterion behaviors to which an examinee's performance is referenced. If such a description is clear, then a test score can be interpreted accurately. If the description is unclear, then score-based interpretations will be less accurate. It is apparent, therefore, that the clarity with which a criterion-referenced test's behavioral domain is described constitutes the single, most important aspect of a properly constructed criterion-referenced test.

Although there are a number of ways in which test developers might describe the examinee behaviors[8] being measured by a criterion-referenced test, the most common technique for circumscribing examinee behavior is the use of *test-item specifications*. Test-item specifications set forth the rules to be used in generating the test's items. They therefore *operationalize* the nature of the examinee behavior being assessed. In essence, a thorough review of a set of test-item specifications should answer the question: "What is this test actually measuring?"

A distinction must be drawn between *test-item specifications*, which focus on the form of the test's items and *test specifications*, which focus on the overall composition of the test itself. To illustrate, suppose you were developing a criterion-referenced test in which you wished to measure the examinee's ability to distinguish between statements of fact and statements of opinion. The *test-item specifications* for such a test would be used to describe the requirements of the items themselves, such as the sorts of stimulus materials and response options that would be eligible for inclusion in the items. The *test specifications* for such a test would be used to describe the constitution of the test itself, such as the proportion of "fact" items versus "opinion" items, the number of items on the test, the time allowed for the test, and so on. The distinction, then, between these two sets of specifications is as follows:

> *Test specifications* = The rules to be followed in constituting the overall nature of a test
> *Test-item specifications* = The rules to be followed in constructing the test's items

Ideally, a test developer would create a detailed set of test-item specifications as well as test specifications for any criterion-referenced test. In actual practice, however, the degree of descriptive rigor for either of these sets of specifications depends on the importance of the test. For a high-stakes test, such as a test used for denial of high school diplomas, then, detailed test-item specifications *and* test specifications should be created. For a teacher-made criterion-referenced test to be used as a final examination, on the other hand, the test-item specifications might appropriately be less than totally detailed, and there might be no need whatsoever for test specifications. Educational evaluators should press for the degree of descriptive rigor in criterion-referenced tests warranted by the situation.

To repeat an oft-repeated point, remember that although the most common form of assessment involves paper-and-pencil tests, there are numerous other forms of assessment that should be routinely considered, such as actual performance tests. When evaluators think of tests, therefore, they should think of a great array of assessment devices.

Test-Item Specifications

Because the most pivotal element in a criterion-referenced test is the set of test-item specifications, we shall spend a fair number of paragraphs familiarizing you with such specifications. Each of the key components of a set of test-item specifications will be described. In addition, several examples of test-item specifications will be provided as models. Because educational evaluators need to be well versed in the nature of criterion-referenced test construction, be sure to attend carefully to this section of the chapter.

The most frequently used types of test-item specifications typically contain the following five components:

1. *General Description:* A brief one-paragraph overview of the attribute (behavior) being measured.
2. *Sample Item:* An illustrative test item for the test.
3. *Stimulus Attributes:* The rules to be followed in constructing the stimulus segments of a test item.
4. *Response Attributes:* The rules to be followed in (a) constructing the response segments of a selected-response test item or (b) scoring an examinee's response to a constructed-response test item.
5. *Supplement* (optional): For some criterion-referenced tests it is useful to list separately, in an appendix or supplement, certain content such as the set of punctuation rules eligible for test items dealing with the mechanics of writing. Such specification supplements are usually employed for tests in which substantial amounts of content need to be identified.

Although the particular names of these five sections of test-item specifications may vary, as may the form in which they are used, test-item specifications containing these components can suffice to explicate the important dimensions of the behavioral domain being assessed. The key word in the previous sentence, however, is *can*. The mere fact that a set of test-item specifications happens to contain sections such as those listed above does not mean the behavioral domain to be measured has been well defined. As we shall see shortly, the two most critical components of a set of test-item specifications are the descriptions of stimulus attributes and response attributes. If those two segments rigorously define the genuinely important aspects of the test's items, then the measured behavioral domain will have been well described. Contrarily, if the stimulus attributes and response attributes sections (1) define relatively unimportant aspects of test items or (2) provide ambiguous or superficial descriptions of important aspects of test items, then the test-item specifications will have done little to advance the cause of clarity regarding what is being measured.

Let's turn to a brief description of each of the five major components in a set of criterion-referenced test specifications. You will then find it useful to read through the illustrative set of test-item specifications that follows. The specifications focus on a reading skill (identifying a selection's main idea) measured by multiple-choice items.

After the illustrative test-item specifications, we'll close out the chapter with a discussion of the *educationally* appropriate level of specificity to employ in criterion-referenced test-item specifications.

General Description   The initial component of a set of test-item specifications is a brief statement, ranging in length from a simple sentence to a short paragraph, which provides a succinct summary of the behavioral domain being
measured. In some instances the general description resembles what is typically
referred to as an instructional objective. Yet, because criterion-referenced tests may
be used both *after* an instructional sequence (to determine whether an objective has
been achieved) and *before* an instructional sequence (to gauge learners' entry status),
it is preferable to use the label "general description" rather than "objective."

Whereas most statements of instructional objectives are single sentences, the
general description for a set of criterion-referenced test-item specifications will often contain several sentences in order to convey more fully an overall notion of what
the test is designed to assess.

Sample Item   The second component of a set of criterion-referenced test
specifications is an illustrative item, that is, a sample item drawn from those that
would be eligible for use on the test.

Whether the test consists of selected-response items, such as binary-choice
(e.g., true-false) and multiple-choice items, or constructed response items (e.g., an
essay-writing assessment), the test-item specifications should provide an actual example of the type of item that will constitute the test.

Usually, after reviewing the general description as well as the sample item,
both evaluators and decision makers will be able to secure a fairly decent idea of
what the test actually assesses.

Stimulus Attributes   An examinee responds to stimuli in the completion of
an examination. In the typical multiple choice test, for example, the "stem" of the
multiple-choice item is the stimulus for which the examinee selects an appropriate
choice. In the following multiple-choice example, the stimulus portion of the item is
in italics:

57. *In which year did the United States*
    formally enter World War II?
    A. 1945
    B. 1495
    C. 1941
    D. 1491

For many multiple-choice items, of course, the stimulus segment of the item is
far more elaborate. Having considered a test item's stimulus, the examinee either (1)
selects a response from options provided (such as true versus false or, even more
common, four alternative answers such as those seen above), or (2) *constructs* a
response such as an essay, short answer, or an oral response as in the case of an
impromptu speech.

The stimulus attributes section should lay out the really significant features of the stimulus segments of test items. Of course, considerable judgment is required to determine which rules should be set forth in test-item specifications. Those creating the specifications must attempt to isolate the truly important features of an item's stimulus segments yet not overwhelm specifications users with a tirade of trivia. Not surprisingly, therefore, there is a good deal of artistry associated with the isolation of the rules to be included in a set of test-item specifications. The determination of the elements to include in these specifications is, unfortunately, an area in which we are currently short on technology.

Response Attributes   Response attributes focus on the elements of test-items that provide examinees with response options, as in multiple-choice items, or provide examiners with ways of scoring examinees' responses. The response attributes section varies considerably depending on whether the test consists of selected-response items or constructed-response items.

For selected-response items, the response attributes must list all of the key rules for generating both correct and incorrect response options. To the extent possible, the specifications should set forth the distinguishing characteristics of both correct and incorrect answer choices. It is inappropriate to do this job cavalierly. Some test-item specifications, shabby ones to be sure, merely indicate that the correct answers will be "right" and the incorrect answers "wrong." More enlightened thought is requisite.

For constructed-response items, the response attributes should focus on the criteria to be employed in judging the acceptability of an examinee's constructed response. For example, if the test under consideration deals with an individual's ability to present an extemporaneous speech, then the response attributes should set forth, as precisely as possible, the criteria to be used in judging the quality of such extemporaneous speeches.

Supplement   An optional component of some test-item specifications is a supplement or appendix in which additional content is presented. Such content, had it been presented earlier in the specifications, might be deflective to users because of its length. In essence, the supplement typically provides a reference source for item-writers.

As you read the illustration of criterion-referenced test-item specifications that follows (Box 6–1), think about how you would be constrained by such specifications if you were attempting to write test items congruent with those specifications.

(This illustrative set of test-item specifications, for a key skill in reading, is taken from a high school graduation test. The specifications were prepared for the Texas Education Agency by IOX Assessment Associates. The specifications are used here with the permission of both those organizations.)

BOX 6–1 • *Texas Educational Assessment of Minimum Skills Reading Skills Test*

General Description

Students will be presented with selections containing information that they might encounter in school, at home, or in their community. Selections may be drawn from textbooks, magazines, newspapers, pamphlets, letters, and fiction or non-fiction books. The students will be required to select from among four choices the best statement of the main idea of the selection.

Sample Item

> Burns are one of the most painful and damaging of all injuries. They are also very common. Burns are now the leading cause of death for people under 40. They are the third leading cause of death across all age groups.
>
> The standard treatment for even the most severe burns formerly involved only the skin. Today, however, we know that burns can affect almost every organ in the body. Medical care for the entire body must be provided quickly to prevent further harm to the burn victim.
>
> A few years ago, there were only a few medical centers that could provide care for burn victims. Today, a special burn center can be found in almost every large city. This has led to great advances in both research and the clinical treatment of burns.

Which of the following is the best statement of the main idea of this selection?

   A. Burns are among the most painful and severe injuries an individual can have. (inappropriate in scope)
   B. The most effective treatment for a burn is to place a protective covering on the damaged area of the skin. (contradicted)
   C. The costs associated with a successful recovery from a severe burn can be quite high. (irrelevant)
   D. Much progress has been made in our ability to understand and treat the serious problem of burn injuries. (correct)

Stimulus Attributes

   1. A test item will consist of a boxed reading selection followed by the question, "Which of the following is the best statement of the main idea of this selection?"
   2. Reading selections will be drawn from any of the following types of eligible materials:
      a. textbooks
      b. magazines
      c. newspapers
      d. pamphlets
      e. letters
      f. fiction books

BOX 6–1 • *Continued*

    g. nonfiction books

3. The selection will communicate a single central idea. This idea may be expressed in a single sentence in the selection, or it may be implied by the selection as a whole. Main ideas which are implied by a selection will synthesize pieces of information explicitly stated in two or more places in the selection.
4. The selection will contain a minimum of 100 and a maximum of 200 words.
5. The selection will contain no sentences longer than 20 words.
6. The readability of the reading selection will range from 9.3 to 11.3 as assessed by Harris-Jacobson Wide Range Readability Formula.
7. The selection will be developed using only words on the Texas Education Agency (TEA) Cumulative Vocabulary List through grade 12. Proper nouns and words explained in the reading selection are excluded from this requirement. The correct answer to the test question will not depend exclusively on the meaning of any words in the TEA Cumulative Vocabulary List above grade 10.
8. Each reading selection will be used as a stimulus for only one item.

Response Attributes

1. Each question will be followed by a set of four answer choices. One answer choice will be a correct statement of the main idea of the reading selection. Three answer choices will be incorrect statements of the main idea of the reading selection.
2. Each answer choice will be a single sentence related to the content of the reading selection. Answer choices will be no more than 20 words in length and will contain no words which exceed grade 12 as judged by the TEA cumulative vocabulary list, unless such words appear in the reading selection.
3. The correct answer for an item will be the statement that is accurate, relevant, and of the most appropriate scope in relation to the other answer choices. For a selection in which the main idea is explicitly stated in one sentence, the correct answer will paraphrase the main idea sentence from the selection. For a selection in which the main idea is implied, the correct answer will represent that implied main idea.
4. An incorrect answer choice must be one of the following types:
   a. *contradicted*, that is, a statement that is contradicted by information in the text;
   b. *inappropriate in scope*, that is, a statement that is (1) too narrow, hence, does not account for all the important information in the selection, or (2) too broad, hence, accounts for a more general viewpoint than is presented in the selection; or
   c. *irrelevant*, that is, a statement that introduces information not included in the text. The statement must contain at least one concept from the selection.
5. Each set of answer choices will include incorrect answer choices from at least two of the categories described in Response Attribute 4.

An Educationally Appropriate Level of Specificity

Because criterion-referenced test-item specifications spell out so lucidly what is eligible to be tested, in the 1980s many educators were able to design effective instructional sequences that were accurately targeted at clearly described targets. In many instances, such instruction yielded substantial boosts in students' scores. Highly detailed test-item specifications for criterion-referenced tests led to the generation of some truly successful instructional programs. Given clear assessment targets, skillful teachers designed instructional sequences that scored numerous bulls-eyes. During the 1980s, in fact, there were a number of well-documented reports of targeted and successful instruction. Scores on many criterion-referenced tests, because of the provision of ample on-target guided and independent practice for students, rose dramatically.

However, as with many aspects of life, the greatest strength of criterion-referenced test specifications was their greatest weakness. The very clarity that fostered the creation of on-target and effective instructional sequences also tended to drive out off-target *but worthwhile* instruction. Students were taught how to perform Skill X as set forth in the criterion-referenced specifications, but *only* as set forth in the criterion-referenced specifications. Teachers became so singularly focused in their instructional efforts that students were not taught to generalize. For many a teacher, the greatest virtue of criterion-referenced test specifications became their greatest vice. Such teachers succumbed to a thoughtless skill-and-drill mentality in which students were taught to master a specified set of knowledge or skills, but only in the particular fashion explicated in the criterion-referenced specifications. If the specifications called for students to display their multiplication competence by solving sets of double-digit, vertically arranged multiplication problems, then the teacher provided instruction and practice in dealing *exclusively* with double-digit, vertically arranged multiplication problems.

Because of the intense pressures to have students perform well on high-stakes tests, too many teachers began providing students with preparation only for skills as defined in the test specifications. Alternative conceptualizations of a skill received short shrift or, all too often, no shrift at all.

An ancient Roman proverb suggests that "in the middle stands virtue." With respect to test specifications, it is time that we heeded our Roman forebears. In today's educational setting, with high-stakes tests and the attendant pressures on teachers to boost students' test scores, we dare not build tests that incline teachers to short-change students by teaching only to narrow, nongeneralizable targets. Nor dare we return to the era when amorphous norm-referenced test specifications ruled the realm. For today's test specifications, we need a middle level of detail, that is, a level of specificity amenable to the delineation of *multiple*, not single, assessment tactics.

Today's testing requirements oblige educators and test developers to strive for a mid-level of detail, not so general (as with norm-referenced tests) that instructional targeting is impossible and not so detailed (as with criterion-referenced tests) that only unitary assessment targets are fostered instructionally.

Given today's educational realities, high-stakes educational tests need to be based on specifications that permit a number of eligible assessment tactics, thus inclining teachers to promote students' *generalizable* mastery of the skills or knowledge tested. Yet, because if exceedingly detailed test specifications were set forth for a variety of multiple assessment strategies, such specifications would turn out to be truly voluminous. Few people would read hyperdetailed specifications, hence the clarity embodied in such specifications would be wasted because no one would have the patience to wade through them.

A mid-level of specificity is, therefore, required. Because one example is often worth a pile of paragraphs, *exemplification* (i.e., the use of illustrative sample items) should be employed as the key communicative mechanism. By providing actual samples of different sorts of test items that are eligible to be tested (but would not, in fact, all be tested on any given form of the test), both item developers and the users of educational tests can be provided with an educationally meaningful level of detail. It must be emphasized, however, that the illustrative items are *nonexhaustive* exemplars.

The key elements of this form of criterion-referenced test-item specifications are (1) a brief *verbal description* of the skill or knowledge being assessed and (2) several *illustrative items* that might be employed for assessment purposes. The verbal description must capture the intellectual essence of that which is to be assessed. In other words, the verbal description must lay out as clearly as possible what cognitive activities must be engaged in by the examinee to answer correctly the described type of test item.

It is imperative that the verbal description be sufficiently clear so a teacher could design relevant instruction for the skill or knowledge being assessed. The illustrative items should assist teachers to understand what is being assessed, but those items should not exhaust the potential types of items that might be used. Other item types that are consonant with the verbal description could be utilized on the actual test. To create the type of test-item specifications described here, it is likely that revisions based on "specifications tryouts" with typical teachers would be required. This test-specification strategy leads to the need for formal verification, via judgmental procedures, that test items are congruent with the verbal descriptions in the specifications.

Box 6–2 presents an example of the *in medio* type of test-item specifications for "initial holistic understanding of a reading selection." Such specifications would be provided to item developers along with several differently formatted test items that were clearly consonant with the nature of the cognitive capability described. Because the items to be used in assessing this capability would be either selected-response or constructed-response in nature, sample stems for the items are also provided.

The appropriate level of detail in this form of criterion-referenced test specifications will be far more circumscribing than the early norm-referenced nonspecific test specifications. The appropriate level of detail would be far less circumscribing than the carefully delineated rules commonly seen in well-developed specifications for criterion-referenced tests. As with most new tools in education, such mid-level

---

BOX 6–2 • *Mid-Level Test-Item Specifications*

Items may call for students to create or choose the most accurate summary of the selection or part of the selection, to identify or state the topic of all or a part of the selection, or to identify or state the main idea or central point of a selection or part of that selection. Students may have to condense explicit information or to paraphrase or restate points, but should not have to make an inference in order to select or construct the appropriate answer. Items can be phrased in a variety of ways, but they all *must require the student to have recognized the central message or overall point of the selection* (or designated part of the selection).

Sample Stems

What is this selection mainly about?
Write a brief paragraph summarizing this passage.
Which of these options *best* summarizes the article?
Describe, in one sentence, the passage's central message.
What is the main point of this passage?
What is the main idea of the passage's fourth paragraph?

---

specifications will take some time to develop properly and some time for item writers as well as educators to master.

Yet, in recognition of today's prevalent pressures on educators to increase students' scores on high-stakes tests, and in view of the potential perils of nongeneralizable skill-and-drill instruction for highly detailed criterion-referenced test specifications, it is time for a gentle paradigm shift. Excessively detailed criterion-referenced test-item specifications may, in certain instances, be educationally counterproductive. A level of specificity should be sought for high-stakes educational tests that fosters generalizability of students' skills and knowledge.

Discussion Questions

1. How would you characterize the differences between earlier norm-referenced measurement specialists and more recent criterion-referenced measurement specialists with respect to their views regarding (a) the role of measurement and (b) the potency of instruction?

2. What are the essential features of the conception of criterion-referenced measurement endorsed in the chapter? What advantages accrue to the evaluator who uses measures that satisfy this definition?

3. For purposes of educational evaluation, what do you think is an appropriate level of specificity for the rules to be employed when creating criterion-referenced tests? Why?

4. What are the truly important differences between typical test-item specifications for criterion-referenced tests and the midlevel test-item specifications recommended in the chapter?

5. How are educators apt to view criterion-referenced tests as opposed to the more traditional norm-referenced tests? Why?

Practice Exercises

1. Determine which of the following would be classified as criterion-referenced tests according to the conception of a criterion-referenced measure presented in the chapter.
   a. A nationally standardized test of specific reading skills, both word attack and comprehension, in which students' scores are reported and interpreted in terms of percentiles.
   b. A teacher-developed test of mathematics skills in which an attempt is made to explicate the class of learner competencies assessed by each group of test items.
   c. An objectives-based test developed so that each of 15 items is based on objectives such as the following: "Students will learn to recognize basic sound discriminations."
   d. A written spelling test constituted by randomly selecting 25 words to be spelled from a particular list of 200 "spelling demons."
   e. An individually administered test of intellectual aptitude that yields comparative scores.

2. If possible, try your hand at developing test-item specifications for criterion-referenced tests using either the midlevel of specificity described later in the chapter or the more detailed level of specificity described earlier. Ask a classmate, or a colleague who is familiar with criterion-referenced testing, to critique your test-item specifications.

Answers to Practice Exercises

1. Only items b and d are consonant with the conception of measurement presented in the chapter. Although item c is described as "objectives based," the objectives apparently are too loose to serve as explicit descriptors of what is being assessed. Both items a and e result in norm-referenced indicators; that is, both percentiles and "comparative scores" are interpretable only in relationship to performance of a normative group.

2. Because parents are often excessively proud of their progeny, you'll be better off asking someone other than you (the parent of your specifications) to review your efforts. The key factor that your colleague should emphasize in the analysis of your specifications is the *clarity* of the descriptive information you provide.

Notes

1. A stanine score is a type of standard score derived by dividing a distribution of scores into nine equal parts, with the 1/9 segment around the mean designated as the fifth stanine, the highest 1/9 segment designated as the ninth stanine, and lowest 1/9 segment designated as the first stanine. In recent years, educators have been employing stanines more frequently in the reporting of test scores.

2. Robert Glaser, "Instructional Technology and the Measurement of Learning Outcomes: Some Questions," *American Psychologist*, 18 (1963), 519–21. Glaser had used the phrase "criterion-referenced measurement" in an earlier essay with David Klaus, but the 1963 *American Psychologist* article was read far more widely: R. Glaser, and D. J. Klaus, "Proficiency Measurement: Assessing Human Perfor-

mance," in R. M. Gagne (Ed.), *Psychological Principles in Systems Development* (New York: Holt, Rinehart and Winston, 1962), pp. 419–74.

3. For example, R. L. Ebel, "Content Standard Test Scores," *Educational and Psychological Measurement*, 22 (1962), 15–25.

4. A. J. Nitko, "Defining Criterion-Referenced Test" in *A Guide to Criterion-Referenced Test Construction*, ed. R. A. Berk (Baltimore: The Johns Hopkins University Press, 1984), pp. 8–28.

5. Ralph W. Tyler, "General Statement on Program Evaluation," in *Evaluation and Education: At Quarter Century*, ed. M. W. McLaughlin and D. C. Phillips (Chicago: University of Chicago Press, 1991), pp. 3–17.

6. American Educational Research Association, American Psychological Association, and the National Council on Measurement in Education, *Standards for Educational and Psychological Testing* (Washington, DC: American Psychological Association, 1985).

7. R. A. Berk (Ed.). *A Guide to Criterion-Referenced Test Construction* (Baltimore: The Johns Hopkins University Press, 1984). Also, although the author and publisher of the current volume are far from unbiased in the matter, you could consult, W. J. Popham, *Modern Educational Measurement* (Englewood Cliffs, NJ: Prentice Hall, 1981).

8. Technically, for many sorts of tests such as the typical multiple-choice variety, the examinee *behaves* by merely making a mark on an answer sheet. Yet, because that mark (say, the choice of A, B, C, or D) is made in response to a particular stimulus (say, a specific type of mathematics problem), when we refer to examinee "behavior," that reference focuses on the examinee's "making a mark in response to a specified stimulus."

Selected References

Glaser, Robert. "Instructional Technology and the Measurement of Learning Outcomes: Some Questions." *American Psychologist*, 18 (1963): 519–21.

Gronlund, Norman E., and Robert L. Linn. *Measurement and Evaluation in Teaching* (6th ed.). New York: Macmillan, 1990.

Haertel, E. H. "Construct Validity and Criterion-Referenced Testing." *Review of Educational Research*, 55 (1985): 23–46.

Hambleton, R. K. "Advances in Criterion-Referenced Testing Technology." In C. R. Reyonds and T. B. Gutkin (Eds.), *The Handbook of School Psychology*. New York: Wiley, 1982.

———. "Criterion-Referenced Measurement." In T. Husen and T. N. Postlethwaite (Ed.), *International Encyclopedia of Education: Research and Studies*. Oxford, England: Pergamon Press, 1984.

Hambleton, R. K., H. Swaminathan, J. Algina, and D. B. Couslon. "Criterion-Referenced Testing and Measurement: A Review of Technical Issues and Developments." *Review of Educational Research*, 48 (1978): 1–47.

Hambleton, R. K., H. Swaminathan, and H. Jane Rogers. *Fundamentals of Item Response Theory*. Newbury Park, CA: Sage, 1991.

Harris, C. W., Marvin C. Alkin, and W. James Popham (Eds.). *Problems in Criterion-Referenced Measurement*. CSE Monograph Series in Evaluation, No. 3. Los Angeles: Center for the Study of Evaluation, University of California, 1974.

Hively, W., G. Maxwell, G. Rabehl, D.

Sension, and S. Lundin. *Domain-Referenced Curriculum Evaluation: A Technical Handbook and a Case Study from the Minnemast Project.* Los Angeles: Center for the Study of Evaluation, University of California, 1973.

Hopkins, Charles D., and Richard L. Antes. *Classroom Measurement and Evaluation* (3rd ed.). Itasca, IL: F. E. Peacock, 1990.

Nitko, A. J. "Distinguishing the Many Varieties of Criterion-Referenced Tests." *Review of Educational Research*, 28 (1980): 95–104.

Popham, W. J. *Modern Educational Measurement.* Englewood Cliffs, NJ: Prentice Hall, 1990.

Sax, Gilbert. *Principles of Educational and Psychological Measurement and Evaluation* (3rd ed.). Belmont, CA: Wadsworth, 1989.

Wiersma, William, and Stephen G. Jurs. *Educational Measurement and Testing* (2nd ed.). Boston: Allyn and Bacon, 1990.

CHAPTER SEVEN

Assessing Affect: Strategies and Tactics

Educators have always paid homage, typically at a lip-service level, to the importance of affective education. Through the ages pupils have heard teachers extol the virtues of patriotism, honesty, thrift, and the like. The nice thing about the promotion of such high-sounding notions, at least from the teacher's point of view, was that, because there was no way to tell whether the students had incorporated such laudable leanings, the teacher could shut down classes at the close of the year with the comforting conviction that pupils were, indeed, more patriotic, honest, and thrifty.

But sought-for learner attributes that are undetectable exercise modest if any influence on the nature of an educational undertaking. It is too tempting to assume that good, if undiscernible, things are happening to learners. Such assumptions breed complacence, not a willingness to evaluate and improve. Indeed, only during the past decade or two have we found educators displaying genuine distress about the underemphasis on affect in curricular, instructional, and evaluation endeavors.

Perhaps the first substantial factor triggering this concern about affective education was the 1956 publication of the *Taxonomy of Educational Objectives* by Bloom and his associates.[1] Even though the bulk of that volume was focused on the cognitive behavior of learners, the distinctions among the three behavior domains — cognitive, affective, and psychomotor[2] — stimulated considerable interest in all three domains. When in 1964 Krathwohl and his co-workers published the second *Taxonomy of Educational Objectives,*[3] dealing the affective domain, interest in affective education and its measurement was greatly intensified. Educators began to toss around the term *affect* with greater frequency, if no greater understanding. By the late 1960s any upstanding educator who didn't at least make an occasional nod in the direction of affective education was under some suspicion as an old-line cognitivist.

Although there has been a good deal more banner waving by affective advocates during the last few years, however, one wonders whether this burgeoning zeal will be followed by actual changes in the schools. Talk is notoriously inexpensive, and until it is backed up with tangible techniques for promoting and measuring important kinds of learner affect, there is considerable danger that the current vocal support for affective education will, like so many educational fads, fade quietly as more fashionable contenders appear.

In a modest effort to counteract such tendencies, this chapter will consider several salient aspects of measurement in the affective domain. Without defensible and practical measures of learner affect, it will be literally impossible for the educational evaluator to offer affectively oriented educators anything other than good wishes and, depending on the evaluator's religious fervor, a pile of prayers.

Analyzing Affect

Just what do we mean when we talk about the affective domain? Typically, when someone is asked to explain what is meant by the term *affective,* an explanation will be given in terms of examples. For instance, we might hear that affective learner behaviors are those that reflect one's attitudes, interests, and values. This kind of an explanation, though incomplete, is helpful to most educators because it distinguishes between affective behaviors and those cognitively based behaviors that abound in the schools. But when we try to pin a more adequate descriptive label on affect, we discover that terms such as *attitudes, values,* and *interest* are themselves in need of clarification.

For example, some scholars distinguish between attitudes and values mainly in terms of the specificity of the *referent* to which such sentiments are directed. We have attitudes regarding specific referents, such as the United Nations; we have values regarding less specific referents, such as justice. But whole books have been written about values, attitudes, interests, emotions, and all the other dimensions of learner behavior normally lumped under the affective rubric. We can deal with the measurement of affect without probing these issues intensively. We can do so, that is, *if* we abandon the typical psychologist's strategy of trying to figure out what's going on inside somebody's head. For purposes of educational evaluation, such a thoroughgoing understanding of the covert meaning of overt behaviors is not necessary.

Measuring instruments that permit valid inferences about individuals will, of necessity, permit valid inferences about groups. The reverse, however, is not true. Let's examine some practical illustrations to see the implications of this point. Suppose you were developing a new affective paper-and-pencil self-report instrument that you thought would provide a reliable and valid estimate of how pupils felt about a certain set of values. The instrument was so well designed, in fact, that you believed it would provide for *each learner* an estimate of how that learner regarded the value question under consideration. Because the measure would permit one to draw valid inferences about each learner, it is clear that it would also permit a valid estimate of group performance. On the other hand, suppose you had devised a new attitude technique that seemed likely to work for most learners but would probably be misconstrued by a few of them whose backgrounds (unknown to you) might cause them to interpret certain items aberrantly. Therefore, even though you could not use the measure to help you make decisions about individual learners, you still might use the device to help you decide whether an affective education program, as reflected by group performance, was working.

A number of years ago I directed a project to develop affective measuring devices dealing with students' (1) attitudes toward school and (2) self-concept. There was precious little literature available for guidance then (and not too much more now) regarding how to produce defensible measures of pupils' self-concept and attitudes toward school. Our general approach was to assemble our development staff and, in as permissive an environment as possible, generate all sorts of techniques—standard or bizarre—to measure the affective dimensions of interest.

Early in these idea-generating sessions, however, a common problem began to recur. Just when someone had proffered an original but zany measurement ploy, another staff member would always say something like this: "Well, that would work well for most kids, but what about the kid who. . . ." Thereafter would be recounted a description of one or more types of youngsters whose experiences would so distort their responses to the measuring device being proposed that the meaningfulness of the resulting data would obviously be vitiated. With resignation, we would say, "That's right," and abandon the new approach to search once more for measures that would stand the validity test for all human beings—plus any moderately divergent mutants in the neighborhood.

We lost some good assessment ideas during the early phase of that project, because we constantly steered clear of any measurement ploys that wouldn't work for everybody. Often, in an effort to satisfy this universal validity requirement, we ended up with the most drab self-report devices imaginable. Learners could fake them with ease, but at least *if* they answered truthfully, the measure would be suitable for everyone. That is a fairly significant *if*.

Then, after weeks of sputtering, the insight came crashing through. We were trying to devise measures for educators working in the field of *program* evaluation. They weren't going to be using these measures to make decisions about individuals. Teachers weren't going to give Johnny an *F* if he did well on all cognitive tests yet had a lousy self-concept. A teacher doesn't fail Mary if she can multiply like a magician yet doesn't feel yummy about fractions. The teacher wants an estimate of the class's attitude toward math, not just Mary's. The measures we were developing, therefore, didn't have to be valid for every child. As long as there weren't too many aberrant responses, we could get a good *group estimate* and help evaluators make recommendations regarding a program's impact on a group of students.

The liberating impact of this understanding was enormous. We could return to developing clever little measurement devices designed to work with most but not all youngsters. The range of our assessment devices expanded accordingly. We were able to contrive instruments that might yield invalid inferences for a handful of learners, but that would most likely be far more suitable for an entire group of learners than the bland self-report devices we had previously produced.

In selecting and/or generating affective measuring instruments, the evaluator should identify the decision-making context and, if it concerns groups rather than individuals, temper more customary conceptions of validity requirements.

Generation Strategies

There are relatively few measuring devices in the affective arena that have been developed specifically for purposes of educational evaluation.[4] It is hoped that, as time goes by, we will see the emergence of many such instruments. In the meanwhile, however, it seems likely that many evaluators will have to devise their own measurement schemes to assess the affective status of learners. How can this best be done?

The first thing to recognize is that the creation of valid affective measuring devices is a difficult and ingenuity-taxing enterprise. In contrast to the more pedestrian chore of churning out a cognitive achievement test, creating affective measures is much harder. This difficulty stems from the problem of trying to discern an individual's *typical* performance in situations (generally speaking, measurement situations) that do not truly replicate the situations in which we are ultimately interested. For instance, how could we possibly equate a student's performance on a paper-and-pencil attitude inventory regarding citizenship with that same student's postschool citizenship activities? The trick is to design the measurement situation so that we secure data that permit us to make reasonably solid inferences regarding the learner's future dispositions.

Another difficulty arises from the fact that when we poke around in the affective domain we are dealing with the unseen. We can't fondle an attitude or box up a value. These things are tumbling around inside people. We're always obliged to deal with overt behavior that we believe is reflective of the influence of such unseen factors. It is true that to a large extent cognitive test constructors, and to a lesser extent psychomotor test constructors, are faced with similar difficulties. Yet, these problems are easier to hurdle (a psychomotor behavior) if one is dealing with maximum rather than typical performances.

The Basic Approach

In general, the individual responsible for generating an affective measuring instrument must try to secure evidence from learners, either products they have created or behaviors that can be observed. The stimulus situations in which these products or behaviors are generated must be such that we can make reasonably confident inferences about the learner's dispositional tendencies in similar or identical future stimulus situations. We can represent this basic approach graphically as seen in Figure 7–1 when we initially measure learners in such a way that we can make predictions regarding their behavior dispositions in comparable situations.

For instance, we might try to measure the quality of an elementary school child's relationships with peers (perhaps by observations or self-report techniques), hoping that such measurement evidence would be useful in predicting how well the child would get along with other people in later life. Note that it is not crucial that the initial affective measurement situation *appear* to be comparable to the later situations about which we wish to generalize. For example, a child's answers to a self-

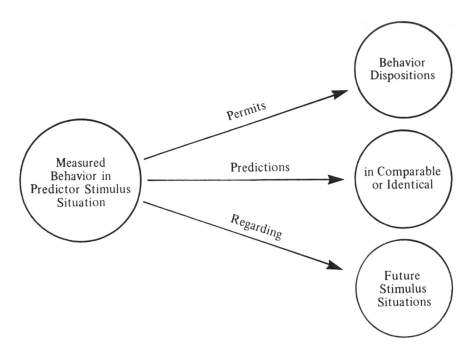

FIGURE 7-1 • *A Basic Affective Measurement Prediction Approach*

report inventory regarding relations with other children is obviously unlike the child's actual relationship with other people later in life. Yet, the intellectual or emotional choices presented on paper may be comparable to those that must be faced later. It is this similarity that permits us to make predictions regarding the child's future dispositions. Without at least some comparability between the nature of an individual's responses in situations to which we wish to make dispositional predictions, there is little likelihood that such predictions would be defensible.

A Four-Step Generation Scheme

The most difficult task in generating defensible affective measurement devices is typically associated with the initial identification of the measurement situations that might provide the evidence for making dispositional predictions. One scheme that has proved helpful involves a four-step generation scheme.

Step 1: Identify an Imaginary Individual Who Possesses the Desired Affective Attributes   The first thing to do is to consider the general affective dimension of interest, such as a learner's attitudes toward government, and then try to conjure up an image of an individual who possesses the desired attitude in complete fullness. For example, imagine a person who is truly positive toward government, so positive that friends would even tend to characterize the individual's dominant motives as reflecting a positive disposition toward government. Similar imaginary individuals could be created with values regarding truthfulness (conjure up an ardent truth teller) or interest in sports (imagine a sports fanatic).

Step 2: Identify an Imaginary Individual Who Does Not Possess the Desired Affective Attribute   The second step is to dream up the counterpart of the first imaginary individual. We now must create an imaginary opposite for our desired affective attribute possessor. If we were originally thinking of a person who was inordinately positive regarding government, then it is now necessary to conceive of a person who is thoroughly negative, or at least indifferent, toward government. If, in Step 1 we had imagined a full-blown music lover who had an incredibly positive disposition toward music, then in Step 2 we would imagine an individual who was disinterested or even hostile toward music.

Step 3: Generate Potential Behavior-Differentiating Situations   Now that we have our two hypothetical individuals representing extremes of the affective dimension under consideration, the next step is to think of as many situations as possible in which these two imaginary human beings *would behave differently*. Try to generate situations, natural or contrived, in which our two fictitious people would display some different responses. In the case of music lovers/haters, it might be volitional attendance at a free school band concert, or responses to an open-ended essay assignment on the topic "Music and Me," or the number of musical recordings purchased over a 12-month period. In the instance of the two fictitious individuals positively and negatively oriented toward government, we might think of voting behaviors at school or city elections, or responses to paper-and-pencil self-report inventories consisting of a variety of statements regarding the merits of governmental participation.

This is the most interesting phase of the four-step generation scheme, for the idea is to generate all sorts of possible behavior-differentiating situations with, at least for the moment, no careful analysis of their defensibility or practicality. This is truly a brainstorming session with a minimum of penalties associated with new ideas, no matter how unusual. Try to think of all possible ways of distinguishing between a positively and negatively inclined individual, including test-like situations, natural situations, situations simulating reality, situations requiring accomplices. No matter how wild, if there is a chance that the situation might yield differences between the two contrasting archetypes, then get it on the table. The spirit of this phase of the four-step model is best characterized as *unrestrained*.

Step 4: Select Practicable and Valid Situations   But restraint is lurking around the corner. The final step in this scheme requires us to reexamine all situations produced in Step 3 and to consider them in terms of both validity and measurement practicality. Those situations that pass these two screens should be eminently eligible contenders for our affective measuring instruments.

With respect to validity, we have to reconsider whether there are any factors in the situation that might diminish its behavior-differentiating qualities. Is there some doubt, on second thought, that the sorts of positively and negatively inclined individuals (represented by our two imaginary archetypes) would really respond differently? Which are the situations that we are most confident would produce differences? It is often helpful to have colleagues examine our list of behavior-differentiating situations at this point, for a creator's confidence is often excessive. More sober external judgments can help us spot the defects in some of our ideas.

As far as practicality is concerned, we have to review our potential measurement situations realistically to see whether they can actually be used. To illustrate this point, suppose there was evidence that certain differences between positive and negative attitudes could be detected via surgically implanted electrodes. Not too many evaluators would seriously propose that we wire up a number of students. Not only would that sort of measurement not be permitted in the schools by either educators or parents, but too many students would also get tangled. Or perhaps a possible behavior-differentiating situation might require the participation of many trained assistants. The costs of such training for a support staff might exceed the available financial resources. However, after screening the possible measurement setting for both validity and practicality, the evaluator ought to end up with the essence of a number of potentially useful affective measurement devices.

We can graphically depict this four-step scheme for generating affective objectives, as seen in Figure 7–2. Though its use will not invariably yield the kinds of affective assessment devices we seek, there are occasions when it may prove helpful.

Reducing Cues that Trigger "Expected" Responses

As previously noted, when evaluators are concerned with the affective domain, they are less interested in what learners *can* do than in what they *will* do. To get a good index of what a person will do, we typically need to see how the individual behaves volitionally, that is, without real or imagined constraints that might impede natural behavior. For instance, if a child were directed to fill out an attitude inventory regarding the quality of teaching in a school, but first was admonished by the school's principal that negative responses would lead to serious repercussions, the child's responses would obviously be influenced by the principal's threats. Similarly, if students were asked to complete a signed questionnaire regarding their own experiences with illegal drugs, they might falsify their responses because of the fear that a law-enforcement agency might examine the questionnaire results.

If we are to secure a realistic estimate of the ways in which individuals are truly disposed to act, we have to design our affective measurement approaches so that we secure volitional, not coerced, responses. This is not as simple as it sounds.

For example, in our society there are major cultural forces that create in children the disposition to "do what they are supposed to." This inclination to behave according to the expectations of others can seriously influence the responses of individuals to affective measures, even when the evaluator least expects it. There is the lingering doubt among individuals, even as they respond to anonymous attitude in-

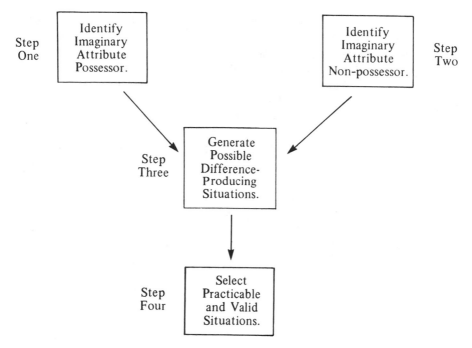

FIGURE 7–2 • *A Four-Step Strategy for Generating Affective Measures*

ventories, that someone will monitor, and perhaps disapprove of, their responses. Accordingly, they may distort their responses in such a way that the responses are more acceptable.

Maybe such thinly masked paranoia is not unwarranted. Think of the teacher who asks pupils to evaluate anonymously the quality of instruction prior to the time that grades are given. Most sensible students will realize that even though they might submit a seethingly negative evaluation without being individually identified, a teacher who is offended by one or two such critical evaluations might retaliate at grading time against the entire "ungrateful" class. The cautious student will often play it safe in such cases and massage the teacher's ego a bit with evaluations of "super," "divinely inspired," or equivalent messages of approbation.

Besides, there is some doubt that our society fosters the merits of truth telling to such an extent that most people will automatically respond to questions, such as those in an affective measuring device, with unwavering candor. In too many situations citizens have been made to feel that little "white lies" are not only acceptable but even desirable. Evaluators should not naively assume that they will always be getting totally truthful responses to their questions. We are, after all, measuring human beings, not archangels.

Many of the affective measuring devices used by evaluators will be some form of self-report device, merely because such approaches are more economical and practical. Some measures will be more elaborate, involving observed learner behavior under natural or manipulated stimulus conditions. No matter what the setting, simple self-report or elaborate observation, students' responses will tend to be distorted to the extent that they can discern socially desirable responses. If even subconsciously aware of how they *should* respond in particular settings, many people will not report their more typical behavior dispositions in favor of reporting those they perceive to be socially acceptable. Thus, the astute evaluator will strive to remove all cues regarding socially desirable responses from any affective measurement instruments. The less likely it is that learners will figure out what others would like to hear, the more likely the evaluator will be to get undistorted responses. Such responses, unwarped either by conscious or subconscious alterations, will be more reflective of an individual's true dispositions.

There are some techniques the evaluator can use to reduce the fakeability of the measures being used. For example, we can ask the respondent to react in terms of how "Most people feel . . ." instead of asking how "*You* feel. . . ." We can also ask about past behavior rather than present feelings. But, if such niceties still lead us to believe that the inventory to be used is fakeable, then it makes good sense to use the more fakeable instruments *after* using those we think are less fakeable. We are then less apt to sensitize respondents to the dimensions of interest that will appear in subsequent measures.

The foregoing discussion leads to the proposition that in many instances the evaluator will be obliged to camouflage the true purpose of a measuring instrument so that the person completing it will not be cued to respond according to perceptions of desired social expectations. By masking the true intent of an affective measure, we can often obtain more candid self-report responses from learners. Procedures such as these are treated in most standard measurement textbooks.

There are also instances when we wish to observe the behavior of learners, perhaps in a natural setting. If the learners are aware that they are being observed, they might behave in a nonvolitional manner, posturing according to what they think the observers want to see. Many times, therefore, evaluators will find that surreptitious observations, that is, observations in which individuals are unaware that they are being observed, will yield more valid data regarding the true dispositions of learners.

Triangulation Strategies

Affective constructs are genuinely elusive. They are covert. They are hard to define. They are devilishly difficult to measure. Just what, for example, is the real nature of a student's self-concept? Where does it exist? How is it created? Or what are the essential ingredients of a pupil's attitude toward school? Can we ever devise one measuring device that will, in itself, adequately snag these elusive dimensions? Probably not. Affective attributes are too shifty to let us capture them without a chase. We must employ more diabolical strategies. The most promising of these involves a *triangulation* approach.

A single measuring instrument will ordinarily not, all by itself, tell us what we need to know about student status with respect to an affective attribute. We can, however, use several different measures and "triangulate" on the sought-for affective dimension. As anyone knows who has watched World War II espionage movies, the enemy army was always able to isolate the allied agents' secret radio transmitter by setting up two or more directional finders, plotting the directions of the signals, then seeing where the line plots intersected. In contrast to such straightforward detection techniques, evaluators who attempt to ferret out a student's dispositions face a far more complex task.

The general approach can be represented pictorially as seen in Figure 7–3. It is apparent that no one of the three measures involved is capable of providing an adequate picture of an individual's status with respect to the affective attribute involved. In concert, however, the three measures give us a far better idea of what we are trying to assess. The measurer of affect is always well advised to tackle the assessment task with more than a single measure. Two, three, or even more assessment devices are preferable.

Validity Evidence for Affective Measures

The kinds of affective measures needed by educational evaluators will be criterion-referenced instruments. This is particularly important in the affective realm, for without explicit test-item specifications there is too much likelihood that we will end up having measured something that we really don't understand. Because of their illusory nature, affective states of learners are, of course, particularly difficult to measure or even to define. For this reason, it is particularly important that there be a most rigorous scrutiny of the measure's definition of the behavior domain to be assessed. Test items or observational situations should be closely matched with test-item specifications. The judged congruence of the measuring device with the test-item specification that guided its creation should be reported.

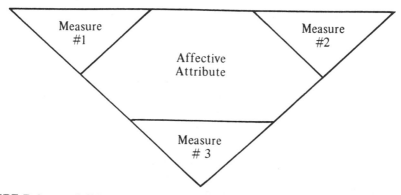

FIGURE 7–3 • *A Triangulation Assessment Strategy for Measuring an Affective Attribute*

In addition to such information, the evaluator will find that *construct-related validation* strategies have much to offer in validating affective measures. Whereas with cognitive or psychomotor objectives we have a fair idea of what really constitutes the behavior domain we are trying to assess, such is not the case with affective assessment. We know pretty well that a set of test-item specifications focusing on descriptions of certain types of math problems does, in fact, deal with the learner's quantitative competence. With test-item specifications for an affective attribute, we may have missed the mark altogether. A series of self-report items that we thought would reveal something about a learner's attitude toward other ethnic groups may, in fact, not tap that disposition at all. In some sense we might refer to *all* general learner skills, attitudes, and knowledge as *hypothetical constructs,* as even a person's capability to perform certain computational operations is inferred from overt manifestations of that capability. Yet with affective attributes the fact that we are dealing with hypothetical constructs is far more obvious.

The choice of a suitable domain is therefore much trickier with respect to affective measurement operations. For this reason, evaluators will find themselves assembling more construct-related evidence of validity when working with affective measures. Again, we can employ traditional construct validation strategies in this regard. For example, predictions can be posited, then tested, regarding how our affective measuring instrument should function under certain conditions such as before, during, and after instruction.

Perhaps we might correlate the performance of individuals on several measures, ostensibly assessing the same affective attribute (as in the triangulation strategy). If the measures constitute different ways of tapping the same affective dimension, we might expect to get moderately positive correlations among such measures, for example, .40 to .60. The correlations should be only moderate (not, for example, .90 or higher) because the several measures represent different procedures for measuring the affective attribute.

Suppose we found that several such measures intercorrelated positively but that one of the measures registered negative correlations with the other devices. Here would be an instance where our construct validation approach had yielded information suggesting the possible inappropriateness of the negatively correlated measure.

A common case of applying a construct validation approach to affective measures involves measuring a group of learners, then having individuals who know them well supply ratings (or rankings) of the learners with respect to the affective dimension being measured. For instance, we might have pupils complete a self-report form dealing with their curiosity tendencies, then ask their teachers to rate the pupils according to their apparent curiosity. A correlation between the pupils' performances and the judges' ratings would offer pertinent construct validation evidence. Typically we would expect a moderate positive correlation in such instances.

There is a sense in which *criterion-related evidence of validity* is needed for certain affective instruments. We sometimes measure a proximate dispositional tendency of learners in the belief that this present evidence will be predictive of future dispositions. Often doing this is our only realistic option, for we cannot afford the luxury of waiting a decade or two in order to apply measurements to the situations in which we are most interested. Too many learners might suffer in the meanwhile. Thus our affective measure administered, say, at the conclusion of an instructional program is often supposed to function as a prediction of some future dispositional tendencies of our learners. Evidence that can be gathered over an extended period of time regarding the accuracy with which such predictions were made will yield *criterion-related evidence of validity*. Such evidence is extremely useful, because, even though we must operate for the present with measures that reflect our best guesses regarding the future, it would be preferable to have these guesses confirmed (or disconfirmed) by evidence.

Common Classes of Affective Measures

It is sometimes helpful in thinking about potential affective measuring instruments to consider as possible options the typical kinds of measurement ploys that have been used in the affective realm. Although, as was seen in Chapter Four, which offered several ways of classifying educational measures, there is no one best method of grouping these sorts of measures, we will now toss in a slightly different classification wrinkle or two, with the hope that the reader's options are thereby augmented.

Low-Inference Self-Report Devices

Without a doubt, the most common type of affectively oriented measurement device used in education is the self-report instrument. Typically these are paper-and-pencil devices, but they can also involve orally-supplied self-report information gathered via interviews. These devices are prevalent because they are so convenient to administer and score.

It is possible to distinguish between two basically different types of self-report measures according to the degree of inference required to interpret the data they yield. The first is *low-inference self-report* measures. Such devices present questions, statements, or similar verbal stimuli to an individual who then supplies self-report responses. These responses, *if truthful*, can be readily interpreted without the evaluator's making any major inferential leaps. For instance, if we were getting at a student's disposition regarding future educational experiences, we might present a series of statements regarding the pros and cons of future educational endeavors. The task of the student would be to indicate a degree of agreement or disagreement with each statement. If the self-report responses are truthful, then anyone examining the statements and the student's responses could, with almost no required inferences, gather a reasonably good impression of how the learner felt about future education.

The distinct advantage of low-inference self-report devices is that they can capture, via a relatively small behavior sample, what people believe and value. The major drawback of such devices, of course, is that respondents may supply untruthful information because the purpose of the low-inference self-report measure is so apparent. There are a few techniques that can reduce this weakness to some extent, but not eliminate it. This topic will be discussed in greater detail later.

Let's consider some typical low-inference self-report devices. They might include:

1. A questionnaire asking students to indicate how personally interesting they found various parts of the curriculum. Such a measure might be used to assess one aspect of students' attitudes toward school.
2. A series of subject matter pairs (e. g. history versus art) in which the student was obliged to choose the more preferred subject. These sorts of devices are used to assess learner interest in particular subject fields.
3. A set of statements, some positive and some negative, regarding the role of government in our society. Such an inventory could be used to get at one's political attitudes.
4. An interview in which students are asked a series of questions regarding their self-esteem. Measures of this sort could prove useful in detecting the way in which school may be affecting pupils' self-concepts.

Almost unlimited kinds of low-inference self-report devices could be generated by the inventive evaluator. Over the years a moderate number of such instruments have been developed by teachers for use in their own classrooms. Most of the carefully developed instruments of this sort have been constructed in connection with individual personality measurement, typically by clinical psychologists and psychiatrists. There are really very few low-inference self-report instruments that have been devised *specifically* for purposes of educational evaluation. It is hoped that that situation will be corrected in the coming years.

Improving Low-Inference Self-Report Measures   Because of the great likelihood that the respondent will falsify, or at least partially distort, the data yielded by low-inference measures of this sort, we must look for ways to improve the instruments. The first and most obvious thing to do is to make certain that all responses to such measures are supplied anonymously. In our surveillance-conscious society, we must strive to remove any elements that will suggest that the responses can be traced or otherwise associated with the individual supplying them. For example, some evaluators employ mailed questionnaires they have numbered in order to send follow-ups to nonrespondents. Even though the questionnaire's directions may assert, "Your responses will be treated anonymously," the appearance of the number on the questionnaire, and the possibility of identifying one's responses via that number, will dissuade some respondents from answering candidly. In such cases it is better to get a smaller return of frank responses than a larger return of potentially phony ones.

Another improvement technique for such measures is to try to shift the focus of the respondent from one that will, in all likelihood, contaminate the learner's responses to one that will not. Sometimes we can accomplish this by phrasing the introductory information of a self-report device so that the essential purpose of the instrument is at least partially concealed. Sometimes we can shift the locale where the instrument is to be administered (from a history class that is being evaluated) to another setting (homeroom). Sometimes a teacher in another class can administer the measure. Perhaps questionnaires can be mailed to respondents from a different agency, totally unconnected to the program being evaluated. All these techniques should be considered with respect to the degree to which they would increase the probability of truthful responses.

Often we can camouflage the self-report items that we really wish to use by employing a *submerged-question* technique. In this procedure a number of questions are first given the learners to create a desired expectation regarding the focus of the instrument. For instance, in a 10-item self-report inventory only items number 6 and 9 might be the ones in which the evaluator is interested; the remaining 8 items are present solely for obfuscation purposes.

To reiterate, the advantage of low-inference self-report affective measures is that they can be readily interpreted if we can be confident that the person responding to them has been able and willing to supply truthful answers. The chief strength of these low-inference measures is, of course, their major liability. It is because the items in such measures can be so readily interpreted, not only by the evaluator but also by the individual responding to the measure, that the prospect of faked responses is so high. This problem has led to the use of a different sort of self-report device.

High-Inference Self-Report Devices

Because we have been considering low-inference self-report devices for several paragraphs, it should not come as a stunning surprise that the class of measures to be discussed now consists of *high-inference self-report instruments*. The difference between the two, obviously, is that with high-inference self-report instruments we sometimes have to make a pretty healthy inferential jump to interpret the data as being reflective of an individual's affective dispositions. The chief advantage of such measurement tactics is that, just as they require an inference on the part of the evaluator, they also require a comparable inference from the individual responding to the measure. As a consequence, they are less fakeable; the respondent cannot be certain what the true purpose of the measure is, hence cannot discern what the "appropriate" answers are.

There are few high-inference self-report devices available for use in educational evaluation. To understand why this is so, the reader will have to recall the discussion earlier in the chapter regarding group versus individual validity. As long as measurement people had to develop affective measures for clinical, counseling, or other *individual* decisions, few risks could be taken in affective instrument development. Indeed, the shakiest strategy for making valid inferences about individuals would be to rely on high-inference instruments, self-report or otherwise. However, as was indicated before, educational evaluation is a totally different game with substantially different ground rules. Because we normally use affective measures to get at a group's dispositional tendencies, the use of high-inference self-report devices should be most attractive. It is chiefly because so few evaluators have recognized the less-stringent validity demands of group-focused measures that we have almost no high-inference self-report devices from which to select. Many more measures of this sort will have to be created in the next few years if evaluators wish to attend to the full range of important learner behaviors.

Let's consider a few examples of high-inference self-report devices drawn from the self-concept measures developed some years ago. The first of these, "Television Actors," was originated by my good friend and colleague, John D. McNeil. It is designed for primary-age children.

> *This inventory asks respondents to consider television roles that they would be willing to play in a fictitious television show. Twenty items are presented, some of which would be generally considered aversive, for example, a "dirty-faced child." The respondents' scores are computed simply by determining the number of roles they would be willing to play.*
>
> *This inventory is based on the assumption that individuals who possess a positive self-concept will be willing to project themselves into a wider variety of roles than individuals who have a less strong self-concept. Individuals who are secure in aspects of their own identity can play a make-believe role without threat.[5]*

The complete inventory is presented in Figure 7–4.

As a second illustration of a high-inference self-report instrument, let's consider a self-concept measure called the "Choose a Job Inventory."

> *This inventory consists of forty items in which the student is asked to consider a list of want-ads for jobs such as the ones found in classified sections of newspapers. The respondents are asked first to read all of the want-ads, then put a check next to the ten jobs which they think they would most like to get if they were adults. The job descriptions are ranked as high, middle, or low, depending on social perception of each job's esteem. Three points are given for high-esteem selections, two for middle-esteem selections, and one for low-esteem selections. The maximum number of points available, therefore, would be thirty, which could be attained by an individual who selects only high-esteem jobs. The lowest score available would be ten.*
>
> *The rationale for this device is based on the assumption that the individual with a relatively high self-concept will generally select positions which are associated with socially approved vocational pursuits. The dimensions used to rank the esteem of jobs are the following: salary, educational requirements, creativity requirements, aggressiveness requirements, and venturesomeness attributes.*
>
> *While there are obviously differences in the degree of self-esteem associated with various positions in different geographic locales, that is, a job which might be considered high esteem (three points) in one community might be considered middle esteem (two points) in another community, the total score should be reflective of an individual's general self-concept as it is reflected by these selections.[6]*

It should be quite clear from the foregoing discussion and examples that the creation of high-inference self-report devices is risky business. Not only is there danger that our inferences will be erroneous but we may also have difficulty con-

---

Television Actors

Directions: (To be read aloud). Let's pretend we are going to put on a television show. If you will play the part I ask you, mark through "yes" on your answer sheet. If you will not play the part I ask you, mark "no" on your answer sheet. You may play as many parts as you wish.

(Use practice items as needed for class to understand procedure.)

1. Will you play the part of a dirty-faced child?
2. Will you play the part of a tree that talks?
3. Will you play the part of a pig?
4. Will you play the part of Batman?
5. Will you play the part of a cry baby?
6. Will you play the part of a funny child?
7. Will you play the part of a sad child?
8. Will you play the part of a mean child?
9. Will you play the part of a happy child?
10. Will you play the part of a worm?
11. Will you play the part of a silly child?
12. Will you play the part of a crying child?
13. Will you play the part of a smart child?
14. Will you play the part of a messy child?
15. Will you play the part of a slow-poke?
16. Will you play the part of a child whose birthdays are always remembered?
17. Will you play the part of a child who never gets dessert?
18. Will you play the part of a policeman?
19. Will you play the part of a hurt child?
20. Will you play the part of a butterfly?

FIGURE 7-4 • *A High-Inference Self-Report Affective Measure*

vincing others that such inferences are warranted. In fact, the very decision makers for whom we are assembling affective measurement data may reject our high-inference approaches altogether. For these reasons the evaluator will find that construct validation strategies are particularly helpful in deciding whether our measures yield valid inferences and, if so, in convincing others of that fact. In such cases there are particular advantages in employing triangulation strategies that involve both low-inference and high-inference measures.

The Likert Technique

One of the most common self-report approaches to the assessment of individuals' affective status is the scheme devised 60 years ago by R. A. Likert.[7] Anderson has provided us with a succinct, step-by-step description of how to create a Likert-type scale.[8] Anderson's eight steps in the development of a Likert scale are presented in Table 7–1.

TABLE 7-1 • *Eight Steps in Constructing a Likert Scale*

Step 1:	Write or select statements that are clearly either favorable or unfavorable with respect to the underlying affective characteristic.
Step 2:	Have several judges react to the statements. These judges should examine each statement and classify it as positive, negative, or neutral.
Step 3:	Eliminate those statements that are not unanimously classified as positive or negative (since neutral statements are not acceptable for inclusion on a Likert scale).
Step 4:	Decide on the number of alternative choices to be offered for each statement. (*Note:* The original Likert scale had five alternatives: SD, D, NS, A, SA.)
Step 5:	Prepare the self-report instrument. Include directions. The directions should indicate that the respondents should indicate how they feel about each statement by marking SA if they strongly agree, A if they agree, NS if they are not sure, D if they disagree, and SD if they strongly disagree.
Step 6:	Administer the scale to a sample of the audience for whom the instrument is intended. (*Note:* You should have at least five times as many persons as statements.)
Step 7:	Compute the correlation between each statement response and the total scale score.
Step 8:	Eliminate those statements whose correlation with the total scale is not statistically significant (Likert's Criterion of Internal Consistency).

As presented by L. W. Anderson, *Assessing Affective Charactistics in the Schools* (Boston: Allyn and Bacon, 1981). Used with permission.

The eight-step procedure in creating a Likert scale concludes with the application of a "criterion of internal consistency." Many novice evaluators attempt to create Likert scales merely by whipping up a batch of statements to which respondents can register varying degrees of agreement or disagreement. Note that by requiring that items on the scale must correlate significantly with total-scale scores, Likert made sure that his scales possessed a degree of homogeneity, that is, they were *related* statements.

Although the original Likert scales allowed five response options – Strongly Agree, Agree, Not Sure, Disagree, and Strongly Disagree – subsequent scale developers have varied the number of alternatives with any number of options from two to seven are sometimes found in such scales. Even-numbered responses are typically used so that respondents will not use a midcategory response such as "not sure" or "uncertain" to avoid registering an agreement or disagreement. Fewer response options are frequently used where Likert scales are to be employed with younger or less educated respondents.

The Likert approach to the construction of affective scales represents a useful weapon in the evaluator's assessment arsenal. Likert scales are relatively easy to create and, if all eight of Anderson's steps are followed, are capable of yielding meaningful inferences about respondents' affective dispositions.

The reader who wishes to learn more about Likert scales, as well as other scales used in the assessment of affect, is encouraged to consult Anderson's highly readable introduction to the assessment of affect.[9]

Behavior Observations

A particularly useful affective measurement strategy involves systematic observation of learner behavior. There was a previous discussion of observational techniques, but in connection with affective assessment the stress should be on surreptitious observations. We must be particularly careful in observing an individual's behavior lest, because of the presence of the observer, unnatural behaviors be displayed.

For instance, if you want to discover whether secondary-school boys display good sportsmanship (as reflected, perhaps, by voluntary handshakes with opponents after a losing game, or by the absence of postgame profanity), then the physical education teacher had best stay out of eyesight and earshot, for that presence will most likely inhibit the behavior of the boys.

Because observed learner behaviors are typically those resulting from volitional acts, they will often tend to correlate better than anything else with the true affective dispositions of the learner. For example, when I taught English classes in an eastern Oregon high school, my students displayed glittering proficiency in grammar during written and oral drills yet walked outside the classroom observing that "He don't never give us enough time." I should have been measuring the out-of-class behavior of my students if I really wanted to know whether my instruction was altering their dispositions to speak in certain ways.

The skilled evaluator will recognize that the kind of behavior that learners will display can occur, as was discussed earlier, under natural or controlled stimulus conditions. If we wait for a particular form of behavior to occur under natural stimulus conditions, we will sometimes be obliged to gather an excessively high rate of wasted data (referred to as the *dross* rate); therefore, it is often more sensible to try to trigger the desired types of behavior by manipulating the stimulus situation. We might, for example, persuade a student to make some particularly inflammatory remarks in order to see how fellow students respond to such remarks.

On the other hand, there are many natural settings in which, if we could only observe people's normal behavior, we would secure some highly useful indications of their dispositional tendencies. To alter the natural situation would, in fact, destroy the very setting we want. In such cases, typically, the only difficulty we encounter is in gathering observations without sensitizing individuals to the fact that they are being observed.

Using Observation Instrumentation   One way to gather observation data surreptitiously is to employ hidden recording instrumentation such as videotape or audiotape recorders. These devices can often be situated so that the person being observed becomes oblivious of their presence. The invasion-of-privacy ethical issue is, of course, critical in such instances. Evaluators should certainly have considered carefully the moral appropriateness of such observation techniques for the purposes at hand. If, for the evaluative function involved, a positive decision is reached regarding the ethical issue, then the use of mechanical instruments to gather observation data surreptitiously can prove most efficient.

Another way of using mechanical instrumentation to gather observation data while avoiding invasion of privacy is to set up the recording equipment quite visibly, even notifying the students to be observed that the equipment will occasionally be used to observe their behavior. If it is possible, the recorder's operating sounds might be muffled so that the students are unaware of when it is functioning. There is some evidence that, after students get used to the presence of the device, they revert to normal behavior patterns. Obviously, this reversion to more natural behavior will not occur during the early days after recording instruments have been installed.

Using Accomplices   Another way of unobtrusively observing an individual's behavior is to enlist the aid of accomplices, such as fellow students, who can gather observational data without the awareness of the individual being observed. Such accomplices can be trained not only to gather observational data reliably, but to do so in an unobtrusive manner. Accomplices can also be employed, of course, to modify the nature of the stimulus situation in which an individual is being observed. It is possible in such cases for the accomplice to play the role of stimulus-evoker as well as unrecognized observer. Some of the most useful data in social science research have been obtained in investigations where accomplices were utilized. Again, concerns about the ethics of data gathering loom large in any assessment approach that involves the use of accomplices.

Learner Products as Affective Indicators

As was indicated previously, there are occasions when evaluators can discern much about a learner's capabilities or affective dispositions by examining the products they create. Such products can be generated under either natural or controlled stimulus conditions. There are a limited number of situations in which such products will be indicative of a student's affective learnings. For example, in an example involving the measurement of students' playground litter we get at the students' tendencies to disregard anti-littering regulation. Such tendencies are clearly dispositional in nature.

In other cases we may want to examine students' products prepared for one class situation in order to detect their dispositions regarding other phenomena. For example, we might examine autobiographical essays written by students in an English course to discern something about their self-concepts.

A Costly Enterprise

Throughout this chapter we have dealt with a variety of issues related to the creation of affective measurement devices. The reader will surely have sensed that in the assessment of student status with respect to the elusive affective domain, simple-minded tactics are apt to yield data in which we have only limited confidence. Considerable sophistication has to be employed in the creation of valid affective measures, often involving the use of atypical measurement ploys and complex inferential chains. The creation of such measures is costly, both in actual personnel sala-

ries and in the psychic energy a staff must devote to this sometimes unrewarding pursuit. We have to recognize, unfortunately, that we will not always be successful in our attempts to create defensible affective measures.

For these reasons, evaluators will find it eminently sensible to capitalize on the availability of any existing affective measures that might, in their present form or with adaptation, be used for the task at hand. Unfortunately, there are relatively few of these devices available at present. One of the evaluator's responsibilities, therefore, should be to stimulate the creating *and sharing* of such instruments so that we can, in subsequent years, be judiciously selecting from a wide range of affective measures well suited for the purposes of educational evaluation.

Discussion Questions

1. Why do you think we have seen an apparent contradiction between (a) educators' vocal support of the importance of affective goals and (b) the frequency of measuring affective outcomes as an index of educational success?

2. What are the most fundamental reasons that individuals completing self-report types of affective measures are influenced by cues as to socially expected responses? How should the evaluator deal with these problems?

3. What important differences, if any, exist between the construction and use of affective measuring instruments designed for individual decision making and those designed for decision making based on group performance? How does an evaluator measure individuals, describe individual performance collectively, and use such data for decisions about such things as instructional treatments?

4. Putting yourself in the role of an evaluator who is faced with a choice be-

tween (a) securing meaningful data via subterfuge or (b) securing less-meaningful data without subterfuge, how would you behave? What are the most important ethical issues facing an evaluator in such instances?

5. What sorts of validation approaches are most appropriate for affective mea-

sures? How do these differ, if at all, from those used for the validation of primarily cognitive or psychomotor measures?

6. Why are high-inference measurement tactics more appropriate for use by educational evaluators than by psychiatric workers?

Practice Exercises

1. Determine whether each of the following measuring devices is chiefly *affective, cognitive,* or *psychomotor* in nature.

   a. An essay test in which the pupil is to describe a personal experience of great emotional impact. The essays are to be graded on the basis of the expository effectiveness.

   b. An end-of-unit debate in which each student is to defend a value-based proposition as persuasively as possible. The propositions are randomly assigned to the students two hours prior to the debate.

   c. A self-report inventory requiring the respondent to register agreement or disagreement with a series of statements regarding good and bad aspects of religion in our society.

   d. A quasi-projective test in which students are shown a series of illustrated slides containing either positive, negative, or neutral depictions of educational situations. The students are asked to indicate the relative degree to which each slide is reflective of their school.

   e. A test of how fast young men can run the 100-yard dash while fervently whistling the national anthem.

2. Decide whether each of the following self-report devices can be more appropriately designed as a *low-inference* or *high-inference* measure.

   a. Pupils are asked to write a short essay describing their feeling regarding the quality of education in their school.

   b. A self-concept inventory consisting of a series of statements such as the following are given to pupils, who must mark each as true or false:

      (1) I feel fairly comfortable about myself.

      (2) Most people don't think I am very capable.

      (3) I know what to do in most situations.

      (4) I am often ill at ease in new settings.

   c. A group projective test consisting of a series of audiotaped dialogues involving a teacher and a pupil. Students are to listen to each taped vignette, then write whatever comes to their minds.

   d. A questionnaire that is designed to measure the respondent's attitudes but that asks students to answer a series of questions about citizenship matters "as their best friends might feel."

   e. A brief questionnaire asking students to answer three questions regarding their interest in the topics treated during the work of the semester in a U. S. government class.

Answers to Practice Exercises

1. *a.* cognitive; *b.* cognitive; *c.* affective; *d.* affective; *e.* psychomotor.
2. *a.* low inference; *b.* low inference; *c.* high inference; *d.* high inference; *e.* low inference.

Notes

1. Benjamin S. Bloom et al., *Taxonomy of Educational Objectives: Handbook I: Cognitive Domain* (New York: David McKay, 1956).

2. Remember that in the cognitive-affective-psychomotor context the term *domain* refers to a much broader type of learner behaviors than is the case in describing the domain of criterion behaviors for a criterion-referenced test.

3. David Krathwohl et al., *Taxonomy of Educational Objectives: Handbook II: Affective Domain* (New York: David McKay, 1964).

4. Exceptions include the affective measures developed by IOX Assessment Associates, P. O. Box 24095, Los Angeles, CA. 90024, regarding such dispositions as attitudes toward school, tolerance, self-concept, and drug use.

5. *Measures of Self Concept,* orig. ed. (Los Angeles: IOX Assessment Associates, 1972).

6. *Measures of Self-Concept K-12,* rev. ed. (Los Angeles: IOX Assessment Associates, 1972).

7. R. A. Likert, "A Technique for the Measurement of Attitudes, *Archives of Psychology,* no. 140, 1932.

8. L. W. Anderson, *Assessing Affective Characteristics in the Schools* (Boston: Allyn and Bacon 1981).

9. Ibid.

Selected References

Anderson, Lorin W. *Assessing Affective Characteristics in the Schools.* Boston: Allyn and Bacon, 1981.

Fishbein, M., and I. Ajzen. *Belief, Attitude, Intention, and Behavior: An Introduction to Theory and Research.* Reading, MA: Addison-Wesley, 1975.

Gronlund, Norman E., and Robert L. Linn. *Measurment and Evaluation in Teaching* (6th ed.). New York: Macmillan, 1990.

Messick, S. J. "Potential Uses of Non-Cognitive Measurement in Education." *Journal of Educational Psychology,* 71, (1979): 281–292.

Popham, W. James. *Modern Educational Measurement.* Englewood Cliffs, NJ: Prentice-Hall, 1990.

Rokeach, M. *The Nature of Human Values.* New York: Free Press, 1973.

Sax, Gilbert. "The Measurement of Interests, Attitudes, and Values." *Principles of Educational and Psychological Measurement and Evaluation* (3rd ed.). Belmont, CA: Wadsworth, 1989, pp. 467–504.

Webb, Eugene J., Donald T. Campbell, Richard D. Schwartz, Lee Sechreat, and Janet Belew Grove. *Nonreactive Measures in the Social Sciences* (2nd ed.). Boston: Houghton Mifflin, 1981.

Wiersma, William, and Stephen G. Jurs. *Educational Measurement and Testing* (2nd ed.). Boston; Allyn and Bacon, 1990.

CHAPTER EIGHT

Measuring the Hard to Measure

Following on the previous chapter's overview of factors to consider when devising affective assessment approaches, in this chapter we will look at several assessment procedures that can be used by educational evaluators to measure affective variables and other sensitive behaviors such as the degree to which students use illegal drugs or engage in sexual practices that place them at risk of infection.

First, we will deal with a commonly employed but frequently misused assessment scheme, namely, the participant-satisfaction evaluation form. Such forms are sometimes given to students at the close of an instructional program and almost always given to teachers and/or administrators at the conclusion of staff-development workshops. Next, we will consider two schemes to increase students' honesty in reporting sensitive behaviors. Finally, we will illustrate how to employ an indirect assessment scheme to obtain estimates of students' status regarding particularly difficult-to-assess variables.

How to Construct End-of-Program Participant-Satisfaction Forms

Just as many school days traditionally begin with the Pledge of Allegiance, many instructional programs traditionally end with the distribution of participant-satisfaction evaluation forms. On such forms participants (whether children or adults) register their satisfaction or dissatisfaction with the overall program and/or its parts. Indeed, for most adult-education programs the use of participant-evaluation forms is so prevalent that a failure to employ such forms almost constitutes a violation of sacred ritual.

Therein, however, lies a problem. Many participant-satisfaction evaluation forms are more ritualistic contrivances than realistic contributions to the program's evaluation. Often, too little thought is given to the construction of participant-satisfaction forms employed to evaluate instructional programs. As a consequence, the data obtained from such forms frequently fail to prove useful in determining the program's effectiveness or in making decisions regarding how to improve the program. Measuring participants' satisfaction is more difficult than most evaluators realize.

Five rules for the generation of participant-satisfaction forms are presented here. By adhering to these rules, forms can be created that can be effectively used with participants (children or adults) at the close of an instructional program. Participants' satisfaction can be solicited regarding such aspects of the program as logistics, organization, content, materials, presentations, and so on. Clearly, the creation of such evaluation forms is a highly particularistic endeavor that will vary from setting to setting, depending on the nature of the instructional program being evaluated. Nonetheless, there are a number of general factors that should be attended to in the construction of any participant-satisfaction evaluation form. Such factors are the focus of the following rules.

Rule 1: Clarity—Adhere to the customary canons of clear writing when creating an evaluation form.

The first rule is that the language employed in a participant-satisfaction evaluation form must be sufficiently simple and clear so that participants understand their evaluative task well enough to provide sensible responses. The specifics of the participant's task must be spelled out in straightforward terms. Each item in the form must lucidly convey what is being sought. Ambiguities of phrasing and complex language must be avoided. Instead, simple, direct statements and questions should be employed. (This is particularly important when soliciting the reactions of young students.) It is also helpful to indicate the purpose of an evaluation form in the directions for completing that form. A description of the form's intended use frequently fosters clarity on the part of the participant when responding.

The usual standards of clear communication must be subscribed to in the use of mechanics, punctuation, spelling, and word usage. Admittedly, one rarely encounters an evaluation form in which the word *form* is spelled *farm*. On the other hand, there are numerous evaluation forms in which punctuation problems or syntax flaws can lead to confusion among participants and, as a consequence, can contribute to potentially misleading data.

Prior to using an evaluation form, the form should be carefully edited by an individual *other* than the person who constructed the form. This external reviewer should scrutinize the form from the perspective of the typical individual who will be asked to complete it. Any shortcomings in the quality of the writing, of course, should be rectified.

Rule 2: Decision Focus—Make every aspect of the evaluation form focus on a program-relevant decision.

Far too many participant-satisfaction evaluation forms are created in order to collect information that is interesting or nice to know. Although there may be a place for such forms of inquiry, program evaluation is not one of them. *Program evalua-*

tors exist in order to promote more defensible decisions regarding programs. Thus questions of idle interest should not be found in a well-constructed participant-satisfaction evaluation form.

The standard by which every item in an evaluation form should be judged is straightforward, namely: "Will the information yielded by the item bear directly on a program-related decision that is at issue?" In other words, every question asked of participants should produce information that can be used in making a decision about the program. One simple way to see if an item on an evaluation form really satisfies this standard is to hypothesize the way in which various sorts of data might turn out, then ask yourself "What decision would I recommend if the responses turned out this way?" or, having hypothesized the opposite result, "Now, what decision would I recommend?" If the data to be gathered don't make a meaningful difference in the nature of the decision, then abandon the item.

There are three decision categories that are apt to cover most of the judgments to be asked of participants regarding an instructional program: (1) *program content*, (2) *instructional activities*, and (3) *logistical arrangements*. Participants can often provide decision-relevant insights regarding each of these categories of concern. For instance, participants can register their satisfaction with a program's content by indicating which of the topics treated were of practical relevance to them. Similarly, participants can signify which instructional activities were helpful and which ones were not. Finally, participants are in a particularly advantageous position to indicate how satisfied they were with such logistical arrangements as seating arrangements, room temperature, ventilation, and so on.

In most instances, participant-satisfaction evaluation forms provide data of value for formative evaluation purposes so that different aspects of the program can be improved. For example, such forms often ask participants to rate the quality of various instructional activities carried out during the program. It is also possible to ask participants to supply a more overall summative evaluation focused on the general quality of the program. For example, participants could be asked to supply an overall grade for the program on an *A-B-C-D-F* scale. Whether formatively or summatively oriented, however, every item on a participant-satisfaction evaluation form should be unequivocally directed toward a program-related decision.

One common section of a participant-satisfaction evaluation form provides an opportunity for participants to indicate the aspect of the program with which they were "most satisfied" as well as the aspect with which they were "least satisfied." The decision implication of such most/least reactions is clearly that the least satisfactory elements of the program will be modified or jettisoned whereas the most satisfactory elements will be retained and, if possible, emulated elsewhere in the program.

In short, those who are charged with constructing a participant-satisfaction evaluation form should be governed chiefly by the extent to which the resultant data contribute to improved program-relevant decisions. An evaluation form that does not contribute to such decisions is a dysfunctional evaluation form.

Rule 3: Brevity—Require participants to provide responses to the smallest possible number of items.

The adage that "less is more" certainly applies to the construction of participant-satisfaction evaluation forms. It is much wiser to ask participants to provide responses to a small set of important questions than it is to ask them to respond to a seemingly endless litany of questions. Far too many novice evaluators err by attempting to ask participants about every imaginable aspect of the program. What these evaluators fail to recognize is that there is an almost perfect *inverse* relationship between the number of questions that participants are asked and the quality of participants' responses. A participant who is asked 5 or 6 clearly important questions about a program will typically supply thoughtful responses to those questions. On the other hand, a participant who is asked to supply responses to 30 questions will often fail to respond at all or, more commonly, will race through the task by supplying only superficial responses.

I have personally observed several instances in which workshop instructors distributed evaluation forms that resembled midsize novellas. Yet, in almost all instances, participant-satisfaction evaluation forms are completed at the *end* of an instructional program—a time when most participants are eager to get on with their next activities. The prospect of a lengthy evaluation form will incline many participants to supply rushed responses that are likely to be of little value. For valid participant-satisfaction evaluation forms, the evaluator must be truly selective in deciding what questions to include. Less, in truth, will turn out to be more.

If there are large numbers of participants in an instructional program, and the evaluator is truly interested in securing responses to more questions than brevity would permit, different versions of the evaluation form (with different items on each) can be distributed to participants. For example, two different evaluation forms might be employed so that half of the participants complete one form while half complete the other. This type of *item sampling* will, with reasonably large numbers of participants, still yield useful group-aggregated data for program evaluation purposes. We will consider item sampling in Chapter Eleven.

This third rule may be difficult for some evaluators to accept. After all, they may contend, "Because we are often interested in many aspects of a program, why shouldn't we be permitted to ask participants questions about all these aspects?" What such evaluators fail to recognize, however, is the marked reduction in the *quality* of participant data when participants perceive the evaluative task to be either excessive or aversive. To choose a somewhat silly example only for illustrative purposes, how would you react if, at the end of a one-day workshop, you were asked to complete a 1,000-item evaluation form? Unless you possessed a mildly masochistic bent, you'd probably not give genuinely thoughtful attention to each of the 1,000 items. In much the same way, when a program participant believes an end-of-program evaluation form to be excessively lengthy, there is a tendency to devote less than careful thought to some or all of the items on the form. Sometimes the choice facing the evaluator is something as simple as "Do I want meaningful responses to a half-dozen questions or less meaningful responses to a dozen questions?" Rule 3 suggests that fewer items will yield evaluative dividends.

> *Rule 4:* Anonymity — Construct at least part of the evaluation form so that responses can be totally anonymous.

The use of participant-satisfaction evaluation forms rests on the assumption that participants will truthfully indicate their satisfaction or dissatisfaction with the program. Untruthful responses, obviously, are apt to be misleading to decision makers. Great attention should therefore be given to designing an evaluation form that is likely to elicit honest responses from participants. In general, to counter the tendency of participants to supply "socially desirable" responses (that is, responses that participants believe the program staff wishes to receive), the evaluation form should be completed with *total* anonymity.

Total anonymity is promoted when participants supply no form of identifying information, even handwritten comments, on the evaluation form. If participants believe that there is *any* way by which their reactions can be linked to them, then the likelihood of their candor is diminished. For example, if an evaluation form for students asks for answers to several questions dealing with such dimensions as gender and ethnicity, some students may believe their demographic responses can be used to identify them. Incidentally, the practical uses of demographic data are often nonexistent. Many novice evaluators ritualistically toss such questions into an evaluation form without ever considering whether this type of information will really influence a program-relevant decision.

Regarding handwritten responses, such as comments regarding key components of the program, these responses should be supplied on a *separate* sheet (not attached to the truly anonymous part of the evaluation form). The evaluation form itself should consist of items that are exclusively answerable via checkmarks, circling the appropriate answer, or some similar type of response. Students who write comments on a participant-satisfaction evaluation form will, with reason, believe that their teacher can identify their handwriting. (If teachers are working with their own classes, and certain students employ distinctive types of pencils or pens, then standard pencils should be supplied when the evaluation form is to be completed.) In other settings, such as workshops for teachers, although it is unlikely that a participant's responses can be identified merely via an inspection of the participant's handwritten comments, the mere *possibility* that such responses are recognizable will, for some participants, reduce forthrightness. By using *separate* check-off forms and *separate* respond-in-writing forms, the likelihood of securing candid responses on the check-off form is increased. If possible, all "check-off-only" questions should be placed on the totally anonymous, no-handwriting form.

Participants should also be informed, *prior* to their completion of the forms, that they will personally be depositing their forms in a box at the rear of the room. Again, to enhance perceptions of anonymity, we do not wish participants to think that they will be identified while handing a negative evaluation, in person, to a teacher or other member of an instructional program's staff.

To repeat, anonymity enhancement is an important feature of a properly constructed participant-satisfaction evaluation form. Meticulous attention should be given to the promotion of such anonymity.

Rule 5: Suggestions—Provide an opportunity for participants to supply additional suggestions regarding the program.

Although it may seem contradictory to provide an opportunity for participants to supply handwritten suggestions regarding the program, and thereby reduce respondents' anonymity, use of the aforementioned separate check-off and separate respond-in-writing forms will alleviate this difficulty by making the check-off form totally anonymous. Even though some participants may be reluctant to supply "potentially recognizable" handwritten suggestions regarding the program, other participants will be quite honest in providing such reactions. Moreover, it is difficult for the constructor of a participant-satisfaction evaluation form, particularly a brief form (as recommended in Rule 3), to anticipate all potentially significant reactions by participants. Thus there is virtue in providing an opportunity for participants to offer suggestions dealing with those aspects of the program not addressed on the check-off evaluation form.

The typical item used for this purpose is phrased approximately in this matter: "Please provide any suggestions regarding ways of improving the quality of the program." As indicated earlier, in the discussion of Rule 2, another way of providing participants with an opportunity to offer less-structured reactions is to allow them to identify their "most favorite" and "least favorite" aspects of the program, then supply any additional comments they wish.

As indicated earlier, the focus of participant-satisfaction evaluation forms should be on the accumulation of information that will be helpful in making program-related decisions. In designing participant-satisfaction evaluation forms, evaluators should give careful *advance* consideration to the most meaningful ways in which to analyze, organize, and present the data supplied on such forms. Too many evaluators give little or no prior attention to the issue of data analysis and data presentation. The result is, all too often, an array of information ill-suited to the decision-maker's needs. An in-advance analysis of how to present the data from an evaluation form will often lead to alterations in the form itself.

In the next section of the chapter we will turn to a useful technique for securing information regarding topics about which students are typically unwilling to supply truthful responses.

Using Camouflaged Answers to Increase Respondents' Anonymity

There are numerous instances in which educational evaluators wish to secure information from individuals via a self-report inventory, but those individuals are reluctant to supply honest responses. For example, suppose that you are evaluating a semester-long sex education program for high school students focused on the reduction of students' sexual behaviors that put those students at risk of becoming infected with a sexually transmitted disease (STD). By measuring students at the beginning and at the end of the semester, you wish to discern if there has, in fact, been a reduction in the frequency of students' high-risk behaviors. Such information will be pivotal in judging the program's effectiveness *if* the information is accurate. And that, of course, is where the difficulty lies. Students are generally reluctant to report their sexual behaviors candidly. Even if the evaluator creates an anonymous inventory and employs anonymity-enhancing procedures such as those suggested in the previous section of the chapter, many students will still be reluctant to respond honestly because *other students might see how they respond*. For example, if students are asked to circle one of four response options regarding their sexual behaviors (such options ranging from *A*, total celibacy, to *D*, rampant promiscuity), many students will fail to answer honestly because they believe that a nearby student will visually observe how they are responding.

An Alphabet-Soup Response Scheme

To combat respondents' fears that other respondents will observe how they respond, an *alphabet-soup* response scheme was developed in 1991 by IOX Assessment Associates.[1] Although respondents are still asked to supply answers to sensitive questions by selecting from a limited number of choices, such as *A* through *D*, the respondents supply their answers by placing a small *X* through a letter imbedded in a string of alphabetized letters such as the following:

S T U V W X Y Z A B C D E F G H I J K L M N O P Q R

The individuals being surveyed are given a form that shows them sample items using this response scheme. They are also informed that there are *different* forms of the survey being distributed. (At least three different forms are recommended.) For each question asked, the string of alphabetically sequenced letters is different, and for each form of the inventory the alphabetical sequences for each question commence with different letters. In other words, an attempt is made to provide a response scheme so that individuals' answers are visually camouflaged. Although respondents still mark an *A B, C,* or *D,* the location of those responses varies from item to item and from form to form.

Because of the variation in the location of the response choices and the variation of the letter sequences on the different scoring forms, it is practically impossible for other respondents to observe, even surreptitiously, how a given respondent is answering a particular question. And this, of course, is the whole point of the response scheme—namely, to increase respondents' forthrightness by giving them a system in which their responses are unknown not only to those who collect the survey forms but also to those individuals who are sitting around them.

The scoring scheme has been used successfully with students at the junior and senior high school levels as well as with adults. Both students and adults report no difficulty in using the alphabet-soup response scheme and, more importantly, indicate that they believe their responses cannot be seen by others sitting nearby.

Figure 8–1 illustrates the explanatory page of self-report inventory in which an alphabet-soup response scheme is used. The assessment instrument, designed for senior high school students, solicits information about students' sexual behaviors that place them at risk of becoming infected with STDs. The teacher (or other person who administers the inventory) reads the directions aloud to students and shows them how to place their *X* responses carefully *between* the two parallel lines so that

FIGURE 8–1 • *The Explanatory Page of a Self-Report Inventory Using an Alphabet-Soup Response Scheme*

SUPER SECRET SURVEY

DO NOT put your name on this survey. Your answers will be kept secret. No one will know how you answered these questions.

Directions: This survey asks you personal questions. To make sure your answers are secret, you will complete this survey in a special way. Read each question and find the answer that is *most* true for you. Then find the letter that goes with that answer in the row of letters between the lines. Put an *X* through the letter in that row (between the two lines).

Example No. 1: Which of the following statements is *most* true for you?

    A. I get up before 6:30 A.M.
    B. I get up between 6:30 A.M. and 7:30 A.M.
    C. I get up later than 7:30 A.M.

O P Q R S T U V W X Y Z A B C D E F G H I J K L M N

Example No. 2: Which of the following statements is *most* true for you?

    A. I walk to school.
    B. I take a bus to school.
    C. I ride a bicycle to school.
    D. I ride to school in a car.
    E. I usually get to school in another way.

S T U V W X Y Z A B C D E F G H I J K L M N O P Q R

To Protect Your Privacy: Your classmates have *different* versions of this survey than you do. *For the same question*, the letters are in a *different* position on your paper and on your classmate's paper. This is done so that no one will know your answers. Some of the questions in this survey ask about "having sex." This means having sexual intercourse. Some of the answers refer to "sexual abstinence." This means not having sexual intercourse.

(Form K)

the responses are less visible. The teacher also describes the other conditions intended to heighten students' perceived sense of anonymity. Such other conditions might include (1) asking for no student names or written comments of any kind in an inventory, (2) providing a receptacle where students can put their completed inventories, (3) indicating that the teacher will not be walking around the room during the completion of the inventories, (4) discouraging students from looking at any inventory other than their own, and (5) reminding students that the alphabet-soup response scheme was deliberately designed to keep responses confidential.

The actual items on the inventory, then, might take the form of the one presented below in which a question is asked about students' sexual practices. (Incidentally, if phrases such as *had sex* or *sexually abstinent* are used in the inventory, these phrases must be explained in the inventory, or by the teacher, so that students have a common understanding of the key terms being used.)

---

1. Which one of these statements is *most* true for you?
   A. During my life, I have always been sexually abstinent.
   B. During my life, I have had sex with one person.
   C. During my life, I have had sex with two people.
   D. During my life, I have had sex with three or more people.

   O P Q R S T U V W X Y Z A B C D E F G H I J K L M N

Procedural Particulars

As is apparent, use of the alphabet-soup response scheme requires hand scoring of individuals' responses because on different forms of the inventory the location of the response options vary. Although the responses need to be scored with care, this is a small cost for the heightened honesty that stems from the use of the response scheme.

When designing an inventory using an alphabet-soup response scheme, be sure that the letters of the actual response options are not split (for example, with *A* and *B* at the far right side of the letter row, while *C* and *D* are at the far left side). Also, do not place the actual response letter near the extreme left-hand or right-hand position in the letter row, because respondents may believe their answers might be more easily seen by others. The actual size of the letters in the letter-row is also a matter of some importance. In general, keep the size of the letters as small as possible, because respondents' choices are then less visible. Finally, be sure that each of the different forms of the inventory is clearly identified. (See Figure 8–1.) This is done not only so that responses can be accurately scored but so that respondents will recognize that there are, indeed, multiple forms of the instrument being used.

The Randomized Response Technique

Another approach that can be used by educational educators to ascertain respondents' answers to highly sensitive questions is called the *randomized response technique*. This procedure, developed almost four decades ago, is not used all that frequently because it requires a relatively large number of individuals, say, 500, to take part in completing a rather special type of self-report instrument. However, there are instances in which educational evaluators, particularly those working in midsize or large school districts, have access to the needed number of students. If you wish to make sensible inferences about students' sensitive behaviors and believe that more conventional self-report instruments will fail to yield accurate responses, then you should give serious consideration to the randomized response technique.

Rationale

The logic underlying the randomized response technique is quite straightforward. If sufficient individuals take part in a truly anonymous survey in which each individual "mentally" chooses between pairs of questions about the individual's behavior (one of questions dealing with benign behaviors and one dealing with sensitive behaviors), it is possible to make a *probabilistic* estimate regarding the proportion of respondents who engage in the behavior asked about in the sensitive question.

Although there are many variations in the way that the randomized response procedure is operationalized (see the pertinent references at the close of the chapter), we will deal with one of the most simple versions of the approach to illustrate how the general assessment strategy functions. Imagine that we are trying to get an accurate fix on the proportion of students who are the victims of parental child abuse. Having been abused by one's parents, of course, is a topic about which many students are reluctant to be candid.

Students are presented with a *pair* of questions, one of which is a nonthreatening yes/no question and one of which is a yes/no question about whether the child has been parentally abused. If the nonthreatening question yields responses that can be probabilistically estimated, then we can also estimate the proportion of yes and no responses made to the child-abuse question.

The nonthreatening question might take the following form: "Think of the name (first or last) of someone you know. Is there an *even* number of letters (2, 4, 6, 8, etc.) in that person's name?" We can refer to this question as the *odd/even question*. You will note that, on average, the answer to the odd/even question will be yes about 50 percent of the time and no about 50 percent of the time. The other question in a two-question pair can be referred to as the *personal question* because it asks a sensitive question that also can be answered by a yes or no.

Now, the only missing element in our little probability drama involves the way in which respondents decide whether they are to answer the odd/even question *or* the personal question. One simple way of making this determination is to allow respondents to shake a coin in their cupped hands (so that no one else can see) to decide which of the two questions to answer. Then, because there is a 50 percent probability of choosing the odd/even question because of the coin shake, and because there is a 50 percent probability of answering the odd/even question with a yes response, it is possible to estimate the percent of yes responses to the personal question in a question-pair.

An Illustration

In Figure 8–2, an illustration is provided of the directions to respondents that might be used when employing the response technique. In the figure the directions for completing *The Hidden-Response Survey* are provided. The survey deals with students' high-risk behaviors associated with becoming infected with HIV (the AIDS virus). In Figure 8–3, an illustrative response sheet is supplied for *The Hidden Response Survey* referred to in Figure 8–2.

FIGURE 8–2 • *An Illustration of Directions for Completing a Randomized Response Survey*

THE HIDDEN-RESPONSE SURVEY

Directions: The survey that you will soon receive contains several personal questions about behaviors related to someone's becoming infected with HIV (the AIDS virus). In view of the seriousness of AIDS, it is necessary to get honest answers from people about these behaviors. However, because the questions are so personal, people often feel uncomfortable about supplying honest answers. Therefore, a special hidden response survey is being used so that you can answer the questions honestly, yet nobody can ever connect you with your answers. As you will see, your answers can be honest because they will be *absolute secret*. There is no way to link any responses to a particular individual.

The survey you will receive contains several pairs of questions. You are to answer *only one* question in each pair. The first question in each pair will ask you a yes-or-no odd/even question about whether there is an even number of letters (2, 4, 6, 8, etc.) in the name of some person that you know. The second question in each pair will ask you a yes-or-no personal question. Remember, you are to answer only one question in each of the pairs. *Only you will know* which one of the questions in each pair you have answered. Presented below is a sample of one of these question pairs. As you can see, the first question (Heads) is an Odd/even question and the second question (Tails) is a personal question.

Sample Question Pair

(Heads)   *Odd/Even:* Think of the name (first or last) of someone you know. Is there an even number of letters (2, 4, 6, 8, etc.) in that person's name?

(Tails)   *Personal:* Have you ever *deliberately* lied to a friend?

Your answer to the question in this pair (check one):   Yes ☐   No ☐

FIGURE 8 .2 • *Continued*

You will need to use a coin to determine which question in each pair to answer. If you do not have a coin, please ask the person administering the survey to loan you a coin.

To decide which of the two questions in each pair you should answer, put the coin in a space formed by cupping your two hands together. Shake the coin vigorously, then look carefully into your cupped hands so that *only you* can see whether the coin shows heads or tails. If it shows heads, answer the first question in the pair. If it shows tails, answer the second question in the pair. Once you know which question you are to answer, check the box that matches your answer. As you see in the sample question pair, there is only one yes box and one no box for each pair of questions. These boxes can be used for either question in the pair. You are to repeat this process for each pair of questions on the survey form. Remember, *only you will know which question you are answering* in each question pair.

If your coin shows heads and you need to answer the odd/even question, think of anyone you know, for instance, a friend, family member, or teacher. You can use either the person's first name or last name. For example, if you were thinking of a friend whose name was Frank, then you would answer no to the odd/even question because there are five letters in Frank's name, and five is an odd number, not an even number. If you aren't sure how to spell the person's name, make your best guess. If you need to answer more than one odd/even question, please use the name of a different person for each new question.

Because there is a 50-50 chance that a person's name contains an odd (or even) number of letters, it is possible to estimate the yes/no responses to the odd/even questions. And because only you will know the name of the person you are thinking about, it should be clear that nobody can tell what any one student's yes or no response means. For large groups of students, however, it is possible to make reasonably accurate estimates based on probabilities.

Now, practice responding to the sample question pair on the previous page by using the cupped-hand coin shake. Remember, it is important for you to answer the odd/even question or the personal question based on whether the coin comes up heads or tails. If the coin comes up heads every time, then you should answer the "heads" question (the odd/even question) in each pair.

Remember, don't choose which of the questions in a question pair to answer. The question that you answer *must* be determined by probabilities, that is, by whether the coin comes up heads or tails. It is by using probabilities that the yes or no responses to each question can be accurately estimated for groups of students (not for an individual student).

When you have supplied a yes or no answer for all question pairs, immediately fold the survey form once that your answers cannot be seen. Your completed survey form will be personally placed by you in a box or large manila envelope. Students' surveys will then be shuffled before being taken from the room. Do *not* put your name on the survey. As you can see, your answers will be absolutely secret. So, please answer honestly.

FIGURE 8–3 • *An Illustrative Response Sheet for the Randomized Response Technique*

THE HIDDEN-RESPONSE SURVEY

Please do *not* put your name on this form.

Question Pair Number 1

(Heads)   *Odd/Even:* Think of the name (first or last) of someone you know. Is there an *even* number of letters (2, 4, 6, 8, etc.) in that person's name?

(Tails)   *Personal:* Have you had any kind of sexual intercourse *in the last 30 days?*

                                                Yes No

Your answer to the question in this pair (check one): ☐   ☐

Question Pair Number 2

(Heads)   *Odd/Even:* Think of the name (first or last) of someone you know. Is there an even number of letters (2, 4, 6, 8, etc.) in that person's name?

(Tails)   *Personal:* Have you had sexual intercourse with two or more different partners *in the last year?*

                                                Yes No

Your answer to the question in this pair (check one): ☐   ☐

Question Pair Number 3

(Heads)   *Odd/Even:* Think of the name (first or last) of someone you know. Is there an *even* number of letters (2, 4, 6, 8, etc.) in that person's name?

(Tails)   *Personal:* Have you *ever* shared needles or other equipment to inject (shoot up) drugs such as heroin or steroids?

                                              Yes No

Your answer to the question in this pair (check one): ☐   ☐

Question Pair Number 4

(Heads)   *Odd/Even:* Think of the name (first or last) of someone you know. Is there an *even* number of letters (2, 4, 6, 8, etc.) in that person's name?

(Tails)   *Personal: In the last year*, have you injected (shot up) heroin, steroids, or any other drugs?

                                              Yes No

Your answer to the question in this pair (check one): ☐   ☐

Determining Estimated Responses to Personal Questions

Once responses have been collected, the next task is to arrive at estimates of the number of yes and no responses to the personal question. Using the same example as presented in Figures 8–2 and 8–3, the following scoring directions could be employed:

> By following the step-by-step procedure presented below, the percentage of yes responses to the personal question in each pair can be estimated. For ease of illustration, it will be assumed that 1,000 total responses are involved.

> *Step 1:* Sum the number of yes and no responses for both questions in a question-pair. To illustrate, for 1,000 respondents, let's say there were 300 yes responses and 700 no responses to a question pair.

> *Step 2:* Determine the estimated number of yes and no responses that were made to the odd/even (heads) question. To do so, divide all responses in half then multiply the resulting number by .50 to get an estimate of the no responses to the odd/even question and .50 to get an estimate of the yes responses to the odd/even question. In this illustration, we would have divided the 1,000 by 2, then multiplied the resulting 500 by .50 to estimate the no responses and by .50 to estimate the yes responses. This yields 250 estimated no responses and 250 estimated yes responses for the odd/even question.

> *Step 3:* Subtract these odd/even response estimates (Step 2), from the total responses (Step 1). In this example, we would have:

700 No	(total responses)	300 Yes
−250 No	(estimated responses to odd/even questions)	−250 Yes
450 No	(estimated respones to personal question)	50 Yes

> *Step 4:* The estimated yes/no rates should be regarded as approximate response rates for the personal question. In the example, this yields a 10 percent positive estimated response rate (50 yes responses out of 500) to the personal question.

> Allowances must be made for respondents' reluctance to report sensitive behaviors accurately and for imprecision in the probability estimates. Nonetheless, even though the percentage estimates for personal questions are based only on probabilistic estimates, with a relatively large number of respondents, it has been shown that the use of the randomized response technique often yields more accurate estimates of respondents' sensitive behaviors than would be obtainable by more conventional self-report assessment devices. Figure 8–4 graphically depicts this scoring procedure.

Applications

As was noted earlier, the randomized response technique has not been widely used in educational evaluation. Among the reasons that the technique has not been

FIGURE 8-4 • *How the Randomized Response Technique Works (Using an Illustration of 1,000 Respondents)*

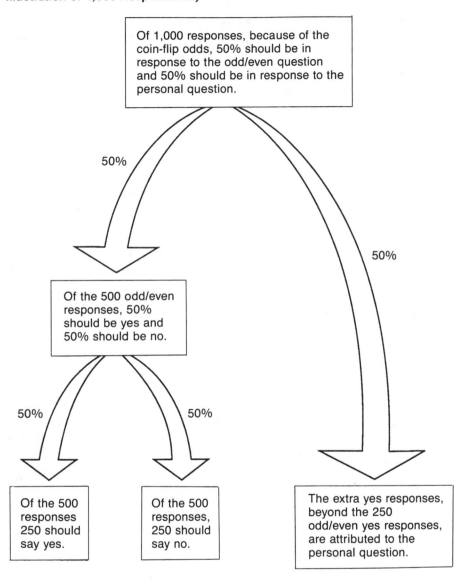

applied are the need for large samples and the relative infrequency with which educational evaluators must gather data regarding highly sensitive questions. After all, for every evaluation survey about students' sexual practices, there must be a hundred tests dealing with reading achievement. However, under the appropriate circumstances, the randomized response technique can be a highly useful assessment approach for educational evaluators.

Indirect Assessment

Sometimes an educational evaluator will need to measure a variable that, quite literally, eludes assessment. In such circumstances, the evaluator is often obliged to employ indirect assessment tactics because direct measurement schemes simply will not work. To illustrate this general approach, an example will be drawn from the experiences of those evaluators who are working with school-based HIV education programs for students.

The Problem

It is generally conceded that individuals' perceptions of their personal vulnerability to potentially undesirable consequences play an important role in their adoption of behaviors that will help them avoid such consequences. With respect to HIV infection, this means that individuals who perceive themselves to be genuinely at risk of becoming infected with HIV will tend to engage in fewer high-risk behaviors than those who perceive themselves to be at little or no risk of HIV infection.

Experience suggests that young people often tend to regard themselves as invulnerable to health calamities; that is, they see themselves at no risk of becoming seriously ill. Yet, students' adoption of reduced HIV-risk behaviors would seem to hinge, at least to some extent, on their recognition that young people who engage in such behaviors as unprotected sexual intercourse or needle sharing are at a substantial risk of becoming infected with HIV. Not surprisingly, therefore, HIV education programs often emphasize that many students are truly at risk of being infected with HIV. It is assumed that if students believe they are actually at risk of HIV infection, they will tend to adopt behaviors to reduce the perceived risk.

Unfortunately, direct attempts to measure students' perceived vulnerability to HIV infection have proved strikingly unsuccessful. In contrast to asking students to estimate their personal vulnerability to *treatable* health problems such as, for example, obesity or high blood pressure, when we ask students to estimate their likelihood of becoming infected with HIV, we are asking about what is currently an *irreversible*, terminal disease. Faced with the gravity of such an illness, most students simply are unable or unwilling to supply realistic estimates of their current vulnerability even if they intellectually recognize that prior high-risk behaviors might have put them at risk of HIV infection.

An Indirect Assessment Technique

To circumvent this assessment obstacle, the Past and Future Survey was created to supply an indirect indication of students' perceptions of their vulnerability to HIV infection. Students are simply asked three questions, each of which deals with an important HIV-risk behavior. Each question asks students to compare their intended behavior in the next three months with their actual behavior during the past three months. Each question is followed by response options that allow inferences to be made about whether students intend to be: (1) more careful, (2) less careful, or (3) about as careful as they were before. If students' responses indicate that they

FIGURE 8–5 • *Questions from the Past and Future Survey*

---

1. Choosing Sexual Partners: In the next three months, compared with the way I've acted in the last three months, I plan to:
A. be sexually abstinent.
B. have fewer sexual partners than before.
C. have the same number of sexual partners as before.
D. have more sexual partners than before.

P Q R S T U V W X Y Z A B C D E F G H I J K L M N O

2. Using Condoms (during Sexual Intercourse): In the next three months, compared with the way I've acted in the last three months, I plan to:
A. be sexually abstinent.
B. use a condom with my partner(s) more often than before.
C. use a condom with my partner(s) just as often as before.
D. use a condom with my partner(s) less often than before.

T U V W X Y Z A B C D E F G H I J K L M N O P Q R S

3. Needle Sharing (to Inject Drugs or Steroids): In the next three months, compared to the way I've acted in the last three months, I plan to:
A. share no needles at all.
B. share needles less often than before.
C. share needles just as often as before.
D. share needles more often than before.

I J K L M N O P Q R S T U V W X Y Z A B C D E F G H

---

intend to be more careful, it can be argued that one factor in their heightened intentions to behave more safely is their heightened perception of vulnerability. It is surely the case that other variables might influence students' increased intentions to engage in safe behaviors, but this assessment device is predicated on the belief that *one* major determinant of an individual's intention to behave more safely is that individual's perception of vulnerability. This instrument, therefore, represents an indirect way of gauging individuals' perceptions of vulnerability to HIV infection. Although it may appear to yield an estimate of behavioral intent, it really uses students' behavioral intentions as vehicles for ascertaining the extent to which students believe themselves to be at risk of becoming infected with HIV.

An effective HIV education program, then, would generally lead to heightened (and, typically, more realistic) perceptions of students' HIV vulnerability. The major exception to this would be if the program were provided for students whose behaviors, in fact, place the students at relatively low risk of HIV infection. Such would be the case, for example, if the prevalence of students' HIV-risk behaviors was exceedingly low. The prevalence of HIV-risk behaviors, of course, would need to be established through other assessment instruments such as the Super Secret Survey and The Hidden-Response Survey described earlier in the chapter.

In Figure 8–5 the three questions presented in the Past and Future Survey are given. Note that the alphabet-soup response scheme is employed with this instrument. For each of the instrument's three questions, one response indicates an intention on the part of the respondent to engage in safer practices. For all three questions, that "safer" response is option B. To score this instrument, simply calculate the percentage of students who choose response B for each question, then compare these percentages on a preprogram to postprogram basis. The more movement toward safer responses (determined on a question-by-question basis or, if desired, by averaging all three "safer" response percentages), the more it would appear that students believe themselves to be at potential risk of becoming infected with HIV.

The indirect assessment approach represented in this illustrative measuring device should make it clear that there are times when educational evaluators will need to be more than a little circumventious. If direct assessment doesn't fill the bill, then opt for less direct measurement schemes. Clearly, in some instances this will oblige evaluators to get their creative juices bubbling.

Reprise

To review, this chapter has illustrated that educational evaluators must frequently employ assessment tactics that are decisively different than the run-of-the-mill multiple-choice achievement test or the one-size-fits-all Likert attitude inventory. The more elusive the assessment target, the more creative that the evaluator will need to be; however, dealing creatively with challenges is where most of the evaluator's fun really resides.

Discussion Questions

1. Participant-satisfaction evaluation forms are routinely, if unthinkingly, used at the close of workshops and other short-duration instructional programs for adults. Either from your personal experience, or based on your reactions to this chapter's rules for constructing such forms, what do you think are the greatest shortcomings in such forms or in the way that they are used?

2. In your view, what kinds of information would be "sensitive"; that is, what kinds of information would students (or adults) be reluctant to supply honestly?

3. What ways can you think of, other than those described in the chapter, to gather sensitive information so that decision makers have confidence in the accuracy of the information?

4. Can you think of situations in which educational evaluators might wish to employ the randomized response technique? What are those situations?

5. In your view, what are the advantages

and disadvantages of the randomized response technique?

6. Can you think of several situations in which the assessment of Variable x is so difficult that it becomes necessary to assess it indirectly via Variable y? What do these situations have in common?

Practice Exercise

To gain some practice in applying the five rules for constructing participant-satisfaction evaluation forms described in the chapter, a specially created participant-satisfaction evaluation form has been provided on the following page. Please review that form and decide which, if any, of the chapter's five rules have been violated. After reviewing the form, you may refer to the Answers to Practice Exercises in which there is a discussion of the extent to which the illustrative evaluation form was consistent with the five rules presented in the chapter. For purposes of this exercise,

assume that the evaluation form is to be used at the close of an HIV staff-development program for teachers and principals of a midsize rural school district. The class met on three Saturdays for four hours each session.

The evaluation form was constructed specifically to provide an opportunity to apply the five rules previously described. It should *not* be regarded as an exemplary participant-satisfaction evaluation form for an HIV staff-development program. Indeed, violations of certain rules were deliberately incorporated in the illustrative form.

Answers to Practice Exercise

Each of the five rules is considered below in relation to the illustration form:

Rule 1: Clarity—Although much of the form is clearly written, question 5, which deals with logistical arrangements, is particularly unclear. (Such polysyllabic obfuscation is to be eschewed!) Also related to Rule 1, note that the response format used for the demographic items (check-mark spaces to the right) has been altered for the program evaluation questions (check-mark spaces to the left). Such inconsistencies, although minor, can confuse respondents.

Rule 2: Decision Focus—The evaluation form seems a bit schizophrenic in relationship to this rule. A few of the questions (e.g., 3 and 4) seem potentially relevant to a program-related decision that might be made. Most questions, however, are not. For example, given the considerable generality of question 1, of what practical value will participants' ratings of relevance be? Surely, some content of the workshop was more relevant than other

content. We won't be able to tell, from participants' responses, which is which. In addition, participants may have varying perceptions of the distinction between somewhat relevant and moderately relevant, rendering the response classifications in Question 1 ambiguous.

Incidentally, question 2 is a good example of an item that is not decision focused for a rather unusual reason, The question asks participants (who are supposedly being *taught* about a topic) to rate the technical accuracy of the workshop's content. If educators are being taught about a topic, they are surely not in a position to comment on the technical accuracy of the workshop's content. Although the technical accuracy of a workshop's content should be scrutinized by competent personnel, those individuals are invariably *not* program participants. Question 2 is not decision focused because it's really quite absurd.

Rule 3: Brevity—This one-page form wins with respect to terseness. Participants will be apt to take seriously a short docu-

Continued

AN ILLUSTRATIVE PARTICIPANT-SATISFACTION EVALUATION FORM

Directions: Please evaluate this staff-development program in order that future programs can be made more effective. *Do not* place your name on the form. All of your answers are to be totally nonymous. When you are finished, please deposit the form in the box marked "Evaluation Forms" as you leave the room.

Participant Demographic Data (Check one response for each item.)
Age: Under 25 ____, 26–35 ____, 36–45 ____, 46 or over ____
Sex: Male ____, Female ____
Ethnicity: Black ____, White ____, Hispanic ____, Other ____
Position: Administrator ____, Teacher ____   Grade Level: K–6 ____, 7–9 ____, 10–12 ____

Program Evaluation Questions (Check *one* response per question.)

1. What was your general impression of the relevance of the workshop's content for your own work?
   ____ Highly Relevant, ____ Somewhat Relevant, ____ Moderately Relevant,
   ____ Moderately Irrelevant, ____ Somewhat Irrelevant, ____ Highly Irrelevant
   Comments:

2. What was your impression of the technical accuracy of the workshop's content?
   ____ Accurate, ____ Somewhat Accurate, ____ Inaccurate
   Comments:

3. Which one of the following workshop features, in your view, was *most* effective?
   ____ General Session Lectures, ____ Small-Group Discussions, ____ Paired-Participant Exercises
   Comments:

4. Which one of the following workshop features, in your view, was *least* effective?
   ____ General Session Lectures, ____ Small-Group Discussions, ____ Paired-Participant Exercises
   Comments:

5. In pondering the logistical arrangements for the workshop, particularly those aspects that, though not directly related to the workshop's instructional foci, were nonetheless germane, how would you characterize them?
   ____ Appropriate, ____ Uncertain, ____ Inappropriate
   Comments:

6. Do you have any additional suggestions for improving the workshop? If so, please supply your suggestions on the reverse side of this sheet.

Thank you for completing this evaluation form.

Note: This form was specifically developed to illustrate certain strengths and weaknesses in form-construction.

ment such as this. Even so, however, note that at the close the participants are still thanked for completing the form. That's a nice touch because, whether a one-page or a multi-page form, evaluators are asking participants to help them by evaluating a staff-development program. Evaluators owe participants a thank you.

Rule 4: Anonymity—This illustrative form loses out on Rule 4 in two ways. First, by asking for handwritten comments on the form itself, anonymity is reduced. Second, because the fictitious workshop was being offered in a midsize school district, responses to the demographic data section would almost certainly enable one to identify the individual who completed the evaluation form. Although the demographic data section is fairly standard, one has to wonder what the relevance of most of the data would be to actual program-related decisions.

In the introductory "Directions" paragraph, however, there was a plea for anonymity (no names, please) as well as a nice notion about depositing completed forms in a box upon leaving. Unfortunately, these anonymity-enhancing ploys were overwhelmed by the two anonymity-reducing problems previously noted.

Rule 5: Suggestions—The evaluation form closed out with question 6 asking for additional suggestions. If that request had been on a *separate* form, that is, a form separate from a check-off-only form, then participant anonymity would have been better preserved and Rule 5 would have been sensibly satisfied.

On balance, although there are several positive features in this illustrative form, overall it is unlikely to yield the sort of participant-satisfaction data apt to improve a staff-development program. Distressingly, the sorts of deficits noted in this form are found far too frequently in such evaluation forms. Participant-satisfaction evaluation forms must be crafted with care. If not, evaluators should not waste participants' time with them.

Note

1. This was developed as part of the project funded by the Division of Adolescent and School Health of the Centers for Disease Control, U.S. Public Health Services.

Selected References

Boruch, Robert F. "The President's Mandate: Discovering What Works and What Works Better." In Milbrey W. McLaughlin and D. C. Phillips (Eds.), *Evaluation and Education: At Quarter Century*. Chicago: University of Chicago Press, 1991, pp. 147–67.

Campbell, C., and B. L. Joiner. "How to Get the Answer Without Being Sure You've Asked the Question." *The American Statistician*, 27 (1973): 227–31.

DeVellis, Robert F. *Scale Development:* *Theory and Applications* (vol. 26). Newbury Park, CA: Sage, 1991.

Ewell, Peter T. "To Capture the Ineffable: New Forms of Assessment in Higher Education." In Gerald Grant (Ed.), *Review of Research in Education*. Washington, DC: American Educational Research Association, 1991, pp. 75–126.

Greenberg, B. G., R. R. Kuebler, Jr., J. R. Abernathy, and D. G. Horvitz. "Application of the Randomized Response Technique in Obtaining Quantitative Data." *Journal of the*

American Statistical Association, 66, 1971, pp. 227–31.

Gronlund, Norman E., and Robert L. Linn. *Measurement and Evaluation in Teaching* (6th ed.). New York: Macmillan, 1990.

Hopkins, Charles D., and Richard L. Antes. *Classroom Measurement and Evaluation* (3rd ed.). Itasca, IL: Peacock, 1990.

Martin, G. L., and I. A. Newman. "Randomized Response: A Technique for Improving the Validity of Self-Reported Health Behaviors." *The Journal of School Health* (1982): 222–226.

Sax, Gilbert. *Principles of Educational and*

Psychological Measurement and Evaluation (3rd ed.). Belmont, CA: Wadsworth, 1989.

Shimizu, I. M., and G. S. Bonham. "Randomized Response Technique in a National Survey." *Journal of the American Statistical Association*, 73 (1978): 35–39.

Warner, S. L. "Randomized Response: A Survey Technique for Eliminating Evasive Answer Bias." *Journal of the American Statistician Association*, 60 (1965): 63–69.

Wiersma, William, and Stephen G. Jurs. *Educational Measurement and Testing* (2nd ed.). Boston: Allyn and Bacon, 1990.

CHAPTER NINE

Focus Groups: A Potent Qualitative Data-Gathering Procedure

During the last few decades, behavioral scientists have been increasingly drawn to the virtues of *focus group interviews* as a method of securing useful qualitative data. Focus groups have been employed for diverse purposes such as market research regarding how well a newly created product is apt to sell: "Is the world really ready for Guacopops, a new avocado-flavored cereal shaped like tortilla chips?" Focus groups have also been used to determine how television audiences are likely to respond to new commercials such as one touting the virtues of Bland, a nonalcoholic, noncaloric, and essentially nonflavored soft drink.

Beyond these more obviously commercial applications of focus group interviews, researchers and evaluators have found that a focus group represents an efficient method of gathering needed data. Focus groups, for example, can provide particularly useful *qualitative* insights regarding those research questions or program-related decisions that cannot be adequately addressed by *quantitatively* oriented data-gathering schemes. Because educational evaluators can employ focus group interviews to help illuminate a number of program-related decisions, this chapter will be devoted to a description of this increasingly popular data-gathering strategy and how it can be used in the formative and summative evaluation of educational programs.[1]

More specifically, we'll be taking a look at three major topics in the chapter. First, we will consider a formal definition of focus group interviews, then take a brief look at their origins as well as their strengths and weaknesses. Second, we'll dig into the nuts and bolts of focus groups, that is, how to plan and conduct a focus group interview. Finally, we'll face the practical problem of how to analyze a focus group's qualitative data.

If you don't already know all that much about focus groups, this chapter obviously will not transform you into a focus group wizard or even a focus group groupie. However, the chapter should provide you with sufficient understanding and insight regarding the role of focus group interviews in educational evaluation so that you will know whether you wish to acquire a deeper understanding of this technique. (There are several excellent treatments of focus groups listed at the close of the chapter that dig more deeply into the innards of this group-interview procedure.) You may also be stimulated to try a hand at personally running a focus group interview to see how comfortable you are in planning and conducting focus groups. As with swimming, some folks find that jumping into the focus group waters is a wonderful way to find out whether they're floaters or sinkers.

Focus Group Fundamentals

The Nature of Focus Groups

What are focus groups and where did they come from? Although there are some variations in the definitions supplied by focus group specialists, the following description of a focus group is fairly standard:

> A focus group consists of a relatively small number of homogeneous individuals who provide qualitative data during a moderated, interactive group interview.

Typically, there are between 8 and 12 participants in a focus group interview (typically referred to merely as a *focus group*). Most focus group sessions last from $1^{1}/_{2}$ to $2^{1}/_{2}$ hours. The focus group is almost always made up of people who are homogeneous, the nature of the group's similarity being determined by the evaluator's purpose. For example, if the evaluator were attempting to secure reactions of students to a newly installed high school curriculum dealing with sexually transmitted diseases, then the participants in the focus group would obviously be high school students.

It is especially important for the individuals in focus groups not to know each other. People who know one another tend to let the nature of their past interactions influence how they behave during the focus group session. When people know one another, this also tends to inhibit their forthrightness during the discussion. Using the previous example about high school students discussing sexually transmitted diseases, for instance, suppose that there were participants present who had previously been romantically linked. Might not Molly be just a mite reluctant to speak candidly in the focus group if she knew that *two* of her former steady boyfriends were also focus group members?

Although an ideal focus group is composed of total strangers, there are situations in which this is a practical impossibility. Nonetheless, no close friends, people who work together, or members of one family should be permitted to take part in the same focus group. Although, as we shall see, practical realities often oblige those using focus groups to bend focus group rules when actually carrying out such sessions, adherence to the "strangers-only" rule is particularly important. Experience with countless focus groups has shown that when participants do not know one another, they are more likely to address with honesty the questions introduced by the moderator. When participants *do* know one another, personal histories often get in the way of candor.

Each focus group is led by a moderator (and often an assistant moderator) who attempts to keep the discussion targeted at the issues of interest but encourages participants to respond to each other's views. In other words, a focus group interview is not a series of question-and-answer interchanges between the moderator and different participants. Instead, the moderator strives to nurture a lively, illuminating discussion among those present. The moderator, as we shall see later in the chapter, plans carefully for the focus group interview so that all key points to be addressed by the group are, in fact, considered. The effective moderator, well versed in interviewing ploys and group dynamics, might be rather directive or quite the opposite. A nondirective moderator, for example, would allow a discussion to proceed with no interruptions if the group interchanges remain on the topic to be addressed.

As noted in the definition of focus groups, the thrust of these activities is to garner *qualitative*, not quantitative, data. Focus groups should not be sessions in which the moderator, or the moderator's assistant, count the number of times that participants make certain kinds of comments about Product X or Topic Z. At the close of the chapter, we will consider ways of analyzing the sorts of qualitative data typically yielded by focus groups. Rest assured that "counting" will not be the cornerstone of such data-analysis procedures.

The Ancestry of Focus Groups

Focus group interviews were born over a half-century ago, but only in the last couple of decades have focus groups captured the imagination of behavioral scientists. How did this data-gathering methodology come into existence?

The stage was set for focus groups in the late 1930s when psychologists and other behavioral researchers began to recognize the data-gathering limitations of highly structured one-on-one interviews. Some rumblings began to be registered among social scientists regarding the virtues of these structured interviews. Such interviews were, in fact, little more than orally administered questionnaires containing selected-response options for the interviewee. Because interviewees were limited in the number of response options available to them, it was believed that potentially valuable information was not being supplied to the interviewer. Nondirective interviewing, embodying open-ended versus closed-ended responses, were offered as a way of combatting the shortcomings of traditional interviews by a number of social scientists, including Carl Rogers.

It was against this backdrop of a search for alternative interviewing methods that Columbia University's Robert Merton and Paul Lazarsfeld devised a research technique that, in time, became the focus group interview. Lazarsfeld and Merton employed a studio audience to gauge the responses of listeners to recorded radio programs. As the program was played, those in the studio audience were to press a green button whenever they experienced a positive reaction to the program and a red button whenever they experienced a negative reaction. By recording the audience's responses and linking them to the time that certain parts of the radio program had been presented, it was possible to isolate those segments of the radio program evoking positive or negative responses. When the radio program was concluded, members of the audience were asked to *focus* on the positive and negative segments they had identified. Thus was born the focused group interview.

During World War II, Merton and his associates applied focus group interviews to the appraisal of training films being created by the armed forces. Merton's work led to the publication of a journal article[2] and, later, a book dealing with focus group procedures.[3] Not surprisingly, although the essentials of today's focus group interviews are similar to those developed by Merton and his co-workers, there have been numerous modifications over the years. With greater experience, decisive improvements took place in the way to carry out focus groups.

Moreover, focus groups began to be used in all sorts of arenas. Even though focus groups are widely used in market research, particularly for the preliminary appraisal of new products or services, focus group methodology has also been applied to a range of advertising, public policy, and program evaluation settings. Focus groups are also sometimes used to help film directors decide how to end their movies. A film may be created with two or more possible endings, then the alternate endings are tried out to determine which conclusion the focus groups find more satisfying. The focus groups in this instance clearly function as a surrogate for the "real" movie audience. If Ending C is preferred over Ending A and Ending B, then future filmgoers can expect to see Ending C at their neighborhood theaters.

Clearly, because focus groups have become so widely used during the last 20 years, they must have something to commend them. Focus groups are not a fad that, previously regarded as a cherished technique of only qualitatively oriented researchers, passed out of favor after a few years in the spotlight. Focus groups have had genuine staying power. Therefore, we should consider what the advantages of focus groups are. Having done so, of course, fairness demands that we set forth some of the disadvantages of focus groups. After looking at the strengths and weaknesses of focus groups, we'll then see how to plan and carry out a focus group interview.

Advantages of Focus Group Interviews

When considering the advantages of focus group interviews, it is important to recall that some of these virtues are also associated with individual interviews. For example, moderators of focus groups can listen to a group member's comment, then follow up with probing questions in order to understand more fully what the individual means. One-on-one interviewers can do the same. Similarly, focus group moderators can observe group members' nonverbal responses such as smiles, grimaces, and so on. One-on-one interviewers can also make such observations. Focus group interviews can be quite open ended and nondirective in nature. One-on-one interviews can be too. In other words, whether conducted in a group or individual basis, *interviews* have some decisive advantages over questionnaires. By the same token, when compared to the use of questionnaires, there are disadvantages of interviews such as an increased cost per respondent and the necessity to use properly trained interviewers. In isolating both the strengths and weaknesses of focus groups, we'll try to stress those features that stem from the group-based nature of this data-gathering technique.

Inhibition Reduction   The first advantage of focus groups derives from the presence of 8 to 12 interviewees. As you will soon see, members of a focus group are usually not required to respond to a question. In other words, people can "pass" on any question they don't wish to answer. This reduction of pressure to respond makes it possible for participants to respond only when they really wish to—thus engendering a degree of spontaneity so that responses tend to be more reflective of an individual's real beliefs.

Moreover, if a focus group is properly moderated, participants will not feel that they are forced to defend their views. They can derive a degree of security from recognizing that their feelings are often similar to those of other participants. In a one-on-one interview, interviewees may be reluctant to reveal that they are "different" from others, hence suppress their most fundamental views. In a group setting, however, the support—whether real or perceived—from other members of the group often reduces inhibitions and leads to more candid responses than can be obtained from almost any other type of data-gathering procedure.

Synergism   The interaction of discrete agents such that the total effect exceeds the sum of the individual effects is referred to as *synergism*. If you ever want to see synergism in action, simply drop in on a properly conducted focus group. The synergistic payoffs of focus group interviews constitute a *distinctive* advantage of this data-gathering technique. The group's combined insights will often exceed by far the total of individual members' insights because a comment by one participant will trigger a new insight for another participant whose comments will, in turn, stimulate another member's new way of viewing the problem.

The interactive nature of focus group interviews is, indeed, pivotal to the payoffs of this data-gathering approach because a wider array of insights and information will often be yielded by the collaborative *social* nature of the data gathering. Human beings are social creatures. We become civilized on the basis of our interactions with family, friends, and strangers. The focus group interview capitalizes on participants' social strengths by allowing them to function as members of a short-duration mini-society. The synergistic payoffs are often quite astonishing.

Understandability of Results   The third advantage of focus groups is that the results from such sessions can be portrayed in a readily understandable form. As you will see later in the chapter, the results of focus groups are frequently described in a manner that is easily comprehended by decision makers. Because focus group data are based on the comments of typical individuals, such data are far easier to understand than, say, a raft of exotic statistical results accompanied by significance tests and confidence intervals. Moreover, because the data from focus groups are qualitative in nature, it is possible to present subtle shadings and nuances that would be difficult to represent by quantitative schemes.

Later in the chapter it will be pointed out that there is often substantial difficulty in accurately depicting what really goes on in a focus group session. However, if properly reported, the results of focus groups are easily understood by decision makers who, in general, wish to be guided by understandable evidence. Because group discussions have been a part of almost everyone's experience, the results of such discussions are readily comprehended by most people.

Rapidly Implementable   A fourth advantage of focus groups is that the evaluator can put them into operation in relatively short order. The stress in the former sentence should be on the word *relatively*, for it will be seen later that you can not devise a sensible focus group during your morning tooth brushing. However, when you compare the time needed to set up and carry out focus groups with the time to implement almost any competing data-gathering strategy, focus groups turn out to be far quicker.

Think about the time that you would need to devote to designing and conducting something as simple as a self-report questionnaire in order to gather data from a group of school administrators. Not only are there sometimes all sorts of obstacles in simply getting permission to poll the administrators but the development of the questionnaire itself takes time. Then, when the myriad permissions have finally been secured to distribute the questionnaires, the response rate is often paltry. School administrators, after all, are a busy lot. In other words, to secure truly credible data from almost any data-gathering approach, you will find that most of these approaches take far longer than focus groups to set up, carry out, and report. Focus groups, on the other hand, can be carried out in comparatively short order, yet yield evidence that can often be quite compelling. Although there are numerous instances in which quicker is not better, there are some data-gathering settings where quicker wins. In those settings, focus groups are frequently first to the finish line.

Low Cost   The fifth and final advantage of focus groups that we will address is their relatively low cost. Again, the emphasis must be on *relative*, for focus groups cannot be conducted for a pittance. However, when you stack up the cost of conducting a set of, say, six focus groups against the cost of carrying out a raft of one-on-one interviews, focus groups win hands down. If evaluators have a sharply limited budget for their data gathering, then the potential of focus groups should be considered. It is not that focus groups are cheap. Rather, it is that in order to yield credible data, many other data-gathering schemes are far more costly.

There are, of course, other virtues of focus groups, such as they are one of the few forms of data gathering suitable for use with illiterate populations (including very young children). However, the five advantages of focus groups identified above should give you a good idea of the payoffs of this qualitative data-gathering strategy. To review, then, the chief advantages of focus groups are set forth below.

Advantages of Focus Groups

1. Because focus groups are rooted in social interactions, they lessen participants' inhibitions.
2. The collective contributions of focus-group participants often yield synergistic gains.
3. The results of focus groups are readily understandable.
4. Focus groups can be quickly implemented.
5. Focus groups are relatively inexpensive.

Disadvantages of Focus Group Interviews

With focus groups, as with most aspects of life, the greatest virtue of a particular approach often turns out to be its greatest vice. Certain of the previously cited advantages of focus groups can, with a twist or two, be seen as a disadvantage of focus groups. Let's look at five disadvantages of focus groups to counterbalance their five previously cited advantages. (Five strengths versus five weaknesses seems so enormously equitable.)

Less Control   The initial disadvantage of focus group interviews is that the data gatherer clearly relinquishes a degree of control. Because the focus group moderator is relying on group interactions, there's less certainty about which direction the group interaction will take. A skillful moderator, of course, can get the group back on target. After all, that's why it is called a *focus* group interview. However, it sometimes requires the moderator to expend serious energy in impeding a stampeding discussion that's heading off in an undesired direction. With printed survey forms or with standard one-on-one interviews, of course, there's much more control by the data gatherer.

In some focus groups, particularly those with a few strong-willed participants, it is exceedingly difficult for the moderator to keep the group on task without being abrasive. Thus, although control ultimately resides in the hands of focus group moderators, there's no doubt that focus groups carry with them a reduced degree of control.

Labor-Intensive Data Analysis   As with most qualitative data-gathering strategies, there are substantial obstacles in reducing the data to a usable form. In focus groups, after all, even if the session is tape-recorded (as it often is) or even if there is an assistant moderator taking copious notes, there are still all sorts of difficulties in deciding what is important to report and what can be forgotten. What one has at the close of a round of focus group sessions is a gigantic pile of words, some of which are significant and most of which are not. The trick is to sort out which is which in an objective, accurate manner, then portray the results in a form palatable to busy decision makers. After all, one could simply place verbatim transcriptions of a dozen focus group interviews on a decision maker's desk, but such a don't-lose-a-word approach is certain to be viewed with disdain by any sensible decision maker.

Until you have personally been faced with a stack of focus-group transcripts or detailed summaries of focus groups, it is difficult to comprehend the difficulty of engaging in accurate data reduction. When you have been through that sort of data-analysis trauma a time or two, however, you'll truly understand why data analysis constitutes a not insuperable but clearly prominent disadvantage of focus group interviews.

Distortional Effect of Interactions The third disadvantage of focus groups is, not surprisingly, the flip side of the advantages that focus groups gain from their interactive nature. Focus groups operate because of their participants. If there are dominant or opinionated members in a focus group, those individuals may excessively influence other members or even intimidate them into reticence. Although a skilled moderator will try to minimize the adverse impact of such strong group members, it may be difficult to do. In the same vein, the collective direction of a group may disincline certain participants to express their views because those views seem out of step with the remainder of the group's views. In other words, even if there aren't any dominating group members present, the subtle pressure of the group's dispositions may incline some participants to succumb to the group's preferences or, at least, to avoid disagreement.

Limited Generalizability Focus groups are idiosyncratic in their composition. Often, in fact, the members of focus groups have been selected because they are willing to take part in a two-hour interview session. Such factors disincline some decision makers to generalize from focus group results. For instance, it could be argued that the individuals who would agree to take part in an extended interview session are not typical of the general populace. Then, too, the actual numbers of individuals who take part in a round of focus groups is usually quite small in relationship to the group of individuals to whom one wishes to generalize the focus group findings. Many decision makers are downright skeptical of the generalizability of focus group findings.

Self-Service A fifth disadvantage of focus groups, and one closely related to the concern about the generalizability of focus group findings, is that focus groups can be used to justify almost any view desired by the focus group researcher. For example, suppose an advertising agency is trying out a new series of early-version television commercials with a number of focus groups to forestall expensive investment in full-blown television production. In the focus group sessions, the ad agency only uses printed scripts and story boards (simple artistic renditions) of what the commercials will ultimately be. If the focus groups find the prospective commercials inappropriate, then theoretically the ad agency will look for alternatives. Yet, and this is important, the ad agency personnel who are sometimes influential in the interpretation of focus group results are the very same ad agency personnel whose "creativity" is on the line. In such circumstances, it is far more likely that the focus group data will be interpreted as supporting the advertising agency's proposed commercials. In other words, in the hands of unscrupulous individuals, a focus group can be viewed as a way of creating the "Emperor's new clothes"; that is, creating an imaginary set of garments even without cloth. Because focus groups yield rich qualitative data that can usually be interpreted in different ways, decision makers must be attentive to the possibility that self-service on the part of the data analyst is operative.

In review, then, here are the five disadvantages of focus group interviews that have been identified.

Disadvantages of Focus Groups

1. Because focus groups are interactive, the interviewer (moderator) has less control than in many other data-gathering procedures.
2. Focus group data analysis is highly labor intensive.
3. The nature of the interaction that takes place in focus group interviews may distort certain participants' contributions to the interview.
4. Focus group data only permit inferences with highly limited generalizability.
5. Because of the qualitative nature of focus group data, some researchers interpret the data to support predetermined views.

Looking back over the advantages and disadvantages of focus groups, you might conclude that there is a need to determine whether focus groups have more virtues or vices before deciding to use them in an evaluation study. That's not necessary. In reality, *all* data-gathering procedures have their advantages and disadvantages. Whether evaluators gather data via questionnaires, achievement tests, one-on-one interviews, or classroom observations, any data-gathering scheme that is selected will be accompanied by strengths and weaknesses. We've spent more time reviewing the positive and negative features of focus groups because many prospective evaluators are not familiar with this form of data gathering. To decide whether to use focus groups in an evaluation study, you need to consider whether a focus group interview, with all the advantages and disadvantages we have noted, is apt to yield the kind of information that decision makers will need to arrive at more defensible decisions. Let's take a look at some of the sorts of situations when an educational evaluator might opt for focus groups.

Applications of Focus Groups in Educational Evaluation

There are a number of settings in which educational evaluators can profitably employ focus groups. We'll consider four different functions for which focus groups are useful, but there are certainly other evaluative applications of focus group interviews. It is important to note, however, that the data gathered via focus group interviews, just as all data gathered during the course of any educational evaluation, should contribute directly to improved decision making. Although educational *researchers* may sometimes wish to employ focus groups as relatively unstructured ways to generate hypotheses, educational *evaluators* should carry out focus groups with a clear set of decision options in mind. Focus groups can be used as the only data-gathering procedure in an educational evaluation study or, more commonly, can be used in concert with quantitatively oriented procedures. Let's consider, briefly, four of the more likely evaluative applications of focus groups.

Needs Assessment   In Chapter Three we dealt with the process of needs assessment wherein educational evaluators help decision makers isolate suitable targets for instruction by identifying the difference between a desired status, such as the hoped-for achievement levels of students, and the current status, such as the present achievement levels of students. An appropriate use of focus groups would be to help determine what educational aspirations a given set of individuals really have. It would be possible, for example, to set up a series of focus group interviews, each of which attempted to elicit educational preferences from different sets of individuals who have a stake in the schools. Those individuals might be, for instance, parents, business executives, educators, governmental officials, students, and so on. Two or three focus groups should be conducted with each type of stakeholder. Thus insights would be derived regarding the kinds of educational outcomes that various constituencies believe our schools should be accomplishing. In addition to the more quantitatively oriented needs-assessment methods described in Chapter Three, focus groups can provide deeper insights into the views of various groups regarding what our schools should be accomplishing.

Formative Evaluation   Formative evaluation is intended to improve yet-malleable instructional programs. What better way to derive some sensible ideas about how to improve a program than to conduct focus group interviews with the students who were the recipients of the program? Focus groups dealing with students who have recently undergone all or part of the instructional program being evaluated can offer insights regarding a program's shortcomings that might never occur to the designers of the program simply because they're on the wrong side of the teacher's desk.

Summative Evaluations   Focus groups can also be used in more summatively oriented educational evaluations, but in such situations the chief function of focus group interviews is to better understand the results achieved by the program as well as those program aspirations that were not achieved. Again, focus group sessions with students who have gone through the program can prove illuminating. Focus group sessions with students are particularly useful in the detection of unanticipated side effects, that is, those outcomes of the program (positive as well as negative) that were not expected by the program staff.

Instrument Refinement   It is often the case that new assessment instruments must be created for a particular educational evaluation study. Frequently these assessment instruments deal with affective outcomes such as students' confidence in their ability to use a newly acquired set of refusal skills or students' attitudes toward certain aspects of mathematics or science. In such instances there is value in subjecting early-version assessment instruments to small-scale tryouts with groups of students (similar to those for whom the instruments will ultimately be used), then holding a relatively short focus group interview to secure students' reactions regarding how to improve the instruments. Such sessions can prove enormously informative to instrument developers because assessment instruments dreamed up in armchairs often collapse when used with real students. Focus group interviews can help eradicate a new instrument's most egregious shortcomings.

Focus Groups and Quantitative Approaches

Too frequently it is thought that an educational evaluator should rely *either* on quantitative or qualitative data-gathering methods. In truth, we often find that most social scientists are strongly inclined toward one of these two data-gathering approaches. However, the most defensible approach to educational evaluation, more often than not, would be to use qualitative and quantitative data-gathering methods in tandem. Qualitative methods such as focus group interviews will usually yield certain insights and understandings that are simply not obtainable through quantitative methods alone.

In general, qualitative data-gathering strategies provide in-depth, rich information about a smaller number of individuals, whereas quantitative data-gathering strategies provide broader information about a larger number of individuals. One key difference between the two approaches, of course, is associated with the costs of the two data-gathering strategies. Even though focus groups are relatively inexpensive (in contrast, for example, with one-on-one interviews or participant observations), they still take more time and money than a series of self-report questionnaires administered by mail or in person. More accurately, focus groups would cost more money to reach the same number of individuals.

Focus groups, then, are frequently used as a low-cost adjunct to quantitative data gathering. It would be just as wrong for educational evaluators to think that they *always* had to use focus groups as it would be to think that they *never* should use focus groups. The most defensible stance for educational evaluators is to determine if the data-gathering needs of a given evaluation study can be best met by quantitative methods alone or perhaps by quantitative approaches plus a set of focus groups. More often than not, such an "in concert" use of focus groups and quantitative approaches will yield the most useful data for decision makers.

Planning and Conducting Focus Groups

In this next section of the chapter, we'll deal with selected particulars of how to carry out focus groups. The particulars clearly have been *selected* because this is, after all, an introductory treatment of focus group interviews. Those who wish to probe focus group procedures more deeply can consult the additional readings cited at the close of the chapter. The focus topics to be addressed will be how to (1) formulate the focus group's data-gathering purpose, (2) identify and recruit participants, (3) develop the interview guide, and (4) moderate the focus group session.

Framing the Focus Group's Mission

A Decision Focus   A focus group interview, by definition, must focus on something. When focus groups are used in educational evaluations, either as the only data-gathering procedure or in conjunction with other quantitatively oriented methods, that focus will usually be on the decisions that need to be made by those who are operating the program or, perhaps, who are deciding whether the program should be continued. It is imperative, therefore, that evaluators who opt for focus groups be particularly clearheaded about the data-gathering procedure's focus.

To become clearheaded about a focus group's mission, evaluators should make certain that they understand the information needs of the decision makers who are supposed to benefit from the focus group's data. Who are the decision makers? What kinds of insights and understandings would really aid them as they wrestle with program-relevant decisions? This is not a time for gathering "nice to know" information. On the contrary, the mission of focus groups used for purposes of educational evaluation should be unashamedly decision driven. Thus the very first step in planning for a focus group is to isolate with clarity what the mission of the data gathering truly is.

Hyperapplication   It is in connection with this first step of focus group planning that we can address an all-too-common tendency on the part of those who have recently learned about focus group methods — namely, the disposition to overuse focus group methods. According to the well-established Law of the Hammer, if you give a child a hammer, the child will find a galaxy of things in need of hammering. Similarly, some evaluators who have just discovered the potential of focus group interviews often attempt to apply focus groups to every conceivable evaluation study.

Focus group interviews, just as any data-gathering method, should be used for the particular situations in which their advantages outweigh their disadvantages. The adoption of focus groups for an educational evaluation study should hinge on whether the decision makers require the kinds of in-depth understandings apt to emerge from focus groups. If not, then quantitative methods may fill the data-gathering bill satisfactorily.

There are too many new converts to focus group interviews who, with the same fervor that is often seen in recent converts to any religion, automatically attempt to apply focus group interviews to any research or evaluation study. Focus groups should not, of course, be part of a knee-jerk response to the question: "How shall I gather data for this evaluation study?" Instead, *if* the evaluation study will genuinely benefit from the sort of information apt to be yielded by focus groups, then strive to become particularly clear about the nature of the information that would best abet decision makers.

How Many Groups?   Typically, an application of focus groups in an educational evaluation study will involve more than a single group. The exact number of focus groups depends on the significance of the evaluation study, the complexity of the questions to be considered, and the number of different categories of individuals who will be involved in the focus groups. As a rule of thumb, you should continue to hold focus groups until the new information you receive is minimal (often referred to as *saturation*). In practice, this often translates to three to five focus groups per application. It is sometimes the case, however, that a single focus group will provide decision makers with all the information they need.

Identifying and Recruiting Participants

Earlier we noted that limited generalizability is one of the disadvantages of focus groups. Focus groups are not intended to provide sample-based insights that can be applied to populations. Therefore, focus groups should be used to garner insights and understandings, not generalizable truths. Rather than trying to recruit focus group participants on the basis of careful probability-based sampling schemes, it is perfectly acceptable to use "convenience" or "opportunity" samples when constituting focus groups. Although convenience samples (see Chapter Eleven) are typically disparaged for a number of evaluation or research purposes, such schemes represent the most frequently used method for identifying the members of focus groups.

Group Compositions   Even though the participants in focus groups need not be identified through the use of sophisticated sampling methods, the kinds of individuals who take part in a given focus group is still of great concern. As you will recall, the homogeneity of participants was a feature in the definition of focus groups. Usually, the variables in which focus group participants should be similar are those that are likely to influence the nature of the discussion process—for example, age, educational level, occupation, socioeconomic level, and so on. For instance, if a focus group planner placed a set of male school custodians in the same focus group as a set of female assistant principals, it is possible that a less-than-lively discussion would ensue.

Although for most purposes it is acceptable to have mixed-sex groups, there would be some evaluation studies in which single-sex focus groups should be used. For instance, if a formative evaluator were attempting to determine the impact on students' behaviors of a new sex education instructional program, then mixing boys and girls in a focus group might prove inhibiting. For many educational uses of focus groups, it is also important to assemble students from the same grade levels.

The names of the individuals who will be invited to take part in a focus group can often be obtained from existing lists such as might be found in school district offices or, if noneducators are to be involved, in the possession of civic or religious organizations. Recalling that it is important to recruit focus group participants so the members do not know one another well, care must be exercised to minimize the amount of previous interactions among participants. For example, if you were assembling several sets of teachers from a reasonably large school district, you should make sure that no two teachers in any group were drawn from the same school.

If existing lists of possible participants are not available, then recruitment via telephone solicitations is often necessary, or perhaps face-to-face recruitment of passers-by in shopping malls. More often than not, such recruitment tactics are not necessary for the types of focus groups employed in most educational evaluations.

Recruiting   Once you have identified a set of potential participants, there is still the task of contacting those individuals and making reasonably certain that they actually show up for the scheduled focus group session. Presented below is a list of steps that you should consider when recruiting participants.

Focus Group Recruitment Steps

1. *Establish Convenient Meeting Times and Places.* Be sure that you schedule a time for the focus group sessions that is not apt to be in conflict with the schedules of your intended participants. Similarly, the location for the focus group session should be easily reached by participants. Unless you resolve the "time and place" issue satisfactorily, your efforts to recruit participants are not likely to be successful.

2. *Invite Potential Participants about Two Weeks Prior to the Session.* Extend a *personal* invitation to participants via a mail, telephone, or face-to-face request approximately two weeks before the focus group is scheduled. The general purpose of the group discussion and any important information about the session should be spelled out – for example, the time involved, location, and so on. Usually, one or two extra participants are invited in order to account for no-shows. The invitation should emphasize the contribution that the invitee can make to the group discussion. In some instances, such as when participants are being recruited by telephone, it may be necessary to screen individuals to make sure that they will not inappropriately reduce the desired level of group homogeneity. When using students in focus groups, it is often necessary to satisfy district policies regarding obtaining parental permission for students' participation in data-gathering activities.

3. *Establish Appropriate Incentives.* Although for certain sorts of focus groups in education it is not necessary to provide monetary incentives, for many focus groups it is entirely appropriate to provide financial incentives for group attendance. To illustrate, suppose that you wish to involve teachers in Saturday or after-school focus groups. In such instances it is altogether proper for you to provide sufficient financial reimbursement so that these busy people will actually take part in your session. Incentives, of course, need not always be financial. Sometimes there will be other payoffs for those attending. Many individuals will be thoroughly gratified to be invited to offer their opinions about issues related to, for example, an educational program. Then too, focus group sessions with students are often held when students are excused from their regular classes, so the student participants are essentially captives. However, participant captivity is often the exception rather than the rule. Thus be sure to give serious attention to the incentive issue. Focus groups may turn you on, but not everyone suffers from your atypical motivational state.

4. *Send a Follow-Up Letter One Week Before the Scheduled Session.* Even if the initial invitation was extended via letter (and provision for a mail or telephone response was provided), a personalized follow-up letter should be sent to participants one week in advance of the session. This letter should contain all of the necessary information and a reemphasis of the importance of the individual's participation. If there is travel time involved, you should recommend that individuals try to arrive 15 minutes early.

5. *Telephone Each Potential Participant a Day or Two Prior to the Session.* A personal telephone call, stressing the importance of the evaluation study and the invitee's part in it, should be made one or two days before the scheduled session. This step would not be necessary if the participants are required to be present, such as when students are released from

their regular classes or teachers are provided with substitutes and expected to attend the session as part of their regular work day.

Developing the Interview Guide

The Guide's Function   A particularly important step in planning for focus groups is the creation of an *interview guide*, that is, a carefully conceived set of questions that will help the moderator maintain the group's appropriate focus. The interview guide usually consists of a dozen or fewer questions that the moderator will attempt to cover during the session. The questions, organized in a logical sequence, typically are more general at the beginning of a session and more specific toward its end. However, because it is often impossible to raise all questions in the guide, it is important to be sure that all truly significant questions are included in the interview guide's early sections.

An interview guide is just that — a guide. It is not an oral version of a questionnaire. Because focus group sessions are, by design, less structured than one-on-one interviews, there should be no attempt to make participants toe the line by answering every question in the order presented. Indeed, in some instances the questions in the interview guide will be addressed out of order (the interview guide's order) and without the moderator's having raised the question.

Moreover, once the interview guide has been developed, it should be committed to memory by the focus group moderator. Moderators should *not* refer to notes or to the interview guide during the session. The information that is sought in a focus group is best fostered if the moderator appears to be asking questions spontaneously rather than reading from a prepared script.

It is in the process of thinking through the nature of an interview guide that the educational evaluator really has an opportunity to make sure the information being requested is the appropriate information for decision makers. Care should be given not only to the substance of the guide's questions but also to the form in which those questions are posed.

The Qualities of Good Focus Group Questions   Because asking good questions typically takes careful preparation, the preparation of the interview guide allows the evaluator to hone the wording of the questions so that they are more likely to yield the desired responses. Questions in the guide should be open ended so that they serve as stimuli for group discussion rather than evoking discussion-suppressing factual or yes/no responses. Lengthy, complex, or ambiguous questions should be avoided. Esoteric vocabulary terms should be avoided. In developing an interview guide for focus groups, it is often helpful to imagine how you might respond to a question if you were a focus group member who had never previously heard the question.

Because the substance and phrasing of questions in the interview guide is so pivotal to a focus group session's success, it is only sensible for the designer of the interview guide to seek reactions from trusted colleagues. (If you don't have any trusted colleagues, try running with a different crowd.) Get one or more persons to scrutinize the guide with the purpose of detecting its deficits. Make revisions as warranted.

Ideally, an interview guide can be tried out in a shakedown focus group session intended chiefly to make sure that the interview guide is well conceived and the moderator is able to use it appropriately. Sometimes, when a series of several focus groups is being used, changes will be made in the guide to take advantage in later groups of experience-derived insights regarding how to structure questions most effectively.

Moderating the Focus Group

Now we'll briefly sketch a number of considerations associated with the actual conduct of a focus group. Attention will be given to the moderator and the moderator's behavior because, without question, the moderator's conduct is the most important factor in the entire focus group enterprise. You can skillfully isolate the function of a focus group, adroitly recruit the perfect participants, and insightfully create a flawless interview guide. Yet, if you choose a clod to moderate the focus group, you can be assured of clod-like results. A focus group's moderator is like a symphony orchestra's conductor. Unrelenting attention should be given to the selection, preparation, and conduct of a focus group's moderator.

A Moderator Team   If possible, try to assign a moderator *and* an assistant moderator to every focus group. The moderator will, in general, lead the discussion while the assistant moderator concentrates on note taking. The moderator also takes notes, but the presence of an assistant moderator permits the moderator to concentrate on the dynamics of the discussion. The assistant moderator can also help in leading the group by raising occasional questions or clarifying participants' responses. The division of labor between the moderator and assistant moderator is fairly clear.

Qualities of Effective Focus Group Moderators   Some skilled moderators are born and some are made. Whether the qualities of the moderator are a function of formal training or stem from a lucky gene pool, focus group moderators should be able to (1) express themselves clearly, (2) be good listeners, (3) quickly comprehend the essence of what participants are communicating via verbal or nonverbal means, (4) be spontaneous and lively, (5) be empathetic regarding the way that participants feel about the issue being discussed, (6) keep the group on task, and (7) be flexible in the face of unanticipated events. Because focus group moderators must be scrupulously careful not to lead participants, dominating individuals typically do not make good moderators.

Preparing for the Session   Moderators should make sure that they are able to concentrate on the group discussion, hence should strive to minimize distractions that might deflect their attention from the group. The interview guide should be completely mastered by the moderator so that if, during the discussion, the group leaps ahead to a later question on the guide, the moderator can mentally delete that question from those to be covered. Because conducting a focus group properly requires a substantial expenditure of mental energy by the moderator, individuals should rarely moderate more than two sessions a day. If two sessions are moderated, ample time between sessions should be allowed so that the first group's discussion can be properly summarized before proceeding with the second group.

Presession Activities   As participants arrive, the moderator and assistant moderator should greet them and, before participants take their seats, engage them in casual conversation for 10 minutes or so about general topics other than the topics that are to serve as the focus for the discussion. Sometimes, arriving participants are also asked to complete anonymous forms that supply demographic information about the group. During this informal conversation period, the moderator attempts to identify those individuals who are talkative, shy, or seem to consider themselves experts. The moderator will often assign the participants to their seats based on these presession conversations.

Prior to the session, be sure that "table tents" (once-folded 5 × 8 cards) have been prepared with participants' first names on them. After noting participants' verbal behaviors during the presession conversation (and, if possible, confirming perceptions with the assistant moderator), the moderator will then, without appearing to be doing so, set out the table tents so that the experts or talkative individuals are placed on either side of the moderator and the shy individuals are placed directly across from the moderator. This kind of seating arrangement allows the moderator to turn slightly from the potentially dominating individuals on either side, hence not notice them as often. It also permits maximum eye contact with those shy individuals who are less apt to speak without prompting.

Recording   If possible, focus group sessions should be tape-recorded so that a complete record can be made of the proceedings. Because tape recorders sometimes malfunction, it is important for the moderator and assistant moderator to also take careful notes regarding the discussion. If the session is to be tape recorded, the moderator will need to ask the participants for permission to record the discussion. Rarely do focus group participants fail to grant such permission.

Because it is often difficult to tape-record group discussions, care should be taken to select a meeting room in which the noise of the ventilation or heating system does not preclude audio recording. Usually, an omnidirectional or stereo microphone placed in the middle of the table will prove satisfactory for recording purposes. The moderator should test the equipment in advance to make sure that there is a reasonable likelihood of capturing on tape what most people will be saying.

Opening the Session   The first few moments of a focus group session are critical because it is during this time that the tone of the session is usually established. Typically, the session begins by the moderator's welcome to the group, followed by a brief overview of the topic and the kinds of information sought. The moderator then sets forth any important ground rules that will govern the discussion, such as whether individuals can "pass" if asked a question they do not wish to answer. Usually, group members are asked to introduce themselves and tell a bit about themselves, such as their occupations. Some moderators then pose an "icebreaker" question for all to answer, that is, a fairly innocuous question that everyone will feel comfortable responding to (so that people can get used to participating). Finally, the first question on the interview guide is presented—and the focus group session is underway.

Adhering to the Guide   Because the interview guide was carefully planned, in general the moderator will wish to follow the order of questions set forth in the guide. Given the nature of group discussions, of course, there is likely to be some degree of unpredictable wandering at various points during the discussion. The moderator will therefore need to keep track of the group's movement through the guide's questions to make sure that all key questions have been adequately addressed in the available time.

Probing   One technique that moderators will rely on during the discussion is the probe, that is, the request for additional clarification or more information. Probing is particularly important during the early part of a discussion because it signifies that the moderator is seeking precise, unambiguous comments from participants. Probing might take the form of the following questions: "Could you elaborate on what you mean?" or "Would you please give us an example of what you're suggesting?

Pausing   Another useful technique for moderators is to pause briefly, for five or six seconds, after a participant has commented. The brief pause frequently elicits additional points of view from other participants. If the moderator speaks instantly after someone's comment or, even worse, "steps on" the last few words of a participant, it is unlikely that other participants will thrust their views forward. Although it sounds simple to pause briefly, we are socialized not to allow silent periods in discussions. Beginning moderators typically will need to practice the brief pause for a while until they master this useful technique.

Neutral Responses   Moderators must be careful not to influence the nature of the discussion by voicing or otherwise displaying approval or disapproval of participants' views. The moderator should strive to maintain a totally neutral response during the entirety of the discussion. If possible, head nodding by the moderator should be avoided because even this nonverbal act can signify approbation by the moderator of certain participants' views. The personal opinions of the moderator should, of course, never be given. *Neutrality* should be the watchword for focus group moderators.

Closing   At the end of the discussion, the moderator may or may not wish to summarize the session's main events, but in any event should thank participants for their participation. If financial incentives have been promised, then they should obviously be distributed at this time. Sometimes a moderator will use the closing moments of a focus group session to ask participants if there's anything that participants think has been omitted. This "last chance" opportunity sometimes elicits comments that are both unexpected and highly worthwhile.

Analyzing Focus Group Data

Social scientists possess many decades' worth of experience in analyzing quantitative data. For the analysis of qualitative data, however, our experiential base is far shorter. Thus techniques for the analysis of focus group data are, when contrasted with quantitative data-analysis schemes, fairly rudimentary. However, during the last decade or so we have seen some significant advances in the applications of computer technology to the analysis of focus group data. Because educational evaluators will typically be relying on fairly uncomplicated data-analysis strategies, we will leave the consideration of computer-based analysis schemes to others.

Because the analysis of qualitative data is regarded by skeptics to be the point at which people can support any view they wish, the analysis of focus group data must be as systematic, verifiable, and credibility inducing as possible. In a sense, those analyzing focus group data should proceed as if they were going to be called on in a court of law to defend every data-reduction decision and every interpretation that they have made.

Preparing for the Analysis

One of the most incontestable truths of both quantitative and qualitative research is that you cannot analyze data if the data do not exist. Accordingly, as soon as a focus group has been concluded, make sure that the tape recording captured what was said. (Try out the tape at several points to be certain.) Then the moderator and assistant moderator should hold a postsession debriefing meeting to prepare a collaboratively written summary of the session's key results. Such summaries can be prepared as though there were no tape recorder available. If possible, these debriefing sessions should themselves be recorded so that the nature of the decisions reached by the moderator and assistant moderator can be documented. The chief function of a debriefing session is to allow the moderator and assistant moderator to determine if there are any major discrepancies in their notes or in their perceptions of the session's key events.

If the tape recording is to be transcribed, this should be done as soon as possible. The virtue of transcriptions, of course, is that they yield a more or less verbatim record of the verbal interchanges that took place in the discussion. (The less-than-verbatim record is often a function of inadequate quality in the tape recording.) The downside of written transcriptions, of course, is their cost. It typically takes a competent word processor at least a full day to generate a decent transcription of a two-hour focus group.

In addition to assembling all summaries of a session as well as the tape recording or transcript of the session, prior to initiating the analysis the analyst should have access to the interview guide and to any demographic data regarding the group whose data are about to be analyzed. Optimally, the analysis will be carried out by the moderator and/or assistant moderator as soon after the session as feasible. These two people will have the best insights regarding what went on at the sessions. Sometimes, however, other individuals will need to analyze the data. It is particularly important for such individuals to read and reread the transcript or to hear and rehear the tape recording of the session. Even the moderator and assistant moderator should read the transcript or listen to the tape recordings before tackling the analysis itself.

The Analysis

In analyzing the various summaries and recordings, try to focus on only one question at a time. If you have transcripts available, you might apply the oft-used and still valuable cut-and-paste technique in which you first go through the transcript and mark sections that deal with the same question, then cut the sections apart and group them under the appropriate headings.

If you are working only with tape recordings, try to isolate individual questions/comments by stopping the tape and noting the nature of the comments. What you are striving to do is to isolate major themes as they relate to the information you are attempting to provide to decision makers. If you can find some quotations that illustrate one of these major themes, you may wish to use the quotations in your report.

As you listen to the tape or review the transcript, try to attend to the words *in context* because that's the real payoff of qualitative approaches. You can identify the nature of the interchange leading up to a given comment, then make a more defensible judgment about the comment's true meaning than if you were obliged to judge that same remark in isolation. When interpreting focus group results, the connotations of words are given stronger weight than the denotations of words.

You can, and should, weight the significance of certain comments based on, for example, their specificity and degree of personalization. In other words, you might take more significantly the comment "I think this is the most exciting curriculum I've ever seen in my 20 years of teaching" than you would the comment "Research results tend to show that a curriculum with these features is strongly correlated with student achievement." As you wade through the immense number of words that typically are uttered during focus group sessions, you are trying to capture a set of group viewpoints or, quite often, disagreements regarding the questions on the interview guide. Remember, you will draw your conclusions as sensibly as you can—but you should draw only those conclusions that you think would be drawn by other reasonable data analysts. This is no time for you to impose your own world view on the data. Systematic and objective data analysis can yield the kind of credibility-inducing conclusions that will prove useful to educational decision makers.

A Personal Observation

When the first edition of this textbook was written, your congenial author had never even heard of focus groups, much less seen them in action. Since that time, I've had an opportunity to watch oodles of focus groups as well as moderate a fair number. I've observed focus groups that yielded insightful information and focus groups that obscured key issues in order to support researchers' preordained conclusions. I am now a strong supporter of focus groups as a tool for educational evaluators. There are disadvantages and abuses of focus group interviews, but, in my experience, the advantages and the payoffs of focus groups decisively outweigh those shortcomings. If you are thinking about becoming an educational evaluator, do some more reading about focus group interviews. Focus group techniques can be, and should be, a potent addition to your methodological repertoire.

Discussion Questions

1. Thinking back over the advantages and disadvantages of focus group interviews that were cited in the chapter, or other advantages and disadvantages that you might identify, what do you regard as the single most important advantage and disadvantage of focus groups? Why?

2. Drawing on your own experiences in education, what sorts of evaluative settings do you believe would be most appropriate for the use of focus group interviews?

3. What is your personal view regarding the compatibility of focus group interviews and more quantitatively oriented approaches?

4. How can objectivity and accuracy be achieved in the analysis of focus group data?

5. If you were trying to explain the nature of focus group interviews to members of a school board who were unfamiliar with such interviews, how would you describe the chief features of focus groups?

Practice Exercise

The very best way to apply the content of this chapter is to plan and carry out an actual focus group interview. If you are using this text as part of a college course, it shouldn't be too difficult to corral some classmates and set up a one-hour focus group. If you can, try to get the group to deal with a topic of relevance to them, such as some aspect of education on which they are apt to be interviewed. Obviously, under those circumstances, you will have to violate the rule about participants who know one another well. The session is, after all, only intended as a practice activity.

Follow the procedures set forth in the chapter: (1) formulate a data-gathering purpose, (2) assemble participants, (3) devise the interview guide, and (4) moderate the session. If there is insufficient time for everyone to moderate a focus group or to serve as an assistant moderator, some students can provide formatively oriented evaluations of other students' focus group efforts. If possible, try to supply a solid critique of your own or someone else's

planning and conduct of an actual focus group.

Notes

1. Appreciation is expressed to Dr. Elizabeth A. Hall, a qualitative research specialist, who was kind enough to review an early version of this chapter.

2. R. K. Merton and P. L. Kendall.

"The Focused Interview." *American Journal of Sociology, 51* (1946): 541–557.

3. R. K. Merton, M. Fiske, and P. L. Kendall. *The Focused Interview* (New York: Free Press, 1956).

Selected References

Fetro, J. V. "Using Focus Group Interviews to Design Materials." *Getting the Word Out: A Practical Guide to AIDS Materials Development.* Santa Cruz, CA: Network Publications, 1990.

Greenbaum, T. L. *The Practical Handbook and Guide to Focus Group Research.* Lexington, MA: D. C. Heath, 1988.

Higginbotham, J. B., and K. K. Cox (Eds.). *Focus Group Interviews: A Reader.* Chicago: American Marketing Association, 1979.

Krueger, Richard A. *Focus Groups: A Practical Guide for Applied Research.* Newbury Park, CA: Sage, 1988.

Krueger, Richard A. "Focus-Group Interviewing: New Strategies for Business and Industry." In Colleen L. Larson and Hallie Preskill (Eds.), *Organiza-*

tions in Transition: Opportunities and Challenges for Evaluation. San Francisco: Jossey-Bass, 1991, pp. 41–50.

Merton, R. K., M. Fiske, and A. Curtis. *Mass Persuasion.* New York: Harper and Row, 1946.

Merton, R. K, M. Fiske, and P. L. Kendall. *The Focused Interview.* New York: Free Press, 1956.

Morgan, D. L. *Focus Groups as Qualitative Research.* Newbury Park, CA: Sage, 1988.

Patton, Michael Quinn. *Qualitative Evaluation and Research Methods* (2nd ed.). Newbury Park, CA: Sage, 1990.

Stewart, D. W., and P. N. Shamdasani. *Focus Groups: Theory and Practice.* Newbury Park, CA: Sage, 1990.

CHAPTER TEN

Data-Gathering Designs

The conditions and procedures arranged by evaluators to collect data are referred to as *data-gathering designs*. Most educators who hear this phrase will automatically think of some sort of research design they have encountered, such as a pretest-posttest design. Though such designs are often employed by evaluators, it is more useful to conceive of the evaluator's data-collection tasks in a larger context.

Educational evaluators, as we have seen, attempt to assemble information that will illuminate the options faced by educational decision makers. Evaluators try to go about their business systematically, relying on evidence rather than intuition. The kinds of evidence they call on are diverse, ranging from pupil performance on conventional tests to recorded observations of behavior by learners, teachers, and others. The frameworks guiding the focus of the evaluator are also varied; we can recall the several evaluation models described in Chapter Two. Although these models help the evaluator isolate the types of decisions to be made, they do not provide procedural guidelines regarding how to gather information relevant to those decisions. A consideration of alternative data-gathering designs will help the evaluator to determine how to secure the data necessary to make more defensible decisions, irrespective of the particular evaluation model being used.

The most common need for evaluative data arises from an interest in the effectiveness of an instructional treatment, such as an innovative program to teach preschool children how to read. By and large, the kinds of designs we shall be examining in this chapter will be useful in collecting data required for evaluating such interventions. However, we should not lose sight of the fact that there are other classes of data needed by evaluators. For example, as has been stressed earlier, there are occasions when evaluators are called on to help appraise the worth of a set of educational goals. For such a task, no classic experimental design fits the evaluator's needs. Yet, unless the evaluator wishes to indulge in data-less goal appraisal, information must still be collected that bears on the goals' worth.

Whether the data are collected as part of an elaborate needs assessment, as part of a classic experimental design, or according to a chapter out of a detective novel, the evaluator is always faced with the problem of deciding what data to collect and under what conditions such information should be gathered.

We have already considered a number of measurement techniques that might be employed to secure evidence as to the effectiveness of typical educational programs. Typically, the evaluator will rely on one or more of these measurement ploys to secure the data perceived to be relevant to the problem under consideration. But the chief trick in designing an evaluation study is to set up the conditions under which such measurements are taken so that meaningful interpretations of the measurement data can be made. In a moment we shall consider a variety of factors that reduce the interpretability of evaluative data, as well as procedures for dealing with such factors.

Designs with a Decision Focus

No matter what sort of data-gathering design is ultimately selected, the paramount consideration should be *the decisions that will be made as a consequence of the data.* There are too many evaluators who, probably suffering from the cerebral damage that comes from carrying out too many hypothesis-testing research studies, gather any and all data they can rake in. Too much information can mask the really crucial data in an evaluation study. We don't know where to start looking. We are inundated with mountains of computer printouts. We are choked by piles of means, standard deviations, and correlation coefficients. Our intercorrelation matrices runneth over.

Evaluators should be highly selective in their decisions regarding data collection. They should always be asking themselves the "So what?" question. Will this information, collected under these conditions, really make any difference? If such a question can be honestly answered in the affirmative, then the evaluator will generally have selected a suitable design.

Textbook versus Real-World Designs

Before proceeding to a consideration of the techniques by which one can set up defensible conditions and procedures for collecting data, we must pause briefly to consider the educational milieu in which those techniques will be used. The world of evaluation is a frighteningly real world. It is not populated by a host of teachers modeled after Mr. Chips who, with docility, will accept the evaluator's assignment to an experimental or control group. Its pupils are not all eager to probe the intellectual nuances of each new course. Its administrators are not charismatic paragons of educational expertise. The actors in the educational drama are strikingly human, with all the attendant frailties of real people. Thus it would be foolish to conclude that the reasons for initiating an educational evaluation always represent a desire to improve the quality of an educational endeavor. It would be equally naive to assume that, once an educational evaluation has been carried out, its results will (1) be greeted with enthusiasm or (2) make an immense difference in the educational program. Evaluators who steel themselves against the probable perils of reality will be less shocked when they try out their shiny new evaluation skills. They may, by anticipating some of these difficulties, be better able to cope with them.

Reasons Underlying the Conduct
of Educational Evaluations

We would like to believe that most educational evaluations stem from a genuine desire to improve the quality of the educational enterprise. For example, we might evaluate an instructional intervention in order to improve it (formatively) or, after it was concluded, to decide whether (summatively) to employ it again. We might also evaluate the merits of a set of educational goals to decide whether to modify them. All these operations sound so splendidly rational. And educational evaluations are often rational. But sometimes they aren't. Let's look at some of the real seeds from which evaluation studies sprout.

Some federal and state funding programs for education require that an evaluation be conducted to determine how effective a funded project has been. Unless each project is evaluated, there won't be any governmental dollars the next year for the local recipients of such funds. Hence, many of the local educators (whose educational programs would suffer without such extramural financing) carry out educational evaluations not because they want to but rather because they have to in order to continue receiving these external finances. For some of these educators, evaluation is viewed as an imposition they must ritualistically perform, often at a superficial level, in order to get their annual dollar rations. Evaluators who unknowingly step into one of these ritual-only evaluation settings will surely encounter problems if they try to do a first-rate evaluation job.

Sometimes, when a school program is under attack by external critics, educational evaluations will be initiated simply to temporize. By telling the critics that "an evaluation is underway," it is often possible to allay the critics' concerns until, after an appropriately elongated "evaluation," the furor subsides.

Sometimes educational evaluations will be initiated merely because they are fashionable and the initiators of such evaluations will be esteemed more highly as progressive and evidence-conscious educators. Such evaluations often lend a form of professional validity to an educational undertaking.

Evaluations will sometimes be undertaken as a blatant power play to get rid of an administrator or teacher perceived to be incompetent or, perhaps, uncooperative.

The fledgling evaluator would do well to try to sort out the motives underlying the initiation of an evaluation project, both the announced motives and those that may really be behind the project. Recognition of such hidden agendas can help the evaluator decide not only what kind of an evaluation design to install but perhaps whether to undertake the project at all.

Seeds, Sterile Soil, and Fertilizer

There is a biblical parable about seeds that fall upon barren rocks; they don't grow well. Beginning evaluators sometimes assume that the results of their efforts will, like seeds sown in a lush meadow, blossom so brilliantly as to change the shape of an educational endeavor. The appraisal of the real world, however, suggests the evaluator's efforts may more often be directed toward a gravel heap than a fertile field. Many educators couldn't care less about the results of an educational evaluation. Their minds are made up regarding what's good or bad about their programs. Evidence is unnecessary.

Sometimes such people are simply lazy, unwilling to expend the intellectual energy required to reconsider and possibly revise an instructional undertaking. Certain individuals are so genuinely convinced that their current approach is praiseworthy that no evidence to the contrary could ever shake them. Sometimes, and these people are the most difficult to cope with, it is in individuals' *vested interests* to keep things as they are; any evaluation evidence that runs counter to those interests is viewed with disdain.

For example, several years ago the federal government set up some heavily funded innovative school projects around the country, each of which permitted local school staffs to add a large number of new workers. Now even though some of the initial evaluations of these projects suggested that they were dismal failures, the local school people resisted the evaluation results with a vengeance, for to accept the results might have meant chopping off a huge financial resource. Such political realities must be anticipated.

There will also be individuals who have an almost religious conviction in the value of their special innovation, such as cross-age tutoring, team teaching, or learning centers. No matter if evaluation evidence suggests that their pet procedure is sickly, they will always find some way to rationalize away distasteful evidence.

About the only thing evaluators can do in such circumstances is to design their studies so that they are as free as possible from defects that might be used to wash away unwanted results. But no matter how flawlessly an evaluation study is designed, evaluators will still have to operate within the political, often irrational, world of education. As important as it is to gather and analyze data, it will probably be more important to engage in the sensitive, intelligent acts that incline people to attend to the results of an evaluation investigation and to act subsequently as a consequence of such results.

If it were possible to identify them, this book would include medication prescriptions that, if taken three times a day, would promote the analytic skill, tact, social sensitivity, and wisdom needed to have one's evaluation results heeded. Although no simple medication guides of this sort exist, one suspects that such attributes are requisite for the successful evaluator.

Internal and External Validity

Characteristically, an evaluation seeks to determine whether individuals have changed as a result of their participation in a program. Can observed changes in the status of participants be attributed to the program? Could other factors such as participant maturation, familiarity with the measures used in the evaluation, or external influences such as a mass media campaign account for the observed changes? Such questions revolve around the *internal validity* of the evaluation — that is, the validity with which we can infer that the program actually caused the effects we find. Ideally the data-gathering design should help to rule out explanations, other than the program, for measured effects. Threats to internal validity weaken the evaluator's ability to attribute observed effects to the program.

Another important issue involves the *external validity* of evaluation studies. Can the findings from a specific evaluation be generalized to the next group of participants or to variations of the program (for example, to a similar education program held in a different place or during the following year)? Could we expect the program to have the same impact in other settings or at other times? What would be its effects with different participants, modes of presentation, or program personnel? External validity focuses on the need to demonstrate that the observed program effects can be expected to occur under conditions other than those associated with the specific program being evaluated. If evaluations possess external validity, they can serve as more than tributes to successful programs or postmortems for unsuccessful ones. Such evaluations can provide useful information as program personnel look to the future.

The distinction between the internal and external validity was introduced in 1957 by Donald Campbell.[1] Although the impact of that distinction on data-gathering designs did not become influential until some years later, it must be clearly comprehended by a skilled educational evaluator.

One reason that it is important to distinguish between internal and external validity is that different information may be required to establish each one. A data-gathering design that increases internal validity may weaken external validity. Experimental control, for instance, which enhances internal validity, must be weighed against feasibility and generalizability. Evaluators must try to balance the problems associated with threats to internal and external validity by selecting a data-gathering design that best addresses the information needs of the program and allocating evaluation resources accordingly. These priorities must come from the context of the program itself, because there are instances in which an evaluator should stress one type of validity rather than the other. Emphases on internal or external validity will vary as a function of the program decisions to be made.

Since the inception of substantial concern about educational evaluation in the late 1960s, there has been an interesting disagreement about the relative importance of internal versus external validity. In 1963 Donald Campbell and Julian Stanley authored an influential chapter on data-gathering designs in the *Handbook of Research on Teaching*,[2] and that chapter was later published as a separate monograph in 1967. By the time educational evaluation became popular, the Campbell-Stanley recommendations were widely accepted by educational researchers as well as educational evaluators.

Campbell and Stanley heavily emphasized the importance of internal validity. Although external validity was not totally discounted, it definitely was regarded as being less significant. In other words, Campbell and Stanley stressed the importance of being able to tell that a program did, in fact, cause certain effects and they were less concerned about the generalizability of a cause-effect relationship. To oversimplify a mite, in the choice between (1) warranted attributions of causality and (2) likelihood of generalizability, Campbell and Stanley clearly chose the former.

Having been persuaded by Campbell and Stanley that any threats to a study's internal validity must, if possible, be eliminated, most educational evaluators touted the virtues of data-gathering designs that bolstered a study's internal validity even if, in the process, the study's external validity was thereby reduced.

An illustration may make this point more clear. As will be seen shortly, one of the most powerful approaches to the design of data-gathering schemes is the use of randomization. Let's say that, even though in a typical school setting it would be impossible to assign students randomly to different programs, for the sake of a study's internal validity the evaluator was able to persuade school officials to allow one-time-only randomized assignment of students to programs. Now let us assume that a set of genuinely delicious data were yielded by this data-gathering design, a set of data that revealed that one of the programs was decisively superior to the others. However, in future years when students were not randomly assigned to programs but could select the program of their choice, it might well be that the program-selection patterns of students would be more important than the relative potency of the programs. The evaluation had set up a design with powerful internal validity but weak external validity. Although valid cause-effect inferences could be drawn about programs in the randomized-assignment study, the study's results could not be generalized to the real world of schooling in which youngsters' choices of programs prevailed. Internal validity had been purchased at the cost of external validity.

Lee J. Cronbach has, for many years, been one of the most influential figures in U.S. educational evaluation, educational measurement, educational research, and on and on. In the 1970s Cronbach began to caution evaluators about the perils of overemphasizing internal validity, arguing persuasively that whereas Campbell's concern with basic science would naturally lead to an emphasis on internal validity, his own background as an applied psychologist led him to be more concerned with external validity. In two important books on educational evaluation, published in 1980 and 1982,[3] Cronbach eloquently argued for the virtues of external validity, contending that evaluation studies that could not be meaningfully generalized at the very least to subsequent years would be of little practical utility.

In essence, the choice for the evaluator is whether to create a data-gathering design that allows causal inferences at the cost of generalizing one's results versus a design that is more directly generalizable but whose causal inferences are shakier. Although there are instances in which data-gathering designs can be selected that do not rob Peter to pay Paul, but there are far more in which the designer will have to shortchange either Paul or Peter.

In a recent essay,[4] Cook has insightfully drawn distinctions between the ways that Campbell and Cronbach view the constructs of internal validity and external validity. As Cook's analysis makes clear, not only are there differences in the ways that those two individuals wish evaluators to emphasize the two forms of validity but there are even differences in the ways that Cronbach and Campbell define the constructs. Readers who wish to probe this topic further will find Cook's observations informative.

Common Factors That Reduce Internal Validity

In the process of setting up a data-gathering design, the evaluator should be attentive to the most common threats to internal validity. As noted earlier, these threats can sometimes be overcome only by weakening a study's external validity, that is, the extent to which the study's results can be generalized. That, of course, is where the skillful evaluator will need to make some trade-offs.

In their 1963 treatise,[5] Campbell and Stanley identified eight different types of extraneous variables that can make the results of the investigation difficult to interpret. We shall initiate our analysis of data-gathering designs by familiarizing the reader with an adaptation of Campbell and Stanley's threats to the validity of a research study.

1. *History.* When instructional treatments extend over a period of time, it is possible that other events occur that may account for end-of-instruction results. For instance, if a special remedial mathematics program is initiated in an elementary school while, at the same time, the local educational television station is offering a six-month cartoon extravaganza emphasizing mathematics concepts, it may be unclear whether the remedial program was the cause of any mathematics improvement on the part of the children.

2. *Maturation.* While an instructional treatment is in progress, there may be natural growth occurring in the learners (biological, psychological, or sociological) which is more instrumental than the instructional treatment in producing desired results. Did this year's first-graders do better on reading achievement tests after an academic year's worth of reading instruction because of the instruction or because they're nine months older?

3. *Testing.* Students who take the same test twice, as in a pretest-posttest design, sometimes perform differently on the posttest as a result of their having taken the pretest. Educators often assert that such pupils have become "test wise."

4. *Instrumentation.* If the measuring instruments are changed during an evaluation study, any apparent changes in pupil performance might be more directly associated with the shift in measuring devices than with the educational phenomenon being evaluated. For instance, if two different achievement tests are being used in an evaluation study, with the more difficult instrument being employed as a pretest, any resulting "increase" in student performance is more apt to stem from the differential difficulty of the two tests than from any intervening instructional program.

5. *Instability.* Most measures used in evaluation investigations are less than perfectly reliable. If the performance of pupils on particular measures is sufficiently unstable, then chance fluctuation in scores that are independent of the phenomenon being evaluated may erroneously suggest the presence (or absence) of a treatment effect.

6. *Selection.* In evaluation studies where the performance of two or more groups is being analyzed, the effect of an educational intervention can be confounded if the students constituting the groups are selected differentially. For instance, if highly motivated pupils were assigned to Treatment X while apathetic pupils were assigned to Treatment Z, then Treatment X might look more effective merely because of the zeal of the students assigned to it.

7. *Mortality*. If two or more groups are involved in the evaluation study and pupils drop out of one or more of the groups differentially, the results of the study may be confounded. To illustrate this defect, often referred to as *attrition*, we might imagine that two treatment groups were being measured with respect to their affect regarding school, but children in one of the groups who were most positive toward school transferred out of the district. Obviously, the other group would look better because of this differential loss of learners.

8. *Statistical Regression*. When learners are selected for an evaluation study because of their extremely high or (more often) extremely low scores on a test, their performance on subsequent tests will tend to "regress" toward the mean of the distribution because of statistical unreliability of the measuring device used. In the early days of systematic educational evaluation studies this particular defect in designs popped up again and again. Designers of federally supported programs for the "educationally disadvantaged" would identify a crop of youngsters at least one or two standard deviations below the mean of an achievement test, give them some type of supposed amelioration treatment, then crow with pride when a subsequent testing showed much higher performance. Yet, because of the statistical regression effect, the children would most likely have shown the same progress *without any treatment* whatsoever. Evaluators working with extremely strong or extremely weak learners should be particularly attentive to this design defect.

For more comprehensive treatments of threats to internal validity, see Cook and Campbell's updating of the original threats to internal validity.[6] Although such advanced conceptualizations of such threats are doubtlessly more comprehensive (it's good to know just how many ways a data gatherer can sin), the eight big-bopper threats just described will account for most of the problems that the typical educational evaluator will encounter.

General Strategies for Strengthening an Evaluation Design

There are two techniques that are generally incorporated in evaluation designs in order to eliminate the sources of extraneous variation we have just examined. The first of these is the use of control or comparison groups. The second is randomized assignment of subjects to the groups involved in the study, or randomized assignment of class groups to different treatments.

Control and Comparison Groups

The use of control groups in behavioral science research has a long and honored tradition. For decades, educational researchers have been whomping up experiments in which they tested the differences between "the experimental and the control group." Most people, therefore, are familiar with this procedure.

By deftly employing control groups, one can eliminate most of the eight classes of extraneous variables previously described. For example, if the effects of history or instrumentation might distort the interpretability of our results, then by adding a control group we can identify, hence discard, the influence of such factors.

However, whereas researchers are often interested in the reactions of (1) a group of subjects who has received a specified treatment and (2) a control group having received no treatment, such "control group versus treatment group" studies should usually be eschewed by the educational evaluator. Remember, educational evaluators are concerned with improving education, and improvements are best nurtured by having educators make better decisions. Better decisions typically call for the selection of the best alternative action plan available. In general, when educators choose whether to install a particular instructional intervention, they should *not* be faced with a choice between an instructional treatment and no treatment at all. Rather, they should be considering *alternative* types of treatments. Thus the designer of evaluation studies should ordinarily not scurry about to create an untreated control group condition, but should instead try to present a range of comparison groups that represent real options open to the educational decision makers. Some have suggested that the evaluator should become skilled in generating "cheapie" versions of an instructional treatment under appraisal so that the program being evaluated can be compared with a very low-cost alternative. Often, under such circumstances, the evaluator will discover that pupils in the comparison group receiving the cheapie version will perform as well as if not better than the splendiferous innovation funded for a decade at a multimillion-dollar level.

There will be instances when an untreated control group will be needed in an evaluation study, but such situations will arise far less frequently than the novice evaluator imagines.

Randomization

In order to constitute comparison groups with subjects who are essentially equivalent, the best technique is to *assign the subjects randomly*. To illustrate, if we wished to compare the relative merits of three new approaches to the teaching of a certain unit of physics, then we might draw students' names from a hat or use a table of random numbers (a procedure explained in the next chapter) so that each student has an equal chance of being assigned to one of the three groups.

Randomized assignment is the optimum way to ensure group equivalence, even though educators have historically leaned toward the procedure of matching. To match two groups of pupils, an educational researcher would laboriously juggle students according to their age, IQ, sex, socioeconomic background, color of eyes, number of eyes, and so on. There *are* problems with matched groups, however, other than the fact that researchers who are obliged to match groups for an extended time run the risk of an emotional breakdown. (How many brown-haired females are there with an IQ of 108.5 whose parents earn $30,875 per year?) For every factor on which the groups are matched, there may be other *equally salient* variables on which they are unmatched. These unmatched variables may, in fact, exert more influence on the results of the study than any variables on which the groups are supposedly equated. Also, matching typically results in the loss of a large number of subjects, which might lead to attendant biasing effects.

Randomization, on the other hand, works more effectively to equalize groups because even if randomly constituted groups appear different (in favor of one group) on one or more factors, there will typically be other undiscerned factors that cancel out these apparent differences. By assigning pupils randomly to different comparison groups, the evaluator can legitimately proceed as if the groups were equivalent for all practical purposes. And evaluators should, above all, be practical people.

In most educational settings, of course, randomized assignment of pupils to different treatment groups will be impossible. Pupils will have already been assigned to classes on the basis of scheduling considerations, not the evaluator's preferences. In many instances, school people will present indisputably sound educational arguments against randomized assignment for a particular situation. In such instances the evaluator will have to make the best of the situation and may have to work with already constituted comparison groups. Comparison groups that are somewhat equivalent are better than those that are wildly disparate.

Yet, if randomized subject assignment can be effected along with the constitution of meaningful comparison groups, educational evaluators will have headed off the major defects in most evaluation designs.

Even in situations where complete random assignments of students cannot be made, it is still possible to use randomization to the evaluator's advantage. Suppose, for example, you were unable to randomize students to different programs, hence chose to select matched pairs of classes based on students' aptitudes, prior achievements, or whatever. Having scrutinized all of a school district's class descriptions, you were able to isolate 10 pairs of classes that were well matched on the basis of several key variables. At that point, you could flip a coin, role a die (one rarely has a chance to roll less than two dice, hence seize the opportunity!), or use a table of random numbers to decide which program will be given to which class. By using a randomized procedure to assign one classroom from each matched pair, the evaluator removes the perception that biased assignment of subjects to treatments occurred. And, as was true with Caesar's wife who, it is said, had to be above suspicion, educational evaluators must sometimes engage in activities to dispel any impression that they may be biased in one direction or another.

Anticipating the Unit of Analysis   After information is collected, it usually has to be analyzed in order for any sense to be made out of it. In a subsequent chapter we shall consider alternative ways of analyzing the data collected during evaluation studies. Even before that discussion, however, it is important to note that analyses of such data must involve the *smallest independent unit* of information. In many evaluation investigations we are appraising an instructional treatment in classrooms where the teacher plays a prominent role. In these instances, inasmuch as the teacher's influence makes pupils' learning teacher-dependent, the smallest independent unit is the class, not the student. Typically, the mean of the class would constitute the datum that, along with each class means, would be analyzed.

The reason for mentioning this analysis consideration here is that in some cases the evaluator, if the unit of analysis is to be the class instead of the pupil, must assign intact classes to different treatment conditions. For such studies, of course, a large number of pupils will be needed, because each class of 30 to 35 pupils will contribute only one unit to the analysis. However, because class averages are less variable than individual pupil scores, a smaller number of units may be needed, for instance, as few as 10 or 15.

Not every evaluation study carried on in classes needs to be analyzed by classroom units, for there are many instances when, even though pupils are working in classrooms, they individually constitute the smallest independent unit of interest. For instance, suppose pupils were working through different series of self-instruction programmed booklets in an evaluation study designed to appraise the booklets. In such an instance it could be the individual pupils who would constitute the appropriate unit of analysis; hence the pupils would be randomly assigned to the different treatments. Smaller numbers of pupils would therefore be needed.

In a situation where a group approach to instruction is involved, for example, when a class is subdivided into four subgroups of seven or eight pupils who jointly complete a simulation gaming exercise, then it would be the subgroup mean that would constitute the analysis unit. In such instances, not only should the subgroups be constituted randomly but the subgroups should be randomly assigned to different treatments thereafter.

In setting up evaluation designs, therefore, evaluators need to be cognizant of the analysis requirements associated with the resulting data. Such requirements, as we have seen, may warrant substantial differences in the basic designs, particularly with respect to whether randomization is focused on individual learners or intact groups.

Particularistic Ploys

In addition to the more general strategies involving the use of randomized assignment and control or comparison groups, there are other tricks the evaluator will find suitable for particular evaluation situations. Remember that the overall purpose of designing evaluation studies is to set up conditions and procedures for data collection such that meaningful interpretations can be made about the merits of the educational phenomenon under consideration. In given instances we can design a study that has no control groups nor any randomized assignments of subjects, yet still derive defensible inferences from the investigation.

For example, when we are evaluating an instructional treatment of short duration, such as a few hours, the threats posed by maturation or history can be discounted, even without the use of a control group. When subjects are selected from the middle range of a distribution, we need not worry about statistical regression. If we employ only unobtrusive measurement tactics, then the threat of testing as an extraneous variable can be discarded. There are also some data-gathering designs in which control groups are not required. We shall examine such designs shortly.

The major point is that evaluators need not approach the task of designing evaluation studies with only two arrows, randomized assignment and control groups, in their quivers. Common sense will reveal additional schemes to be installed. Besides that, unless evaluating archery instruction, evaluators who walk around carrying a quiver will be considered somewhat bizarre.

Alternative Evaluation Designs

We now turn to a consideration of a number of formal evaluation designs that should be mastered by the educational evaluator. Each of these designs has special features that warrant its use in different types of evaluation situations. Some are easier and less expensive to install than others. Some are well suited for formative evaluation assignments but less so for summative evaluations. Others are suitable when randomized assignment of subjects is impossible. Still others can be used when control groups cannot be constituted. In brief, all the following designs have attributes that must be known to evaluators.

The designs described here have been adapted from the widely used description of research designs provided by Campbell and Stanley.[7] Though their focus was on the isolation of designs suitable for research on teaching, the relevance of these designs for purposes of educational evaluation will be apparent.

The names used to describe each design will be identical to those used by Campbell and Stanley. In addition to being named and described, each design will be presented symbolically, according to the Campbell and Stanley symbol system. Because Campbell and Stanley rely on Xs and Os in their designs, the designs have been referred to as excursions into tic-tac-toe. The following symbols will be employed here:

R = Random assignment
X = Treatment (that is, an instructional intervention)
O = Observation (that is, a measurement)

In these instances, the term *treatment* refers to a program, policy, or practice being evaluated. *Observation* (measurement) is used in the widest possible sense, as we have seen in previous chapters. Let's turn now to a consideration of a number of these data-gathering designs.

The One-Shot Case Study

Although some purists contend that the *one-shot case study* hardly qualifies as a respectable data-collection design, there are instances when evaluators might employ it. Essentially, the design involves the administration of measuring devices to a group of learners who have received some sort of educational treatment. Schematically, the design looks like this:

X ⟶ O

One-Shot Case Study

The design is referred to as a *case study* because it more closely resembles a clinical case study than anything else. The evaluator merely notes what happens to learners who have received the instructional treatment being evaluated.

The threats to internal validity associated with this design are several, and they are significant. Extraneous variables stemming from history, maturation, selection, and mortality can becloud the interpretability of data gathered under conditions of the one-shot case study.

Yet, with all the frailties of the one-shot case study, there are instances in the early stages of a formative evaluation project where one might use it to secure a rough idea of what happens to learners after they experience a certain kind of treatment. Maybe only one or two learners are involved at that. The formative evaluator makes no claims that the inferences gathered under such conditions are unflawed. No effort would be made to have a school board adopt a major new program on the basis of such shaky data. However, an instructional developer yearning for some kind of feedback as to whether an early version of an instructional prototype is working may find data from a one-shot case study quite helpful.

If the need for the data is balanced with the potential sources of invalidity associated with this design, there may be instances during formative evaluation when the one-shot case study may prove useful. Its applications in a more summatively oriented evaluation, because of its weaknesses, are obviously limited.

The One-Group Pretest-Posttest Design

Another design is *the one-group pretest-posttest* design which, as its name implies, consists of pretesting and then posttesting a single group that, between the two testings, has been exposed to some sort of treatment:

$$O \longrightarrow X \longrightarrow O$$

One-Group Pretest-Posttest Design

This design is particularly susceptible to the following threats to interval validity: history, maturation, testing, instrumentation, and the possible interaction of selection with other factors. For instance, it is easy to see how, if the interval between the two tests is a long one, history (an external event) or maturation (pupils' natural growth) could be operating. If the same test is used both times, there could be a testing effect. If different tests are used, then an extraneous instrumentation effect may be present. Finally, because there is no comparison group present, we can't tell whether we are studying an aberrant group of learners.

Yet, with all its problems, there may be occasions, particularly in a formative evaluation context, when the evaluator will find this design helpful. If the interval between the pretest and posttest is kept short, then history and maturation should not be concerns. If the pretest is not likely to influence learners' posttest performance or the nature of their interaction with the treatment, then the threat of testing as an extraneous variable can be discounted. If two identical tests or two properly equated tests are employed, then instrumentation is not a problem. If the learners involved in the study are carefully selected so that they are representative of the learner population of interest, then safeguards against the selection defect are present. In other words, for certain purposes, the one-group pretest-posttest design might be extremely useful for educational evaluators.

The design is particularly handy for formative evaluators who wish to gather data regarding the effectiveness of subcomponents of an instructional program. For instance, if a formative evaluator were assisting a group of instructional developers preparing a series of sound-filmstrip programs, then useful information regarding early versions of each sound-filmstrip program might be accumulated via the use of the one-group pretest-posttest design.

For summative evaluation applications, however, even though variants of this design are used quite frequently for that purpose, designs involving comparison groups should be preferred to the one-group pretest-posttest design. Even in formative evaluation settings the evaluator will find that comparison groups can prove helpful because the decision will often involve a choice between two (or more) possible instructional approaches. As we have previously noted, the use of control or comparison groups can markedly strengthen a data-gathering design against threats to internal validity. Let's turn to some of those data-gathering paradigms.

The Nonequivalent Control Group Design

One commonly employed data-gathering design involving a control group is one in which the assignment to groups is not accomplished randomly. The *nonequivalent control group design* employs two or more groups, all of which are administered a pretest and, following an instructional treatment, a posttest. In its simplest form, with one group serving as an untreated control, the design looks like this:

Group 1: $O \longrightarrow X \longrightarrow O$
Group 2: $O \longrightarrow O$
Nonequivalent Control Group Design

Because educational evaluators will, more often than not, be engaged in *comparative* analyses, the forms of this design most frequently used will be something like this:

Group 1: $O \longrightarrow X_1 \longrightarrow O$ Group 1: $O \longrightarrow X_1 \longrightarrow O$
Group 2: $O \longrightarrow X_2 \longrightarrow O$ or   Group 2: $O \longrightarrow X_2 \longrightarrow O$
Group 3: $O \longrightarrow X_3 \longrightarrow O$ Group 3: $O \longrightarrow O$
Typical Evaulation Variants of the
Nonequivalent Control Group Design

In the design at the left, three different instructional programs are being compared with each other. In the design at the right, two different programs are being contrasted with each other, as well as with all untreated control group.

The major applications of this design arise in situations where it is impossible to constitute comparison groups randomly. Although the advantages of randomization cannot be secured, the dividends of control or comparison groups are present. The more similar the comparison groups, the more straightforward will be the interpretations of data collected via this design. The less confidence we have in the initial equivalence of the comparison groups, the less likely we will be to make defensible inferences from such data.

Obviously, the key deficit in this design is the possibility that the initial selection of individuals constituting the comparison groups might result in essentially dissimilar groups. If one group consists of dedicated and eager learners whereas the other group consists of recalcitrant rascals, a comparison of their pretest versus posttest performance will yield a misleading estimate of the program's worth.

The need for this particular design arises often in the practical school world where randomization cannot be employed. As we have seen, the use of randomization *plus* control or comparison groups relieves most of the evaluator's design headaches. With this design we apparently have only half an aspirin, yet there are numerous occasions where we must use it.

Now, how do we increase the likelihood that the groups involved in the design are sufficiently equivalent that we can make meaningful interpretations from the resulting data? Well, if the pretest, administered prior to the treatment, indicates that the comparison groups are really different, then we can selectively eliminate discordant learners for purposes of the posttest analysis. Let's say, for instance, that we are comparing two instructional procedures and are using two intact groups of pupils, which we believe are comparable. Suppose, on the basis of the pretest, we find 15 very high scorers in Group A and 7 very low scorers in Group B. We can continue with the treatment as scheduled, administering the posttest to all learners, but never analyze the results of the 22 aberrant learners.

Even better, we can gather other data deemed relevant to posttest performance, such as previous grade-point averages or scores on scholastic aptitude tests, and match the comparison groups even more closely. Most evaluators agree that the single most influential factor in designing studies without randomization is the difference between the pupils involved. It would be better, therefore, to discard half the potential pupils from the analysis on the basis of pretreatment matching considerations if, as a result, we ended up with nonequivalent groups that were "less nonequivalent."

The Pretest-Posttest Control Group Design

When randomization is possible, then a commonly used design is the *pretest-posttest control group design*, which is the first design we have encountered that incorporates both control groups and randomization. Because it does, it takes care of almost all eight threats to a study's validity cited earlier. In its most basic form this design can be depicted as follows:

Group 1: $RO \longrightarrow X \longrightarrow O$
Group 2: $RO \longrightarrow O$

Pretest-Posttest Control Group Design

Because, as we have seen, educational evaluators will often wish to engage in comparative analyses of the merits of different programs, this design can be varied so that there are two or more treatment conditions. The untreated control group may or may not be employed.

The pretest-posttest control group design is a particularly useful design for educational evaluators because of the ease with which the data collected can be interpreted. The only real defect in the design is that if the pretest is *reactive*, its influence may confound the picture. A reactive test is one that, when completed by learners, influences their response to the treatment condition. It is easy to think of examples of reactive tests that are used in educational evaluation studies. For instance, suppose we were attempting to evaluate the extent to which two different films influenced youngsters' attitudes regarding foreigners. If, prior to the viewing of a film, we administered a questionnaire to the pupils, which asked all sorts of questions regarding their feelings about foreigners, then the pupils would most likely be sensitized to those aspects of the film that focused on one's response to people from other nations. In other words, any postfilm measurement might reveal something about the pupils' responses to the film *plus* the pretest and the "set" it produced.

If there is any likelihood that reactive effects may be yielded by a particular pretest, then another design (to be introduced momentarily) should be adopted. Although the problem is not limited to the affective domain, evaluators will find that measurement procedures attempting to assess the learner's affective status will more often be reactive than will cognitive measuring devices. For example, if we use a cognitive measure of a pupil's ability to solve simultaneous linear equations, and the pupil doesn't perform well, the pretest experience will probably not dramatically influence that learner's interaction with a subsequent instructional treatment. Yet, even with cognitively oriented instructional treatments, it is possible that the "organizing set" induced by taking a pretest may facilitate the student's successful interaction with an instructional sequence.

The Posttest-Only Control Group Design

When randomization is possible yet there is the fear that the pretest may be reactive, a particularly useful design is the *posttest-only control group* design. As can be seen from its most basic form, this design is the same as the pretest-posttest control group design, except that there is no pretest:

Group 1:RX $\longrightarrow$ O
Group 2:R O
Posttest-Only Control Group Design

Many educators will abandon a pretest only with scratching and screaming, for without the *demonstrated* equivalence of comparison groups (as indicated by similar pretest performances) they will not know "for sure" that the groups are essentially the same. Yet, "the most adequate all-purpose assurance of lack of initial biases between groups is randomization."[8] By randomly assigning learners to different comparison groups, we actually have a better chance that the groups will be equivalent than if we tried to match them carefully on the basis of relevant variables. Thus, particularly when there is the fear of a reactive pretest (but by no means limiting its use to such settings), the posttest-only control group design is a winner.

The basic dividend of the posttest-only control group design is that by measuring an untreated, randomly assigned control group, we secure an estimate of how our treated group would have responded on a pretest, but without introducing the potentially reactive effects of a pretest. Although the diagram for this design suggests that the measurements be made for both groups at the conclusion of the treatment, it is possible to obtain measurement on the untreated control group earlier if doing that seems advisable.

Because educational evaluators will typically be comparing two or more programs, the posttest-only control group design will generally be set up for multiple groups in an evaluation contest, such as this:

Group 1: RX_1 ⟶ O
Group 2: RX_2 ⟶ O
Group 2: R O

A Typical Evaluation Application of the
Posttest-Only Control Group Design

Remember that, unlike the case with previously discussed multiple-group designs, we cannot avoid using an untreated control group in this instance, because it is that group's performance that provides us with an estimate of how untreated learners perform, that is, how our treated learners would have performed if they had been tested prior to the treatment.

With each of the data-gathering designs discussed here, the evaluator need not slavishly adhere to the "pure" form of the design. Occasions will arise when it will be advantageous to modify a design so that it better suits the evaluator's purpose. For instance, an instructional intervention may be viewed as so potentially beneficial that local educators cannot bring themselves to withhold it from pupils. There are even governmental funding programs that require that an externally funded program be given to *all* pupils. What does the evaluator do under such circumstances? How can a comparison group or untreated control group be assembled?

If it is not necessary to give the instructional treatment simultaneously to all pupils, then the posttest-only control group design can be modified to handle this situation. Suppose, for example, that the program to be evaluated is a new two-month multimedia unit dealing with drug abuse. We can designate this drug program as X_d. If the evaluator can round up a second instructional program of the same duration, say, a unit dealing with environmental education (designated as X_e), a modified posttest-only control group design can then be set as follows:

Group 1: $RX_d \longrightarrow O_d \quad O_e \longrightarrow X_e$
Group 2: $RX_e \longrightarrow O_e \quad O_d \longrightarrow X_d$

Modified Posttest-Only Control Group Design

In this modification we see that one of the randomly constituted groups first receives the drug abuse unit, then gets the environmental education unit. The reverse is true for the second group. Note that measurements on both units are taken after the initial treatment. In essence, the drug abuse measurement (O_d) taken for Group 2 is the same as that which would be taken on an untreated control group. The appropriate comparisons to make in this type of design are as follows:

Group 1: $RX_d \longrightarrow (O_d) \; (O_e) \longrightarrow X_e$
Group 2: $RX_e \longrightarrow (O_e) \; (O_d) \longrightarrow X_d$

Appropriate Posttest Comparisons for
the Modified Design

The programs added after the measurements satisfy the condition that all learners receive the program. It would be possible, of course, to measure the learners after the second program to pick up an estimate of retention, if this is of interest. As with the other designs, because more than one treatment condition is usually under consideration in evaluation studies, additional groups can be added as logical extensions of the modified posttest-only control group design.

In review, the posttest-only control group design is a particularly serviceable design for educational evaluators, especially when there is the danger that a pretest might produce reactive effects. If those initiating the evaluation believe strongly that pretest information is needed, and if that pretest is not likely to be reactive, then the pretest-posttest control group design is a sound alternative to the posttest-only model. Taken together—for they both incorporate randomization and the use of comparison or control groups—these two designs will probably be used more frequently by summative evaluators than will any other data-gathering designs.

The Interrupted Time-Series Design

The last design to be presented is somewhat different from the previous models. It can be diagrammed as follows:

$$O_1 \longrightarrow O_2 \longrightarrow O_3 \rightarrow X \rightarrow O_4 \longrightarrow O_5 \longrightarrow O_6$$

Interrupted Time-Series Design

In the *interrupted time-series design* a series of measurements (the more, the better) is taken both before and after the introduction of the program being evaluated. Frequently these measurements will be drawn from existing records, such as regularly administered achievement tests, attendance reports, or disciplinary referrals. Such so-called *archival* data are particularly well suited for the interrupted time-series design, but are by no means the only kinds of data to be used with the design. Although the procedures for statistically analyzing data yielded by this design are rather complicated, there are many instances in which a reasonable judgment regarding the impact of the treatment can be made from an inspection of graphically represented results. For instance, assume that in the examples in Figure 10–1 we have measured pupil performance on equivalent problem-solving tests every two months during the year and have introduced a three-week teaching unit on problem-solving procedures during the middle of the year. In which, if any, of these three situations would a beneficial influence of the teaching unit (i.e., the treatment) be reflected?

Even though in all cases there has been an *identical* improvement in performance from the third to the fourth measurements, that is, the measurements immediately preceding and following the treatment. Although certain types of results from the interrupted time-series design are difficult to interpret, many are quite straightforward and are easily interpreted when represented graphically.

The greatest advantage of time-series designs is not that they offer an alternative to traditional comparative designs but that they provide a markedly different perspective for evaluating the effects of an educational intervention. Many treatments of interest to an educational evaluator produce their effects across time, not in a single instant as measured by a posttest. Often an *effect pattern* is yielded by such treatments; if only the more common simultaneous comparison designs were to be employed, such a pattern would be undetected. Because the interrupted time-series design is ideal for studying longitudinal effects, it is most appropriate when long-term payoffs of an instructional treatment are likely.

Another advantage of the interrupted time-series design is that it provides a *post hoc* tool to evaluate educational interventions for which no comparison-group contrasts were preplanned. For example, suppose a school district had initiated a

FIGURE 10–1 • *Sample Interrupted Time-Series Design*

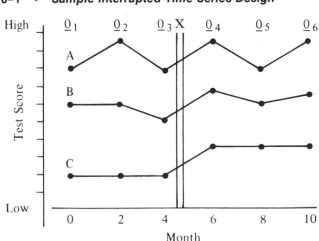

special extramural club program designed to make students' attitudes toward school more positive. If the school officials didn't get around to deciding on the importance of an evaluation of the program until several months after it had been in operation, then an after-the-fact evaluation strategy is the only one possible. If the evaluator can get access to data that can be considered reflective of pupils' attitudes toward school, such as tardiness or attendance records, then an interrupted time-series design might be profitably employed.

This type of design can also be used when it is impossible, for ethical or other reasons, to withhold a given treatment from any learner. By setting up a series of measurements prior to and after the program's introduction, it is possible to get a fix on its effects.

If conditions permit, the simplest form of this design can be modified so that two or more groups can be involved. It is even possible to randomize the assignment of learners as follows:

$$\text{Group 1: } O_1 \longrightarrow O_2 \longrightarrow O_3 \rightarrow X_1 \rightarrow O_4 \longrightarrow O_5 \longrightarrow O_6$$
$$\text{Group 2: } O_1 \longrightarrow O_2 \longrightarrow O_3 \rightarrow X_2 \rightarrow O_4 \longrightarrow O_5 \longrightarrow O_6$$

A Variation of the Interrupted Time-Series Design

Such a variant of the interrupted time-series design is obviously more powerful than the more basic form of this design.

A complete consideration of time-series experiments, including their design and the analysis of the data they yield, has been prepared by Glass, Willson, and Gottman.[9] The evaluator who wishes to master the nuances of this most useful family of designs should consult the excellent discussion provided by these writers.

Rights of Program Participants

In all of this discussion about data-gathering designs, it may have been overlooked that educational evaluators, by and large, gather data from people. In general, education programs are designed to improve individuals' educations, that is, their well-being. When we evaluate those programs, therefore, we typically focus on their impact on human beings. Some evaluators, however, become so caught up with the importance of appraising an education program that they overlook the *rights* of the participants.

Above all, an evaluator should be guided by a respect for human dignity and hence should not engage in data-gathering activities that in any way demean an individual's rights. Prominent among the principles that should guide evaluators is *informed consent*. The principle of informed consent requires that an evaluator secure, in advance of the study, agreement of all participants in an investigation. This consent is obtained after the potential participants have learned about the nature of the investigation, at least insofar as their participation is involved. This principle properly reflects the evaluator's concern for human dignity, because it rules out the possibility of making individuals serve unknowingly as subjects in an evaluation. Although there may be exceptions to this requirement when the nature of the program being evaluated is so patently benign or would otherwise be experienced by participants whether or not there was an evaluation, informed consent should routinely be obtained by evaluators if any additional data gathering is required of participants. In the case of children, such consent should be obtained from parents or guardians.

A key tenet in most ethical codes insists on the *confidentiality* of all information gathered about participants. Because the evaluator is not concerned with an appraisal of individual participants but, rather, with the worth of education programs, the principle of participant confidentiality usually poses no problems. Evaluators must be careful, however, to devise protective safeguards, such as anonymous completion of forms and careful handling of data, that ensure the confidentiality of the data.

In Retrospect

There is a temptation, when describing data-collection schemes that might be used by evaluators, to cite a good many more designs than the six basic approaches described here. After all, educational researchers have been about their business for a good many years and they have sharpened and multiplied their methodological tools to an impressive degree. There are many other designs the evaluator might want to call on in certain situations, but these will be the exception rather than the rule. In general, the half-dozen designs described in this chapter should take care of the evaluator's design requirements 95 percent of the time. For those readers wishing to become better versed in advanced data-collection designs, the references cited at the close of this chapter offer excellent avenues for initiating that inquiry.

My decision to describe only a handful of designs was a deliberate choice, predicated on a belief that if a writer attempts to "cover the waterfront" by describing an endless array of anything, the reader may "cover" the topics but lose sight of the most crucial components therein. Having mastered the six designs described in this chapter, you may wish to pursue the study of alternative data-collection schemes. That more advanced pursuit need not be forced on you here.

The real trick, of course, is deciding what data-gathering designs to use in particular situations. A reconsideration of the six evaluation designs described here will reveal that each one of them has particular properties that render them suitable for given evaluation situations. Sometimes several of the designs could be reasonably used. Often there is only one design that is appropriate. The practice exercises at the close of the chapter will help you decide whether the special features of each design have been mastered or whether a review of certain segments of the chapter is in order.

Discussion Questions

1. In many analytic discussions someone assumes the role of "the devil's advocate" in order to ask all those sticky questions that never get raised by proponents of an argument. We have considered a number of data-collection designs that might be employed in evaluation settings. For a moment, assume the role of "the practitioner's advocate" and try to identify all those practical obstacles that might interfere with the installation of particular evaluation designs. Can you think of any way to overcome such impediments?

2. Of the eight factors that can weaken the validity of an evaluation design, which two or three do you think are most likely to contaminate the typical evaluation investigation?

3. If you were trying to identify the factors that would incline an evaluator to select one design (of the six treated in the chapter) over another, what design features would you isolate?

4. What are the contributions of random-ization and the use of control or comparison groups to the quality of evaluation designs?

5. Try to imagine hypothetical evaluation situations in which you could employ each of the six designs examined in the chapter. Then mentally try to plan the particular steps to be followed in implementing the designs, that is, when to randomize, how many groups to select, when to measure, and so on.

6. What factors can you think of that would weaken an evaluation study's external validity?

7. In deciding between data-gathering designs that contribute to external validity versus internal validity, the evaluator must often decide which of these two forms of validity is more important. Which of the two types of validity do you believe to be more significant?

8. What are your views about the necessity of obtaining *informed consent* from program participants?

Practice Exercises

1. Below are five brief descriptions of evaluation studies, each of which probably suffers from one or more of the eight threats to an evaluation study's validity. Following each description, four possible sources of invalidity are presented. Choose the *one* factor that is most apt to be operative. (Other threats, not cited, may also be present.)

    a. In this evaluation study there was an effort to contrast the merits of three different approaches to the teaching of reading. Pupils in three randomly assigned groups were tested at the beginning of the academic year with a California Achievement Test and at the close of the year with the Iowa Test of Achievement. Comparisons were made among the groups with respect to their progress as reflected by these measures. Which one of the following threats to this study's validity is most prominent? (1) statistical regression; (2) history; (3) instrumentation; (4) selection.

    b. A formative evaluator attempts to provide an instructional developer with "rough and dirty" data regarding one component of an instructional sequence by trying the component out with a group of children who are friends of the

evaluator's daughter. After the
children complete the 60-minute
instructional component, they are
given a posttest covering its major
objectives. Which of the following
threats to this study's validity is
most prominent?
(1) testing; (2) instrumentation; (3)
selection; (4) maturation.

c. A Chapter I program is directed
toward improving the reading proficiency of the worst readers in the
school district. Accordingly an
innovative program is set up for all
children who score below the 15th
percentile on a nationally standardized test of reading achievement.
Twenty of these children are randomly selected from the 200 low-
scoring learners, then these 20
children complete the special program to ameliorate their reading
deficits. The children are tested
before and after the 10-week treatment. To the delight of the project
staff, the pupils display considerable improvement over the 10-week
period. Which one of the following
threats to this study's validity is
most prominent?
(1) instrumentation; (2) statistical
regression; (3) mortality; (4) instability.

d. The measuring instruments used in
this evaluation study were constructed by teachers in the district,
most of whom have little familiarity
with the procedures used in devising tests. The district superintendent directs the evaluation staff to
use these tests even though their
reliability has never been verified.
The general design used is a posttest-only control group approach.
Which one of the following threats
to the study's validity is most prominent?
(1) instability; (2) selection; (3)
testing; (4) history.

e. During the semester in which an
innovative program in history instruction was introduced in the local
high school, a series of first-run
historical movies was shown during
prime-time hours on the local television station. Affective scores
reflecting interest in history, administered at the beginning and end of
the semester, reveal more positive
student attitudes toward history as a
subject. Which one of the following
threats to this study's validity is
most prominent?
(1) maturation; (2) instability;
(3) instrumentation; (4) history.

2. For each fictitious situation given
below, decide which one of the follow-
ing six designs should probably be
employed by an educational evaluator
who was concerned with reducing the
threats to internal validity:
One-shot case study
One-group pretest-posttest design
Nonequivalent control group design
Pretest-Posttest control group design
Posttest-only control group design
Interrupted time-series design

a. An evaluator is called in well after
an innovative counseling program
has been initiated by an inner-city
school. The major thrust of the
program is to counsel students into
more relevant coursework that is
suited to their interests and abilities
as revealed during the counseling
sessions. The overall goal of the
program is to make students happier
in school as a consequence of the
more relevant curriculum. The
principal reports to the evaluator
that the staff is willing to use attendance as an index of pupil's satisfaction with school.

b. An evaluation consultant has been
asked to recommend a design for a
comparative study of two new
biology textbooks, particularly as
they affect the attitudes of students

toward sexual concepts. There are many students who can be used in the study, and the district officials indicate it is acceptable to assign the students to groups randomly. Upon inspecting the attitudinal measures to be used in the study, the evaluation consultant concludes that they are definitely reactive in nature.

c. A curriculum development staff wants some fast feedback on one section of a new set of economics materials they are developing. They want to see whether these materials, in their present form, can help students accomplish some prespecified cognitive objectives. They are particularly interested in the amount of growth that the learners display after interacting with the two-hour instructional component that they want evaluated. Because only 15 students have completed the earlier phases of this new program, they are the only youngsters suitably prepared for the new unit. The project staff wants to see all 15 pupils respond to the unit, realizing thereby that they run the risk of

possible invalidity in the study.

d. In evaluating the merits of two new approaches to the teaching of basic mathematics, the school staff wants to see pretest-to-posttest growth data, because they are anxious to provide the school board with some influential information regarding what kind of program to adopt next year for the district. It is possible to constitute treatment groups randomly, because the study is being designed during the summer, well in advance of the start of school.

e. Although the school principal wishes to compare two new social studies filmstrip series, prior assignments to classes preclude the random assignment of learners to different treatment conditions. Yet, on the basis of prior achievement test scores and scores on aptitude tests, the principal is confident that 10 or so classes can be used in which the pupils are of essentially comparable ability. A pretest and posttest are to be used, and the principal believes the pretest will definitely be nonreactive.

Answers to Practice Exercises

1. *a*. instrumentation; *b*. selection; *c*. statistical regression; *d*. instability; *e*. history.
2. *a*. interrupted time-series design; *b*. posttest-only control group design; *c*. one-group pretest-posttest design; *d*. pretest-posttest control group design; *e*. nonequivalent control group design.

Notes

1. Donald T. Campbell, "Factors Relevant to the Validity of Experiments in Social Settings," *Psychological Bulletin*, 54 (1957), 297–312.

2. Donald T. Campbell and Julian C. Stanley, "Experimental and Quasi-Experimental Designs for Research on Teaching," in *Handbook of Research on Teaching*, ed. N. L. Gage (Chicago: Rand McNally, 1963).

3. L. J. Cronbach et al., *Toward Reform of Program Evaluation: Aims, Methods, and Institutional Arrangements* (San Francisco: Jossey-Bass, 1980); L. J. Cronbach, *Designing Evaluations of Educational and Social Programs* (San Fran-

cisco: Jossey-Bass 1982).

4. Thomas D. Cook, "Clarifying the Warrant for Generalized Causal Inferences in Quasi-Experimentation," in *Evaluation and Education: At Quarter Century*, ed. M. W. McLaughlin and D. C. Phillips (Chicago: University of Chicago Press, 1991), pp. 115–44.

5. Campbell and Stanley, "Experimental and Quasi-Experimental Designs."

6. T. D. Cook and D. T. Campbell, "The Design and Conduct of Quasi-Experiments and True Experiments in Field Settings," in *Handbook of Industrial and*

Organizational Psychology, ed. M. D. Dunnette (Chicago: Rand McNally, 1976); T. D. Cook and D. T. Campbell, *Quasi-Experimentation: Design and Analysis Issues for Field Settings* (Chicago: Rand McNally, 1979).

7. Campbell and Stanley, "Experimental and Quasi-Experimental Designs."

8. Ibid., p. 195.

9. Gene V Glass, Victor L. Willson, and John M. Gottman, *Design and Analysis of Time-Series Experiments*. (Boulder, Co: Laboratory of Educational Research, University of Colorado, 1972).

Selected References

Campbell, Donald T. "Factors Relevant to the Validity of Experiments in Social Settings." *Psychological Bulletin*, 54 (1957): 297–312.

Campbell, Donald T., and Julian C. Stanley. "Experimental and Quasi-Experimental Designs for Research of Teaching." In N. L. Gage (Ed.), *Handbook of Research on Teaching*. Chicago: Rand McNally, 1963.

Cook, T. D. "An Evolutionary Perspective on a Dilemma in the Evaluation of Ongoing Social Programs." In M. B. Brewer and B. E. Collins (Eds.), *Scientific Inquiry and the Social Sciences: A Volume in Honor of Donald T. Campbell*. San Francisco: Jossey-Bass, 1981.

Cook, T. and D. T. Campbell. "The Design and Conduct of Quasi-Experiments and True Experiments in Field Settings." In M. D. Dunnette (Ed.), *Handbook of Industrial and Organizational Psychology*. Chicago: Rand McNally, 1976.

Cook, T. D., and D. T. Campbell. *Quasi-Experimentation: Design and Analysis Issues for Field Settings*. Chicago: Rand McNally, 1979.

Cronbach, Lee J. *Designing Evaluations of Educational and Social Programs*. San Francisco: Jossey-Bass, 1982.

Glass, Gene V, Victor L. Willson, and John M. Gottman. *Design and Analysis of Time-Series Experiments*. Boulder, CO: Laboratory of Educational Research, University of Colorado, 1972.

Greene, Jennifer C., Valerie J. Caracelli, and Wendy F. Graham. "Toward a Conceptual Framework for Mixed-Method Evaluation Designs." In James W. Guthrie (Ed.), *Educational Evaluation and Policy Analysis*. Washington, DC: American Educational Research Association, 1989, pp. 255–74.

Kerlinger, Fred N. *Foundations of Behavioral Research* (3rd ed.). New York: Holt, Rinehart and Winston, 1986.

Lee, Barbara. "Statistical Conclusion Validity in Ex Post Facto Designs: Practicality in Evaluation." *Educational Evaluation and Policy Analysis*, 7:1 (Spring 1985): 35–45.

Reiss, Albert J., Jr. "Some Failures in Designing Data Collection That Distort Results." In Leigh Burstein, Howard E. Freeman, and Peter H. Rossi (Eds.), *Collecting Evaluation Data: Problems and Solutions*. Beverly Hills, CA: Sage Publications, 1985.

Rossi, Peter H., and Howard E. Freeman.

"Randomized Designs for Impact Assessment." *Evaluation: A Systematic Approach* (4th ed.). Newbury Park, CA: Sage, 1989, pp. 271–308.

Rossi, Peter H., and Howard E. Freeman. "Non-Randomized Designs for Impact Assessment." *Evaluation: A Systematic Approach* (4th ed.). Newbury Park, CA: Sage, 1989, pp. 309–74.

Sirotnik, K. A. "Psychometric Implications of the Unit-of-Analysis 'Problem' (with examples from the measurement of organizational climate)." *Journal of Educational Measurement*, 17 (1980): 245–81.

Worthen, Blaine R., and James R. Sanders. "Collecting Evaluation Information." *Educational Evaluation: Alternative Approaches and Practical Guidelines*. White Plains, NY: Longman, 1987, pp. 298–327.

CHAPTER ELEVEN

Sampling Strategies

Everyone knows what sampling is. Almost all of us, in fact, have been involved in one or more sampling operations such as being interviewed by Gallup or Harris pollsters. Further, most people recognize why anyone adopts sampling procedures. By sampling a population of U.S. voters, we can get an idea of how the whole group is apt to behave.

Sampling in Assorted Settings

Sampling in Daily Life

In reality, even if someone has not been interviewed (whether in person or by telephone) as part of a sample-based survey, that person undoubtedly uses sampling on a far more frequent basis than is usually recognized. We all form opinions about things such as whether "politicians are more interested in personal fame than in public service." We do not form those opinions on the basis of an exhaustive study of all politicians. Rather, we use our limited experiences with the actions of some politicians to form a judgment about the general tendency of politicians. In essence, we *sample* all possible interactions with politicians so that we form an opinion based on our own, typically limited, sample of such interactions. Indeed, most of the opinions held by people are based on sampled experiences.

Sampling for Research

An educational researcher engages in sampling because the researcher wishes to generalize a set of findings based on the sampled data to a larger population. This is only natural because researchers are in the business of making generalizations from samples to populations. They want to discern the nature of relationships between variables. The more generalizable the finding, the better. A researcher's dream, in fact, would be to identify such a strong and generalizable relationship among a set of variables that predictions could confidently be made about one variable on the basis of another.

The educational researcher will often expend considerable energy on defining a population clearly, then sample from it carefully, because it is to the population that generalizations from the sample are made. Drawing a representative sample from that population, such as is used when one conducts an educational experiment on a small number of learners, is obviously important. If the sample is not truly representative of the population, the generalization from sample data to the larger population is clearly unwarranted.

Sampling for Evaluation

Evaluators will also engage in sampling operations. In many ways their reasons for doing so are identical to those of the researcher, but on a far more limited scale. The population of learners with which evaluators are concerned is typically more modest. Such a population might be, for example, all the high school seniors in a particular school district. The reasons that the evaluator engages in sampling are more often associated with questions of economy and practicality than of generalizability. There is a sense, of course, in which the educational evaluator needs to generalize to a population of future students who might interact with subsequent replications of the instructional program being evaluated.

In many educational situations there is no feasible way for the evaluator to gather large amounts of data from each child. Teachers and administrators would balk, for example, if an evaluator asked for several hours of testing time each week from each pupil. Whether their view is warranted or not, most educators believe that this much time away from their normal instructional endeavors would irreparably damage pupils.

But evaluation is a data-based enterprise. Evidence regarding the status of learners (such as before and after instruction) is often viewed as indispensable to certain varieties of well-conducted evaluations. Yet, because evaluators cannot intrude excessively on the ongoing school program, they must gather their data as economically as possible. Sampling is the answer.

Major approaches to sampling will be described in this chapter. Several are conventional sampling techniques used for several decades, notably by survey researchers but also by experimentally oriented investigators. We shall also consider newer approaches to sampling, approaches well suited to educational evaluation applications.

Sampling and Representativeness

Technically, *sampling* consists of considering any segment of a population or universe to be representative of that population or universe. Note that in this definition the term *considering* is used. The fact that we consider a sample to be representative of a population does not automatically render that sample representative. A sample may or may not be representative of the population from which it was drawn.

Representativeness means that a sample is typical of a population; that is, it accurately embodies the important characteristics of the population. If the important characteristics of a given population of pupils are (1) their current state of reading skills and (2) their attitudes toward reading, then a representative sample drawn from that population should reflect the reading skills and attitudes present in the population.

Remember, we sample from populations — typically for economy's sake — in an effort to generalize to the population. Yet, if the sample is not truly representative of the population, then sample-based generalizations are apt to be erroneous. The trick in sampling is to be able to make sensible judgments about the representativeness of our samples.

Customary Sampling Techniques

The most commonly used sampling procedures are typically those that, within the constraints of the situation at hand, offer the most likelihood of selecting a portion of a population that will be representative of that population. Obviously, not every situation will provide the evaluator with total freedom to choose any of the many sampling procedures available. Sometimes compromises will have to be made. In the past, educational researchers have generally opted for one of the following sampling plans.

Simple Random Sampling

A *simple random sample* is one in which each individual in the population has an equal chance of being included. Because of this equality of opportunity for inclusion in the sample, random sampling offers an excellent way to reduce the likelihood of a seriously unrepresentative population sample. We often refer to a *simple* random sample, not to denigrate the sample as unintelligent but to signify that no additional sampling operation (such as stratification) is involved.

Although there are several ways of securing a random sample, the most popular is to employ a table of random numbers. Such tables will be found in the appendixes of most statistical texts. These tables typically consist of an extensive series of five-digit numbers, randomly generated by a computer, such as these:

10478
75510
22039
65959
64819
68531
09599
80130

To use a table of random numbers in constituting a simple random sample, one assigns sequential numbers to all members of the population at hand, then employs the tabled numbers to select the proportion of subject desired. To illustrate, suppose we had a group of 90 first-grade pupils from which we wished to select a sample of only 15. We would first number all our pupils, 01 through 90, then enter the table of random numbers at any point (from top to bottom, bottom to top, sideways, etc.) and pick the first 15 numbers that appeared. If we had started at the upper left two columns of numbers in this instance, we would select the students whose numbers were 10, 75, 22, 65, and so on. Numbers 91–99 (and 00) would be ignored.[1]

Another commonly recommended technique for constituting a random sample is to place the number of all subjects on disks (statisticians appear to have access to an unlimited supply of disks), thoroughly mix the disks, then select the disks from a container until the appropriate number of them has been chosen. Because of the imprecision associated with disk mixing by hand (few mechanical disk mixers have been financially successful), this procedure is less appropriate than employing random-number tables.

One of the writer's less-talented, but no-less-creative graduate students once suggested a variant on this procedure. When asked, on the final examination in a statistics class, to describe a common sampling procedure, she responded as follows.

> First you take small slips of paper and put every subject's name on them. Then you put all of the slips in a brown paper bag. Next you blindfold yourself. Now shake the bag vigorously. Then while still blindfolded, you pull out the appropriate number of slips. This gives you an unbiased *rambling* sample.

As one might guess, sampling experts have never been sufficiently excited by this suggestion to substitute *rambling* for *random* samples in their recommended procedures.

A more formal definition of *random sampling* is that it is a method of drawing a portion of a population or universe so that each member of the population or universe has an equal chance of being selected. Suppose, for example, we were trying to select a sample of 50 pupils randomly from a population of 500. If, using a table of random numbers or some comparable technique, we selected the first pupil (Johnny Jergins) in the sample, that pupil had a 1/500 chance of being selected. If we return Johnny Jergins's number to the original pool, then the next chosen pupil also has a 1/500 chance of being selected. Putting once-selected sample members back into the population prior to the next selection is called *sampling with replacement*.

If we had not put Johnny Jergins's number back into the original pool, then the next chosen pupil would have had only a 1/499 chance of being selected. This technique is called *sampling without replacement*. Although sampling with replacement is one of those technical niceties that make statisticians joyful, it probably is not requisite in most of the sampling chores faced by educational evaluators. After all, if Johnny Jergins's number is randomly chosen again, you'll need to toss it back in the original pool, like an undersized trout, and draw again.

As you will see, random sampling is a particularly useful procedure because it precludes our consciously or unconsciously allowing some factor to lead us to select a biased, hence unrepresentative, sample. If a teacher is asked by an evaluator to select a representative sample of 10 students, there is a high likelihood that the teacher may select not 10 typical students but perhaps the 10 most talented, most docile, or most unruly (if the evaluator is going to take them away for a while). Random sampling does not allow us to bias our samples in that fashion.

The reason that random sampling works is that the characteristics that are typical of the population will be present in greater frequency in a random sample and hence are most likely to be selected. Although we hope that a randomly selected sample will, indeed, be representative, there's no way to be absolutely certain that the sample is truly representative. Random sampling, however, eliminates the possibility of the sampler's biases messing up the sample's representativeness.

Stratified Random Sampling

Although simple random sampling can provide us with representative samples, we can add greater representativeness to sampling estimates by drawing a *stratified random sample*. Stratified random sampling utilizes supplementary information about the population so that samples drawn are more apt to be representative of that population.

The population is first divided into any subpopulations whose nature would appear to be relevant in some way to the measures we are making. (Don't, therefore, ritualistically subdivide a population into age, sex, and socioeconomic subgroups unless there is some reason to believe that these dimensions are relevant to the things you're measuring.) This technique assumes, of course, that you have access to the information that will permit you to make these decisions. For example, you would have to know that in the population of learners under consideration there are approximately 47 percent males and 53 percent females.

The subpopulations are called *strata*, and from each *stratum* (singular) there is typically drawn a proportional number of subjects by random sampling. Drawings are made independently in each of the strata. The strata selected, incidentally, should be mutually exclusive and exhaustive.

To illustrate the application of stratified random sampling procedures in an evaluation context, we might think of an "end-of-instruction attitude toward school" measurement that we wished to secure for an entire school district. Because there are many pupils in the district (10,000), the evaluator decides to draw a sample, thereby conserving both the students' time and the money required to administer and score tests. To make the sample more representative of the entire district than a random sample might be, the evaluator decides to employ a stratified random sample. First, the variables in the population of potential relevance (to attitudes toward school) are isolated. Suppose previous studies in the district have suggested that ethnicity seems to be related to learners' attitudes toward school. Accordingly, the evaluator checks the central office to determine that the ethnic percentages of all schoolchildren in the district are as follows:

Anglo   42%
Hispanic   21%

Black	20%
Oriental	11%
Others	6%

In constituting a 500-student stratified random sample of the district's 10,000 pupils, the evaluator then determines that 210 (42 percent) will be Anglo children, 105 (21 percent) will be Hispanic youngsters, and so on. The specific pupils for each stratum, their number predetermined by the percentage of pupils in the population, are drawn randomly. The result is a more representative sample than would have been derived from simple random sampling that ignored the ethnic strata. If we wish to make statements about all strata, then we may want to oversample the smaller group (that is, overrepresent the proportion of individuals in a given stratum) and, in forming estimates for the total group, reduce the contribution of such oversampled strata accordingly.

It is possible, of course, to add additional strata to the sampling plan. If the stratified sampling plan becomes very complicated, the evaluator would be well advised to consult one of the references on sampling cited at the close of this chapter. Another alternative is to secure the services of a sampling expert who can aid in the design of a complex sampling plan.

It should be noted that when we refer to a sample as a *simple random sample* or a *stratified random sample*, we are really describing one *procedure* by which all samples are computed, not a characteristic of the sample. One can't tell whether a sample is random merely by looking at it — even looking at it closely. Because simple random sampling does not guarantee a sample that will be representative in terms of some important characteristic(s), stratified random sampling (which does) is seen as a more refined method of sampling.

Varieties of Samples

Thus far we have considered two varieties of random sampling: simple and stratified. Simple random sampling is the model on which all scientific sampling is predicated. In reality, however, educational evaluators will not be employing simple random samples all that often.

There are two fundamental categories of samples. Those that employ some form of random sampling at one or more stages are called *probability samples*. Samples that do not employ random sampling are called *nonprobability samples*.

Nonprobability Samples

Because nonprobability samples do not use random sampling, it is impossible to make probabilistic estimates regarding the degree of their accuracy, that is, the confidence we can place in their representativeness (of the population). Nonprobability samples, however, must often be used by educational evaluators. The deficiencies of such samples can be partially alleviated if sensitivity and care are used in determining the sample. Remember, educational evaluators must function in a decisively practical real-world arena. If, employing real-world wisdom, evaluators can use samples that are as representative as possible, this approach will usually be sufficient for the needs of most decision makers.

Quota Sampling   One frequently used form of nonprobability sampling is *quota sampling*, wherein the evaluator relies on knowledge regarding key population strata such as sex, ethnicity, income, and so on. As might be surmised, quota sampling calls for the assignment of quotas, that is, proportions of types of people, to the sample. Thus, for instance, interviewers of students in a cafeteria might be directed to interview 30 Hispanic girls, 25 Hispanic boys, 30 Asian girls, and so on. Quota sampling is used a good deal in the conduct of opinion polls.

Purposive Sampling   Another form of nonprobability sampling is *purposive sampling*, in which an attempt is made to secure a representative sample by deliberately selecting groups (or regions) thought to be typical of the population. Thus, for example, if there were many elementary schools in a metropolitan school district, a purposive sample would be chosen by the evaluator's including students from a smaller number of schools deemed "most typical."

Accidental Sampling   *Accidental sampling* is the weakest form of sampling. Unfortunately, it is probably the most frequent type of sampling in the field of education. Although the term *accidental* makes it appear that the members of the population fell off a bicycle and into the sample, it's not all that whimsical. In essence, one takes *available* samples at one's disposal. Thus, if a convenient sample of high school sophomores is at hand, plus a number of school board members, then such individuals are used in the sample. Sometimes referred to as *samples of convenience* or *opportunity samples,* accidental samples are to be avoided unless the evaluator can't get any better samples. Often, that is precisely the case. If accidental samples must be used, be wary in your interpretation of the data. The representativeness of the sample is clearly questionable.

Probability Samples

Cluster Sampling   A useful form of probability sampling is *cluster sampling*, in which the unit of sampling is not the individual but a naturally occurring group of individuals. This procedure is often used when it is more convenient to select preformed groups of individuals than it is to select individuals from a population. To illustrate cluster sampling, imagine that you are attempting to draw a 300-pupil sample of ninth-grade English classes from a large district with 100 ninth-grade English classes, each of which has 30 pupils per class. To get the sample, you could draw 300 youngsters randomly from the 3,000 pupils in all 100 classes. But, if that process is impractical because of the measurement interruption to all 100 classes, you might *randomly* select 10 of the 100 classes, thereby picking up your sample of 300 learners. Note that cluster sampling becomes a form of probability sampling when we randomly select the intact groups.

The disadvantage of cluster sampling is that it sometimes yields a less accurate estimate of population's performance than would be provided via a random sampling scheme. On the other hand, the savings in time and money offered by this approach are almost always attractive trade-offs for the evaluator.

The decision to use cluster rather than random sampling often hinges on the unit of analysis to be employed when the data are analyzed. Recalling the brief discussion in Chapter Ten, there are instances when the appropriate unit of analysis must be the classroom, that is, a single average of pupil performance calculated for each class of pupils involved in the evaluation study. If this were the case, instead of having an *n* of 10, it might be preferable to draw randomly 10 students from each of 30 randomly selected classrooms, then compute an average for each of the 30 classes (represented by the 10 pupils). If the pupil, rather than the classroom, is the appropriate unit of analysis, then cluster sampling is an economical way for the educator to round up a sample.

Systematic Sampling   A convenient form of probability sampling involves drawing the subjects for the sample *systematically* from a list of the population. For example, if a 100-learner sample is to be drawn from a list of 1,000 learners, then the evaluator might *randomly* decide which number (1 through 10) to start with, then draw every tenth person from the list thereafter. For instance, if the number 8 was randomly drawn, then the *systematic* sample would be constituted by the 8th, 18th, 28th, 38th (and so on) learners. Systematic sampling can be used instead of random sampling if the evaluator is certain that the population list is in a reasonably aperiodic order. If there is any possibility that there is *periodicity* in the list — that is, if every *n*th person on the list shares a characteristic not shared by others on the list — then simple random sampling should be preferred. Periodicity, however, doesn't occur all that often.

Sample Size

The question of how to determine sample size is one of the evaluator's most difficult problems. The key, of course, is to draw a sample large enough so that those making the educational decisions will have confidence that the sample results are truly indicative of those that would be present had the entire population been measured.

A better way to put this might be to say that we must determine the uncertainty in the estimate that one would tolerate before changing a decision. For example, would the decision be different if our estimates were off by *x* percent or *y* points? At the point at which the decision changes, we need sufficient precision to be sure we don't make a "wrong" decision because of sampling variability. Looking at the problem this way, evaluators can often get by with much smaller samples than they might normally think.

Often, therefore, the evaluator will have to gauge the decision maker's receptivity to various sample sizes. Suppose, for example, that on the basis of some small-scale statistical analyses it was determined that a sample of 100 would yield a reasonably accurate estimate of the student population's preferences regarding a particular school program. Yet, it becomes apparent that the members of the school board (who would use the report to reach a program revision decision) would be convinced only by a sample of 200 or more. If unable to persuade the board that the smaller sample would do the job, the evaluator ought to opt for the sample size that will make a difference, in this case the sample of 200.

Sometimes it is possible to gather measures for an entire population, then randomly select samples of different sizes from the population, with the purpose of demonstrating (for future evaluations involving samples) what kind of accuracy is yielded by samples of varying sizes. For instance, in the previous example the evaluator might have been able to persuade the school board that the 100-student sample would be sufficient if it could be demonstrated that the mean performance for the entire population was 81.2 percent and three successively drawn random samples of 100 pupils fell within 3 percentage points above or below the population mean.

Given the relatively small numbers of participants in some education programs, is it always appropriate to sample persons? How large must groups be before sampling procedures can be sensibly used? Although an unequivocal answer to this question would be desirable, such a definitive answer does not exist. Some texts on sampling do provide rules of thumb for estimating the size of samples needed for detecting group differences in relation to the magnitude of differences sought and the nature of the groups being sampled. At best, though, those are rough estimates. It is important to recognize that the task of identifying a sufficiently large sample is more difficult than is usually thought.

Intuitively, we may recognize that when we start with a very small group of program participants, the use of sampling is risky. For instance, if there were only nine pupils involved, few educators would try to split these participants into three groups of three each for the purpose of testing different programs. Even though each group represents one-third of the total population, there is too much likelihood that a sample of three individuals does not properly represent the total group.

The variability of participants' anticipated performance on the measures is the primary influence on the sample size necessary. The following example illustrates the effect of population variability on sample size. If a man's socks were all stored in a drawer and there were only gray and white pairs, he wouldn't need to draw out too many pairs until he had a reasonably good idea of the characteristics of the total population of socks in his drawer. But suppose he had socks in 10 different colors. Then he would most likely have to take out many more pairs until he could reach an accurate estimate of the colors of socks in the drawer. In much the same way, if it is expected that participants' scores on a test will be relatively homogeneous, a smaller number of respondents will be needed than if participants' scores are expected to vary widely.

It is possible, as we shall see, to compute *confidence intervals;* these serve as ranges which (on the basis of sample data) span the "true" population performance at specified probability levels. This procedure will be examined in more detail in Chapter Twelve.

Sample Precision

It is apparent that although we would prefer to be perfectly precise in estimating population data from our sample data, there is a degree of imprecision associated with sampling. An expression often used in connection with sampling operations is *standard error*, which provides an estimate of the possible magnitude of error present in some obtained statistic. The larger the standard error, the less confidence we have in the precision of our sample-based statistics. The smaller the standard error, the more likelihood that our sample estimates are precise reflectors of values in the population. Measures based on *samples*, such as the mean or standard deviation, are often referred to as *statistics*. Those same measures, when computed for the entire *population*, are referred to as *parameters*. It is important to determine how closely our sample's statistics match the population's parameters. The extent of this match provides us with an idea of the sample's representativeness.

We can illustrate the meaning of standard error of measurement by referring to Figure 11-1, in which two sets of score distributions are presented, where the *scores* are really *means* obtained by repeatedly sampling the population. Each of the distributions (A and B) has been produced by plotting the means yielded from each of 500 separate sampling operations. The population mean is, as seen, 20. Now,

FIGURE 11-1 • *Fictitious Distributions of Sample Means Based on 500 Replications of Two Different (A and B) Sampling Schemes*

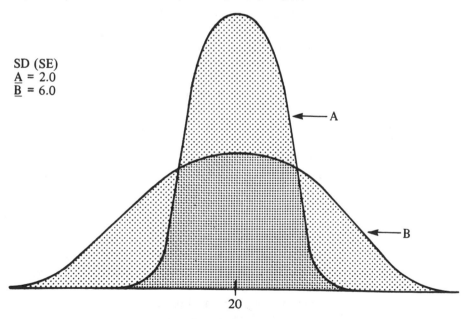

SD (SE)
A = 2.0
B = 6.0

20
Population Mean

note distribution B, which results from sampling procedure B. Its distribution is much more spread out than that of distribution A. The standard deviation of distribution B is 6.0, reflecting the fact that it is more dispersed than distribution A, which has a standard deviation of only 2.0. This indicates that a greater number of the sample means drawn via sampling procedure B missed the mark (the population mean of 20) by any given amount than did those produced from procedure A. Sampling procedure A is the more precise.

The standard deviations of those two distributions are referred to as *standard errors* and it can be seen, therefore, that the smaller the standard error of a sample statistic, the greater confidence we can have in its accuracy.

We don't have to draw 500 samples to get an estimate of the sample's standard error. It can be calculated on the basis of a single sample. However, it is a useful concept to employ when we deal with various types of sampling procedures. For example, cluster sampling typically yields a somewhat larger standard error than a simple random sample of the same size drawn from the same population. As we shall see later, there are other sampling techniques that can shave the standard error even more.

Randomized Assignment

Thus far we have focused on random *sampling*. Another use of randomization occurs when we engage in *randomized assignment* of individuals to treatment groups. Randomized assignment constitutes an effort on the part of the evaluator to make as equivalent as possible the individuals who are instructed via different programs. Sometimes, although not often, educational evaluators have such a luxury. More frequently, of course, ongoing educational activities preclude the use of randomized assignment procedures.

The two procedures of random selection and randomized assignment are illustrated in Figure 11–2. Note that we randomly select participants from the pool of potential participants, then randomly assign those individuals selected to either Program A or Program B.

Use of randomization techniques does not necessarily create equivalent groups. For example, if we were to randomly distribute 100 potential participants in an education program into a treatment and a no-treatment group, it is still possible that one of the groups would end up with individuals who, when pretested, turned out to be significantly different in relation to characteristics of interest than those in the other group. In such instances evaluators must rely on statistical procedures in an effort to compensate for such disparities. In most instances, however, use of randomization will create groups of sufficient equivalence that such statistical adjustments are not needed.

As was indicated earlier, program personnel often may not be able to constitute groups via random selection or randomized assignment. In some situations, in fact, program personnel would not want to use such procedures. When randomization is not used, it is especially important to collect and examine descriptive data carefully in order to determine where preexisting differences occur and to consider the ways in which they may influence outcome data. Even if randomization is impossible, attempts to constitute comparison groups with individuals as equivalent as possible can help minimize the influence of preexisting participant differences.

Matrix Sampling

During recent years a new approach to sampling, which can be of particular use to the educational evaluator, has been devised. Known as *matrix sampling*, this procedure was developed chiefly by Frederic Lord,[2] who in the mid- and late 1950s authored a series of theoretical papers regarding the approach. In 1965 Lord spelled out even more clearly the rationale and potential advantages of matrix sampling.[3] Since that time a number of other psychometricians have advanced the technical procedures needed to employ matrix sampling methods more effectively.[4]

Sampling Examinees and Sampling Items

In the conventional sampling procedures described earlier, it was apparent that we were selecting different individuals (or, in a measurement context, *examinees*) from a population. What Lord and his associates recognized is that for purposes of estimating a group's performance on a particular measure it is not necessary to have all the sampled examinees complete all of the items in a test. If every examinee completed every item, we would refer to the process as *census testing*. Yet, not only can one engage in *examinee sampling* (only some examinees complete all items) but in *item sampling* (only some of the items are completed by all examinees) as well. For many people this is a revolutionary idea. We have been nurtured on the

FIGURE 11-2 • *Randomized Selection of Participants from Pool of Potential Participants and Randomized Assignment of Participants to Programs*

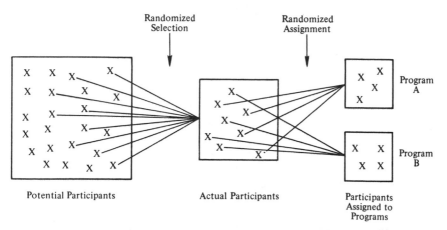

idea that sampling involves the selection of certain individuals who, having been selected, typically complete an entire test. After all, if such examinees didn't complete the entire test, how could we determine their score on the whole test? Sometimes we don't need to.

The educational evaluator is often faced with situations in which the task is not to establish how individuals perform on a test but, instead, to determine how a group performs. Indeed, the evaluator is characteristically more interested in the quality of educational programs as reflected by their impact on a group of examinees. Learner data, as was noted previously, are gathered from individuals but treated collectively. To secure accurate estimates of a group's performance, it is absolutely unnecessary to have individuals complete the entire test. In fact, with a relatively large group of learners the most accurate way to secure an estimate of the group mean is to administer one test item to each examinee.

I used this procedure for a number of years in large lecture classes at UCLA. When wishing to evaluate the effectiveness of 30-minute tape-slide instructional programs on a pretest-posttest basis, I would devise criterion-referenced tests of 10 to 20 items, one test per program, then have each of the items printed on a 3-by-5-inch card. Having shuffled the cards adroitly with all the flourish of a Las Vegas blackjack dealer, I would distribute them, *one card at a time*, to the 150–200 students enrolled. No one objected to these 30-second tests, for they took such a small bit of time. Yet, when I assembled the data collectively, the results gave me a good idea of how the total class could perform before and after the instructional program. For each item, I typically had 10 to 20 individual responses, enough to supply some evidence regarding how the entire class might perform on the item.

Because it is convenient to consider one's examinee-sampling and item-sampling options at one time, research specialists often display their data in a box or *matrix* such as that seen in Figure 11–3, where the horizontal axis refers to test items

FIGURE 11-3 • *An Illustrative Matrix Representing Examinee Performance on Test Items*

Test Items

	1	2	3	4	5	6	etc.
1	1	0	0	1	1	0	
2	1	0	1	0	1	1	
3	1	0	1	1	0	1	
4	0	1	1	0	1	1	
5	1	1	0	1	1	1	
etc.							

Examinees (left vertical axis label)

and the vertical axis refers to examinees. The zeros and ones in the matrix indicate whether the examinee answered the item correctly (1) or incorrectly (0). Different gradations of responses could also be used, such as is frequently seen with affective measures (3 = agree, 2 = neutral, 1 = disagree).

Multiple-Matrix Sampling

Now imagine a larger data matrix such as that seen in Figured 11–4, where we have 50 items across the top and 100 examinees on the vertical axis. It would be possible to sample some examinees and some items simultaneously. Doing this results in an *item-examinee* sample, customarily referred to as a *matrix sample*. To illustrate, suppose we had randomly identified individuals 1, 4, 28, 37, 42, 50, 75, and 80 to represent our examinee sample. Then suppose that we randomly select items 4, 9, 17, 26, and 37 to represent our item sample. By having the selected examinees complete the selected items, we constitute a matrix sample. If we repeated this process, we would secure a second matrix sample. Several such matrix samples are symbolically represented in Figure 11–4, although in reality if we sampled the examinees and items cited above the matrix, samples would be scattered out rather amorphously.

By repeating the initial operation several times, that is, drawing new item-examinee samples, we can constitute a *multiple-matrix sample*. Multiple-matrix samples are significant because they provide the most accurate estimate of popula-

FIGURE 11–4 • *An Illustrative Data Matrix Reflecting Multiple-Matrix Samples*

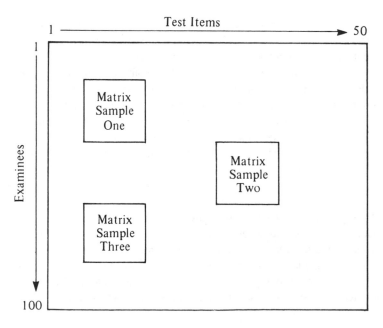

tion parameters of all the sampling procedures we have considered thus far. For example, if we were to compute the means for 10 separate matrix samples used in a multiple-matrix sampling approach, and then average out the 10 separately derived sample means, the resulting value would be our best bet for estimating the population's mean.

There is some disagreement among matrix-sampling methodologists regarding whether the samples that constitute matrix sampling should be drawn *with* or *without replacement*. Most people appear to favor sampling without replacement, that is, once items or examinees are assigned to one matrix sample they are no longer available for assignment to another matrix sample.

Advantages of Matrix Sampling

Particularly for purposes of educational evaluation there are some advantages associated with matrix sampling that should be noted.

Reduced Testing Time per Student   Since today's educational evaluator relies heavily on measurement data, typically measurement data derived from test administrations, any procedure to reduce the time needed to test learners is a boon. Matrix sampling really fills this need. Because not all examinees need be tested and those who are tested need not complete all the items, matrix sampling represents a considerable economy for evaluators, saving the testing time taken away from an individual learner's instructional activities and the supervisory time required of those administering the tests. Overall, however, more students must be tested or more items must be administered to achieve the same level of precision as if we were using sampling procedures other than matrix.

Smaller Standard Error of Estimate   It has been demonstrated both algebraically and empirically (postmortem sampling for known populations to verify the accuracy of different sampling schemes) that *multiple-matrix sampling* will generally yield a smaller standard error of estimate than either examinee sampling, item sampling, or a single item-examinee or matrix sample. This assumes, of course, that the numbers of observations[5] are comparable in the different sampling approaches. We would almost always get a more accurate estimate from, for example, simple random sampling (a form of examinee sampling) if we used a large sample of the population—as opposed to a very small multiple-matrix sample. But, if the magnitude of the data gathered is comparable, multiple-matrix sampling gives us the best estimate available.

Measuring Large Item Domains   In some cases the number of test items constituting a domain will be so numerous that if we want to know how a group performs on the total domain, there is no alternative to matrix sampling. For instance, suppose a foreign-language teacher wishes to test a class's knowledge of 600 vocabulary words. It would be unlikely that any procedure other than matrix sampling could be practically used to secure information about all the words.

Less Threatening to Individual Examinees   There is plenty of evidence that some people become so threatened by the prospect of being tested that they perform below their capabilities on the examination. Because in a matrix-sampling setting it is obvious that most examinees cannot be compared (most of them are completing different sets of test items), those individuals who freeze under typical test conditions may thaw out a bit.

Limitations of Matrix Sampling

Not all is euphoric, however. There are some difficulties with matrix sampling that should be weighed along with its positive features.

Performances of Individuals Unknown   Although for many evaluation applications there is no need for data regarding individual learner performance, there are instances when it would be useful to have such data. For example, certain states are moving to a matrix sampling statewide educational assessment plan. This scheme provides the statewide decision makers with the requisite information, but a good many teachers find themselves yearning for some sort of pupil-by-pupil test scores. The evaluator will have to reckon with the fact that no individual learner-performance data will be available from this group-oriented sampling procedure.

Logistics of Administering Multiple Tests   There is something incredibly straightforward about having every person complete every item in a test. Everybody gets the same test form. Every test is scored with an identical scoring key. Even students who lean toward cheating find real advantages in having all examinees receive the same tests. Those evaluators considering the use of matrix sampling procedures should recognize that the juggling of many different test forms—their administration, scoring, and assimilation—represents a nontrivial problem. For the very young learners (or foreign students), whose lack of reading skills requires tests to be administered orally, the time required to administer tests via matrix sampling is awesome.

Context Effects for Speeded Tests   There have been several studies conducted in which the way an examinee responds to an item in a total set of test items is contrasted with the way the examinee responds to items in a matrix sample. If there are substantial differences in the examinee's performance under the two conditions, then *context* effects are said to be present. For unspeeded tests—that is, those in which there is no maximum time limit set on student performance—there appears to be little or no context effects associated with matrix sampling items. For speeded tests, however, context effects logically appear to be operative. Hence, matrix sampling should typically not be used for speeded tests.

Data-Processing Requirements   For certain kinds of data-processing operations involving matrix sampled data, the evaluator must employ electronic computers to treat the data. Although for the bulk of evaluation requirements these more sophisticated analyses will not be needed, the evaluator who contemplates use of matrix sampling should make sure that the requisite data-processing equipment is available. An abacus is usually not sufficient.

Impersonal Measurement and Optimal Performance   One advantage of matrix sampling is that individuals may not feel threatened by the items they are obliged to complete, inasmuch as the fact that other examinees complete other items renders comparisons impossible. But this positive feature has a negative side. Some people only perform their best when they have a personal stake in the testing situation. There is a possibility, therefore, that some examinees who sense the essentially noncomparative nature of matrix sampling may fail to perform at their optimal levels. This is an unstudied question thus far.

On Balance

Although the application of matrix-sampling methodology is not without its problems, a consideration of its pros and cons would strongly suggest that there are a number of situations in which the evaluator will find it strategically advantageous to use this technique. Its saving of time for any one examinee, the ability to sample a domain widely, and its reduced standard error of estimate are particularly compelling advantages.

It is important for those who would employ matrix-sampling procedures to keep abreast of the technical developments associated with the procedure. The step-by-step procedures needed to decide, for example, how many examinees, items, or matrix samples to select are beyond the scope of this treatment. More technical references should be consulted. Used as a substitute for, or in connection with, some of the other sampling procedures described in this chapter, matrix sampling can prove a useful ally for educational evaluators.

Discussion Questions

1. Why do evaluators engage in sampling? Are their reasons for sampling basically different from those of educational researchers? If so, how?
2. Can you think of educational situations, not necessarily those associated with evaluation endeavors, in which different kinds of sampling procedures would be appropriate? What are the distinguishing features of such situations?
3. How would you present the major strengths and weaknesses of matrix sampling if you were reporting to a school board regarding this sampling procedure?

Practical Exercise

1. Eleven descriptions of sampling procedures follow. Decide which of the following descriptions is most appropriate for each:
   Simple random sampling
   Stratified random sampling
   Cluster sampling
   Systematic sampling
   Quota sampling
   Purposive sampling
   Accidental sampling
   Item sampling

Matrix sampling
Multiple-matrix sampling
Census testing

a. The evaluator studies the status of 10 percent of the state's pupils by randomly sampling 10 percent of the state's school districts — measuring every pupil within each district sampled.

b. A class of 50 pupils is randomly assigned 25 of 500 spelling words to determine whether pupils can properly spell the words after oral presentation by the test administrator.

c. Bob Harris, a high school principal, draws a 20 percent sample of his school's student body by selecting every fifth name from the school's master roll book. He chose the first student to start with by using a table of random numbers.

d. The 50 students whose I.D. numbers appear first in a table of random numbers are included in the sample.

e. The data base for this evaluation project involves all examinees. Each examinee is required to complete the entire test instrument.

f. In this random sample a provision is made to ensure proportional representation of students representing different socioeconomic status groups.

g. This nonprobability sampling plan hinges on the evaluator's use of convenient-to-measure intact classes of sixth-grade pupils.

h. This sampling plan can be described as a series of item-examinee samples.

i. Pupils' names are placed on cardboard disks, placed in a box, then selected until the proper size sample has been chosen.

j. Some of the examinees and some of the items are randomly identified, then those examinees selected complete the items selected.

Answers to Practice Exercise

1. *a.* cluster sampling; *b.* item sampling; *c.* systematic sampling; *d.* simple random sampling; *e.* census testing; *f.* stratified random sampling; *g.* accidental sampling; *h.* multiple-matrix sampling; *i.* simple random sampling; *j.* matrix sampling.

Notes

1. There is hardly a statistics textbook on the market that doesn't contain a table of random numbers. Indeed, if you were thumbing through the last 20 or 30 pages of a statistics text, you would be apt to encounter such a table, almost at random. Random-number tables are disgustingly common. But not everyone knows that!

Upon joining the faculty at UCLA in the early 1960s, I took on any consulting assignment that came my way. Assistant professors, as has been empirically established, need to eat. On one of these con-

sulting excursions I was in the process of advising the faculty of a nearby dental school that they could assign students to an experimental or control group by using a table of random numbers. Unfamiliar with random-number tables, the dental professors asked me to describe one. Pointing out the utility of such random-number tables, I described them. The dean of the dental faculty paused thoughtfully, then asked the key question: "Dr. Popham, do you have *access* to such a table?"

Suppressing my surprise, as is appropriate for novice consultants, I responded that, with effort, I could "put my hands on one." In any library, of course, I could have put my hands on half a hundred such tables.

2. F. M. Lord, "Estimating Norms by Item Sampling," *Educational and Psychological Measurement*, 22 (1962), 259-67.

3. F. M. Lord, *Item Sampling in Test Theory and Research Design* (Princeton, NJ: Educational Testing Service, 1965).

4. D. M. Shoemaker, *Principles and Procedures of Multiple Matrix Sampling* (Cambridge, MA: Ballinger, 1973). Also K. Sirotnik, "An Introduction to Matrix Sampling for the Practitioner," in *Evaluation in Education: Current Applications* (Berkeley, CA: McCutchan Publishing, 1974).

5. Defined as the product of the number of examinees tested and the number of responses per examinee.

Selected References

Berry, Sandra H., "Field Sampling Problems in Data Collection for Evaluation Research." In Leigh Burstein, Howard E. Freeman, and Peter H. Rossi (Eds.), *Collecting Evaluation Data: Problems and Solutions*. Beverly Hills, CA: Sage, 1985.

Cochran, William G. *Sampling Techniques*. New York: John Wiley, 1953.

Feldt, L. S. and R. A. Forsyth, "An Examination of the Context Effect in Item Sampling. *Journal of Educational Measurement*, 2 (1974): 73-83.

Gressard, Risa P., and Brenda H. Loyd. "A Comparison of Item Sampling Plans in the Application of Multiple Matrix Sampling." In James Algina (Ed.), *Journal of Educational Measurement*. Washington, DC: National Council on Measurement in Education, 1991, pp. 119-30.

Jaeger, Richard M. *A Primer on Sampling for Statewide Assessment*. Princeton, NJ: Educational Testing Service, 1973.

Johnson, Palmer O. "Development of the Sample Survey as a Scientific Methodology." *Journal of Experimental Education*, 27 (1959).

Kerlinger, Fred N. *Foundations of Behavioral Research* (3rd ed.). New York: Holt, Rinehart and Winston, 1986.

Kish, L. "Selection of the Sample." In L. Festinger and D. Katz (Eds.), *Research Methods in the Behavioral Sciences*. New York: Holt, Rinehart and Winston, 1953.

Lord, F. M. "Estimating Norms by Item Sampling." *Educational and Psychological Measurement*, 23 (1962): 259-67.

———. *Item Sampling in Test Theory and Research Design*. Princeton, NJ: Educational Testing Service, 1965.

Lord, F. M., and M. R. Novick. *Statistical Theories of Mental Test Scores*. Reading, MA: Addison-Wesley, 1968.

Sadler, D. Royce. "Evaluation, Policy Analysis, and Multiple Case Studies: Aspects of Focus and Sampling." *Educational Evaluation and Policy Analysis*, 7:2 (Summer 1985): 143-49.

Shoemaker, D. M. *Principles and Procedures of Multiple Matrix Sampling*. Cambridge, MA: Ballinger, 1973.

Sirtonik, K. "An Introduction to Matrix Sampling for the Practitioner." In *Evaluation in Education: Current Applications*. Berkeley, CA: McCutchan Publishing, 1974.

Warwick, D., and C. Lininger. *The Sample Survey: Theory and Practice* (Chap. 4). New York: McGraw-Hill, 1975.

Yates, Frank. *Sampling Methods for Censuses and Surveys*. London: Charles Griffing, 1949.

CHAPTER TWELVE

Analyzing Evaluative Data

There is an all-too-common misconception among novice evaluators that, even though distinctive techniques should be applied during earlier phases of an evaluation study, when it comes to data analysis, evaluators are justified in reverting to the traditional statistical analyses employed by educational researchers. An inspection of many reports of evaluation projects reveals a data-analysis section that, for all practical purposes, cannot be distinguished from the data-analysis segment of a classical hypothesis-testing research investigation. Yet, it is precisely for "practical purposes" that evaluators are scurrying around these days. As will be seen in this chapter, the best way to promote practical improvements in education is not necessarily to adopt, almost ritualistically, the statistical analysis techniques used by researchers.

Educational evaluators, even those who have been nurtured on a traditional diet of significance tests, must never lose sight of the fact that theirs is a practitioner-oriented endeavor. The evaluator's task is not to produce technically flawless reports that will appear in the professional journals destined to compete for dust intake with the myriad bound journals on library shelves. Rather, the evaluator should be engaging in worth-determination activities that make a difference in the way education takes place. This position translates into a data-analysis stance that is *decision focused*.

An Impossible Task

Given enough time, and paper, this chapter would provide the reader with a thorough understanding of the conceptual and computational ingredients associated with the statistical analysis of any data the evaluator will encounter. But to do so, of course, would require the creation of a full-blown educational statistics text. Having already written such a book,[1] and suffered the cerebral damage that goes with proofreading the galleys and page proofs of a statistics text, I am unwilling to reenter that battlefield. Besides the present space limitations, there is simply more in a standard statistics text than most evaluators need.

Not that a solid background in statistical methodology is to be avoided; an evaluator who is really conversant with statistical options is undoubtedly more effective than an evaluator who isn't. But in order to function well as an educational evaluator it is not imperative to be a super-statistician. For those readers who do wish to enhance their statistical prowess, and this is highly desirable, then the completion of graduate statistics courses or the reading of the selected references cited at the close of the chapter will be of help.

A Possible Task

Within practical constraints, this chapter will describe those data-analysis procedures that will most often be employed by educational evaluators. The descriptions provided will be designed to give the reader an intuitive understanding of how these various analysis procedures function. No effort will be made to describe the computational mechanics of the procedures to be examined. It is assumed that any reader who wishes to become that well versed in how actually to carry out these analyses will consult a standard statistics text designed for educational or psychological researchers. In other words, after reading this chapter the novice educational evaluator ought to have a pretty fair idea of what data-analysis schemes will be appropriate for handling most, but not all, of the situations commonly faced by evaluators. To carry out these data analyses, it will be necessary to read further or to enlist the services of a statistically competent consultant.

Prior to an examination of particular techniques, there will be a discussion of several important issues that should be understood by those who would analyze evaluative data. For example, a distinction will be drawn between the *statistical significance* and *practical significance* of data yielded by an evaluation study. Implications of this distinction for data-analysis decisions will be considered.

On the basis of this brief preview of the chapter, it should be possible for the reader to decide whether it represents necessary reading or whether to jump ahead to the next chapter. For example, most persons who have recently completed a course in educational or psychological statistics will probably be able to bypass this section. If you are unsure, you might wish to try the discussion questions and practice exercises at the close of the chapter to see how readily you can deal with the chapter's main ideas.

Descriptive Statistics

The chief reason for statistically processing data is that most people can't make much sense out of the kinds of raw data yielded by evaluation investigations. For instance, suppose we were trying to determine the worth of several instructional programs on the basis of such data as (1) pupils' scores on cognitive achievement tests, (2) pupils' responses to affective self-report inventories, and (3) participating teachers' written reactions to the programs. Imagine that there were a couple of hundred pupils involved, plus 20 or so teachers. Now it is obvious that if the evaluator were to leaf through each individual test score, each affective inventory, and each teacher's report, a rough impression of the data could be obtained—but oh how rough it would be.

People generally don't have calibrated eyeballs or mammoth memories. We see what we want to. We selectively forget. We are overwhelmed by many numbers.

In order to reduce mountains of data to manageable molehills, most people employ techniques referred to as *descriptive statistics*. In Chapter Five we described the most commonly used of these procedures—measures of central tendency such as the mean, median, and mode, and measures of variation such as the range and standard deviation.

If an evaluator can display summary statistics that include, for example, the mean and standard deviation of a set of data, then we can secure a reasonable idea of what a whole set of data is like.

Because evaluators often must analyze data and summarize them for relatively unsophisticated (with respect to data analysis) decision makers, there will often be instances where the use of such indices as the standard deviation would be quite out of place. The consumers of such reports might think that a standard deviation was some sort of run-of-the-mill perversion.

To illustrate, in Tables 12-1 and 12-2 two different data descriptions are given. Which would be more readily understood by a typical school board? In general, most school boards would probably be able to make more sense out of results in Table 12-2, even though Table 12-1 may convey more information to those with technical sophistication. Thus, in deciding on a statistical analysis scheme, the evaluator will have to be extremely sensitive to the capabilities of the relevant decision makers to deal meaningfully with the results of the analysis techniques selected. Sometimes more conventional techniques will have to be jettisoned in favor of nonstandard but more readily understood alternatives, such as reporting the average percent correct.

TABLE 12-1 • *Evaluation Results I*

	Mean	*Standard Deviation*
Program A	51.4	4.8
Program B	48.3	6.2
Program C	54.9	5.9

TABLE 12-2 • *Evaluation Results II*

	Average % Correct	*Percentage Scoring Below 50%*	*Percentage Scoring Above 90%*
Program X	71	15	6
Program Y	81	5	13
Program Z	74	2	6

As we saw in Chapter Five, graphic methods of summarizing data are extremely useful. We shall also consider these graphic display procedures in the next chapter.

Inferential Statistics

In addition to the set of procedures known as descriptive statistics, we have access to a much larger array of analytic techniques known as *inferential statistics*. Researchers employ such techniques in order to make inferences regarding the degree to which the statistics (such as the mean) they observe in a sample are accurate reflections of the parameters (such as the mean) present in the total population. It is important for researchers to know how confidently they can make these inferences; as we have seen, they are particularly eager to determine the generalizability of their observed results.

Statistical Significance

Perhaps the most important procedure by which researchers make inferences involves the determination of the *statistical significance* of a set of results drawn from a sample. To determine statistical significance, we calculate the probability that a given event could have occurred as a function of chance. If the probability of occurrence by chance alone is small, then we attribute the results to nonchance factors, typically the research conditions under investigation.

We can illustrate this process with a simple example. Suppose an educator has tested the postinstruction performance of two groups of learners taught by two different instructional methods. The results indicate that there is a 5-point mean difference in favor of one group. Now the question is whether this 5-point disparity was brought about by the different instructional methods or whether it is the kind of difference that one might get by mere chance. There are several statistical techniques for dealing with such data, the most common of which for this situation is the *t test*. A *t* test is a numerical procedure that takes account of the size of a mean difference between two groups, the number of subjects in each group, and the amount of variation or spread present in the scores. By inserting the appropriate numerical quantities in a *t* test formula, we can compute the value of *t* for the data under analysis. We then use a statistical probability table that indicates what the chance probability is of the obtained *t* value. To continue our example, suppose we found, after subjecting the 5-point mean difference to a *t* test, that the resulting *t* value's probability was less than .01. This would indicate that less than one time in 100 the difference we had found would occur by chance alone. Because the probability of chance occurrence is so low, we would usually attribute the observed event to a nonchance cause, in this instance the difference in the instructional methods.

The conventional levels of probability employed by behavioral science researchers are .05, .01, and .001. We often say that a result that has been statistically analyzed and satisfies one of these levels is, for example, "statistically significant beyond the .01 level." Often these results are displayed in terms of probability levels, for instance, $p < .05$, which should be read as "The probability of this event's *chance* occurrence is less than five times in 100."

To repeat, an event that is statistically significant at or beyond a conventional level of probability would, *by chance alone*, occur very infrequently. If a particular set of data's level of statistical significance were .80, then the likelihood of chance occurrence would be high, hence one would be reluctant to attribute the data to anything other than chance.

Evaluators and Inferences

In earlier chapters we made quite a fuss about the fact that while researchers are inclined to make generalizations to other settings, evaluators are more concerned with decisions. Evaluators working in a particular school district should have no illusions that the results of their evaluation studies will be applicable to school districts across the nation. To the extent that other districts are comparable, there may be some applications of the results, but this is surely not the focus of a local evaluation.

There *is* a need to generalize, however, even for evaluators. The generalizations are not to populations of learners or teachers in other locales, but to the subsequent learners who will in the local situation be affected by the educational decisions involved. For example, suppose an evaluator contrasts the merits of two sets of teaching materials, hoping to determine which one has more merit. It is anticipated that an observed result in favor of one set of materials will persist if the "better" materials are used with next term's or next year's pupils. Many of the decisions of concern to evaluators are of just this sort, that is, what seems to work better at this time so we can use it in the future.

Now in this sense it is apparent that an evaluator wants to rule out the possibility (or, more accurately, reduce the probability) that an observed result that appears to favor one instructional approach is due to chance alone. Accordingly, one way of making the inference that future applications of the preferred (i.e., evaluated as superior) program will yield a consistently superior result is to ascertain the statistical significance of the data.

Because educational evaluators should be attentive to alternative courses of educational action, there will be many instances in which the evaluator will wish to establish whether observed differences in favor of one approach are statistically significant. For if the differences favoring one approach, even though they appear to be sizable, are such that they would occur by chance alone very often, then the evaluator should be loath to recommend the superior approach with unbridled enthusiasm.

Sometimes, of course, decisions have to be made even without decisive evidence in favor of one option over another. In such cases, even though we might have to proceed with a statistical significance level approximating .30 instead of .01, the odds may still incline us to act in favor of the apparently (but not indisputably) preferable approach.

Now there are all sorts of inferential statistical techniques ideally suited to testing the probabilistic significance of the kinds of data evaluators gather. Later in the chapter, we shall describe a number of those most commonly used by evaluators.

Practical Significance

Most tests of statistical significance are designed in such a way that they are particularly sensitive to the number of subjects involved in the analysis. This approach is only proper, of course, because a mean difference of 10 score points between two groups with only three or four learners in each group would be more suspect than that same size significance with several hundred learners in each group. The more subjects who are involved in the data analysis, the more stable the results, hence the less likelihood that mere chance is operating. All this attention to the number of subjects is fine, except that it sometimes leads to analyses in which the results are considered statistically significant even though, in any kind of practical terms, they would be judged unimportant. Given enough subjects, even the most trivial difference in treatment effects may turn out to be statistically significant.

Educational evaluators, because they are decision oriented, want to know not only whether an observed set of data departs from chance probability but also whether those results are *practically significant*. Some evaluators erroneously try to discern the degree of practical levels resulting from statistical analyses. For example, if an analysis turns out to be statistically significant beyond the .05 level, they will consider it less practically significant than if the result turned out to be statistically significant at the .01 level. Yet, as we have seen, the only factor operative may be the size of the sample. Some evaluators report their probabilities so that they look like the scoreboard for a no-hit baseball game (e.g., $p < .000000001$).

Statistical and practical significance cannot be equated. There are additional data-analysis schemes evaluators may use to get a better fix on the practical significance of a set of results. We shall examine some of these later in the chapter. Unfortunately, no handy analytic tools exist that will completely eliminate the necessity for the evaluator or the educational decision maker to decide whether a given result is important. By quantifying and massaging our data, we can undoubtedly make better choices, but the sticky judgmental job remains of deciding whether, for example, a 12 percent difference in favor of Program X is sufficiently meaningful to warrant the adoption of Program X over its competitors.

Although we shall return to the matter of estimating practical significance later, it should be apparent to the reader that statistical significance tests alone, though they often seem sufficient for the researcher's purpose, will fail to satisfy the evaluator's requirements. Many analyses of evaluative data will involve three separate operations:

1. Computation of descriptive statistics
2. Determination of statistical significance
3. Estimation of practical significance

Now, clearly, if the earlier phases of this three-step analysis approach indicated that subsequent steps should not be carried out, then the evaluator would stop short. If, for instance, descriptive statistics revealed no difference resulting from three treatment conditions, then it would be silly to subsequently check for statistical or practical significance. Similarly, if a test of statistical signficance indicated that chance rather than any treatment effect was the probable factor contributing to a set of observed differences (for example, $p < .50$), then it would be foolish to muck around with estimates of practical significance. But if earlier stages of this three-step strategy seem to warrant it, then its complete application may prove useful to the evaluator.

In keeping with the evaluator's provision of information to decision makers and other stakeholders, the choice of data-analysis techniques should be governed by the audiences for whom the evaluation report is intended. Alkin states:

> *Analysis procedures that are employed should be appropriate to the data collected, and analyses should always be done in a way that recognizes the evaluator's obligation to communicate to potential users. This communication should be in forms that are meaningful and likely to enhance the possibility of use. The evaluator's job is not to "dazzle" or to impress with sophisticated expertise, but rather to communicate. . . .*[2]

Common Tests of Statistical Significance

Let's now examine some of the more common statistical significance tests that evaluators will employ. Remember, in order to become familiar with all the available significance tests that might be relevant, the reader will have to engage in more detailed study than that provided here.

Relationship Tests

Two kinds of statistical significance tests of particular use to evaluators are those that test for the significance of *relationships* and those that test for the significance of *differences*. In Chapter Five we considered the most commonly employed measure of relationship, the product-moment correlation coefficient. You will recall that correlation coefficients can range in magnitude from $+1.00$ to -1.00, with a coefficient of zero reflecting no relationship between the two variables involved in the analysis. Once the size of the correlation coefficient (r) has been calculated, there are tables provided in statistics textbooks that can be used to ascertain the significance of the particular coefficient. The only real factors in this significance determination are (1) the size of the r and (2) the number of subjects (n) involved in the analysis.

As we have seen, there are a good many instances, particularly in connection with establishing the reliability or validity of measuring instruments, when evaluators will call upon correlational techniques. Several similar but slightly varied forms of correlational analysis can be employed for treating different sorts of data.

There will be other cases when evaluators may wish to employ correlational analyses. For example, suppose some teachers are trying to decide under what conditions different types of pupils prosper best with different instructional programs. It is possible to get an idea of what variables may be important to consider in setting up an evaluation design by running a series of correlational analyses, prior to designing the evaluation study, in order to see what variables (e.g., age, sex, ethnicity), if any, are related to the performance measures being employed.

But, although conversance with correlational approaches will sometimes lead to their use in evaluation investigations, the evaluator's bread-and-butter analysis techniques will be *difference-testing* procedures. We can turn now to several of the more popular tests of whether there are statistically significant differences among groups.

Difference Tests

It should not be surprising that educational evaluators will find difference tests to be most useful. After all, evaluators are engaged in the business of worth determination, typically involving comparisons among competing alternatives. The most common kind of systematic education evaluation seen is the comparison of two or more instructional programs (treatments) according to their observed effects on learners. The results (such as performance on cognitive or affective measures) of learners completing Program I are compared with those of learners completing Program II. This is an obvious case of testing for the significance of differences between results yielded by the two treatments.

It is also possible to apply difference-testing analyses to the goal-preference data supplied by groups involved in educational needs assessments (see Chapter Three). Are the differences between the ratings of various goals statistically significant, or would we get the obtained rating differences by chance alone? Again, we could test for differences among the various goals rated according to the mean ratings supplied by different groups.

In other words, because of their comparative bent, evaluators will usually end up treating their data with analyses designed to answer the question, "Is there a statistically significant difference between these two (or more) sets of data?" Let's take a look at the most widely used statistical tests that can help us answer that question.

Level of Measurement

In choosing among the available difference-testing analysis procedures, one important consideration involves the level of measurement represented by the data. In Chapter Five distinctions were drawn among the following measurement scales: *nominal, ordinal, interval*, and *ratio*. It was pointed out that the form of the data sometimes influences the type of statistical analysis selected. Simply put, if you have data reflecting one level of measurement, such as nominal data, it may be improper to use a statistical technique that would be ideal if interval data were available.

Thus, in our consideration of the several difference-testing analysis techniques, we shall be referring to the level of measurement required. In general a statistical technique designed to treat data representing a *weaker* scale of measurement will be appropriate for data reflecting a stronger measurement scale. The reverse, however, is not true. Recall that the strength of these four scales increases as follows (from left to right):

nominal < ordinal < interval/ratio

Now a statistical test designed for nominal data can usually be employed to treat ordinal or interval data. (We don't have much ratio-scale data in education.) Ordinarily, we sacrifice some precision of analysis when we do so. However, a statistical test that requires interval-scale data is usually inappropriate for the analysis of nominal or ordinal data. Because of the importance of the differences among measurement scales in any consideration of alternative data analysis schemes, the reader may wish to review the descriptions of the three most common measurement scales (nominal, ordinal, and interval) in Chapter Five.

An Illustrative Significance Test

The most common technique for comparing two groups is the *t* test. As was mentioned earlier, the *t* test is based on a formula that involves three factors: the size of the mean difference between the two groups, the amount of variation present within the two groups, and the number of subjects in the two groups. We shall go into a bit more detail than usual with the *t* test in order to provide, for the reader who is unfamiliar with the nature of statistical significance tests, an idea of how such analyses are constituted.

A standard formula for the *t* test, along with an explanation of the symbols used in the formula, follows:

$$t = \frac{\bar{X}_1 - \bar{X}_2}{\sqrt{(S_1^2/n_1) + (S_2^2/n_2)}}$$

where t = the value by which the statistical significance of the mean difference will be judged
$\bar{X}_1$ = mean of group 1
$\bar{X}_2$ = mean of group 2
S_1^2 = variance of group 1 (or its squared standard deviation)
S_2^2 = variance of group 2 (or its squared standard deviation)
n_1 = number of subjects in group 1
n_2 = number of subjects in group 2

Now slowly and carefully look the formula over with this point in mind: The larger the value of *t*, the greater the statistical significance of the data being analyzed. Note first that in the numerator of the *t* formula we have the actual mean difference represented. If there isn't a reasonably large difference between the means, then the value of t will be small, hence nonsignificant. Then notice all the ingredients below the square root sign. The squared standard deviation of each group forms a fraction with the number of subjects in that group. Now, recalling your elementary arithmetic tribulations, remember that when a constant quantity is divided by a smaller amount, the resulting quotient is larger. Thus the smaller the combined values of the ingredients below the square root sign, the larger will be the value of t (assuming the mean difference remains the same). Now how do those ingredients, that is, the two fractions, below the square root sign become smaller?

Well, the larger the n, the smaller the fractions. Also, the smaller the standard deviations, the smaller the fractions. For example, if we were artificially to manipulate the denominators of those two fractions (below the square root sign) by adjusting the sizes of the samples, then $1/100$ is obviously less than $1/10$. This indicates that the larger our n is, the larger the value of t. If we were to manipulate the numerators of those two fractions by adjusting the sizes of the standard deviations, then $1/100$ is obviously less than $5/100$. This indicates that the smaller the standard deviations, the larger will be the value of t:

Recapitulating: because there are three basic ingredients in a t test, if we could hold the other two factors constant, then:

The larger the mean difference, the larger the value of t.
The larger the sample sizes, the larger the value of t.
The smaller the standard deviations of the groups, the larger the value of t.

Now, a careful consideration of these three points will reveal that the t test merely represents a statistician's translation of common sense into a numerical analysis scheme. To illustrate, if we are trying to see whether the mean performances of two groups are significantly different, then the larger the mean difference, the more likelihood that the difference is significant. Further, the larger the sample sizes involved, the more likely our results are to be stable, hence the more likely an observed mean difference is to be significant. Finally, and this is not so readily apparent, the smaller the variability in the two groups, the more likely a given mean difference will be significant.

To clarify this point, consider the two sets of data presented in Figure 12–1. In each case the mean difference is identical, but in the situation at the left there is greater variability in the groups, hence more overlap. With the smaller variability in the groups at the right, we can have greater confidence that the two groups are truly different.

To review, the value of t is based on three factors which common sense would tell us are important in deciding whether an observed mean difference is reliable or just a function of chance. The t value that results from the application of the t formula is then interpreted for statistical significance from a t table, which would be found in the appendix section of most statistics textbooks. For example, with two groups involving 15 learners in each group, it would take a t value of 2.048 or larger to be significant at the .05 level. It would take a t value of 2.763 to be significant at the .01 level.

FIGURE 12-1 • *Identical Mean Differences Between Two Groups in Which Greater and Lesser Variability Is Present*

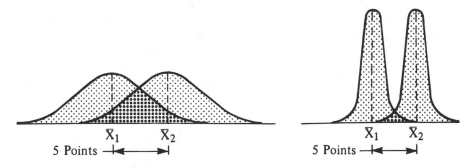

The chief reason we have spent some time dissecting the *t* test is to remove the misconception that statistical significance tests are magical number-jumbling procedures that operate apart from common sense. To the contrary, statistical significance tests represent the efforts of bright people to quantify and systematically incorporate the kinds of considerations that would be important to any clear-thinking individual. Other significance tests work similarly to the *t* test. Statistical significance is far from mystical. If one had sufficient mathematical competence, such tests could all be exposed for what they are, namely, complicated looking but sensible contraptions for handling data so that we can tell how likely it is that chance is operative.

Interval Data

The t Test   As has been indicated, the *t* test is a technique for determining whether the mean performances of two groups are significantly different. It requires that the data used in the analysis be measured on scales that can be considered interval in nature.

Analysis of Variance   To determine whether there are significant differences among the means (interval-level data) of more than two groups, statisticians generally employ the *single-classification analysis of variance*, often referred to as ANOVA. The analysis of variance is a more general form of the *t* test that, in fact, can be employed with only two groups (instead of using the *t* test). In spite of its name, which suggests that we are scrutinizing variation, the analysis of variance tells us whether there are any statistically significant mean differences between two or more groups. By employing a clever statistical perspective, this analysis technique reveals conclusions about *means* by analyzing the variation (*variance*) of groups. Accordingly, it is referred to as the analysis of variance. The ANOVA approach yields an *F* value which is interpreted much like the *t* value, that is, the larger the value of *F*, the more likelihood there is of statistical significance.

At the conclusion of an ANOVA, the single resulting *F* value merely tells us whether there are any significant differences between two or more means in the groups under analysis. If there are none, as indicated by an insufficiently large F value, then that is typically where the analysis stops. But if there is a significant F, then additional analyses are required to determine precisely which groups are significantly different. Most statistics texts describe one or more of these *post hoc* multiple-comparison procedures. There is a certain amount of fashionability associated with such comparison techniques; that is, the multiple-comparison procedures favored by statisticians ten years ago are apt to be out of vogue today.

In general, then, an evaluator who is comparing several groups of learners who have completed different programs would employ a single classification analysis of variance and, if the resulting F value were significant, would follow up with some type of *post hoc* analysis that would isolate which groups were significantly different.

There are also occasions, more common in research than in evaluation, where a *multiple classification analysis of variance* may prove useful. This procedure allows us to check for significant differences among two or more groups that have been subdivided according to a variable of interest. To use a simple example, suppose the evaluator believed that sex differences were potentially influential in the way students responded to three new sets of simulation materials. The evaluator could *block* the design on the sex variable by analyzing the data separately for males and females in such a way that there would be (1) an F test for the three treatments (Are there differences among the means of the pupils taught by three sets of materials?), (2) an F test for the sex factor (Is there a significant difference between the performance of boys and girls?), and (3) an F test for the *interaction* of sex with treatment (Did boys do better on some treatments and girls do better on others?). As with single classification ANOVA, there are *post hoc* multiple-comparison procedures available for further examining the causes of significant F values.

Both single- and multiple-classification analysis of variance models are extremely important statistical tools. They are sensitive to the detection of subtle yet significant differences and are able to analyze a diversity of data yet yield meaningful results. Computer programs are available that make it simple to employ electronic hardware for analysis of variance approaches, a nontrivial consideration when a large amount of data must be processed.

Analysis of Covariance   Another technique that has special usefulness in educational evaluation is the *analysis of covariance* (ANCOVA), which is also available in single- and multiple-classification forms. Essentially, the analysis of covariance performs the same jobs as ANOVA models, except that it can statistically equate groups on relevant variables so that initial disparities among groups can, at least to some extent, be diminished. Because of this feature, ANCOVA is most useful in treating data gathered from intact groups, that is, groups that could not be constituted by randomization.

To illustrate, suppose the evaluator is obliged to use three already constituted groups in an evaluation study, even though there is some evidence that the groups differ with respect to scholastic aptitude. By administering a scholastic aptitude test to the three groups, the evaluator could pump such data into an analysis of covariance so that, when the three groups are contrasted on some subsequent performance measure, the analysis could be carried out as if the groups were equivalent with respect to scholastic aptitude.

The technique for pulling off this minor miracle is fairly straightforward. The statistician uses one or more *control variables* (e.g., IQ, grade-point average) assumed to be relevant to the *criterion variable* (e.g., performance on a postinstruction examination) by first establishing the relationship between the control variables and the criterion variable, then adjusting the actual criterion variable scores so that (on the basis of their relationship to the control variables) they would have resulted had the groups been identical at the outset with respect to the control variables. Like ANOVA, an ANCOVA yields *F* values whose probability levels are determined from previously established statistical tables.

Because educational evaluators are so often obliged to work within contexts in which randomized assignment of learners is impossible, the analysis of covariance procedure can often prove helpful when they are coping with the relevant disparities that often exist in intact groups.

A cautionary note must be added, however, for as Cronbach has pointed out,[3] the use of analysis of covariance rests on assumptions that are frequently not satisfied by the data with which practicing educational evaluators work. Unlike a number of other statistical techniques, ANCOVA is not particularly *robust*, that is, able to yield meaningful analytic results even though its assumptions are not satisfied. Accordingly, it is injudicious to view ANCOVA as an omnipurpose statistical remedy for dealing with initially unequal groups. To decide on whether ANCOVA can be appropriately employed in a given setting, it is prudent to enlist the counsel of a moxie statistical consultant. When the situation permits, ANCOVA is a nifty analytic technique. When the situation is otherwise, ANCOVA will yield potentially misleading results.

Ordinal Data

When one is analyzing data that represent an ordinal scale, such as rankings, the choice among difference-testing procedures depends on whether the subjects in the groups are *independent* or *related*. Choosing a two-sample case for illustrative purposes, suppose the evaluator were working with matched pairs of learners, each pair of pupils having been matched on the basis of sex, age, and IQ test scores. This would be an instance involving two *related* samples. We can also consider a pretest-versus-posttest analysis carried out on the same learners to represent a related sample, because each individual is measured on two separate occasions. We should expect that the same person's test scores on two different occasions would he more alike than two different persons' scores on such tests. In contrast to these related samples, suppose we had randomly assigned two groups to two different treatment conditions. This would be an instance involving *independent* samples.

Sign Test   For analyzing data from two *related* samples the sign test is one of the most widely employed significance tests. It is an easily computed test that simply lines up the pairs of related subjects and determines how many times the paired subjects in one group exceeded the performance of those in the other group. If there is no statistically significant difference present, the superiority of the two groups should be divided about equally. If there is a sizable disparity in favor of one group, for example, if a pretest-posttest comparison indicates that only 20 percent of the learners scored better on the pretest than they did on the posttest, then there are statistical tables that can be readily used to determine the chance probability of that event's occurrence.

Wilcoxon Matched-Pairs Signed-Ranks Test   Whereas the sign test takes into account only the direction of the difference favoring one or the other related sample, the Wilcoxon Matched-Pairs Signed-Ranks Test takes into consideration also the magnitudes of those differences. As a consequence, the Wilcoxon is a more sensitive test than the sign test. Yet, consistent with the previously stressed importance of practical significance, if a difference between two related groups is so small that it would be picked up with a Wilcoxon test but missed by a sign test, then from a practical point of view it's probably a dinky difference anyway.

Mann-Whitney U Test   If two *independent* samples are involved, then the Mann-Whitney U Test is a powerful alternative to the t test for treating ordinal data. Briefly, the U test is predicated on the notion that if scores of two essentially similar groups are ranked together, as though they were one, there will be a considerable intermingling of the two groups' rankings. When these pooled rankings are summed *separately* for the two groups, if there is no difference between the groups, then one would expect the sums of these two sets of individual ranks to be about the same. If the summed ranks are markedly disparate, then there is likely to be a statistically significant difference between the two groups. This straightforward test yields a value, U, whose chance probability of occurrence, as with all our other significance tests, can be determined in the back of a friendly statistics text.

Kruskal-Wallis One-Way Analysis of Variance   If more than two *independent* samples are involved, then the Kruskal-Wallis One-Way Analysis of Variance can be employed to treat ordinal data. Like the Mann-Whitney U Test, this procedure involves the ranking of individuals in several groups as though they were all members of a single group, then comparing the sums of such ranks when added together for each of the individual groups being analyzed. As usual, this analysis yields a value (H) whose likelihood of chance occurrence is established by using a specially prepared probability table.

Friedman Two-Way Analysis of Variance   If more than two *related* samples are involved, as when one might have constituted matched groups of four pupils per group to complete four different instructional sequences, then the Friedman Two-Way Analysis of Variance is a convenient way to treat ordinal data.

Although when ordinal data are involved there are other procedures that can be used to test for differences among two or more groups, related or independent, the few techniques mentioned here will satisfy most of the evaluator's analysis needs for data of an ordinal nature.

Nominal Data

The Chi-Square Test   One of the most serviceable analyses used by statisticians is the chi-square (χ^2) test. Although often used with data of a stronger variety (e.g., ordinal data), the chi-square test can be employed to contrast two or more groups with respect to nominal, that is, nonnumerical, classification data. For example, if we were trying to contrast the effects of three distinctive high-school programs upon students' subsequent choices of career, we could categorize careers into six classifications. Now if the three programs were essentially indistinguishable, then one would expect that about the same proportions of students from each treatment group would select the same careers. For instance, if there were a category labeled "Professional" and another labeled "Manual Labor," we might anticipate that roughly the same percentages of learners from all three treatment conditions would opt for each of these categories.

The chi-square analysis is based on a contrast between the *expected frequencies* per cell and the *actual frequencies* per cell in a grid such as that seen in Figure 12-2. If the actual or observed frequencies are similar to the expected frequencies, then there is undoubtedly no difference between any of the groups under analysis. If there are considerable differences between the expected and observed frequencies, however, then a significant value of the chi-square test will result.

Just to show how simple it is to compute a χ^2 test, the formula for χ^2 looks like this:

$$\chi^2 = \text{Sum of } \frac{(\text{observed frequency} - \text{expected frequency})^2}{\text{expected frequency}}$$

This would mean that in our 3-by-6 grid we would calculate an expected frequency for each cell, subtract it from the frequency that actually occurred (for example, the number of students from Treatment A who opted to be manual laborers), square the difference, and divide by the cell's expected frequency. When we add all the values

FIGURE 12-2 • *A Typical Chi-Square Frequency Table*

CAREER CHOICES

TREATMENT	*1*	*2*	*3*	*4*	*5*	*6*
A						
B						
C						

from each of the 18 cells, we obtain our χ^2 which, as usual, is checked for significance from one of the endless tables cluttering up the rear ends of statistics texts.

Parametric versus Nonparametric Tests

The analysis procedures employed with interval data, such as the *t* test, ANOVA, and ANCOVA, are referred to as *parametric* statistical procedures. The other tests we have been considering for use with ordinal or nominal data, such as the sign test and the chi-square test, are described as *nonparametric* procedures. Although there have been some striking advances in recent years in the field of nonparametric statistics, a classic treatment of these procedures written by Sidney Siegel in 1956, is still one of the most lucid expositions, both of the rationale of these procedures and of how they should be employed for data-analysis purposes.[4] The reader interested in these simply computed analysis techniques should consult not only the classic Siegel text but also some of the more recent references cited at the close of the chapter.

A Summary

Table 12–3 presents a summary of the statistical difference tests we have been discussing. Note that for interval data one can employ the analysis of covariance for two or for more than two groups. Because ANCOVA is employed to compensate for initial group differences, it is often needed by evaluators for difference tests involving only two groups. The *t* test can be used with either independent or related samples. There are slight differences in the *t* test formulas for these two situations. The techniques cited in Table 12–3 are certainly not exhaustive. Almost any recent statistical text will be able to provide additional analysis alternatives.

TABLE 12-3 • *A Summary of Selected Difference Tests for Statistical Significance*

	Two Groups	*More than Two Groups*
Nominal	Chi-square	Chi-square
Ordinal	Sign test (related samples)	Friedman test (related samples)
	Wilcoxon test (related samples)	Kruskal-Wallis test (independent samples)
	Mann-Whitney test (independent samples)	
Interval	*t* test	ANOVA (single or multiple classification)
	ANCOVA	ANCOVA

Procedures for Estimating
Practical Significance

Earlier in the chapter a distinction was drawn between statistical and practical significance. It was emphasized that the educational evaluator, because of a dominant concern with the decision implications of a set of results, should not be satisfied with the determination of mere statistical (nonchance) significance, but should press on to determine whether a set of statistically significant differences is sufficiently meaningful to warrant practical action.

There are several approaches that can be employed by the evaluator who wants to get an idea of the practical significance of a set of results. None of these schemes, unfortunately, is altogether satisfactory. There will still be a large segment of judgment involved when the evaluator tries to answer the question, "Is this result sufficiently important to warrant action?"

Inspecting Summary Indicators

One approach to the problem of estimating the practical significance of a set of results, such as the postinstruction performance of several groups who were instructed via different programs, is to visually scrutinize summary indices of the results. The most common summary indicators for a set of data would be the descriptive statistics we have previously considered, such as measures of central tendency (e.g., the mean) and variability (e.g., the standard deviation). Sometimes these summary indicators can also be translated into proportion or percentage indices, such as the proportion of possible points earned.

In addition, we have seen that graphic display procedures can also help in the summarizing of a given set of data. By inspecting graphs that visually convey a comparative picture of the differential status of the groups under analysis, the evaluator can often get a better fix on the import of a set of results.

Of course, there will still be a goodly amount of looseness associated with visual inspection of summary indicators. For that reason, statisticians have provided other schemes to help estimate practical significance. We shall examine the most popular of these approaches.

The Use of Confidence Intervals

When an evaluator completes a study and discovers that students taught by Innovation X outperformed those taught by Innovation Z to the extent of a statistically significant 9.2 posttest points, the problem typically at hand is to decide whether the 9.2 mean difference in favor of Innovation X is large enough to warrant adopting that innovation for future students.

One of the difficulties of arriving at an answer to the "large enough" question is that the evaluator has only one set of observations, a set that this time resulted in a 9.2 victory for Innovation X. However, any reasonably bright evaluator realizes that the 9.2 mean difference is far from precise. If the same study were replicated, we might be apt to detect a difference in favor of the same innovation, but the chance that it would be exactly 9.2 points is remote.

Therefore, to provide a better estimate of the true magnitude of difference of this sort, statisticians compute a *confidence interval*. A confidence interval can be calculated at different probability levels, usually 90, 95, or 99 percent, to provide a notion of the range of mean differences that might be secured if the study were replicated. To illustrate, a 95 percent confidence interval in the example we are using (the 9.2 mean difference) might be 6.0–12.4. This interval is produced by adding and subtracting a value of 3.2 to our 9.2 mean difference. The procedures needed to calculate these sorts of confidence intervals are described in most of the recent statistics texts.

Now the interpretation of the meaning of a confidence interval is a bit tricky. Let's go through it slowly. Technically, a confidence interval defines a range that, at a given probability level, spans the true *population parameter*. A population parameter, in the case of an evaluation study, would be that value (in this case, a mean difference) that would be present if an *infinite* number of replications of the study were carried out. It would, in a sense, be the *true* mean difference. Inasmuch as evaluators carry out only a limited number of study replications, often only one, the challenge is to provide as accurate an estimate as possible of this population parameter. On the basis of a single study we can compute a confidence interval, for example, a 90 percent interval. Now it is not correct to assert that the odds are 90 out of 100 that the population parameter falls within that interval. The population parameter is a real number and our confidence interval either does or does not contain it. The accurate way to conceive of a confidence interval is to think of the number of replications of our evaluation study that might be run and the number of confidence intervals that might be generated. If we were to replicate the study and crank out another confidence interval, the odds would be 90 percent that the next confidence interval, like our current confidence interval, would span the population parameter.

But technicalities of interpretation aside, the evaluator is obviously advantaged by working with confidence intervals rather than a single set of results. If, for example, the 95 percent confidence interval for an investigation were, as in our present example, 6.0–12.4, and it was believed that any difference greater than 5.0 was worth doing something about, then action would appear warranted. But suppose the 95 percent confidence interval for the observed mere difference of 9.2 turned out to be 2.2–16.2, that is, 9.2 ± 7.0. Then the evaluator who needs at least a 5.0 mean difference in order to feel comfortable gets more queasy about action. Obviously, having access to a range of results with known probability levels makes it easier, but not easy, to get a fix on practical significance.

Confidence intervals can be reported for several probability levels at the same time. For instance, confidence intervals can be simultaneously supplied for 90, 95, and 99 percent probability levels. Confidence intervals can be constructed for most statistics, such as a single mean or a correlation coefficient. The procedures are really quite simple for the most common situations where confidence intervals will be needed. As was indicated, most recently published statistics textbooks describe these procedures. More frequent use of confidence intervals by evaluators should be seen in future years.

Making a Choice

It should be clear that none of the approaches we have been considering completely eliminates the necessity to make sticky choices as to whether an observed difference does indeed constitute a practically important result. The evaluator will probably discover that more than one of these approaches might be useful for reaching the practical significance decision. Different decision-maker audiences will undoubtedly find certain of these procedures more informative than others. The astute evaluator will have to anticipate the sophistication level of the relevant decision makers and match the analysis procedures to the client's consumption capabilities.

Anticipating Data-Analysis Requirements

Too many evaluators design an evaluation study without sufficient consideration of the data-analysis resources that will be needed. As a consequence, at the end of the study a mountain of data erupts without warning. The evaluator may spend the next year or two wading through this information without really understanding it.

Prior to gathering the data, be sure to think through such matters as how the measures will be scored, who will do it, and who will conduct the statistical analyses. What kind of data-processing equipment will be required? Will an electronic computer be needed or can you get by with a roving band of Mongolian abacus experts? Not to foresee these data-analysis requirements, and to gather data consonant with the available analysis resources, will destine an evaluation project to probable failure.

In summary, this chapter has provided a brief introduction to some of the important considerations involved in the analysis of evaluation data. As was indicated at the outset of the chapter, the more sophisticated that evaluators are with respect to data-analysis procedures, the more effectively they can function. Although the tyro evaluator might be able to get by with the rudimentary guidelines provided in this chapter, further study is obviously recommended.

Discussion Questions

1. What is the difference between practical significance and statistical significance? Which, if either, is more important to the educational evaluator?
2. If you were asked by a citizens' group to explain the meaning of statistical significance, how would you present this explanation in language they could understand?
3. What is the relationship between levels of measurement and the kinds of statistical significance tests that the evaluator might use?
4. Several approaches were described in the chapter to help the evaluator estimate the practical significance of a set of results. What are the advantages and disadvantages of each of these methods?

Practice Exercises

1. Presented below are several descriptions of educational evaluators engaged in data-analysis activities. Read each description, and then decide whether the evaluator is engaged in the determination of *statistical significance or practical significance*.

   a. This evaluator has just initiated an analysis of data drawn from intact classrooms where it appears likely that pupils differ substantially on variables relevant to the criterion-referenced tests the evaluator is employing as the chief measure of program success. The evaluator applies an analysis of covariance technique to determine, after adjusting for initial differences between intact groups, how likely it is that the observed differences are attributable to mere chance.

   b. Dr. Fawcett has summarized the data from an evaluation study so that the differences observed between pupils taught by different methods are reported in terms of 95 percent confidence intervals.

   c. After conducting her ANOVA processing of three group's postinstruction, Ms. Snell obtains a significant F value. She then employs a *post hoc* analysis to see which of the three group means are significantly different from the other group means.

   d. This evaluator, having conducted a t test analysis of the difference between means of two groups, calculates a mean-difference confidence interval to provide an estimate of the likely magnitude of the actual mean difference involved.

   e. Because nominal data are involved, Mr. Hager treats the data yielded from his evaluation investigation by chi-square analysis. A statistical consultant has advised him that a

   nonparametric technique is requisite in this instance.

2. In this chapter we considered a number of difference-testing tests of statistical significance. Examine the situations described below and then decide which one of the following statistical procedures would be most appropriate for analyzing the data:

   • t test

   • single-classification analysis of variance

   • multiple-classification analysis of variance

   • analysis of covariance

   • sign test

   • Wilcoxon Matched-Pairs Signed-Ranks Test

   • Mann-Whitney U Test

   • Friedman Two-Way Analysis of Variance

   • Kruskal-Wallis One-Way Analysis of Variance

   • chi-square test

   It is acceptable to refer back to the chapter prior to making a decision regarding which technique to employ.

   a. In this evaluation study the principal criterion measure is the degree major chosen by learners at the conclusion of their sophomore year in college. Four different instructional treatments are being evaluated. Students' subsequent choice of majors according to the following categories constitute the data: (1) liberal arts, (2) sciences, (3) pre-professional, (4) other. What analysis technique should be used?

   b. In this small-scale study of the respective merits of two approaches to the teaching of oil painting, there have been two groups of learners randomly assigned to the two treatment conditions. A group of four art critics subsequently judge the oil paintings produced by students after the conclusion of the treatments. The judges agree to rank the 40 paintings only from best to worst (not knowing with which treatment group the artists were associated). The *average rankings* of these four critics, then, constitute the basic data from this study. What analysis technique should be used?

c. This evaluator is faced with the necessity to analyze scores of three-treatment groups on a criterion-referenced achievement test but, at the same time, must subdivide (block) each treatment group according to sex because there is evidence that this variable may interact with the particular kind of achievement data being studied. What analysis technique should be used?

d. A group of 15 pupils has been involved in a formative evaluation of a new self-instruction program to each elementary harmonica skills. Each pupil makes a three-minute harmonica recording prior to and following

the two-week course. Each pair of recordings is then presented to a judge (sometimes presenting the preinstruction recording first, sometimes the second). The judge is then obliged to say which of the two paired recordings is better. As it turned out in this case, ten of the recordings judged better were postinstruction renditions. What analysis technique should be used?

e. An evaluator wants to compare the differential effectiveness of three new instructional film series but is obliged to employ existing groups of pupils in what is essentially a nonequivalent control group design. Because the evaluator is certain that pupils' scholastic aptitude will influence their performance on the criterion measure to be used, IQ scores are gathered for each pupil from cumulative record files. The evaluator first wants to adjust statistically for any substantial IQ differences among the learners, then test for differences. What analysis technique should be used?

Answers to Practice Exercises

1. *a.* statistical; *b.* practical; *c.* statistical; *d.* practical; *e.* statistical.
2. *a.* chi-square; *b.* Mann-Whitney *U* test; *c.* multiple-classification analysis of variance; *d.* sign test; *e.* analysis of covariance.

Notes

1. W. James Popham and Kenneth A. Sirotnik, *Educational Statistics: Use and Interpretation* (New York: Harper Row, 1973).

2. Marvin C. Alkin, "Evaluation Theory Development: II," in *Evaluation and Education: At Quarter Century*, ed. M. W. McLaughlin and D. C. Phillips (Chicago: University of Chicago Press, 1991), pp. 91–112.

3. L. J. Cronbach et al., *Analysis of Covariance in Nonrandomized Experiments: Parameters Affecting Bias* (Evaluation Consortium, Stanford University, September 1977).

4. Sidney Siegel, *Nonparametric Statistics for the Behavioral Sciences* (New York: McGraw-Hill, 1956).

Selected References

Burstein, Leigh, Howard E. Freeman, and Peter H. Rossi (Eds.). *Collecting Evaluation Data: Problems and Solutions*. Beverly Hills, CA: Sage, 1985.

Kerlinger, Fred N., *Foundations of Behavioral Research* (3rd. ed.) New York: Holt, Rinehart and Winston, 1986.

Knoke, David, and George W. Bohrnstedt. *Basic Social Statistics*. Itasca, IL: F. E. Peacock, 1991.

Levine, Harold G. "Principles of Data Storage and Retrieval for Use in Qualitative Evaluations." *Educational Evaluation and Policy Analysis*, 7:2 (Summer 1985): 169–86.

Marascuilo, L. A., and M. McSweeney. *Non-Parametric and Distribution-Free Methods for the Social Sciences*. Monterey, CA: Brooks/Cole, 1977.

Popham, W. James and Kenneth A. Sirotnik. *Understanding Statistics in Education*. Itasca, IL: F. E. Peacock, 1991.

Siegel, Sidney. *Nonparametric Statistics for the Behavioral Sciences*. New York: McGraw-Hill, 1956.

Wolf, Richard. "Data Analysis and Reporting Considerations in Evaluation." In *Evaluation in Educationa: Current Applications*. Berkeley, CA, McCutchan, 1974.

Worthen, Blaine R., and James R. Sanders. "Analyzing and Interpreting Evaluation Information." *Educational Evaluation: Alternative Approaches and Guidelines*. White Plains, NY: Longman, 1987, pp. 328–40.

CHAPTER THIRTEEN

Reporting Evaluation Results

Imagine that a skilled investigative journalist had spent six months gathering information about a heretofore undetected political scandal that could, in the journalist's estimate, "shake the foundations of the current federal administration." The information was the stuff for which Pulitzer Prizes are awarded. The information was the answer to a journalist's prayers. But, to carry the fiction a bit farther, imagine that the journalist, though effective as an investigator, wrote up the results of the investigation in a bland and unappealing fashion. Although there would surely be some attention given to the scandal (unless our citizens have become inured to such events because of their frequency), the report would fail to do the job the journalist wanted. An ineffectual report of an investigation can, in short, dissipate the utility of the entire endeavor because its impact on those for whom it was intended will undoubtedly be vitiated.

The lesson for educational evaluators is obvious: Considerable attention must be given to the procedures employed to report the results of educational evaluation investigations. Evaluation specialists have, surprisingly, failed to give this significant operation in the evaluation process the attention it warrants. As a consequence, there are only a handful of suggestions to proffer regarding the reporting of educational evaluation studies. It is hoped that in the future there will be more thought given to the reporting of evaluation analyses, thus leading to a more sophisticated technology for reporting such investigations.

A Responsive Orientation

Educational evaluators should never lose sight of the fact that their mission is to facilitate better decisions. Sometimes the evaluator will be the decision maker, such as a teacher who carefully evaluates an instructional sequence in order to shape it up the next time it is offered. More often, however, the evaluator will be supplying evidence to be used by others who make decisions. These "others" might be a school superintendent, a curriculum project's director, a teachers' union, a school board, the public at large, or a combination of those individuals. Even though evaluators may be strongly tempted to write up the results of their investigations so that such reports will be personally satisfying, it is not the evaluator's professional or personal needs that must be satisfied. The people who must be content are the decision makers.

Prior to deciding on reporting procedures, therefore, the evaluator must reconsider (assuming this operation should have been carried out *prior* to designing the evaluation itself) just who the relevant decision-making audiences really are. The activities of the evaluator at this juncture should be highly *responsive* in nature. If the evaluator does not respond to the perceived needs of those making the actual decisions, the evaluator's activities are destined to be ceremonial rather than influential.

Often it is apparent who it is that will be making the decisions. All the evaluator has to do is ask. There will be occasions, however, when the decision makers will be hard to locate. Perhaps the question of who will finally be calling the shots is even in contention. For instance, suppose that a school board and a teachers' organization are battling over whether a particular instructional program should be continued or abandoned. Maybe the teachers' organization has even made the issue a point of negotiation in its annual contract deliberations with the board. Perhaps, until that final moment of negotiated closure, one can't be sure who will be more influential in deciding the program's fate. In such cases, therefore, the evaluator will sometimes have to do a bit of bet hedging by considering both groups as potential decision makers whose information requirements must be serviced. Indeed, as was noted earlier, the evaluator who increases the quality of dialogue engaged in by the decision-making community will have performed a useful service. Thus, in a sense, a reporting strategy should be employed that will accommodate the widest possible set of those who, in one way or another, influence the decisions at issue.

Although one might argue that the evaluator in certain cases should be attentive to the needs of whichever group has put up the money to finance the evaluation, it would seem more beneficial to the learners (who might utimately be helped or harmed by the decision) if all contending parties have access to the evaluation results. If one party is informed and the other ignorant, a less defensible decision will probably eventuate than if both factions are knowledgeable.

Detecting the Decision Makers' Needs

Having figured out specifically who will need the information provided by the evaluation report, the evaluator should then formally engage in an attempt to isolate the kinds of evaluative information those groups really want. It should *not* be a foregone conclusion that the evaluator will know best what the decision maker should want. Although there is often no difference between the decision maker's expectations and the kinds of information the evaluator would have reported anyway, occasions arise when the kinds of data the decision maker desires will come as a genuine surprise to the evaluator.

Though a responsive orientation is being urged as a general strategy for designing one's reporting procedures, this stance should not be equated with blind passivity. Sometimes the evaluator will have to help the decision maker realize the kinds of information that should be considered before a decision is reached. For instance, in the next chapter we shall consider the question of how to analyze the costs of competing decision alternatives. If the decision maker is naive about such matters, the evaluator may have to initiate a dialogue that will expand the decision maker's conception of the relevant information needed in order to choose among alternative courses of action.

One of the most economical ways of getting at the decision makers' information requirements is simply to ask them what it is they want to know as a consequence of an evaluation study—that is, what sorts of data do they really want to see in the report of the evaluation project. This straightforward approach often gives the evaluator sufficient guidance.

To Recommend or Not to Recommend

One issue the evaluator is apt to face when preparing a report is whether to offer recommendations to decision makers. Suppose the pretest-posttest results of a formative evaluation study regarding a one-week unit dealing with refusal skills indicate that the unit was particularly ineffective. Students' skills after the unit are essentially the same as before the unit. A logical recommendation would be that the unit be seriously overhauled. But should the evaluator make such a recommendation? Similarly, if a summative evaluation study indicates that an education program focused on self-esteem is having a decisively beneficial impact on students' self-concepts, should the evaluator recommend that the program be continued?

This is an issue over which evaluation specialists are divided. For some specialists, making decision-related recommendations is a logical extension of the evaluator's decision-facilitation role. Other specialists, however, regard evaluator-generated recommendations as intrusions on the decision maker's prerogatives. These individuals believe that the evaluator should supply evidence only and should offer no guidance regarding actual decisions. There is no clear consensus regarding the recommend versus not recommend issue among evaluation specialists.

It is suggested, therefore, that the evaluator be guided by decision makers' expressed preferences about whether to make recommendations about decisions under consideration. The evaluator will doubtlessly have met with decision makers during the early stages of designing the study, because the evaluator clearly needs to find out what their important decision points really are. At that stage of the process, the evaluator can easily learn whether decision makers wish the report of the evaluation to be prepared with or without recommendations.

The evaluator will frequently be called on to provide an oral report in addition to written reports. Recommendations will often be solicited during such reports even though the evaluator may have been directed to avoid such recommendations in writing. In this case, as well, because the evaluator is attempting to serve decision makers, let them make the call regarding whether they wish recommendations to be offered.

Scriven contends that educational evaluators should key their activities to the client's interests, but that a complete evaluation obliges the evaluator to interpret data, not simply provide fragmentary and uninterpreted information to the client. Recognizing that some writers urge evaluators to avoid any final overall evaluations, Scriven notes that in any serious evaluation there are always explicit subevaluations of what are seen as less important issues. He points out that "balking at the last step — the overall evaluation — is rather like deciding you want to be a virgin after the orgy but before the Day of Judgment."[1]

The Mock Evaluation Report

A particularly useful device that can help an evaluator secure a better fix on the information needs of decision makers is the *mock evaluation report*. This report, written in advance of the actual evaluation report, reflects the evaluator's best guesses regarding what elements the real report should contain.

By working up a mock evaluation report in rough form, using fictitious results, evaluators can test the adequacy of their judgments regarding appropriate reporting categories while there is still time to correct oversights. If the mock evaluation report is prepared very early in an evaluation investigation, it may influence not only the nature of the reporting categories to be used but the actual types of data to be gathered. The mock evaluation report should be submitted to decision makers much as a preview of form, not substance, in advance of the actual report's preparation.

A Diversity of Reporting Mechanisms

With a bare-bones budget, the evaluator will be obliged to get by with whatever reporting procedures can be afforded. In an adequately funded project, however, it is recommended that, just as the evaluator is urged to employ multiple criterion measures, *multiple reporting mechanisms* be utilized.

It is very difficult to select a single medium that will satisfy all people. Some individuals prefer to learn about the news of the day from newspapers, others from radio reports, and others from television news reports. It is as unlikely that a single written evaluation report will satisfy the information needs of educational decision makers as it is that a single news magazine will satisfy the news needs of a diverse citizenry. This means that evaluators should always consider several procedures, not necessarily several media, as possible reporting vehicles. The habitual dependence on a single written evaluation report, laden with technicalities, should be reduced.

For example, in addition to the preparation of a detailed, elaborate evaluation report, the inventive evaluator might put together one or more leaflet-like summaries that contain only evaluation highlights. In addition to a written report, evaluators might set up an oral reporting session where, in news-conference style, evaluators could respond to questions posed by interested parties. Tape-recorded reports, video or audio only, might also be employed. Even sound-filmstrips could be used.

The general idea is that decision makers will be more inclined to act if their information requirements have been satisfied, not only with respect to the substance of those needs but also with respect to manner of information presentation. The more varied the reporting schemes that one uses, the more likelihood there will be that the evaluation results will be provided so that the decision makers can find one fashion consonant with their preferences.

Differential Depth within a Written Report

This same principle applies even within a single written report. Most reports should, at a minimum, contain an introductory section written at a fairly elementary level, plus a more technical report, presented perhaps as an appendix to the initial report. The idea of adding an extremely short *highlights* section at the very outset of the report has been well received by many decision makers.

Whenever possible, the evaluator should employ *verbal, numerical,* and *graphic* reporting techniques within the report. Some people like an expository account of the study. Others are enamored of tabular presentations, loaded with percentages, means, and standard deviations. Still others are enraptured by a well-conceived bar graph or pie graph. The more hooks the fisherman uses, the more apt the fish is to get hooked.

For instance, in addition to the customary expository prose used in most evaluation reports, the evaluator will often find that anecdotal accounts or even verbatim transcripts communicate a sense of reality to the reader that is difficult to achieve via standard exposition. The inclusion of realistic vignettes and actual photographs can go a long way toward enlivening the typically drab written report of an evaluation study. Remember: If the report isn't read, its influence is likely to be nonexistent.

Adversary Reporting Techniques

Earlier in Chapter Two we explored the use of judicial/adversary evaluation approaches, noting that their chief advantage was that when individuals are cast in a partisan role their increased commitment often yields an intensity of effort not associated with routine, nonpartisan evaluator efforts.

In the same vein, different people can look at the same set of evaluation results, yet come up with interpretations that may be quite divergent. As a consequence, some evaluation projects[2] have tried out an adversary approach with respect to the final evaluation report itself. One or more writers are given the charge of writing an evaluation report in which they paint as positive a picture as the data will permit. Other individuals are given the opposite charge. The final evaluation report contains both accounts. The decision makers must weigh both versions before coming to a conclusion. Where several programs are being compared, the adversary reporting model would entail having one advocate (or advocate team) interpret the data in a manner most favorable to one of the programs being considered. Evaluators must be cautious, when using adversary approaches, that the issue is not settled on the basis of which advocate can whomp up the best public relations case, evidence be damned.

Care must be taken in such adversary reporting schemes to keep most of the relevant conditions constant for the adversary reporters. For instance, it would hardly be fair to give a negative evaluator 5 pages and no pictures and give the positive evaluator 20 pages, a 20-minute cinemascopic movie, and two weeks of advertising space on the Goodyear blimp.

Sometimes the same person can write both sections of an adversary report, thereby avoiding the differential effectiveness of having a fledgling Faulkner weaving an award-winning essay on one side while a nonliterate clod carves out grocery-list prose on the opposing side. This approach, however, sacrifices the partisanship-perspective benefits of the whole approach. A preferable alternative may be to have a single person edit both reports so that they reflect a comparable degree of eloquence (or drabness).

Use of Communications Specialists

Most educators haven't been trained to be skilled writers. If resources permit, the evaluator may want to consider hiring a professional communications specialist to help during this phase of the project. Journalists, for example, can typically write a more fetching report than could a statistics professor. Many statistics professors, benumbed by too many numbers, have trouble creating any words-only sentences, much less a full-blown report. A public relations specialist may be able to suggest previously unconsidered mechanisms for reporting a statewide evaluation project's results to the state's citizens. A television director may recommend some attention-arresting ways of communicating a televised evaluation report so that it really sticks with the viewers.

There are firms specializing in such communications enterprises. The evaluator, resources permitting, may pick up a number of useful cues, either from them or from individual communication specialists, which will substantially augment the impact of the manner in which evaluation reports are packaged.

Brevity Wins

Creators typically adore their creations. Evaluators who have staged a lengthy, complex evaluation study will want to tell their story — and tell it at length. But there is an almost perfect *inverse* relationship between the length of a final report and the degree to which it will be completed (not to mention *used*) by consumers.

Evaluators, many of them already familiar with the researcher's strategy of detailing everything in sight, will often create evaluation reports large enough to choke a hippo. Such encyclopedic volumes strike terror in the hearts of most non-masochistic readers. These reports often find their way to a pile of "to be read later" materials. The "later" may end up being postburial.

There are few things that put off a busy decision maker as much as a thick, dull-looking evaluation report. If, upon commencing the dreary volume, readers realize that it will be a marathon battle between their eyes and the endless paragraphs, the report may be set aside or, perhaps worse, receive only a cursory perusal.

For this reason it is imperative that in at least one form a *terse* report of the evaluation study be made available. Perhaps, as we have seen before, this will be only one form of several reporting mechanisms. For example, we might use a one-fold leaflet as our short-form evaluation report and a 200-page monograph as a long-form report. The short form could be used by those busy people who would never plow through the larger version. The long form could be used by individuals, perhaps intrigued by their reading of the short report, who want a more detailed account of the investigation.

Even though many people would be wise to examine the detailed corroborating data, it may be extremely useful to summarize a program-comparison evaluation study as follows:

> Although Program I appears moderately successful as a cognitive instructional sequence, its affective impact was enormously beneficial. Program II turned out to be an abysmally ineffectual sequence on both cognitive and affective dimensions. The cost of Program I is essentially equivalent to that of Program II.

Such summary evaluation statements, to be supplemented elsewhere for sure, can often provide decision makers with the information they need. The more succinct these reports can be made, the better.[3] A 1-page summary is apt to be read. A 10-page summary is apt to be discarded. Such a push toward brevity, of course, always assumes the availability of more detailed supplemental reports.

The Routine Rejoinder

Another way of enhancing the value of an education report is to provide those individuals *whose program is being evaluated* with a preview copy of the evaluation report in draft form. These individuals are then urged to write a rejoinder if they wish to do so, such rejoinders to be included in the final version of the report.

For example, suppose a group of teachers had been evaluated on the basis of their ability to promote students' more positive attitudes toward minority ethnic groups. The specific program they had been employing, a program relying heavily on quasi-sensitivity groups constituted by pupils of diverse ethnicity, appeared to be a dismal failure on the basis of the evaluation procedures employed. By providing the teachers with a preview copy of the report, the evaluator gives the teachers the chance to evaluate the evaluation. If they find deficits in the procedures employed, such reservations can be entered as part of their rejoinder. If they interpret the data differently, if they think that certain data should have been collected but weren't, whatever their complaints, these can be entered in their rejoinder.

Similarly, the publishers of instructional materials being evaluated can also have an opportunity to submit rejoinders to evaluations focusing on their products. Not every publisher will want to take advantage of these invitations, for in some cases the stakes may not be high enough to warrant a response, but at least the opportunity has been provided.

A reasonable but short time period should be provided to would-be rejoinder authors. This step is designed to enrich the final report, not delay its release interminably.

Circulating Exemplars

As was indicated earlier in the chapter, evaluation specialists have not given much systematic attention to the question of how evaluation reports can be most effectively devised. Until they do, one of the best ways to get ideas regarding the format and other ingredients of such reports is to identify actual examples of reporting techniques that have been judged successful. For instance, by inspecting a particularly well-written report, either a short version or a more elaborate technical version, the evaluator will often get ideas regarding how to design similar reports. The more diverse these exemplars, the more useful the reporting ideas that they are apt to stimulate.

The overriding message of this chapter, in spite of its relative paucity of verified guidelines regarding the design of evaluation reports, is that the job of preparing evaluation reports should not be approached offhandedly. Without careful consideration of the available options regarding reporting mechanisms, without attention to the kinds of points mentioned in the chapter, the evaluator is likely to reduce the overall usefulness of an evaluation project by creating an ineffectual report of its results. From the earliest hours of an evaluation study's initiation, the skilled evaluator will begin *planning* for reporting. Such advance planning for effective communication will typically yield big payoffs.

Direct Communication

Evaluators should view with favor the value of direct communication with pertinent members of the decision-making community. Direct and informal, face-to-face reporting of the gist of an evaluation study's results can be powerful and effective. The evaluator's task is to enlighten. By speaking directly to the key decision makers, the evaluator will often be able to make an impact that would be impossible with written reports alone.

If the oral communication route is adopted (in addition, of course, to more formal written reports), the evaluator must prepare for the oral communication session as carefully as for any important speech. Care must be taken not to talk too long or too technically. Even though evaluators realize how complex the actual situation is, they must strive to isolate the crux of the report. Indeed, a good exercise for novice evaluation reporters would be to formulate the most abbreviated depiction of the evaluation's results that they could, then cut that formulation in half! Too many evaluators, enamored of their study's nuances, are inclined to go blah-blah-blah-blah, when a single blah would suffice.

Communicating with the Media

In most evaluators' careers there will be a few instances in which an evaluation's results attract the attention of the media, that is, reporters from newspapers, radio, or television. In a sense, such media attention is consonant with the evaluator's mission as illuminator, and hence it is highly gratifying. After all, the more people who learn of the evaluation's results, the more informed the decision-making community is apt to be.

Yet, there is danger when evaluators muck about in media-land. Novice evaluators, flattered by a call from a reporter, may be seduced into saying something that, although newsworthy, does not accurately represent the evaluation's findings. Caution, caution, and more caution is warranted in dealings with the press. Experienced evaluators can recount instances galore in which a newspaper reporter's story turned out quite differently from what the evaluator thought was being said. Thoughtful phrasing of comments, not glib rejoinders, are required in response to a reporter's queries.

There may also be prohibitions against an evaluator's divulging evaluation results to the press. Often the officials of the agency that has commissioned the evaluation, such as school district or state department of education executives, wish to be the individuals who deal with the media. If so, it is appropriate for the evaluator to engage in lip zipping, no matter how glamorous the opportunity to appear on the five o'clock news.

In dealing with the press, most evaluators will find that they will have to do a fair amount of educating before reporters have an adequate grasp of what's being reported. Most reporters, of course, are honest and conscientious individuals. They are apt to be uninformed, however, about the technicalities of the evaluation's methodology. The skilled evaluator will be able to simplify — without distorting — the fundamentals of the study's design, analyses, and so on. Such simplification is best done in advance of the media interview. It is difficult to simplify at all, and it is almost impossible to simplify in front of TV cameras or when a radio interviewer's audiotape is running.

Discussion Questions

1. Put yourself in the following roles and then decide what kind of information you would require if an evaluation contrasting two sets of elementary reading textbooks were to be reported. What information needs would be the same? What information needs would be different?
   a. A teacher who would use the textbooks
   b. A building principal in whose school the textbooks would be used
   c. A member of the Parent-Teachers' Association of the school in which the textbooks would be used
   d. A member of the district's school board

2. When should an evaluator start contemplating the nature of the reporting mechanisms to be used in a project — that is, at what point in the project's existence should such issues be confronted?

3. How important do you think *brevity of reporting* is for various kinds of deci-

sion-maker groups? Are there some sorts of decision makers who need more elaborate reports? If so, who are they?

4. What kinds of tactics do you think the evaluator should use in trying to detect the information needs of decision makers?

Practice Exercise

Unlike most practice exercises in this text, this one involves a fairly lengthy writing task. Further, because it is impossible to predict the form of the reader's response, no formal feedback (correct answer) has been provided. To secure an idea of the adequacy of one's response, it will be useful to seek the reactions of others, such as classmates or colleagues, to the finished product.

Your task is to prepare a *mock evaluation report* for a fictitious program evaluation study involving a comparison of two sets of self-instruction biology programs for a tenth-grade general biology course. You

can imagine any kind of evaluation design you wish and any kind of results you care to conjure up. The important steps are to (1) describe the decision-maker group or groups who will be receiving the evaluation report, and (2) describe, at least in sketchy form, an evaluation report (fictitious results) as it might be prepared for the decision makers you designate.

Ideally, you should try out the report on one or more people who represent the targeted decision makers, or at least who agree to play the roles of such individuals, such as school board members, parents, or teachers.

Notes

1. Michael Scriven, "Beyond Formative and Summative Evaluation," in *Evaluation and Education: At Quarter Century*, ed. M. W. McLaughlin and D. C. Phillips (Chicago: University of Chicago Press, 1991), pp. 19–64.

2. Robert E. Stake and Craig Gjerde, "An Evaluation of T City," in *Four Evaluation Examples: Anthropological, Economic, Narrative, and Portrayal*, Amer-

ican Educational Research Association Monograph Series in Curriculum Evaluation, Vol. 7 (Chicago: Rand McNally, 1974), pp. 99–139.

3. A 1986 report by Joan Osborne suggests that it is possible to abbreviate such summaries too greatly. "Report Length," *Educational Evaluation and Policy Analysis*, 8:2 (Summer 1986), 205–13.

Selected References

Brown, R. D., L. A. Braskamp, and D. L. Newman. "Evaluator Credibility as a Function of Report Style. Do Jargon and Data Make a Difference?" *Evaluation Quarterly*, 2:2 (1978): 331–41.

Gronlund, Norman E. *Improving Marking and Reporting in Classroom Instruction*. New York: Macmillan, 1974.

Jones, B. Kathryn, and Napoleon Mitchell.

"Communicating Evaluation Findings: The Use of a Chart Essay." In James W. Guthrie (Ed.), *Educational Evaluation and Policy Analysis*. Washington, DC: American Educational Research Association, 1990, pp. 449–62.

Osborne, Joan M. "Report Length: A Factor Influencing Audience Perceptions of an Evaluation Study." *Educa-*

tional Evaluation and Policy Analysis, 8:2 (Summer 1986): 205–13.

Wolf, Richard. "Data Analysis and Reporting Considerations in Evaluation." In *Evaluation in Education: Current Applications*. Berkeley, CA: McCutchan Publishing, 1974.

Worthen, Blaine R., and James R. Sanders. "Reporting and Using Evaluation Information." *Educational Evaluation: Alternative Approaches and Guidelines*. White Plains, NY: Longman, 1987, pp. 341–68.

CHAPTER FOURTEEN

Cost Analysis and the Evaluator

Educational evaluators, as has probably been stressed far too often, are concerned with decisions. Very often, the focus of those decisions involves a choice among alternative instructional programs. For instance, educational evaluators are frequently called on, in a summative context, to help decide whether a particular instructional innovation such as team teaching should, on the basis of its first year's performance, be retained for the next academic year. Or the evaluator might be asked to help a teaching staff that is obliged to choose one of three competing textbooks.

Thus far in our discussion we have emphasized the evaluator's responsibility for gathering information about the effectiveness of the competing programs. We have considered ways of measuring the effects of such programs as well as the types of designs and data-analysis procedures that can be used to obtain and process these measurements. The reader may have acquired the impression, quite understandably, that all there is to establishing the worth of an educational program is to ascertain its effects. Such an impression is erroneous, however, for there is another vital ingredient that must be considered before the worth of an educational phenomenon is established. The missing element is *cost*.

Let's work with a simple illustration. Suppose a school district evaluator is comparing the relative merits of two instructional programs, X and Y. Now imagine that X turns out to be twice as effective as Y, but we also discover the X is *10 times as expensive*. Maybe, in fact, the school district can afford to install Y without much sacrifice, but to install the expensive X program would bring the district to the brink of financial insolvency. Clearly, under such circumstances decision makers would lean toward the less effective but far less costly Y program. The productivity of the Y program, per dollar spent, is greater.

Even though the fact has not been stressed earlier, all decisions involve costs. It is the educational evaluator's responsibility to consider such costs in determining the worth of whatever is being evaluated—not only when contrasting instructional programs but also when evaluating the worth of educational goals. To illustrate, suppose that, on the basis of a needs-assessment program, the evaluator ends up with five strongly advocated instructional objectives. If the first three of these would require the expenditure of far more resources than the educational system has available, then the other two objectives, on the basis of the needs-assessment analysis *and a cost analysis*, might ultimately be recommended.

The Meaning of Costs

If costs must be considered in the rendering of evaluative judgments, then the educational evaluator should be familiar with more appropriate ways of conceptualizing costs than simply "how many dollars we pay for something." Indeed, we have been nurtured on the notion that costs are the undesirable consequences of an event. As economists point out, such a view of costs robs the concept of its usefulness.

There is a fair amount of ambiguity associated with the idea of what constitutes a cost. Even economists differ to some extent regarding how to conceptualize costs. Educators' estimates of a given program's costs often vary wildly, for there is considerable confusion regarding appropriate costing procedures.

In this chapter we shall consider some of the more basic notions most economists employ when treating the topic of costs. In addition, the most widely used cost-analytic procedures will be described, including *cost-feasibility analysis, cost-effectiveness analysis, cost-benefit analysis*, and *cost-utility analysis*. After having been sensitized to some of these concepts and procedures, the educational evaluator should be able to make more enlightened analyses of the costs associated with the educational phenomena being evaluated.

Costs as Benefits Forsaken

Let's warm up to a conception of cost that, for those readers not versed in economics, may represent a somewhat different way of looking at the world. A simple example involving a common homeowner's dilemma will help.

Imagine that you own a home and are contemplating the addition of another room, specifically, a den. Suppose you try to get systematic in your thinking, and deliberately write down all the advantages and disadvantages of building the den. For advantages, you cite (1) the possibility of having a quiet place to read and work—a room relatively insulated from the clamor of children on the prowl as they play that age-old game, "provoke-a-parent"; (2) the room could be furnished with a convertible sofa bed so that it could be used as a guest bedroom for Uncle Henry and other visitors; and (3) the house would be easier to sell, should you want to, because several realtors have advised you that a den adds appreciably to the value of a house. For disadvantages, you list (1) the $10,500 that several contractors have told you it will take to add a den to your house, (2) the two to three months' disruption and turmoil that will eventuate from having a contractor remodel the house, and (3) the likelihood that your property taxes will be raised if the room is added, since it will increase the appraised taxable value of your house.

Thus, you have a constellation of advantages and a constellation of disadvantages, elements that are difficult to contrast because they are set forth in qualitatively different units such as enjoyment, discomfort, and money. But suppose you could somehow convert these positive and negative factors into comparable units. For illustration purposes, suppose your analysis turned out like this:

Advantages	Unit Value
1. Isolated work/study space	50
2. Extra guest room	20
3. Enhanced resale possibilities	10
Total	80

Disadvantages	Unit Value
1. The $10,500 builder's fee	30
2. Two–three months of disruption	10
3. Increased property taxes	10
Total	50

Now it would appear that the cost of building the den could be established merely by subtracting 50 from 80, giving us a figure of 30 units. But this figure, 30 units, is the *net value* of building a den. *It is not the cost* of building a den, at least not unless you have unlimited resources. But, assuming you are like most people, and certainly like most educators, you do not have unlimited resources. Thus, when you choose one alternative, you necessarily give up other alternatives. Suppose, for example, in the process of contemplating the new den you realized that by taking advantage of the space (where the new den would be built) you could instead build other things, the most appealing of which is a swimming pool. Assuming you played the same kind of advantage-versus-disadvantage game with the pool possibility, you might come up with a set of summed advantages totaling 70 unit values and a set of summed disadvantages totaling 50 unit values. The net value of the pool is therefore 20.

Now the cost of the den is *not* 30, its net value, but *20*, the net value of the pool. *The cost of an event is the highest valued opportunity necessarily forsaken.*

Let's apply this conception of opportunity costs to an educational example. Suppose a school administrator wants to refurbish the school's home economics classroom by installing new equipment, in particular, more modern ovens. This decision was triggered by a semester-long series of badly charred biscuits and a now-neurotic home economics teacher. The administrator may hesitate to spend the $5,500 required by the project because that money could also be spent to buy (1) 1,000 hours of teacher-aide time, (2) 500 new workbooks for the algebra teacher, (3) a carpet and comfortable furniture for the teachers' lounge, or (4) some combination of parts of these three alternatives. By renovating the home economics classroom, the administrator sacrifices these other potential benefits. Costs, in fact, are *benefits. Costs are benefits lost* when we adopt one decision rather than another.

Putting it another way, the cost of any educational decision is the forgone benefits that would have resulted if we had decided in favor of the highest-valued alternative. Suppose we were able to estimate the net value associated with several educational decisions as follows:

	Net Value
1. Buy new textbooks	40 units
2. Repaint gymnasium	30 units
3. Provide in-service program for teachers	20 units

Then the cost of deciding to buy new textbooks would be 30 units, because that is the worth of the next highest valued alternative.

Implications of Viewing Costs as Benefits Lost

When an evaluator accepts the "benefits forsaken" conception of costs, then several implications are immediately apparent. The first of these is that in order to calculate the cost of anything, it is necessary to determine the value of *at least one alternative*. To do so will unquestionably require a good deal of estimation, but without defining the consequences of two or more alternatives and then valuing those consequences, it is impossible to isolate the value of the benefits forsaken by not opting in favor of the unchosen alternative.

We have previously emphasized the comparative nature of educational evaluation. This discussion of costs should make that point all the more apparent. It may be that the truly skilled evaluator is one who can generate realistic alternatives to a possible course of educational action so that decision makers can comprehend more meaningfully just what they are giving up if they move forward on a given course of action.

A second implication of viewing costs as benefits lost is that, from an evaluator's point of view, costs are irrevocably and exclusively tied to decisions. It is not teachers' services that constitutes a cost, it is the *decision* to use teacher services in one way rather than in another. A pile of textbooks has no inherent cost. Rather, it was the *decision* to buy those textbooks and to forgo buying alternative sets of materials that constitutes the real cost.

A final implication of this conception of opportunity costs is that it tends to make costs occur in the future. Because of this, such costs must be estimated. Educational evaluators had better get ready to do a ton of estimating because, whereas in estimating the cost of constructing a shortwave radio we can secure reasonably accurate net values for component parts, the difficulty of estimating the value of such things as student instructional time and teacher fatigue are next to overwhelming. Because the decision to implement, for example, a special ethnic studies program will carry costs to be incurred over a long period of time, these costs (that is, the forgone benefits) will naturally have to be estimated.

But just because the evaluator is placed in the role of estimator, and estimations are obviously more subject to error than counting the number of correct answers on a posttest, don't disparage the utility of reaching cost estimates. When we operate on reasonably generated estimates, we are better guided than if we operate without any information whatsoever. Well-reasoned estimates, albeit less than perfect, will typically increase the decision maker's *probability* of reaching an appropriate decision. Although that's all we can hope for, it's a good deal better than having the probabilities unknown or stacked against us.

Measuring Costs

An evaluator can employ any of several methods to measure costs. Although we are familiar with finding costs registered in dollar figures, as we shall see, that constitutes only one of the available alternatives. One way would be merely to describe the resources required for two or more alternative programs, for example, an alternative reading and social studies program. By setting forth the actual resources demanded by these competing programs we have a measure, although a rough one, of each alternative's requirements. We can get a general fix on what we are giving up in one program by choosing the other.

Another, more refined, approach would entail the evaluator's estimating the value of two or inore alternatives under consideration. This would be accomplished much like our example of the homeowner's choice between a den and a swimming pool. First, a constellation of advantages is set forth with values affixed to each, then a constellation of disadvantages is sketched and values once more identified for each. The difference between the values of the summed advantages and the values of summed disadvantages constitutes a net value. The cost of the alternative selected is, as we have seen, the value of the next best alternative to it.

Finally, it is possible to attach dollar values to the resources required by each alternative and, as usual, set the cost of the alternative selected according to the dollar value of the next best alternative that is forsaken. Because dollars, as units of measurement, are generalizable and comparable, there are advantages to translating the values of the required resources into dollar values. For instance, when we exasperatedly observe that $20 is a high price to pay for a tankful of gasoline, we are inadvertently using the concept of opportunity costs in that we let the $20 represent the forsaken benefits we could have acquired with that money.

Opportunity Costs and Cost-Analysis Procedures

We have now considered the notion of costs as benefits forsaken. How does the notion of opportunity costs relate to the work of the evaluator who is attempting to aid decision makers as they tussle with the merits of alternative choices?

Thompson indicates that, as an alternative to using opportunity costs in cost analyses, "the analyst can always (1) specify the true alternatives and (2) calculate the consequences for all affected parties."[1] The fundamental idea of opportunity costs must be transmitted to decision makers in a meaningful manner, for those decision makers must recognize that their adoption of Program X costs them the benefits derivative from the next most valued program. Yet the actual calculation of opportunity costs can be avoided. As Thompson indicates:

> *Identifying and combining all effects is equivalent to using opportunity costs. The former method is often conceptually clearer and may be used to check whether opportunity costs have been appropriately determined. The opportunity cost method may enable quicker and more concise calculations.* [2]

Cost-Analysis Alternatives

For fledgling educational evaluators, the world of cost analysis often appears to be foreboding. Not only are there numbers aplenty but also a ton of intimidating terminology. Expressions such as *cost feasibility, cost effectiveness, cost benefit,* and *cost utility* are frequently encountered, sometimes as synonyms and at other times as distinctive approaches. In the remainder of this chapter we'll consider the most relevant of these cost-analysis approaches as they bear on the work of the educational evaluator. There are important differences among the four cost-analysis approaches to be considered. Although each is a legitimate form of cost analysis, there are key distinctions among these approaches that educational evaluators must comprehend. Let's warm up to this distinction-drawing task by considering the simplest of the four: cost-feasibility analysis.

Cost-Feasibility Analysis

Educational decision makers are characteristically faced with choices among competing programs. Most cost-analysis approaches provide ways of choosing among these programs on the basis of the yield for the investment, that is, the payoff per cost associated with the program. *Cost-feasibility analysis,* however, focuses on only one alternative at a time in order to establish whether that alternative is, on the basis of its cost, even affordable.

For example, suppose a group of newly trained educational evaluators have set up their own private consulting company known as EDEVAL Unlimited. Members of the group decide that they simply must have a company car. After all, what self-respecting company these days doesn't have an auto for executive indulgence? Suppose the members of EDEVAL Unlimited, upon pooling their resources, have come up with $12,000 to purchase the auto.

On the basis of prior experiences with certain autos, as well as their secret desires, the following options were suggested for the company vehicle at an EDEVAL staff meeting.

Potential Company Auto	*Purchase Price*
Ford	$ 10,200
Chevrolet	$ 9,900
Plymouth	$ 10,150
Rolls Royce	$182,000

Note that the final option, the British luxury auto, carries a price tag well in excess of the available $12,000. A cost-feasibility analysis would rule out the Rolls as an affordable option. In essence, cost-feasibility analysis constitutes a formal way of determining whether one can afford certain options.

In an educational context, suppose a newly enacted state law provided for a maximum curriculum-enrichment dollar amount of $125 per gifted student. A cost-feasibility analysis would simply determine the cost per student of alternative curriculum-enrichment programs, then knock out any that cost more than $125 per youngster.

Clearly, although cost-feasibility analysis can help decision makers eliminate certain options, it does nothing to help those decision makers choose among the options that remain.

Cost-Effectiveness Analysis

An expression often used by both laypersons and professionals hinges on the extent to which something is "cost effective." Most people, indeed, have a general idea about cost effectiveness, believing that it reflects the extent to which the use of a product or procedure leads to effects that are worth its cost.

Stated a mite more technically, *cost-effectiveness analysis* refers to the appraisal of alternative programs on the basis of their costs *and* their effects in producing a given outcome or group of outcomes. It is not generally recognized, however, that cost-effectiveness analyses can be applied only to the comparison of programs with identical or similar goals. Moreover, cost-effectiveness analyses must be based on a common measure of effectiveness. Let's look a bit closer at these two important constraints.

A major disadvantage of cost-effectiveness approaches is that they are limited to the appraisal of alternatives aimed at the same or markedly similar goals. Using a cost-effectiveness analysis, therefore, evaluators could not compare the virtues of a science-education program with those of a humanities-education program. Nor, for that matter, could an evaluator employ a cost-effectiveness analysis to appraise the merits of two reading programs that had markedly different emphases, for instance, one focusing on word-attack skills and the other focusing on comprehension skills. In order for a cost-effectiveness analysis to be used properly, programs with essentially identical goals must be involved.

The second key constraint in cost-effectiveness analyses is that there must be a *common* index of effectiveness, such as (1) scores on a test of mathematics achievement, (2) the frequency of school vandalism incidents per month, or (3) the proportion of high school graduates who enter postsecondary advanced training programs. If alternative programs are evaluated according to their effects as reflected by different measures, then cost-effectiveness analysis is not an appropriate cost-analytic approach.

A particularly appealing feature of cost-effectiveness analysis stems from the simplicity with which it can be applied in appropriate settings. Because, typically, effectiveness data are available from most evaluations, all the evaluator has to do is determine each program's cost, and a cost-effectiveness evaluation can be readily conducted.

Let's illustrate the application of cost-effectiveness analysis with an example. Suppose you are an evaluator who has been called on to conduct a cost-effectiveness analysis of three competing instructional programs, all focused on the promotion of pupils' critical-thinking skills. Each of the three programs can be carried out in a one-month period, consisting of 50 minutes of instruction per day for four weeks. To make our example simple, assume that officials of the school district in which you're working have randomly assigned 400 pupils to one of four treatment conditions, that is, Program A, Program B, Program C, or a control group that receives no instruction dealing specifically with critical thinking.

Cost Determination   First, the costs of the three programs are determined, including the actual or estimated costs associated with the implementation of each program. Levin[3] recommends what he describes as an "ingredients method" to help evaluators determine costs. By isolating each ingredient in a program, then assigning a cost to it, we can sum these assigned costs to arrive at a cost per program. Levin recommends the categorization of ingredients into four or five main categories such as (1) personnel; (2) facilities; (3) materials and equipment; (4) other program inputs, that is, any ingredients that do not fit into the first three categories; and (5) client inputs, that is, any contributions required of clients such as the requirement that students who participate in a sports program buy their own uniforms.

Once the set of ingredients has been isolated, the evaluator's task is to calculate their *actual* costs or to make a reasonable *estimate* of each ingredient's cost. The care with which one undertakes such a cost-determination effort depends, of course, on the seriousness of the evaluation task at hand. If the stakes are high—that is, if the decisions riding on the evaluation are quite important—then more care would be warranted than if the evaluation were dealing with less significant matters. In high-stakes evaluations, the evaluator will wish to be attentive to the varied types of costs described earlier in the chapter.

Frequently, the costs-per-program can be translated into a program's cost per student. Some programs, of course, are capable of serving more students than other programs at the same cost. In the present example, because there are 100 students who took each program, we merely divide each program's costs by 100 to arrive at a per-student cost for each program.

Effectiveness Determination   Once the costs have been established for each competing program, then the evaluator's attention must turn to effects. In the current example, because all three programs seek to promote pupils' critical-thinking skills, a straightforward paper-and-pencil test of critical-thinking skills might be employed. To keep our example tidy, let's suppose the evaluator locates a nifty commercially published criterion-referenced test of critical-thinking skills simply bristling with reliability and validity. By administering this heaven-sent test to students at the close of the three instructional programs, the evaluator can calculate a common index of program effectiveness.

Recalling that there was also an untreated control group of 100 students, we can compare the control group's test scores with the postinstruction test scores of students in the three programs to obtain the score-points-gained (as a consequence of instruction) per program.

The Analysis   We now have the necessary grist to grind out an illustrative cost-effectiveness analysis, seen in Table 14–1, which presents, for each of the three programs, (1) the cost per student; (2) the effectiveness, that is, the average test score gain over that of the control group; and (3) a cost-effectiveness ratio obtained via dividing costs by effectiveness.

As can be seen in the table, although Program A was the most effective, it was also the most costly. The cost-effectiveness ratio for Program A is $5, indicating that the cost for students to improve one point as a consequence of Program A is $5.

Although Programs B and C each promote identical effects, the lower cost of Program C leads to a cost-effectiveness ratio of only $2 per one-point improvement in test scores. Thus, Program C is the most cost effective. The next most cost-effective program is Program B. Program A is least cost effective.

It is interesting to note that the most effective alternative (Program A) is ranked last when program costs are taken into account. This sort of situation is surprisingly common, for it is frequently the case that the most effective approaches are substantially more costly than their less effective counterparts. Cost-effectiveness analysis illuminates the yield-per-investment picture for decision makers.

To reiterate, the advantages of cost-effectiveness analysis are that it is readily carried out and provides an excellent cost-based comparison among alternatives. Its disadvantages are that it can be applied only to programs with identical goals on the basis of common indices of effectiveness. These limitations, of course, markedly reduce the applicability of cost-effectiveness analysis for purposes of educational evaluation. There are numerous settings in which these two required conditions are not present.

Cost-Benefit Analysis

Cost-benefit analysis, in contrast to cost-effectiveness analysis, permits comparisons among programs aimed at different goals on the basis of different indica-

TABLE 14–1 • *Cost-Effectiveness Data for Three Critical-Thinking Skills Programs*

Program	Cost (per student)	Effectiveness (test scores)	Cost Effectiveness
A	$40	8	$5
B	$20	5	$4
C	$10	5	$2

tors of program effectiveness. In essence, cost-benefit analysis consists of the evaluation of alternatives according to a comparison of their costs and benefits when both are measured monetarily.

Translating Benefits to Dollars   The greatest strength of cost-benefit analysis stems from the translation of program effects into dollar estimates of the value of those effects. Because cost-benefit analysts transform all costs and all benefits to monetary terms, such analysts can undertake comparisons among very different sorts of programs. To illustrate, a school board might be deciding whether to purchase a new type of school bus. This alternative could be compared via cost-benefit analysis with a new parent-tutoring program for the school district's bilingual education classes. Even though the two programs are obviously designed to accomplish different outcomes, because the cost of each can be determined (as in cost-effectiveness analysis) and the outcomes can be described in monetary terms, a meaningful comparison of the two programs can be made.

However, it is the necessity to translate all program outcomes into monetary terms that represents the greatest difficulty in carrying out cost-benefit analyses. How many dollars is it worth to enhance the self-esteem of those students? How much good will can be garnered from parents by having them take part as tutors? How many dollars is that good will worth?

There is also the problem of placing a price tag on the outcomes associated with the acquisition of a new variety of school bus. How many dollars is it worth, for instance, to have students arrive at school refreshed because of improved features in a new bus? Assuming the new brand of bus is safer, how many dollars is it worth to reduce the risk of accident or possibly death? Obviously, pinning monetary values on program outcomes is not fool's play.

Thus, we see, as with many things in life, the greatest strength of cost-benefit analysis, its focus on translating program effects into monetary values, is also its greatest weakness—the subjectivity that must be used in this translation task is considerable.

In education, cost-benefit analysis is most appropriate when applied to programs that can be appraised according to the additional earnings of students who participated in the programs. Such investigations, of course, call for long-term data gathering in order to sort out program impact on participants' incomes.

The Analysis   To illustrate the application of cost-benefit analysis, let's assume that we are contrasting the virtues of three programs, X, Y, and Z, each of which is aimed at the enhancement of students' writing ability. (Although with cost-benefit analysis we could have analyzed programs focused on dramatically different sorts of outcomes, this example will be messy enough even with identical program goals.) To gauge the effects of the program, we have chosen a criterion-referenced test of one's writing skills, half of which consists of multiple-choice items and half of which calls for an actual writing sample. Scores on this test can range from 0 to 50.

Once more, to keep our example tidy, let's imagine we randomly assign 4,000 students, 1,000 each, to (1) Program X, (2) Program Y, (3) Program Z, and (4) an untreated control group. Preinstruction to postinstruction gain scores of the three groups of program-taught students (that is, gains beyond those of the control group) provide us with an index of each program's effects.

First, of course, we must determine the costs of the programs, as we did in the cost-effectiveness analysis. Remember that the value of all resources required to implement a program must be included in these cost determinations.

Next, we must assign monetary values to the benefits produced by each program. We can either (1) make an *estimate* of participants' increased earning power and productivity per one-point test gain (over the control group) or (2) actually *monitor* the earnings and productivity of participants over a long period of years.

The estimation approach, of course, hinges on the accuracy of the cost analyst's estimates. It is extremely difficult to guess how point-by-point boosts in test scores translate into lifelong earning power. Yet this is precisely what we must do in this instance. The actual monitoring approach, on the other hand, takes too long to be of utility in all but a few instances. Decision makers want to render decisions this year or next, not decades down the line.

Let's opt for the estimation approach in order to move forward with our example. Having estimated the monetary benefits per one-point increase on the test, we are now in a position to complete the analysis. Note the cost-benefit data presented in Table 14–2, where we see that Program X is the most expensive, Program Y is the next most expensive, and Program Z is the least expensive. In regard to the monetary value of benefits for the students participating in each program, we note that Program X produced the greatest benefits, Program Z the next greatest benefits, and Program Y the least benefits. In the cost-benefit ratio column, we see the result of costs being divided by benefits. Note that in the case of Program Y, the ratio is greater than 1.0, indicating that costs exceed benefits. In the final column of the table we see the net benefits. It is this column that yields the most understandable reflection of each program's benefits according to its costs. In this example, it appears that Program X is clearly the winner.

Assuming that we previously had carried out a cost-feasibility analysis to determine that we could, in fact, plunk down $100 per student for the writing program (the $100,000 costs for 1,000 students), it would seem that the cost-benefit analysis clearly favors Program X.

TABLE 14–2 • *Cost-Benefit Data for Three Writing-Instruction Programs*

Program	*Cost*	*Benefit*	*Cost Benefit*	*Net Benefit*
X	$100,000	$220,000	.45	$120,000
Y	$ 70,000	$ 60,000	1.17	–$ 10,000
Z	$ 50,000	$100,000	.50	$ 50,000

Remember that cost-benefit analyses can be applied to programs with different goals because the different effects of the programs can be translated into monetary values. As has been noted, however, that translation operation is fraught with the potential for error. It is tough enough to tie dollars to one-point gains in test scores. Imagine the difficulties of putting meaningful monetary values on outcomes such as the mental health benefits associated with the addition of a school psychologist for each 500 pupils in a school district or the reduced medical costs to society of a high-powered preventive health education program. The chief virtue of cost-benefit analysis, then, its ability to contrast dissimilar programs because of its focus on monetary values, is also the greatest problem in this cost-analysis approach.

Cost-Utility Analysis

The final cost-analysis approach to be considered here is *cost-utility analysis*. This form of analysis compares programs according to their costs as they are contrasted with estimates of the utility associated with their outcomes. Thus, whereas cost-effectiveness analysis employs a common measure of program *effectiveness* and cost-benefit analysis translates program benefits into *monetary values*, cost-utility analysis is based on the assignment of numerical values to the *utility* of program effects. For instance, a 10-point utility scale can be employed to make value assignments to program effects, either those effects that have actually been achieved or those that the programs are predicted to bring about.

The advantage of cost-utility analysis over cost-benefit analysis is that in cost-utility analysis there is no need to estimate dollar amounts for program effects, only the need to estimate the relative utility of these effects. Although we all recognize that attaching a monetary value to a program's impact on children's attitudes is apt to be an exercise in guesswork, it is somewhat less difficult to judge such an attitudinal outcome's value on a 0–10 utility scale. Thus, even though the assignment of utility values to program outcomes calls for subjective judgments, those judgments are more readily rendered than the assignment of dollar amounts to program outcomes.

Cost Determination   In order to carry out cost-utility analyses, it is again necessary first to isolate the costs for each program to be compared. These cost determinations are made in the same way that they are made for the other three cost-analytic techniques. Costs are, as usual, calculated by assigning actual or estimated costs to all ingredients required by each program.

Utility Determination   To determine the utility of a program's effects, we first must consider the concept of utility. Most economists attribute the notion of "utility" to the nineteenth-century British utilitarians who advocated a social theory based on providing the greatest happiness to the largest number of individuals. The leaders of the utilitarian movement believed that social institutions should be evaluated according to their utility in promoting societal happiness. In a sense, then, when we ask individuals to estimate the utility of various program effects, we are asking them to determine the usefulness, value, or contribution to societal happiness of such effects. To permit comparisons among these estimates of utility, we ask people to rate the utility of program effects on a numerical scale.

The Utility Scale   Although the number of points on the scale can vary, in cost-utility analysis a serious effort must be made to employ a scale that has equal intervals between its units. Thus, if a 0–10-point scale were to be used, judges should be instructed *not* to regard the scale as merely an ordinal scale, that is, a scale in which higher numbers represent only "more worth" than lower numbers. Instead, the scale should be viewed as an interval scale, in which a program effect that is given a utility rating of *6*, for example, is viewed by the judge as having twice the utility of an outcome to which a value of *3* has been assigned. The scale to be used should be regarded as a *rating* scale in which units are equal, not a *ranking* scale that signifies only the order of outcomes ranked. Explanations to this effect, in language readily understood by those using the scale, should be provided for those individuals being asked to rate the utility of program effects.

Because cost-utility analysis can be applied to programs aimed at different outcomes, it is possible that the same scale might, when applied to different phenomena, be employed differently. This situation should be avoided. One procedure to use to avoid this problem is to provide "rules of thumb" to those judging the utility of outcomes. For instance, were a 0 to 5 scale employed, it might be accompanied by guidelines indicating that *0* equals no utility, *1* equals modest utility, and so on until *5,* which equals the highest utility.

Utility Judges   The individuals who rate the utility of program outcomes should be those affected by the programs being considered. For example, if several staff-development programs were being considered for adoption in a school district, then district officials might ask the educators who would be on the receiving end of the programs to rate the utility of each program's outcomes. Again, if the programs had actually been tried out with a sample of the district's educators (or with comparable educators elsewhere), then the actual effects of the programs would be rated on the utility scale. If not, then estimates of each program's likely effects would be rated by the judges.

If it is impossible, for practical reasons, to have all potentially affected stakeholders rate the utility of program outcomes, then representative samples of stakeholders can be used. For instance, if not all of the district's educators can rate the utility of the projected outcomes of several staff-development programs, then a representative committee of teachers and administrators could render the needed utility ratings.

Obviously, the composition of the rater group will vary from setting to setting. In some situations, for instance, the decision makers themselves could serve as the utility raters. For instance, if a state board of education were choosing among three alternative programs, each with substantially distinctive goals, then the board members themselves might supply the utility ratings.

The ratings supplied by a given set of stakeholders in a particular setting should not, under any circumstances, be employed in different settings. The subjective and, characteristically, idiosyncratic nature of the ratings supplied by a particular group of raters are not generalizable to other settings in which different subjectivities would be operative.

Aggregating Utility Ratings   The translation of separate utility ratings into a single, overall utility rating for each alternative involves a few difficulties. The most obvious way of aggregating individual ratings is to compute a mean rating based on the sum of the individual ratings. Yet, as has been pointed out,[4] there are instances in which such straightforward methods fail to account for the interactions among individual raters, the significance of different stakeholder groups, and so on.

While recognizing that there are difficulties in simple aggregation of separate ratings, Levin[5] suggests that a straightforward summation approach to a "grand" utility score may be employed. He points out that one must assume (1) the existence of utility scales at least approaching the ideal of interval measurement and (2) the absence of contaminating interactions among individual raters. As Levin observes, cost-utility analysis has "a shakier conceptual base than we would like for a tool that is logically so compelling and easy to use." Nonetheless, he concludes, the virtues of cost-utility analysis are considerable. Levin notes that "there is no *a priori* bias in its use; it is easily and readily implementable; and as a pragmatic matter it has very attractive properties."

The Analysis   We can now illustrate the cost-utility analysis by considering its application to three different programs (I, II, and III), each designed to yield a different set of consequences for a group of college students at a small midwestern college. One of the programs is a psychological counseling service, another consists of tutorial program for low-achieving students, and a third is a series of special-focus seminars featuring invited lecturers from other colleges and universities. To keep the example simple, we need not even identify which program is which.

First, of course, the three programs must be subjected to cost analyses so that, on the basis of each program's required ingredients, the cost per program can be calculated. As is always the case, we can calculate the total cost per program or, by dividing the total program cost by the number of students served, compute a cost per student for each program.

Next, a representative group of 50 faculty members from the college, 50 currently enrolled students, and 50 graduates from the college are assembled to assign utility ratings, from 0 to 10, to each program's predicted outcomes. (The predicted outcomes have been described by each program's designers and have been confirmed by nonpartisan reviewers.) The individual ratings of the 150 raters are then averaged so that an overall estimate of utility for each program's likely outcomes is available.

In Table 14–3 these data are presented, along with the usual "costs divided by something" ratio, in this instance, the cost of a program being divided by the judged utility of that program's outcomes.

TABLE 14-3 • *Cost-Utility Data for Three Diverse College Programs*

Program	Cost	Utility	Cost Utility
I	$20,000	8.3	$2,410
II	$15,000	6.4	$2,344
III	$10,000	7.4	$1,351

As can be seen in the table, the cost-utility ratio for the three programs indicates that Program III has a decisively lower cost-utility ratio than the other two programs. This indicates that the cost of a given level of utility is lower for Program III than for the other two programs. The decision makers would surely choose Program III over Programs I and II.

One Family — Four Siblings

We have considered, then, four different cost-analytic techniques that educational evaluators may employ in an effort to guide decision makers as they consider the respective merits of alternative programs. The first of these, *cost-feasibility analysis*, is a fairly simple approach that answers the fundamental question, "Do we have enough money to afford this program?" The remaining three approaches employ essentially identical methods of determining cost. What makes them different is the way that each procedure determines what those costs yield.

In Figure 14–1 we see a succinct set of distinctions among the four cost-analytic approaches we have considered. As can be noted, the cost-feasibility analysis involves simple subtraction of available resources from each program's cost, but the other three approaches all hinge on a division operation. More specifically, they

FIGURE 14-1 • *Critical Features of Four Cost-Analysis Procedures for Educational Evaluators*

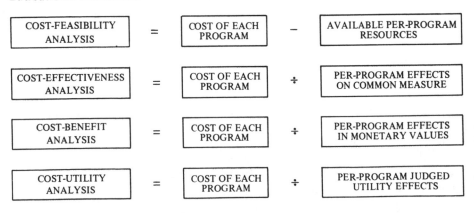

conclude with a ratio resulting from the division of each program's costs by the particular index of program effects employed in that approach.

For *cost-effectiveness analysis*, the divisor is each program's performance on an identical measure of effectiveness such as pupils' average test scores. For *cost-benefit analysis*, the divisor is each program's actual or estimated yield in monetary values. For *cost-utility analysis*, the divisor is each program's payoff in terms of judged societal utility on a numerical utility scale.

Levin,[6] who has supplied an excellent introductory text dealing with cost analysis from the evaluator's perspective, believes that cost-effectiveness and cost-utility analyses have the most applicability to educational situations. He spends the bulk of the pages in his cost-analysis primer clarifying the applications of these two approaches. For those wishing to travel the cost-analytic trail further, Levin's introductory primer is a first-rate next step. In a recent essay regarding cost analysis in educational evaluation, however, Levin argued that "by virtually every standard, there is very little cost-effectiveness or cost-benefit analysis that is carried out in the evaluation arena."[7]

Everything in Its Proper Place　For the novice evaluator who has never previously fondled economic toys, there is a seductive appeal in the group of cost-analysis approaches we have been considering. After all, it should be more than a mite obvious by this time that an evaluator who considers program options without taking cognizance of program costs and program payoffs is a bona fide cluck.

Yet, how much energy should be devoted by educational evaluators to the exotics of cost-analytic machinations? As we have seen, although there are several ways of looking at program costs in relation to program effects, there are technical problems associated with each. No currently available cost-analytic approach so neatly dodges the technical dilemmas that it can be judged a decisive winner.

A major drawback with all of the cost-analytic approaches resulting in cost-effect ratios is that nonmonetary costs must be translated into dollar amounts and, in the case of effects, dollar estimates or some proxy for dollar amounts (such as scores on a utility scale) must be used. The translation operations involve, for the most part, solid doses of subjectivity. Evaluators must always remember that subjectively derived numbers are no better or worse than the subjective judgments from which they are derivative. Too many novice evaluators who rush to the raptures of cost-analytic approaches seem to forget the source of the numbers with which they derive their ultimate cost-effect ratios. Caution is warranted in the adoption of cost-analytic approaches, particularly for the beginner who is not sensitive to the possible shortcomings of these approaches.

As Scriven puts it:

> At first glance, these quasi-quantitative approaches may appeal to the evaluator because they yield such indices as the benefit-cost ratio, which connects neatly to the rule that one should select the option with the highest such ratio. But this rule offers no advantage over its more primitive predecessor: Select the option with the largest net benefits. Indeed, it is less general and will give the wrong answer in many important

and typical cases where the options do not use exactly the same amount of all resources.[8]

Scriven contends that, in many instances, it may be preferable to employ a simple weight-and-sum approach such as that used in *Consumer Reports*, wherein one weighs the importance of various output factors, estimates the performance of these factors, then sums the weighted performance results to choose an alternative. While arguing that cost-analysis approaches should not be abandoned, Scriven reminds evaluators that "some of the more technical apparatus and concepts — in fact, most of the buzz-words of cost analysis — do not pull their weight; they contribute almost nothing analytically, and they constitute a tremendous liability pedagogically."[9]

Educators clearly cannot dismiss the importance of costs or the pertinence of some sort of cost-analytic considerations to aid the deliberations of decision makers. It is imperative, however, for evaluators not to get so caught up in the exotics of cost-analysis procedures (the surface of such procedures having only been scratched mildly in this chapter) that the decision maker's capability to comprehend is forgotten. Even a conscientious decision maker can become befuddled if subjected to an unrelenting barrage of cost-analytic terminology and concepts.

If evaluators wish to help decision makers truly profit from cost-analysis considerations, those decision makers must be educated, in language appropriate to their level of sophistication, to what is really going on in the cost-analytic approach chosen. Educational evaluators should strive to improve the quality of education decisions rendered by those who are responsible for decision rendering. If cost-analysis information is to play a part in the decision makers' deliberations, and it should, be sure that the decision makers thoroughly understand what is involved.

A Defensible Level of Detail

The attentive reader will have recognized that the foregoing discussion of cost considerations could lead to the conduct of an incredibly detailed cost analysis or, at the other extreme, a very rough and dirty cost analysis. The practical problem facing the educational evaluator is just how fine-grained a cost analysis should be.

There is an expression used by contract bridge players who find themselves forced to play with a weak partner. The expression runs as follows: *"Don't play for the best possible result; play for the best result possible."* In other words, instead of trying to bid and make the best possible contract, an effort bound to fall in view of the inept partner, the wise player goes for the best result possible *under the circumstances* (of having been afflicted with a loser on the other side of the table), hence aims for less stunning but more attainable contracts.

In the same way, an evaluator should engage in cost-analysis operations consonant with the circumstances, the two most important of which are (1) the financial resources available to support the endeavor and (2) the evaluator's talents in this arena. If there aren't many dollars available to support a detailed cost analysis, then the evaluator will have to consider costs at a more gross level than might be preferred. But it is also true that one can plow endless energy into estimating the costs of various decision alternatives. Care must be taken not to try to be more sophisticated than the accuracy of estimated data warrant.

Discussion Questions

1. How would you go about explaining to someone else what is meant by thinking of costs as benefits lost?
2. Which cost-analytic procedure do you believe yields the most *defensible* reflection of the output of an educational program in relationship to its cost? Is it cost-effectiveness analysis, cost-benefit analysis, or cost-utility analysis? Why did you make your choice?
3. If you were an evaluator assigned to the task of helping an elementary school staff choose one set of reading texts over another, how would you introduce cost considerations into your work?
4. In the situation described above, just how detailed do you think your cost analysis should be?
5. For cost-effectiveness analysis, cost-benefit analysis, and cost-utility analysis, name each procedure's greatest strength and greatest weakness.

Practice Exercises

1. In each of the following four vignettes an example is provided of one of the following types of cost analyses: *cost-feasibility analysis, cost-effectiveness analysis, cost-benefit analysis,* or *cost-utility analysis.* Identify which cost-analytic approach is illustrated in each vignette.

   a. An evaluator establishes the cost for each of three health education programs focused on the dangers of using illegal drugs. The programs are then tried out on three groups of randomly assigned students. In addition, a fourth group of untreated students is employed for control purposes. All four groups of students are given identical knowledge tests on a pre- and postinstruction basis. The gains of the three "treated" groups of students beyond those of the untreated control group serve as an indication of each program's effects. The costs per program are then divided by the program's average points gained from pretest to posttest. The resulting ratios constitute an index of program success in relationship to program cost.

   b. Evaluator Evelyn compares the payoff of three rather different programs being considerd by a state board of education. Because of the distinctiveness of the three programs' outcomes, she asks the board members to rate the "social good" yielded by the three programs. Board members are to supply their ratings on a 20-point scale. The averages of these ratings are then divided by Evelyn into the cost of each program. The resulting ratios are presented by Evelyn to the board.

   c. A first-year evaluator in a mid-sized school district has helped the district superintendent determine whether certain enrichment programs being considered by the district for possible adoption can be afforded. On the basis of a detailed analysis of the per program cost of the five programs' ingredients, the evaluator indicates to the superintendent that two of the programs are too expensive to be considered further.

d. Theodore Thrift, whose parents pushed him into economics largely because of his name, has compared three program alternatives on the bases of (1) their costs in relation-

ship to (2) their effects as translated into monetary terms. Theodore has employed the latest cost-analytic thinking in calculating the dollar costs (actual and estimated) and the dollar consequences of the three programs.

Answers to Practice Exercises

1. *a.* cost-effectiveness analysis; *b.* cost-analysis; *c.* cost-feasibility analysis;

d. cost-benefit analysis.

Notes

1. M. S. Thompson, *Benefit-Cost Analysis for Program Evaluation* (Beverly Hills, CA: Sage Publications, 1980), p. 116.

2. Ibid. p. 117.

3. H. M. Levin, "Cost-Effectiveness in Evaluation Research," in *Handbook of Evaluation Research*, (Vol. 2), ed. M. Guttentag and E. Struening (Beverly Hills, CA: Sage Publications, 1975).

4. K. J. Arrow, *Social Choice and Individual Values* (New York: Wiley, 1963).

5. H. M. Levin, *Cost-Effectiveness: A Primer* (Beverly Hills, CA: Sage Publications, 1983), p. 122.

6. Ibid.

7. Henry M. Levin, "Cost Effectiveness at Quarter Century," in *Evaluation and Education: At Quarter Century*, ed. M. W. McLaughlin and D. C. Phillips (Chicago: University of Chicago Press, 1991), pp. 189–209.

8. M. Scriven, "Costs in Evaluation: Concept and Practice," in *The Costs of Evaluation*, ed. M. C. Alkin and L. C. Solmon (Beverly Hills, CA: Sage, 1983), p. 41.

9. Ibid.

Selected References

Alchian, Armen A. "Cost." In David Sills (Ed.), *International Encyclopedia of Social Science* (Vol. 3). New York: Macmillan and the Free Press, 1968.

Alkin, Marvin C. and Lewis C. Solmon (Eds.). *The Costs of Evaluation*. Beverly Hills, CA: Sage, 1983.

Anthony, Robert N. "What Should Cost Mean?" *Harvard Business Review* (May 1970): 121–31.

Byrk, A. S. (Ed.). "Stakeholder-Based Evaluation" (Special Issue). *New*

Directions for Program Evaluation, 17 (March 1983).

Chambers, J. "The Development of a Cost of Education Index." *Journal of Education Finance*, 5:3 (1980): 262–81.

Fisher, Gene. *Cost Considerations in Systems Analysis*. New York: American Elsevier, 1971.

Haller, Emil J. "Cost Analysis for Educational Program Evaluation." In *Evaluation in Education: Current*

Applications. Berkeley CA: McCutchan, 1974.

Levin, H. M. "Cost-Effectiveness in Evaluation Research." In M. Guttentag and E. Struening (Eds.), *Handbook of Evaluation Research* (Vol. 2). Beverly Hills, CA: Sage, 1975.

———. "Cost Analysis." In N. Smith (Ed.), *New Techniques for Evaluation*. Beverly Hills, CA: Sage, 1981.

———. *Cost-Effectiveness: A Primer*. Beverly Hills, CA: Sage, 1983.

Quinn, Bill, Adrian Van Mondfrans, and Blaine R. Worthen. "Cost-Effectiveness of Two Math Programs as Moderated by Pupil SES." *Educational Evaluation and Policy Analysis*, 6:1 (Spring 1984): 39–52.

Rossi, Peter H., and Howard E. Freeman. "Measuring Efficacy." *Evaluation: A Systematic Approach* (4th ed.). Newbury Park, CA: Sage, 1989, pp. 375–416.

Scriven M. "Costs in Evaluation: Concept and Practice." In M. C. Alkin and L. C. Solmon (Eds.), *The Cost of Evaluation*. Beverly Hills, CA: Sage, 1983.

Thompson, M. S. *Benefit-Cost Analysis for Program Evaluation*. Beverly Hills, CA: Sage, 1980.

CHAPTER FIFTEEN

Teacher Evaluation — A Special Challenge

Educational evaluators are generally concerned with the appraisal of educational programs, that is, the formative or summative evaluation of an educational treatment. Rarely do educational evaluators attempt to evaluate *individuals* — rarely, that is, with one important exception: the appraisal of classroom teachers.

Educational evaluators may not be called on to appraise the competence of physicians or bricklayers. But individuals who remain in the educational evaluation field for more than 10 or 15 minutes should not be surprised when they are called on to evaluate schoolteachers. Teacher evaluation comes with the educational evaluator's territory. Accordingly, we'll take a good hard look at this sort of personnel evaluation.[1]

Teachers as Treatments

Because of the nature of a typical instructional event in which a teacher is involved, we are obliged to consider the individual teacher as an instructional *treatment*. Of course, a classroom teacher relies on textbooks, as well as a variety of other instructional support devices, to teach the pupils. But inasmuch as it is the teacher who orchestrates the medley of instructional inputs the pupils receive, it is possible to consider each teacher as constituting a unique instructional treatment, and therefore to evaluate that instructional treatment as such.

The quality of a particular teacher's efforts are, of course, dependent on the kinds of supporting instructional resources available. To be sure, given two teachers of equal ability, one with a galaxy of modern instructional devices and the other with only a chalkboard and a half-dozen pieces of chalk, the teacher suffering from resource deprivation will obviously have a tougher time of it. But if we really want to focus on evaluating the teacher as *teacher*, then there are ways of reducing, if not eliminating, the influence of such factors as textbooks and other instructional support devices.

The Long, Sorry Search for
Teacher-Effectiveness Indicators

Since the early 1900s educational researchers have spent endless hours trying to devise a satisfactory measure of teacher competence. In view of the enormous energy expended in trying to identify this elusive prey, some disgruntled researchers have opined that a defensible index of teaching skill ranks third behind two other hard-to-locate targets:

Among Humanity's Perennial Quests

1. The Holy Grail
2. The Fountain of Youth
3. A Valid Index of Teaching Skill

The bulk of the teacher effectiveness research carried on during this century, usually in the United States, was directed toward the isolation of some kind of measure of instructor skill that, for research purposes, could be employed as a dependent variable. It was hoped that such a dependent variable could then be used to discern the influence of independent variables, for example, different instructional techniques.

In the early stages of teacher effectiveness research, in fact, it was thought that there really was a species known as "the effective teacher," and all that researchers had to do was figure out how to identify these all-purpose winners. With few exceptions, the focus of such teacher effectiveness investigations was not on devising assessment techniques to yield information for making decisions about individual teachers. Instead, the teacher effectiveness researcher was interested in discovering relationships between effective teaching and the myriad variables that might play a role in determining one's instructional skill.

A review of the teacher-effectiveness investigations during the first three-quarters of this century reveals a woeful record of unfilled hopes and unrejected null hypotheses. The most frequently occurring phrase in the reports of these investigators has been, without question, *no significant difference*. Nothing seems to have panned out for the teacher-competence researcher. The hundreds and hundreds of studies designed to isolate a defensible index of instructional skill have, almost without exception, failed to yield the anticipated dividends. Later in the chapter we shall consider the major stratagems that have been adopted in these teacher-competence inquiries.[2]

The Increased Popularity of Teacher Appraisal

Evaluating teachers has become increasingly fashionable during recent years. Just as the 1970s found educators preoccupied with program evaluation, and the 1980s saw them embroiled in competency testing for students, the latter part of the twentieth century may well be remembered as the period when our attention was focused on teacher quality.

In numerous localities, policymakers have installed a variety of teacher appraisal programs. In some of these instances, the new teacher evaluation standards represent a thinly veiled attempt to cast out the incompetents. In other cases, the new teacher education requirements are part of an elaborate scheme to reward the meritorious and thereby to improve the quality of schools.

No matter what the rationale, however, all of the recently mandated teacher evaluation programs are predicated on the belief that we know how to evaluate teachers. That belief, in my view, is mistaken. I do not believe that a defensible technology for the appraisal of teachers currently exists. Moreover, I believe that the implementation of large-scale teacher evaluation systems may, in the long term, have an adverse effect on the quality of education.

There are several reasons for my pessimism:

- Large-scale teacher evaluation enterprises are costly. If an expensive evaluation program accomplishes little, then precious educational funds have been wasted.
- The creation of an elaborate evaluation system instills a false sense of confidence in those policymakers who must monitor our schools' progress. Having established a quality-control mechanism, however ineffectual, they become complacent in monitoring the actual effectiveness of our schools.
- Because a good many large-scale teacher evaluation programs employ flawed procedures, a teacher's daily activities may become stultified because of pressures created by such programs. If, for example, teachers are told that to be truly effective they must have at least one high-order cognitive objective per lesson, then they may waste a lot of time whomping up a suitable objective for each lesson plan. Yet there is no evidence that this instructional strategy is invariably effective. There may be some lessons that are best spent on unabashedly low-level memorization.

A Fragile Technical Base

The distressing truth regarding our teacher evaluation technology is that it is far more fragile than most people believe. We simply do not possess the measurement ploys needed to get a good fix on a particular teacher's instructional prowess. There are problems in every one of the data-gathering procedures now in use. Those who think that we can comfortably rely on one or more meaningful measures of a specific teacher's merit are not being realistic.

The shortcomings of specific teacher evaluation systems become most apparent when they are used to make *summative* decisions – such as hiring or firing decisions, and appraisals for merit pay awards and promotions.

I do not oppose the use of certain teacher evaluation procedures when they are used for *formative* purposes – to help teachers improve their instruction. Because formative teacher evaluation promotes discovery and self-education, it is quite acceptable for a supervisor's classroom observation to conclude with the supervisor's telling the teacher, "You might want to try Procedure X."

Although our data-gathering procedures are very shaky, for day-to-day assistance to teachers they can't hurt all that much. Moreover, if applied in a "what-happens-if" context, such procedures may prove quite beneficial. Because formative teacher appraisals should be aimed at "if-then" notions to be tried, the worst thing that can happen is that the teacher may discover a suggested improvement tactic may not work.

The Perils of Particulars

One of the most fundamental impediments to the creation of a first-rate teacher evaluation system is that the bulk of what we know about the instructional process is correlational in nature. If teachers provide ample practice opportunities for pupils, then those pupils *tend* to learn better. If teachers give their students immediate knowledge-of-results, then pupils *tend* to achieve more. But the correlations between particular practices and pupil growth are far from perfect. Translation: A teacher can break the research-based rules yet still come up a winner.

When we evaluate teachers, we do not engage in group-focused assertions such as "teachers who discipline in a consistent manner will more frequently achieve good classroom interest than those who discipline inconsistently." Rather, we must determine whether Cecily Smith, grade 3 teacher in Sunnyside Elementary School, is competent or incompetent. Such a specific appraisal of merit is required, but the appraisal must be made in a plethora of particulars.

Cecily is a *particular* person pursuing *particular* educational goals for *particular* pupils who have *particular* genetic and experiential backgrounds. Moreover, Cecily is using *particular* textbooks in a *particular* classroom under the leadership of a *particular* principal guided by a *particular* superintendent and a *particular* school board. To evaluate Cecily's effectiveness as a teacher, we must take cognizance of all the particulars that bear on her teaching performance.

Teacher effectiveness research makes one thing abundantly clear. There is not an across-the-board "effective teacher." Different teachers can employ thoroughly divergent instructional techniques, yet in their *particular* situations both achieve fine results.

To be oblivious to the particularistic nature of teaching, hence to adopt a "one-size-fits-all" conception of teacher evaluation, is to err fundamentally.

A Litany of Shortcomings

Thus far I have been maligning the data-gathering procedures employed in teacher evaluation schemes, implying that their weaknesses render them unsuitable for use, particularly in a summative context. Although space prohibitions preclude an exhaustive flaying of teacher evaluation data-gathering procedures, let's highlight some salient shortcomings of the more popular techniques.

Administrative Ratings   Although administrative ratings are inexpensive to gather, and they can be used to appraise many teachers in a short period of time, these ratings are often provided by administrators who have only an outmoded and often simplistic view of teaching. Principals, for example, all too often incorporate a variety of irrelevant considerations in judging teachers, such as a teacher's behavior in faculty meetings. Too many principals also use recollections of their own "stellar" days in the classroom as the yardstick against which to rate teachers.

Classroom Observations   Even though classroom observations are almost universally regarded as the *sine qua non* of a complete teacher evaluation system, they are not without serious problems. One difficulty with observational techniques is that they rely heavily on intrinsic criteria (i.e., the *processes* that the teacher employs) in contrast to extrinsic criteria (i.e., the results that the teacher produces in learners). In addition, classroom observations are *incredibly reactive:* By their very nature they usually distort the teacher's performance. In situations where classroom observations are scheduled in advance, particularly in settings where the observational criteria have been made public, observers will typically encounter a canned lesson, one that has been rehearsed repeatedly, sometimes with the aid of a videotape machine. Typicality of teacher performance is nonexistent. Finally, truly effective classroom observations depend on first-rate observation instruments and painstaking, lengthy training of observers, both of which are not found in most teacher evaluation schemes featuring classroom observations. Classroom observations, however, can focus on detailed data categories useful in formative evaluation strategies.

Pupil Test Performance Pupil achievement is often considered the ultimate index of a teacher's instructional proficiency. Yet, as tempting as it is to evaluate teachers chiefly on the basis of their pupils' attainments, there are substantial problems with this approach. For openers, many of the tests employed to assess pupil progress are standardized, norm-referenced achievement tests that are typically insensitive to detecting the effects of differentially effective instruction. Even more important, we have not yet found an effective way to deal with differences in students' entry behaviors. If Teacher A, who has a class full of academically talented and motivated students, is compared with Teacher B, who has a class full of slow and disinterested students, on the basis of year-end test results, the comparison is meaningless. And those who contend that we can deal with such problems via statistical adjustments are promising more than they can deliver. If our schools were populated by essentially homogeneous youngsters who could be randomly assigned to different teachers, then pupil test performance might serve as a suitable indicator of teachers' skills. But the pupils are heterogeneous, and random pupil assignment is often a researcher's pipe dream. The realities of public schooling render pupil test performance far less formidable as an index of teachers' skill than is usually believed.

Student Ratings One difficulty with having students rate their teacher's instructional effectiveness is that the students' estimates of a teacher's instructional skill are often contaminated by the teacher's popularity or the students' interest in the subject matter being taught. If carefully devised student-rating forms are not used, as well as procedures that truly protect the students' anonymity, the validity of student ratings will be diminished. Students will believe that low ratings could lead to poor grades. Finally, there is scant experience and almost no evidence regarding how mature pupils must be before they can supply sensible judgments regarding their teachers' instructional competence.

Tests of Teachers' Competency/Knowledge The recent flurry of interest in competency tests for teachers might suggest that such tests can play a useful role in helping us judge how proficient a teacher actually is. For example, some states now employ tests of a teacher's professional knowledge, such as tests focusing on the teacher's knowledge of classroom instructional principles. It may, indeed, be reasonable for state officials to use such tests as measures of knowledge that is considered precursive to effective teaching. Nonetheless, no empirical basis exists to support the use of such test results as indices of a *specific* teacher's instructional skill. Teachers may know the difference between positive and negative reinforcement, yet choose to use neither in their teaching.

Professional Portfolios In the past few years some teacher evaluation programs have required teachers to submit professional portfolios which, like artists' portfolios, contain varied evidence regarding the teacher's instruction. These portfolios might contain such items as lesson plans, quizzes, and descriptions of classroom projects. Although it is too early to tell whether professional portfolios will turn out to be useful in teacher appraisals, there seems to be at least one salient deficit in using portfolios. If, in the interest of fairness, teacher evaluators make public the criteria on which the portfolios are to be judged, then teachers will fastidiously fashion portfolios designed to gain the maximum evaluative points. The portfolios will be unrepresentative of the teacher's actual instruction, but rather will become contrived extravaganzas designed to win plaudits. Sadly, we will probably see the emergence of portfolio-preparation firms that, for a suitable fee, will create portfolios that make an inept teacher resemble Socrates.

Teacher Appraisal Interviews   Another recent entrant in the teacher evaluation sweepstakes is the teacher appraisal interview. In such schemes interviewers probe the teacher's approach to instruction in an effort to discern the merits of that approach. Again, although it is too early to write off teacher appraisal interviews, they seem to suffer from the same shortcomings as professional portfolios. The difficulty is that teachers really should be informed of the criteria to be employed in making judgments regarding them, yet communicating these criteria to the teachers will heighten the likelihood of contrived, hence meaningless, teacher behaviors during the interview.

Teachers' Self-Evaluations   The problem with asking teachers to appraise their own instructional prowess is that most of us are markedly partisan when we judge ourselves. If there are significant contingencies associated with the teacher evaluation activity, most teachers will provide inflated estimates of their instructional skills. Thus, while particularly useful for purposes of formative evaluation, self-evaluations have no utility in the summative appraisal of teachers.

Contract Plans   An infrequently used teacher evaluation ploy is a *contract plan*. A contract plan calls for the teacher to negotiate a simple sort of contract with the evaluator regarding the kinds of pupil performance to be promoted as a consequence of instruction. The teacher describes the current (preinstruction) status of learners, on the basis of their measured performance, then indicates the kind of evidence that will reflect successful completion of the instructional sequence. Such evidence might include any of the kinds of measures described in Chapter Five, such as pupil responses to affective measures, pupil test performance, or observations of pupil out-of-school behavior.

After the teacher and the evaluator agree as to the targets of the instruction, the teacher instructs the students. Evidence is then gathered from the students, perhaps by the teacher, perhaps by the evaluator, to indicate whether the anticipated learner results have been attained.

It is important in such a scheme to build in some kind of review, perhaps by colleagues, of the quality of outcomes the teacher agrees to promote. There is some danger, of course, that teachers will set their expectations too low in a contract plan in order to enhance the likelihood of attaining the anticipated outcomes.

One of the chief problems with contract plans for teacher evaluation is that, since dissimilar goals will typically be set by teachers, it is difficult to compare the relative proficiency of teachers who pursue different goals with different groups of learners.

The advantage of the contract plan is that it sets forth in no uncertain terms just how the teacher is to be evaluated. No shifting or capricious criteria are used here (such as the teacher's hair length). The needed evidence is specified in advance. Both evaluator and evaluatee negotiate an agreement on such evidence prior to instruction.

A number of districts are currently employing variants of such contract plans. Experience with this approach will suggest whether it is a viable option which teacher evaluators should consider.

Teaching Performance Tests   Another option for teacher evaluators to consider is the *teaching performance test*. A teaching performance test assesses the teacher's ability to accomplish prespecified instructional objectives as reflected by the postinstruction performance of learners. The following steps are required for carrying out a teaching performance test.

1. A teacher is given a specific instructional objective (and any needed background information), then asked to plan a brief lesson that will (a) promote learner mastery of the objective (usually cognitive) and (b) be judged interesting to the learners.
2. The teacher prepares a lesson, using any instructional techniques the teacher wishes.
3. The teacher instructs a small group of learners, typically for 15 to 20 minutes.
4. The learners are posttested with a test previously unseen by the teacher but whose nature is readily inferable from the objective given to the teacher. The learners are also asked to rate how interesting the lesson was.

The learners involved can be either children or, because of greater logistical convenience, adults (such as fellow teachers). The topics employed can be novel, thereby eliminating the necessity of pretesting the learners, or more familiar, thereby requiring the use of pretests to locate sufficiently naive learners.

The chief advantage of such teaching performance tests, sometimes referred to as *mini-lessons*, is that because the teaching task is identical, it is possible to undertake meaningful comparisons of teachers. It is necessary, of course, to keep all other conditions — such as teaching time and preparation time — identical in the conduct of such tests. Learners should also be comparable, a requirement suggesting random assignment of pupils to teachers. It is even desirable to screen the learner pool, at least in general terms, prior to assigning learners to teachers, thus making it possible to eliminate aberrant learners from the potential pupils.

Although there have been a modest number of studies regarding the utility of teaching performance tests as a teacher-evaluation tool, it is still too early to tell whether such measures can be devised with sufficient rigor that they will yield reliable results regarding an individual teacher's performance. It is also true that teaching performance tests are more reflective of optimal rather than typical instructor performance. We must discover the relationship between (1) teachers' competence as measured by performance tests and (2) their competence as reflected by more routine performance over an extended period in classrooms.

There is evidence[3] that teaching performance tests can yield reliable evidence regarding the performance of groups of teachers, but it is not clear whether such devices can provide reliable estimates of individual performance. Evaluators should be aware of this distinction, incidentally, as it may be possible for a measure to function marvelously as an index of group performance yet fall on its face if applied to the assessment of individual prowess. It is unlikely that teaching performance tests can be refined to the point that they provide decent data on the skill of individual instructors. For formative teacher evaluation purposes, however, teaching performance tests may be of use.

First, however, in addition to recognizing the shortcomings of the data-gathering techniques just discussed, it is necessary for those designing teacher evaluation systems to deal with two serious drawbacks in most teacher evaluation approaches.

Summative/Formative Confusion

The initial shortcoming in current teacher appraisal practices, a problem encountered in almost all public school districts, is that the officials of those districts have thoughtlessly merged two different missions of teacher evaluation. These two evaluative functions are splendid if separate, but counterproductive when combined. The first of these two missions, *formative* teacher evaluation, is to help teachers become more effective. A second, and equally important, function of teacher evaluation is to isolate those weak teachers who, if they cannot be improved, should be removed from their teaching positions. This latter mission, of course, is *summative* teacher evaluation.

Summative teacher evaluation, in addition to being used for the dismissal of teachers, can also be employed to help assign teachers to levels of a career ladder (merit pay) program and to grant or deny tenure to beginning teachers. Summative teacher evaluation has as its primary function, however, the determination of a teacher's competence—not the augmentation of that competence. Summative evaluation makes no pretense about helping a teacher get better. Improving the teacher's performance is the job of formative teacher evaluation.

Almost all U.S. teacher evaluation systems attempt to combine these two teacher evaluation functions so that both can be carried out simultaneously. Yet, that combination constitutes a classic instance wherein the coalescing of inherently contradictory functions renders both dysfunctional.

Typical of the language encountered in most public school teacher appraisal procedures is that found in the teacher appraisal law recently enacted by one state legislature. According to that law, "The results of the appraisal of teachers shall be used for career ladder purposes, and may be used for contract renewal and staff development considerations." In the same law, however, legislators require that the evaluation assessment instrument for teachers "be used to assess specific skills primarily for purposes of remediation and improvement." Not surprisingly, a dual-purpose statewide teacher appraisal system was developed consonant with legislative intent.

As we see, a hybrid summative/formative teacher evaluation system has been legislatively mandated, a system that must simultaneously pursue the formative function of teacher appraisal, that is, teacher improvement, and the summative functions of career-ladder assignment and contract renewal. The situation is not atypical.

The reason that formative and summative teacher evaluation cannot cavort together congenially is that their end results are so dramatically different. The decisions riding on formative teacher evaluation are a host of choices focused on "How can I do it better?" The teacher can try out different approaches, either minor or major, to see what works best. The aim of this type of teacher evaluation is to shape the teacher's performance so that it becomes more effective. Summative teacher evaluation, in contrast, can lead to identification of weak teachers who may, if unremediable, be dismissed. In essence, the distinction is between "fixing" versus "firing" the teacher. From the perspective of the teacher who is being fixed or fired, that distinction is not trivial.

In a typical school district, principals serve as dual-function teacher evaluators; that is, they are given responsibilities for both formative and summative evaluation of the teachers in their schools. Even if a principal were skilled at both formative and summative teacher evaluation (and very few are), most principals would probably prefer to engage in formative teacher evaluation. As is true with most of us, principals would prefer to be liked rather than loathed. It is far easier to be approved by a colleague if you're trying to assist instead of eliminate that colleague.

Teachers recognize, however, that despite an abundance of "Let's get better" rhetoric from principals, those principals can also transmit another message, namely, "Look elsewhere for employment!" Because nobody likes to get fired, teachers will naturally be reluctant to reveal their own deficits to a principal, or even to agree with a principal's perceptions of their shortcomings. Such admissions, while indispensable for formative teacher appraisal, could constitute part of the evidence needed in order to dismiss the teacher. Indeed, the weakest teachers—those most in need of improvement—will typically be the very ones least apt to identify or admit their own frailties. The less confident that people are of their own competence, the more guarded they are about admitting to an absence of perfection.

Thus we see that although many principals set out to make their teacher appraisals focus on the improvement of teachers' skills, the contaminating specter of summative teacher appraisal serves to blunt that improvement mission.

With regard to summative teacher evaluation, because principals are so caught up in an effort to improve their staffs' instructional skills, they devote precious little effort to reaching an evidence-based judgment about a teacher's overall instructional capabilities. As a consequence, few teachers are ever rated as weak or incompetent by their principals. Rather, most principals shower their teachers with excessively positive ratings. Teachers who receive an "average" or "satisfactory" evaluation from a principal are, indeed, often outraged. To be rated "average" in the teacher evaluation game is to be regarded as decisively "below average."

One problem, then, with today's teacher evaluation is that its formative function contaminates its summative function, and vice versa. The resultant confusion in mission and method leads to ineffective teacher appraisal systems which neither remove nor improve teachers.

A Flight from Judgment

A second major drawback in today's teacher appraisal systems is a reluctance by the architects of those systems to employ professional *judgment* in order to ascertain a teacher's competence. This problem is encountered in both formative and summative appraisal procedures but is particularly prevalent in summatively oriented teacher evaluation systems.

Because the designers of teacher appraisal systems typically recognize the tentative nature of the knowledge base on which they are operating, they usually go to great lengths to avoid relying on human judgment in the determination of a teacher's skill. The judgmental process is either circumvented altogether or, more commonly, subdivided into a series of such minuscule judgments that no single judgment, by itself, is terribly important.

This subdivision approach calls for a host of mini-judgments such as whether classroom observations reveal that the teacher "stresses important points and dimensions of content" or "specifies expectations for class behavior." Points are assigned by a classroom observer for each such dimension depending on whether the teacher displays inadequate, acceptable, or superior quality. In some teacher appraisal systems there are 50 to 100 of these separate dimensions about which observers must make judgments. On the basis of a galaxy of separate judgments by the observer, an *aggregated* number of points is assigned to each teacher. Before long, unfortunately, these aggregations are treated with respect and deference not warranted by their origins. Indeed, although many of the separate judgments are based on point assignments of arguable consistency and validity, it is somehow thought that the sum of all these little judgments becomes an accurate index of the teacher's skill. Teacher evaluation of this sort may *not* be one of those wholes that is greater than the sum of its parts, particularly if its parts (the tiny judgments) are of debatable defensibility.

In such an approach, evaluators must often fill in myriad little bubbles on some sort of evaluation form, each little bubble representing a specified number of points on a particular dimension. A perusal of these appraisal forms reveals far more bubbles than is found in a glass of sparkling wine, imported or domestic. Thus we can think of this judgment-avoidance approach as a "champagne" teacher evaluation strategy. In the end, all of the little bubbles are added together so as to yield a sum-of-bubbles per teacher. This sum-of-bubbles total is, all too often, regarded with reverence. Sometimes the sum-of-bubbles index is subjected to further mathematical massaging so that, in the end, it comes out simply reeking of (unwarranted) rigor.

Why, one might ask, would the designers of teacher evaluation schemes go to so much trouble? Instead of masking human judgments by fractionating them, why not ask teacher evaluators to render more global judgments regarding a teacher's instructional prowess?

The answer is all too clear. It takes *courage* to assert that a teacher is inadequate. It does not take courage to fill in a bubble indicating that one small aspect of the teacher's instructional delivery is flawed. After all, in a teacher appraisal system consisting of 100 separate judgments, it takes no backbone to indicate that the teacher has a .01 deficit.

In addition, because teacher evaluators are fearful of overlooking any legitimate aspect of a teacher's instructional skill, no matter how minor, many evaluators toss all dimensions of potential relevance to a teacher's skill into a to-be-judged hopper. In the end, therefore, proponents of a champagne judgment strategy ask evaluators to supply so many judgments that serious, insightful attention can be given to none. The evaluator is overwhelmed with a plethora of dimensions to be bubbled. This, too, contributes to the evaluators' rendering less than defensible judgments regarding the galaxy of dimensions to be judged.

A particularly insidious feature of champagne teacher evaluation approaches is that, because the system's designers lack the backbone to say that certain teacher behaviors are more significant than others, all bubbles are treated as equals. Although such a patently egalitarian process should yield satisfactions for lovers of democracy, the all-bubbles-are-equal strategy is silly. Suppose, for example, that one of the dimensions to be bubbled focused on the "teacher uses appropriate vocabulary." Now, picture a teacher who did oodles of good things, all of which earned bubble-points galore, but *spoke over the pupils' heads*. Although the teacher might lose a point or two for the appropriate vocabulary bubble, that fatal omission could thoroughly muck up the quality of the lesson. A competent judge, cognizant of the significance of the instructional impact of such an omission, would be able to accurately reflect its importance, but those who use an all-bubbles-are-equal strategy will be permitted only one bubbly demerit.

The net effect of such myriad-dimensional teacher evaluation schemes is that they provide a *false picture of precision*. Because of their attention to so many factors and their yielding a quantitative summary index, the results of these types of schemes are regarded with too much confidence. In an effort to avoid making hard-nosed professional judgments, architects of such systems have created strategies that yield teacher evaluations of dubious validity.

To review, then, the two most basic shortcomings of today's teacher appraisal system are that (1) they confound the formative and summative roles of teacher appraisal systems and (2) they avoid the use of overall professional judgments to determine a teacher's skill, most typically by obliging evaluators to provide an endless stream of minuscule judgments rather than a more general estimate of the teacher's skill. How can these two deficits be corrected?

Role Separation

Correcting the confounding of the two primary functions of teacher evaluation is easier to accomplish conceptually than practically. From a conceptual perspective, all we need do is keep the formative function of teacher evaluation separate from the summative function. Practically speaking, in many school settings that separation is devilishly difficult to pull off.

The individuals who carry out formative teacher evaluation must be different from the individuals who carry out summative evaluation. It's that simple. Not only should the evaluators be different persons, but the procedures employed and records gathered for the two missions should be kept separate. Information about a teacher gathered by a formative evaluation should not, *under any circumstances*, be made available to a summative evaluator. Violations of this division of functions will deprive the formative evaluator of the candid reports so necessary if teacher weaknesses are to be eliminated. Similarly, the less fine-grained data gathered by the summative evaluator should not be made available to the formative evaluator, for its global nature will often be misleading to the more focused concerns of formative evaluators. The two evaluative activities, although often occurring in tandem, must remain distinct.

If the school staff is large enough to include both a principal and vice-principal, the task is straightforward. One of the two administrators can assume responsibility for formative teacher evaluation and the other can take on the summative chores. The rules for separating the two functions must be made public so that the school's teachers realize the vice-principal's function will be to help teachers get better, and that in such a role the vice-principal promises never to reveal teacher deficits to the principal. Ideally, all of these ground rules will be adopted and promulgated at the district level rather than obliging school-by-school procedures to be evolved.

The choice regarding which administrator is to play the formative versus summative role should depend to some extent on the personal styles and competencies of the two individuals involved. If the principal, for instance, is well versed in the nuances of instruction and possesses effective conferencing skills, then it may be best to assign the principal to the task of formative evaluation.

If a school has no vice-principal, perhaps a senior teacher can be given released time to function in the formative role. Given the stakes involved, however, it is more fitting if a principal assumes the summative assignment. Teachers should not be asked to appraise their teacher colleagues summatively.

What should be done if there simply aren't two individuals in a school who can assume responsibility for the two different teacher evaluation functions? What should a school-site administrator do who must "go it alone? My advice is that one of the two teacher evaluation functions should then be totally abandoned. Because efforts to fulfill both the summative and formative missions of teacher evaluation are destined for disaster, the situation, regrettably, can be dealt with only by discarding one of the two evaluative functions.

Unless there are statutory requirements for a district's teacher evaluation program to provide summative appraisals of teachers, I would recommend that in such situations the summative function of teacher evaluation be jettisoned. In light of the substantial legal difficulties associated with the dismissal of tenured teachers, it makes far more sense to toss all of one's teacher evaluation energy into formative activities. Teaching performances can be improved via a skillfully conceptualized and implemented formative evaluation program and improvements will benefit pupils. On the other hand, Herculean efforts are typically required to terminate a teacher. Therefore, if a choice must be made between formative and summative evaluation, it seems wiser to expend one's efforts in a quest for improvement.

In Praise of Professional Judgment

In any profession worth its salt, the considered judgment of professionals is regarded with respect. This respect given to professional judgment does not stem from the belief that every professional's judgment is flawless. Clearly, lawyers, physicians, and architects sometimes err. Yet, because of the complexity of the phenomena with which professionals typically deal, we often have no alternative but to rely on the best judgments of professionals.

One way to compensate for the possibility that a given professional's judgment may be flawed is to call on more than one professional to render a judgment. For example, it is common practice when an individual must decide about the wisdom of elective surgery to secure a second or even a third opinion from other physicians. Thus, by pooling the judgments of several professionals, we increase the confidence that we can place in a final judgment.

Citizens in general, as well as the courts, place great credence in professional judgment. In a teacher dismissal case, for example, if it can be shown, through a reasonable array of pertinent evidence, that an experienced school administrator has systematically judged a teacher's performance to be inept, such a judgment carries a good deal of weight with the judge or hearing officer. Jurists, indeed, often rely on the opinions of credible professionals as they listen to the plaintiff's or defendant's expert witnesses.

Professional judgment, then, is prevalently employed in many professions to help make important decisions. Why have the architects of teacher appraisal systems gone through such gyrations to avoid the use of professional judgment? The champagne teacher appraisal systems, with their myriad mini-judgments, may give us a clue. By casting as much as possible of the system in a form that yields quantifiable information or, putting it more directly, *numbers*, the designers of champagne systems hope to create sufficient rigor in the system so that its dominantly quantitative product will be viewed with credulity. But numbers, unfortunately, are no protection against nonsense.

These types of approaches to teacher evaluation remind us of individuals who possess such poor self-concepts that they relentlessly seek external proofs of their self-worth. Similarly, most people who have tussled with the complexities of teacher evaluation recognize the shakiness of the ground on which they walked. Such individuals may succumb to the seductive allure of numbers—the more numbers, the better. Yet, what has been created in champagne teacher evaluation systems is an illusion of precision, a façade of defensibility. Multiple, minuscule judgments have been used as a cloak for the system designer's fundamental lack of confidence.

It is time for those of us in the education profession to abandon our pretensions of precision regarding teacher evaluation. It is time to install evaluation systems that are unashamedly judgmental. It is time to believe in ourselves enough to rely on our ability to render sound professional judgments about a teacher's instructional prowess.

Will judgment-based teacher evaluation procedures be flawless? Of course not. Mistakes will be made whenever human judgment constitutes the heart of a decision-making scheme. There are, unfortunately, individuals currently serving sentences in our penitentiaries who are innocent of the crimes they were *judged* to have committed. One suspects that there are at least an equal number of villains striding our streets who, in a court of law, were wrongly *judged* to be innocent. Yes, some mistakes will be made.

On balance, however, judgmentally rooted teacher evaluation systems will be infinitely preferable to the pseudo-quantitative appraisal schemes currently being used. The chief deficit of such champagne teacher appraisal systems is that they are designed to dodge the only instrument capable of dealing with the enormous complexity of a teacher's instructional efforts. That instrument is professional judgment.

A Solution Strategy

I believe there is a reasonable approach to teacher evaluation, an approach which, albeit imperfect, offers the promise of helping us ferret out the truly weak teachers. In brief, such an approach can be characterized as a *professional judgment model* based on multiple sources of data.

The heart of this approach involves a review team of trained, certifiably competent evaluators who render judgments. Review team members would need to become knowledgeable regarding the virtues of various data-gathering procedures so that they could weigh the impact of the particular segments of evidence being used to appraise a specific teacher. The review team, not unlike the *ad hoc* faculty review committees that appraise a professor's promotion case, would be obliged to consider a range of evidence such as that yielded by the data-gathering procedures cited earlier. In essence, a convergent-validity paradigm would be followed as the review team sifted the evidence in an effort to determine the teacher's relative merit.

Yes, I am suggesting that the very same data-gathering procedures I damned only a few paragraphs earlier can be used to provide the evidence considered by the review team. An evidence source that may be untrustworthy in isolation may, in concert with different data sources, help reviewers form a defensible judgment. The review team would look for consistent patterns, attempting to weigh more heavily those data sources that, on the basis of the particular evidence-gathering procedures employed, were regarded as more credible.

Such review teams would need to be carefully trained so that they could be really discriminating in sorting out believable data from data best viewed with skepticism. By and large, few teachers currently possess the sophistication to sort data-wheat from data-chaff. Ideally, these teacher evaluators would need to display their competence to carry out a judgment-based approach to teacher evaluation via some sort of real or simulated performance test.

Mistakes, of course, would be made. There are currently many tenured university professors who should have been sent scurrying to other callings. On balance, however, I believe the overall impact of such an approach would improve the quality of public schooling.

Teacher Evaluation at the Crossroads

Teachers are under ever-increasing scrutiny these days. New statewide and districtwide teacher evaluation edifices are, it seems, being erected every month. If most of these teacher evaluation operations were ever to be appraised themselves, they would be revealed as ineffectual shams.

We must, therefore, abandon our dysfunctional and confused formative-plus-summative teacher evaluation schemes. We must discard the increasingly popular teacher evaluation procedures in which evaluators avoid the obligation of making significant judgments by rendering a plethora of piddling ones. Instead, educators must summon their courage and opt, without shame, for a judgment-based teacher evaluation strategy in which trained, certified educators render professional judgments about the instructional competence of their colleagues. It is the professional thing to do.

Discussion Questions

1. Do you know of any teachers who have been dismissed from a teaching position because of the results of an evaluation of their competence? Do you think that such occurrences are common or rare? Why?
2. Why do you think that the designers of teacher evaluation systems have avoided professional judgments regarding teachers' skills?
3. Numerous indicators of teaching competence were discussed in the chapter. If you were asked by a school board to describe the validity of at least three of these approaches, what would you say?

4. Do you agree that the combining of formative and summative teacher evaluation approaches is dysfunctional? Why or why not?
5. Imagine that you were a member of the staff of a state legislator who wished to draft a bill to establish a statewide system, possibly with local options, whereby all public school teachers would mandatorily be evaluated. What kinds of suggestions would you offer the legislator? What kind of first draft of such legislation might you propose?

Practice Exercises

1. Presented below are several *weaknesses* of the various types of teacher evaluation data-gathering techniques considered in this chapter. Following each weakness are three teacher evaluation data-gathering procedures. Select the procedure that most prominently displays the cited weakness.
   a. This approach relies too heavily on intrinsic criteria.
      (1) teaching performance tests; (2) classroom observations; (3) contract plans.
   b. Differential perceptions of what it is that constitutes effective teaching distort the validity of this approach.
      (1) pupil performance on norm-referenced tests; (2) administrative ratings; (3) contract plans.
   c. This approach may be rejected as too unlike real teaching.
      (1) teaching performance tests; (2) contract plans; (3) classroom observations.
   d. This index has failed to prove sufficiently sensitive to the influence of instruction.
      (1) ratings; (2) pupil performance on norm-referenced tests; (3) teaching performance tests.
   e. It is difficult to compare teachers using this approach.
      (1) classroom observations; (2) administrative ratings; (3) contract plans.
2. Presented here are several *strengths* of the various types of teacher evaluation data-gathering procedures considered

in this chapter. Following each strength are three teacher evaluation data-gathering procedures. Select the procedure that most prominently incorporates the cited strength.
   a. This procedure can be adapted to an individual teacher's goal preferences.
      (1) teaching performance tests; (2) contract plans; (3) administrative ratings.
   b. This procedure can reveal cues for use in formative, not summative teacher appraisals.
      (1) administrative ratings; (2) teachers' self-evaluations; (3) classroom observations.
   c. A school administrator can use this technique to gather evaluative data on many teachers in a relatively short time.
      (1) pupil performance on norm-referenced tests; (2) contract plans; (3) administrative ratings.
   d. This approach permits contrasts among teachers on the basis of their ability to promote learner mastery of objectives holding many other factors constant.
      (1) teaching performance tests; (2) contract plans; (3) classroom observations.
   e. This approach yields heuristic data well suited for formative evaluation.
      (1) pupil performance on norm-referenced tests; (2) teaching performance tests; (3) classroom observations.

Answers to Practice Exercises

1. *a.* classroom observations; *b.* administrative ratings; *c.* teaching performance tests; *d.* pupil performance on norm-referenced tests; *e.* contract plans.

2. *a.* contract plans; *b.* teachers' self-evaluations; *c.* administrative ratings; *d.* teaching performance tests; *e.* classroom observations.

Notes

1. The views expressed in this chapter have been registered in several earlier analyses. I have drawn on material appearing in: "Teacher Evaluation: Mission Impossible," *Principal*, March 1986, pp. 56–58; "The Dysfunctional Marriage of Formative and Summative Teacher Evaluation," *Journal of Personnel Evaluation in Education*, 1988, 1(3), pp. 269–273; and "The Shortcomings of Champagne Teacher Evaluations," *Journal of Personnel Evaluation in Education*, 1987, 1(1), 25–28.

2. In passing, I might note that during the 1960s I spent nearly a decade dealing with the topic of teacher effectiveness. During that period I surveyed state laws to discover, not surprisingly, that the two almost universal grounds for dismissing a tenured public school teacher were "incompetence" and "immorality." I was intrigued to find that in one western state (not identified here) the grounds for dismissal were "incompetence" and "gross immorality." Apparently, in that state, mere run-of-the-mill immorality was condoned. For teacher dismissal, really rocko-socko immorality was requisite.

3. W. James Popham, "Evaluating Teacher Education Candidates with Teaching Performance Tests," Paper presented at the annual meeting of the American Educational Research Association, Chicago, April 15–19, 1974.

Selected References

Bolton, Dale L. *Selection and Evaluation of Teachers*. Berkeley, CA: McCutchan, 1973.

Conley, Sharon C., and Samuel B. Bacharach. "Performance Appraisal in Education: A Strategic Consideration." *Journal of Personnel Evaluation in Education*, 3 (1990): 309–19.

Duke, Daniel L. "Developing Teacher Evaluation System that Promote Professional Growth." *Journal of Personnel Evaluation in Education*, 4 (1990): 131–44.

Ebmeier, Howard; Ronald Jenkins; and George Crawford. "The Predictive Validity of Student Evaluations in the Identification of Meritorious Teachers." *Journal of Personnel Evaluation in Education*, 4 (1991): 341–57.

Harris, Ben. M. *Developmental Teacher Evaluation*. Boston: Allyn and Bacon, 1986.

The Joint Committee on Standards for Educational Evaluation, Stufflebeam, D. L. (Chair). *The Personnel Evaluation Standards: How to Assess Systems for Evaluating Educators*. Newbury Park, CA: Sage, 1988.

Linn, Robert L; Margret Buchmann; Bruce Gould; Thomas Kellaghan; Dal Lawrence; Phil C. Robinson; and Perry Zirkel. "The Development, Validation, and Applicability of the Personnel Evaluation Standards." *Journal of Personnel Evaluation in Education*, 2 (1989): 199–214.

McNeil, John D., and W. James Popham. "The Assessment of Teacher Competence." In Robert M. W. Travers (Ed.), *Second Handbook of Research on Teaching*. Chicago: Rand McNally. 1973.

Millman, Jason, and Linda Hammond-Darling (Eds.). *The New Handbook of Teacher Evaluation: Assessing Elementary and Secondary School Teachers*. Newbury Park, CA: Sage, 1990.

Mitchell, James, V. Jr.; Steven L. Wise; and Barbara S. Plake (Eds.). *Assessment of Teaching: Purposes, Practices, and Implications for the*

Profession. Hillsdale, NJ: Lawrence Erlbaum, 1990.

Morsh, J. E. and E. Wilder. "Identifying the Effective Instructor: A Review of the Quantitative Studies, 1900–1952." USAF Personnel Training Research Center, *Research Bulletin* No. AFPTRC-TR-54-44, 1954.

Peterson, Penelope L., and Michelle A. Comeaux. "Evaluating the Systems: Teachers' Perspectives on Teacher Evaluation." *Educational Evaluation and Policy Analysis*, 12 (1990): 3–24.

Popham, W. James. "Performance Tests of Teaching Proficiency: Rationale, Development, and Validation." *American Educational Research Journal*, 8 (1971): 105–17.

Rosenshine, B. and N. Furst. "Research in Teacher Performance Criteria." In B. O. Smith (Ed.), *Research in Teacher Education: A Symposium.* Englewood Cliffs, NJ: Prentice-Hall.

Stiggins, Richard J., and Nancy J. Bridgeford. "Performance Assessment for Teacher Development." *Educational Evaluation and Policy Analysis*, 7:1 (Spring 1985): 85–97.

Stronge, James H. "The Dynamics of Effective Performance Evaluation Systems in Education: Conceptual, Human Relations, and Technical Domains." *Journal of Personnel Evaluation in Education*, 5 (1991): 77–83.

CHAPTER SIXTEEN

Instructional Considerations for Educational Evaluators

Educational evaluators focus much of their energy on the appraisal of educational programs. In recent years, particularly because of the often inconclusive findings from summative evaluations, much of the evaluator's work has been of a formative nature. Whether working with teachers who are attempting to improve their lessons (as we saw in the previous chapter) or with staff members trying to make a program more effective, today's educational evaluators frequently find themselves smack in the middle of an *instructional* puzzle centering on the question: "How can the quality of instruction be improved?

Although some educational evaluators, as a consequence of previous training and/or experience, will be comfortable when tinkering with instructional approaches, there are many who are not at ease in an instructional arena. If such evaluators are pushed to propose an instructional improvement scheme, they typically rely on their own intuitions in coming up with methods to boost the quality of instruction. That isn't good enough.

A Formative Evaluator at Work

Let's consider a typical situation in which instructional improvements are being sought. For instance, suppose you were called in to assist a school district's educators in their efforts to have higher percentages of students display mastery on a state-administered mathematics test. You would doubtlessly meet with the district's mathematics specialists, consider the instructional materials being used, and talk with a number of district mathematics teachers to discern what kind of mathematics instruction was actually taking place in the classroom. In addition, if you had your wits about you, you would surely spend a fair amount of time analyzing the state-level mathematics test to see what sorts of student skills or knowledge it assessed. After having gained a decent idea of (1) the skills/knowledge being measured by the state test and (2) the nature of the district's mathematics instruction, you would then be in a position to explore possible instructional improvement options.

In essence, you would be working with district educators to identify changes to be made in instruction, changes to be tried out and retained if effective or abandoned if ineffective. You would be engaged in a systematic effort to appraise the quality of an instructional program that you were helping to improve. In conducting such appraisals, you would employ the numerous tricks of the trade we have considered in previous chapters: you would probably devise some scrumptious criterion-referenced assessment devices according to Chapter Six's commandments, monitor student results via one or more of the X and O data-gathering designs dealt with in Chapter Ten, and analyze the very devil out of your data as prescribed in Chapter Twelve. You might even toss in a bit of Chapter Fourteen's cost-analytic razzle dazzle to show the district folks you knew your stuff. If the modifications you were appraising worked well, those alterations would probably be retained. If the modifications flopped, then there would be a search for new ones. The key question, however, is: "What instructional modifications should you be appraising?"

There may be times when, as a formative evaluator, you will find the educators with whom you work already laden with improvement ideas to try out. Often, however, the locals will be stumped. They will be looking to you, as the "expert," to assist them in isolating potential improvement options. Will you be up to that task?

Although it is not realistic for clients to expect educational evaluators to have a total repertoire of expertise at their fingertips, it is reasonable to expect that an *educational* evaluator ought to be familiar with the rudiments of instruction. Instruction, after all, is the heart of education.

This chapter will provide a brief introduction to the fundamentals of instruction. For those readers already well versed in the instructional process, rapid page turning to the next chapter is in order. If you are not certain about your familiarity with instructional matters, then a skim-along is suggested. If you really haven't thought seriously about the instructional process since your sixth-grade teacher confused you about subject-verb agreement, then commit the chapter to memory—or at least memorize a section or two.

For further reading, there are a number of first-rate references cited at the close of the chapter. A particularly useful compendium of instructionally relevant research reviews can be found in the third edition of the *Handbook of Research on Teaching*,[1] a project of the American Educational Research on Teaching. The Handbook's editor, M. C. Wittrock, has assembled an excellent collection of essays which can familiarize you with pertinent research and theory regarding the instructional process. Most introductory educational psychology texts also contain useful treatments of the instructional process, although, if more than a decade old, such books will obviously not incorporate some of the more recent findings.

Through such literature or via formal coursework dealing with instruction per se, you must acquire sufficient knowledge regarding the innards of instruction so that when you are called on, particularly in the course of a formative evaluation, to isolate possible defects in an instructional program or to suggest possible improvement options, you will be able to make useful contributions. Although, as a formative evaluator, you will not be the decision maker regarding how to modify an instructional program, you should be able to present a meaningful array of options for a teacher or an instructional staff to consider. The remainder of this chapter treats the stuff from which such instructional options are born.

Many of the empirical studies dealing with the instructional process that have been carried out since the mid-1970s have dealt with *direct instruction*, that is, the explicit effort to promote students' mastery of a set of well-defined skills or a clearly understood body of content. The bulk of that research has dealt with instruction focused on cognitive outcomes (rather than psychomotor or affective outcomes). Principles of effective direct instruction, then, deal primarily with explicit efforts to promote learner mastery of well-structured subject areas such as the teaching of scientific facts and concepts, mathematical procedures, distinguishable reading procedures such as discriminating between facts and opinions, grammatical rules and concepts, and so on. Most researchers dealing with such direct instruction invoke a host of disclaimers to indicate that their findings do not apply to instruction focused on less clearly structured skills or content.[2] Thus you should size up the nature of the instructional task to make sure you're dealing with an instructional enterprise that, at least dominantly, is direct. (In my experience, you'll be dealing with direct instruction almost 90 percent of the time.) If it is, the following guidelines will have particular relevance.

Eight Instructional Principles

To facilitate your consideration of the eight instructional principles to be treated, each will be cast in the form of a directive. If you find yourself working with an instructional program that is noticeably shy of one or more of these *shoulds*, then remedies based on these principles *may* be in order. Most of the principles are applicable to a classroom teacher's efforts as well as instructional programs less dependent on teachers' involvement.

Principle 1. Clarify purpose. Make certain that students understand what it is that they are expected to learn.

This initial instructional principle is quite straightforward. Learners must be informed, in unambiguous terms, what it is that they are supposed to be learning. An instructional sequence that does not include an explicit effort to communicate such expectations to learners is less apt to be successful than a comparable instructional sequence in which efforts have been made to ensure that learners know what it is that they are supposed to learn.

The precise form in which such expectations are communicated can vary substantially. Some instructional programs relay expectations to learners by supplying them with clearly stated instructional objectives that describe the postinstruction behaviors it is hoped the learners will acquire. Other instructors provide examples of the types of test questions or exercises that it is hoped the learners will be able to master after instruction. In other cases, a detailed outline of content to be mastered may do the trick. The key element, in whatever communication vehicle is employed, is that the learner understand unequivocally what is being sought as a consequence of the instructional sequence. Such clarifications of instructional intent can yield big dividends because, having been made aware of what is expected of them, students can direct their energies during the instructional sequence toward those elements most pertinent to the instruction's intended outcomes.

In communicating to students the nature of what is expected of them at the outset of an instructional sequence, it is particularly important to employ a communication vehicle that is comprehensible to the students. Formalistic statements of instructional objectives that may communicate effectively to members of an instructional staff may be far too abstruse for students. It must be recalled that these students are *as yet untaught*, hence the techniques chosen to communicate the desired outcomes must be consonant with their current "unknowledgeable" status. Given this constraint, considerable skill is often required to devise ways of communicating instructional intents to students. Research evidence strongly suggests, however, that such communication efforts are worth the trouble.

If the instructional sequence is a lengthy one, there is also merit in *reminding* students of the nature of the intended learning outcomes. Students forget. (Teachers' lives would be 200 percent easier, of course, if students never did.) To combat such forgetting, for an instructional program lasting more than a week or two, it is helpful to review with students, even daily, what it is that they are supposed to be acquiring from the instruction.

To repeat, then, if as a formative evaluator you are working with an ineffective instructional sequence and you discover that learners have not been thoroughly apprised of the instruction's intended purposes, you may wish to encourage the instructional staff to consider a dose of early purpose clarification.

Principle 2. Relate prior learnings. Relate to-be-learned material to previously learned material.

The majority of learning is not squeezed into a fresh sponge that lurks in the student's skull. Rather, new learnings are based on earlier relevant learnings. Instructors who recognize this fact can help students achieve new insights by building from earlier learnings. Thus, there are instructional payoffs to be gained from having students review such prior relevant knowledge. Rosenshine[3] argues strongly for the use of daily review by classroom teachers. He suggests that a period of five to seven minutes at the beginning of a class be devoted to reviewing prerequisite skills and knowledge, related homework assignments, and previous learning that the teacher deems relevant.

A sophisticated application of this principle involves the concept of *advance organizers*, introduced by David Ausubel. Advance organizers are short expository passages that link previously learned knowledge to knowledge that is to be learned. Such advance organizers are designed to provide a sort of "ideational scaffolding" that, because of its greater abstractness, inclusiveness, or generality, allows the learner more readily to incorporate and retain the material that follows. In a sense, then, advance organizers can be thought of as previously mastered constructs that can help learners make sense of and retain the more detailed or differentiated knowledge that is to be learned. If learners do not have such constructs available, or would not have referred to them without prompting, then it appears that advance organizers can help them master unfamiliar, technical, or otherwise difficult material.

Whether the instructional sequence, in its early stages, employs advance organizers or more routine reviews of previously learned relevant material, there appears to be a clear instructional dividend to be derived from encouraging the learner to relate new content to content that has already been mastered. Thus, if you are attempting to provide a bit of evaluative medicine for a sickly instructional sequence and you discover that the sequence makes no effort to tie the new to the old, you might suggest that the material to be learned can profitably be linked to materials already mastered.

Principle 3. Present in small steps. Present new material, one point at a time, in steps of gradually increasing difficulty.

If students are to be taught, they must be presented with material so that the material can be learned. The presentation of new material to students requires substantial instructional expertise. The heart of truly skilled instruction occurs during an instructor's presentation of new material. Competent teachers, given a complicated set of material to present, can isolate the key constructs and illumination schemes to make that complexity comprehensible to learners. There is, to be sure, oodles of artistry in instruction.

But beyond general experience-derived maxims such as "make explanations lucid," "employ clear language," and "avoid digressions," there are several research-supported guidelines that tend to enhance the quality of instructional presentations. One of these guidelines is reflected in the suggestion that instructors present material in small steps.

Effective direct instruction focuses on only one point at a time, attempts to get students to understand that point, *then* moves on to another point. Each new point represents only a small increment of difficulty. The essence of this aspect of instruction is gradualism.

Too many instructional designers assume that once a learner has heard (or read) something to be learned, even only once, that something will have actually been learned. Such optimistic views are rarely supported in practice. More often than not, in order to understand new material, students need to be given the new information in small doses of ever-so-slightly increased difficulty. Most instructors, of course, are fairly smart folks who know their material quite well. Such smart and knowledgeable people, however, tend to overestimate the rapidity with which learners can comprehend new information and concepts. The general tendency on the part of instructional designers, as well as classroom teachers, is to dish out too much, too fast.

There is always the possibility, of course, that the presentation phase of an instructional sequence might contain such small-stepped material that learners become bored and hence tune out. Instructors can err, therefore, in the direction of hypergradualism. Of the two pedagogical-presentation errors, however, we encounter far more instances in which step size is too large rather than too small.

If your formative appraisal of an instructional sequence suggests that the presentation of new material is based on large rather than small increments, you may wish to recommend consideration of adding intermediate steps in the presentation sequence.

Principle 4. Use concrete examples. Provide many concrete examples, both positive and negative, during presentation of new material.

The use of examples, both positive and negative, is a particularly important component of effective presentations. Students need to be able to discriminate between appropriate and inappropriate applications of a concept or principle. For example, if the instruction is focused on "when to use *t* tests," it will be helpful for the students to be presented with situations in which *t* tests should be used and situations in which *t* tests should not be used.

There are instructional situations, such as those involving very young learners or particularly complicated concepts, where there is peril in prematurely introducing negative examples. In such cases, it is preferable to have students become familiar with positive examples first, then introduce negative examples.

In some instances, of course, such as when the intent of the instructional sequence is only to promote students' acquisition of knowledge, there may be no negative examples that are really appropriate. In these cases, concrete positive examples will usually suffice. In situations when both negative and positive examples can be meaningfully used, however, they will typically aid the students' comprehension of new materials.

In presentations dealing with the students' acquisition of skills (as opposed to knowledge), one way of providing concrete examples is to employ *modeling* procedures, with the instructor or someone else actually displaying the sought-for student behavior. Thus, for example, if students are being taught how to identify suitable synonyms in a thesaurus, the teacher might model, from start to finish, how to look for and choose appropriate words from a thesaurus.

In general, then, if you are formatively evaluating an instructional sequence and find it bereft of concrete examples (or, if not totally bereft, then at least a little on the light side), you might suggest to instructional personnel that they consider the virtues of supplementing the sequence with a scad of concrete exemplars and nonexemplars.

Principle 5. Check for understanding. Monitor the degree to which students understand the presentation.

Too many instructional designers assume that once a point has been presented, it will invariably be understood by learners. Such instructional designers subscribe to a bizarre belief that a teacher's words, if spoken or written even once, are quickly spirited inside the cranium of the learners and will live happily thereafter as part of the learner's knowledge. Nothing could be less true. It is important, therefore, to routinely check learners to see if they have comprehended the important elements in an instructional presentation.

If a teacher is checking for understanding, then students can be questioned to see if they have accurately grasped the key points in the presentation. As a variant, teachers can ask individual students, or the entire class, to summarize the presentation's major elements.

Teachers should not check for understanding merely by asking students, "Are there any questions?" or "Did everyone understand?" Even worse, some teachers check for understanding by asking, "Who doesn't understand?" The teacher might as well ask students, "Which of you is sufficiently dull-witted that, not only didn't you understand what I just taught you but now will be foolish enough to admit it?" In the absence of student responses to such silly inquiries, some teachers naively assume that the students actually understand what has been presented.

To gauge whether learners are actually comprehending the material being presented, it is necessary to have students display in an *active* fashion that they have understood. Thus, for example, teachers may ask a student to summarize the essence of a presentation, then require all other students to signify visibly (thumbs up or thumbs down) whether the student's response was accurate.

If a teacher discovers that students have not understood important points in a presentation, then those points will need to be retaught. Ideally, the teacher will take a somewhat different tack in the reteaching, not merely reiterate a presentation that, judging from the students' apparent lack of comprehension, seems to have fallen short of the mark. For example, the teacher might employ different explanations and/or use different and, it is hoped, clearer examples.

For instructional sequences involving presentations by other than a "live" teacher (such as printed instructional materials), checking for student understanding requires more ingenuity on the part of instructional designers. One of the best ways to find out if students have understood written presentations is to incorporate self-scorable "learning checks" consisting of brief quizzes that cover the essence of what has been presented, along with correct-answer keys so that learners can determine if they have been understanding what's been taught. If they discover that they have not understood the presentation, then they can be directed either (1) to *reread* the relevant sections (perhaps with a few cues regarding which points are pivotal) or (2) to read additional material designed for those who have scored below a particular point on the self-scorable quiz.

The key element in the checking-for-understanding principle is to make sure that the instructional sequence's presentation has been comprehended by learners. If learners have not understood what's been taught, then something must be done about the situation. Because ignorance builds happily on ignorance, poorly understood presentations will often pile up to the point that learners will soon be totally awash. Inadequate learner understanding of what has been taught cannot be permitted.

If, in your formative appraisal of an instructional sequence, you discern that there have been no checks for understanding during and after a presentation, then you may wish to suggest the addition of routine checks for understanding during the sequence. If checks for understanding are incorporated, of course, it will be necessary to install some sort of reteaching scheme for those students who did not truly understand the first time around.

Principle 6. Provide guided and independent practice.
Give students ample time-on-task opportunities
to learn by supplying both guided practice
and independent practice.

For almost all types of instruction, but particularly for the direct instruction of well-defined subject matters, one of the best ways to have students master what is being taught is to provide them with abundant practice opportunities. It has often been asserted that practice makes perfect. It is equally true that appropriate practice can often salvage even abominable pedagogy. Given an infusion of student practice opportunities, an otherwise pedestrian instructional program can sometimes sparkle.

Two varieties of practice have been used successfully. In the first of these, *guided practice*, the student is given substantial instructional support, either from a "live" teacher or from numerous hints supplied in written, typed, or otherwise prestructured instructional sequences. In *independent practice*, as is suggested by its name, students are largely on their own. After having become reasonably fluent during guided practice, learners are then given an opportunity to solo. During independent practice, relatively few cues are provided to assist the learner.

In both types of practice activity, the learner is given the opportunity to display behaviors consonant with the behaviors ultimately sought by the instructional sequence. Thus, for example, if at the close of a mathematics instructional sequence the learners are supposed to be able to solve a certain type of word problem, then the practice opportunities provided to students should require them to solve the same kind of word problem.

Meaningful practice opportunities for learners must be carefully selected so that the practice situations demand the same sorts of intellectual operations that are required in the behaviors being taught. If the skill sought were psychomotor rather than cognitive, then appropriate practice would involve students' engaging in physical behaviors congruent with those in the sequence's sought-for behavior. In other words, not just "any old practice" satisfies this instructional principle. The closer that the practice activities resemble the behaviors ultimately desired of the learner, the better.

There is, of course, a substantial amount of instructional judgment involved in deciding just how far a practice activity can appropriately depart from an activity that completely coincides with the instructional sequence's target outcome. If, for example, students are required to *write* their answers to problems presented *in writ-*

ing, in some cases it may still be useful to have students respond *orally* to *orally* presented problems. If, in both instances, the intellectual operations demanded of the students are identical, then the practice activity would appear germane. If, on the other hand, students are to synthesize a series of discrete elements into a more complex whole, it may *not* be all that helpful to have them practice doing the reverse, that is, analyzing complex wholes into their subcomponents. It is even possible that such "backwards" practice, for certain skills, will confuse rather than help learners.

One of the key elements in most practice exercises is the frequent questioning of students. A number of empirical studies, both correlational and experimental, have shown that teachers who ask a high frequency of questions, particularly during guided practice, are more effective than those who ask fewer questions of students.

Thus, effective application of this principle would call for students to be provided initially with guided practice in which a fair amount of support and careful monitoring are present so that, if students are practicing incorrectly, those errors can be quickly eliminated. Subsequent to the guided practice, students would be given independent practice opportunities in which, essentially on their own, they engage in practice behaviors consonant with the instruction's sought-for behaviors. During both guided and independent practice, a high frequency of questions helps ensure that students are actively involved in the practice activities.

When evaluating an instructional sequence, formative evaluators will frequently find that learners have been given little or no practice opportunities. One of the most direct ways of boosting an instructional sequence's potency is to beef up the frequency of student practice. As a formative evaluator, you will find that an "increase-practice" prescription often yields big dividends.

Principle 7. Provide knowledge of results. Give students immediate feedback regarding the appropriateness of their responses.

An effective instructional sequence will be peppered with opportunities for students to respond. Instructors must make provisions for students to discover, as quickly as possible, if their responses are acceptable. In this way errors can be corrected and thus eliminated before they become habitual.

Classroom teachers, of course, can usually arrest student errors on the spot. For materials-based instructional sequences, on the other hand, it will typically be necessary for instructional designers to provide some sort of self-scorable quiz accompanied by an answer key (or, for more elaborate student responses such as essays, examples of both acceptable and unacceptable responses).

A host of empirical investigations demonstrate quite clearly that instructional sequences that feature immediate knowledge of results will be more effective than those that do not. Thus, as a formative evaluator, you may wish to make sure that any instructional sequences with which you work contain provisions for students to find out quickly if they're on target or off target.

**Principle 8. Review, review, review. Provide students
with numerous reviews of already learned material.**

Students should not be allowed to forget what they have previously learned
once they move to new lessons. Therefore, a key to effective direct instruction is
review. Classroom teachers should be urged to start each lesson with a short review
of what has been previously learned (including the correct answers to the previous
night's homework). Thereafter, teachers should be urged to review at the beginning
of each week what was learned the previous week and to review at the end of every
month what was learned during that month. For materials-based sequences, similar
attention to review is recommended.

Clearly, this emphasis on review is designed to counteract many instructors'
tendencies to believe that students readily retain most of what they have already
learned. Such is rarely the case. Most students seem to have inherited incredibly
powerful forgetting mechanisms that can be triggered by such stimuli as air, soil, or
water. It is probably more sensible for instructors to think of students as wide-gauge
sieves through which acquired knowledge runs out at blinding speed. To impede
such knowledge erosion, the use of frequent reviews is recommended.

It is rather surprising to discover that many classroom teachers and numerous
instructional materials fail to include any reviews whatsoever. Such omissions probably stem from instructors' reluctance to "teach students things that they already
know." Yet, in the case of direct instruction, particularly in recognition of students'
proclivities to forget, a quest for *overlearning* is desirable.

If you discover that an instructional sequence with which you're working is
light on review, you may wish to recommend providing more such reviews.

The Role of Instructional Principles

We have now considered, ever so briefly, eight powerful principles that can enhance
the quality of an instructional program. There are other factors to consider in analyzing instruction, such as accuracy of content, but evaluators can also become overwhelmed with too many things to which they must pay attention. The eight
principles presented here are based on recent analyses of research that deal with
high-impact instructional variables.[4]

The eight principles are summarized in Box 16–1. Formative evaluators may
wish to consider these principles, or similar evidence-supported sets of such principles, as they work with teachers or program staffs. You can, for example, use the set
of principles as a checklist against which to judge the elements in an instructional
program with which you are working.

Now for a few disclaimers. First, these eight principles should *not* necessarily
be applied in the order treated here. Although there is an inherent order more or less
implicit in the eight principles, departures from that order may work quite well indeed. Second, as was noted above, there are other instructional principles that you
might wish to employ in your formative evaluation toolkit. Finally, as I indicated at
the outset of the chapter, these eight instructional principles may not work as well in

---

BOX 16-1 • *Eight Principles to Consider When Formatively Evaluating Instructional Programs*

1. Clarify purpose.
2. Relate prior learnings.
3. Present in small steps.
4. Use concrete examples.
5. Check for understanding.
6. Provide guided and independent practice.
7. Provide knowledge of results.
8. Review, review, review.

---

the promotion of certain outcomes. Affective changes in learners, such as having the learners acquire more positive values toward cooperative decision making, would not be accomplished best by the eight direct instruction principles treated here.

Will the use of these eight instructional principles always result in an instructional program that works? Unfortunately, no instructional principles are that powerful. If you use these principles, you'll be offering empirically based guidelines capable of increasing the likelihood that a given instructional program will work better. There may be such fundamental flaws in the program, such as a garbled explanation of key concepts, that no amount of principles-based massaging can ever transform the program into a winner. Each principle, by itself, addresses one small element that, considered in concert with the elements represented in other instructional principles, can markedly enhance an instructional program's effectiveness.

The relationship of these eight principles to effective instruction is illustrated in Figure 16-1 in which, hypothetically, 100 instructional programs have been contrasted with another 100 instructional programs. If the first 100 programs (Group *A*) routinely adhered to the eight principles while the second 100 programs (Group *B*) did not, there is no doubt that Group *A*'s programs would outperform Group *B*'s. This does not mean that *all* programs in Group *A* would be effective nor that *all*

FIGURE 16-1 • *A Hypothetical Comparison of the Relative Effectiveness of 100 "Principles-Based" versus "Unprincipled" Instructional Programs*

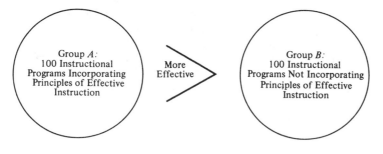

programs in Group *B* would be ineffective. It does mean, however, that *on average* the principles-based programs would be substantially more effective than their principles-lacking counterparts.

Dipping Deeper

As was pointed out earlier, it is difficult for educational evaluators to function effectively in a formative role if they are devoid of knowledge regarding the instructional process. Skilled formative evaluators need to know what makes instruction tick. If you're going to function effectively in a formative capacity, you will need to become as knowledgeable regarding instruction as your energy and inclination will permit.

The treatment given here to eight instructional principles has clearly been short on the shrifty side. If you need some skill building in this crucial area, please dip as deeply as you can into the references listed at the close of the chapter. They're loaded with instructionally sensible stuff.

Discussion Questions

1. If you were to rank the eight instructional principles in order of import, from most to least important, what would your rankings be?

2. Why is it that teachers and designers of instruction do not routinely incorporate principles of effective instruction in their instructional sequences?

3. If you were to guess about the principles of effective instruction that are most frequently omitted in an instructional sequence, what do you think those omissons would be? Why?

4. Try to think of instructional situations for which the eight instructional principles do not apply. What are the common elements, if any, of those situations?

5. To what extent do you believe the majority of the nation's classroom teachers are knowledgeable regarding the eight principles of effective instruction presented here? Why do you think that is the case?

Practice Exercise

As an educational evaluator, you may be called on to appraise an ongoing instructional program so that potential modifications can be considered. To carry out such quality appraisals, it will be useful if you can readily isolate which, if any, of the eight instructional principles treated in the chapter are not present. To give you practice in doing just that, a description of a fictitious instructional program is presented below. First, quickly review the eight principles summarized in Box 16-1. Then, *after only one reading of the description*, see if you can identify which, if any, of the eight instructional principles have been omitted in the instructional program described.

A Description of After-School Peer Tutoring in Unreal Unified School District

Early in the current academic year, officials of Unreal Unified School District (UUSD) installed a districtwide language arts program in grades 5 through 7 featuring peer tutoring. The stimulus for the program's initiation was the low district scores on statewide language arts tests given at the close of grades 5 and 7.

The first activity in the new program was the identification of volunteer participants in the after-school program. All fifth-, sixth-, and seventh-grade students who had scored higher than the 75th percentile on the state language arts tests were asked if they wished to serve as tutors in the new program. The remaining students were asked if they wished to be tutored. Parental approval was also sought for all participants. During the first three weeks of the fall term all tutors were given daily instruction regarding how to tutor other pupils.

One week later the peer-tutoring program began to operate. Each tutor met with two, three, or four tutees for 30 minutes each day at the close of school. The tutoring sessions began by the tutor's summarizing the language arts concepts that had previously been learned by the tutees. Tutors attempted to link this prior learning to the particular lesson that tutees were to be taught that day.

Tutors had been previously given sets of explanations that were to be used with their tutees. These explanations introduced the tutees to new material very gradually, in extremely small increments. For example, when the use of punctuation marks was introduced, tutees were directed to apply a particular punctuation mark, such as the comma, to only one type of sentence, then to another type of sentence, and so on. Only after the punctuation mark had been applied in many settings was a new punctuation mark introduced.

A key element in the tutors' presentations was the use of illustrations. When tutors dealt with commas, for example, they showed tutees a variety of sentences in which commas were used correctly as well as sentences in which commas were used improperly.

As soon as the tutors sensed that tutees were ready, the tutorial lessons focused on practice exercises similar to those on the statewide language arts test. At first, tutors provided considerable support for tutees as they worked through exercise sheets (developed by UUSD curriculum specialists). Later, tutees were obliged to work on their exercises without assistance from the tutor. For both types of exercises, tutors were directed to let tutees know immediately whether responses to the exercises were correct or incorrect. This tutorial feature, the potential for instant feedback for individual learners, was considered by UUSD officials to represent one of the key advantages of the district's peer-tutoring program.

At the close of each week, all tutors were directed to devote the last 15 minutes of a tutorial to a careful recapitulation of the important content treated during that week. Tutees were asked to identify the content areas that they thought had been most difficult for them. Tutors were directed to consider such tutee-identified content areas for possible reteaching.

On the basis of informal reactions from several district observers, the need for a systematic formative evaluation of the after-school peer-tutoring program has now been identified. Although the procedural logistics of the program seem to be functioning satisfactorily, that is, the tutors and tutees seem to be working quietly together for 30 minutes each day, some district observers believe that tutees "aren't learning very efficiently about language arts."

Assume that you have been engaged as the formative evaluator for this program. Which, if any, of the eight instructional principles treated in the chapter have apparently been omitted in the peer-tutoring program? If you identify any such principles, how might they be infused into the program?

Answers to Practice Exercise

According to the description of the peer-tutoring program, it appears that two instructional principles were not attended to in the program. There seems to have been no attempt to clarify the purpose of the instructional activities: Tutees were not routinely informed of the skills or knowledge being sought. Second, there was no formal check for understanding so that tutors could gauge more objectively (rather than merely "sensing") whether tutees had understood what had been presented. All of the other principles seem to have been attended to in the program.

The quality with which each of the other principles was employed, of course, is another matter. As a formative evaluator, you would have to assist in such quality determinations. For instance, the principle of providing guided and independent practice can be satisfied by only two brief exercises, one with help and one without. Clearly, more practice would be needed in order for the principle to have been effectively employed.

To install activities based on the two missing principles would be relatively straightforward. You might suggest that UUSD staff prepare brief statements of purpose for each tutoring lesson, such statements to be formulated in language that tutees could readily understand. Tutors could be directed to read these statements at the outset of each tutoring session in order to communicate to tutees the nature of what was expected for that session.

To check for understanding, tutors could be told to ask one of the tutees, selected at random, to summarize the main points in the tutor's presentation. The remaining tutees should be asked whether the summary is accurate. In this way, the tutor could monitor tutee understanding more accurately so that any reteaching necessary could take place.

These two possible changes, of course, represent decision options for the program staff. If the staff chooses to implement these or other alterations in the program, it will be the task of the formative evaluator to help gather the information necessary to determine whether such alterations added to or detracted from the program's effectiveness.

Notes

1. M. C. Wittrock, (Ed.), *Handbook of Research on Teaching*, 3rd ed. (New York: Macmillan, 1986).

2. I appreciate the caution embodied in such disclaimers. Good researchers are supposed to be cautious by dissuading users from overgeneralizing the results of research. My personal intuition, however, is that a good many of the principles derived from research dealing with direct instruction will apply with equal force to instruction in less structured content areas. In the absence of many empirically supported guidelines for less direct instruction, the direct-instruction principles treated here aren't bad for openers. We might not be treating "one-size-fits-all" instructional principles in this chapter, but the principles will often work in settings beyond those that, in the strict sense of the term, constitute "direct" instruction.

3. B. V. Rosenshine, "Synthesis of Research on Explicit Teaching," *Educational Leadership* (April 1986).

4. Rosenshine, "Synthesis of Research."

Selected References

Ausubel, D. P. *Educational Psychology: A Cognitive View*. New York: Holt, Rinehart and Winston, 1968.

Bandura, A. *Social Learning Theory*. Englewood Cliffs, NJ: Prentice-Hall, 1977.

Bangert-Drowns, Robert L.; Chen-Lin C. Kulik; James A. Kulik; and Mary Teresa Morgan. "The Instructional Effect of Feedback in Test-Like Events." *Review of Educational Research*, 61 (1991): 213–38.

Bank, A., and R. C. Williams. *Improving Instruction Through the Management of Testing and Evaluation Activities: A Guidebook for School Districts*. Report to NIE. Los Angeles: Center for the Study of Evaluation, University of California, 1982. (1983).

Bloom, B. S. "Learning for Mastery." *Evaluation Comment*, 1:2 (1968). Los Angeles: University of California, Center for the Study of Evaluation.

Darling-Hammond, L. "Instructional Policy Into Practice: The Power of the Bottom Over the Top." *Educational Evaluation and Policy Analysis*, 12 (1990): 339–47.

Kulik, C-L.; J. Kulik; and R. Bangert-Drowns. "Effectiveness of Mastery Learning Programs: A Meta-Analysis." *Review of Educational Research*, 60 (1990): 265–99, 1990.

Rosenshine, B. "The Third Cycle of Research on Teacher Effects: Content Covered, Academic Engaged Time, and Direct Instruction." In Penelope L. Peterson and Herbert J. Walberg (Eds.), *Research on Teaching: Concepts, Findings, and Implications*. Berkeley, CA: McCutchan, 1979.

Rothkopf, E. Z. "The Concept of Mathemagenic Activities." *Review of Educational Research*, 40 (1970): 325–26.

Sergiovanni, Thomas J. "Expanding Conceptions of Inquiry and Practice in Supervision and Evaluation." *Educational Evaluation and Policy Analysis*, 6:4 (Winter 1984): 355–65.

Slavin, Robert E. "Mastery Learning Re-Reconsidered." *Review of Educational Research*, 60 (1990): 300–02.

Slavin, Robert E. *Educational Psychology: Theory into Practice* (3rd ed.). Englewood Cliffs, NJ: Prentice-Hall, 1991.

Smith, Mary Lee. "Put to the Test: The Effects of External Testing on Teachers." *Educational Researcher*, 20 (1991): 8–11.

Tyler, R. W. *Basic Principles of Curriculum and Instruction*. Chicago: University of Chicago Press, 1950.

Wittrock, M. C. (Ed.). *Handbook of Research on Teaching* (3rd ed.). New York: Macmillan, 1986.

CHAPTER SEVENTEEN

A Potpourri
of Evaluation Issues

This final chapter will consider a number of issues that are apt to be encountered by educational evaluators. Each issue is discussed, with no reflection of import suggested by the order of presentation, in the hope that the reader will be sensitized to some of the ways of coping with the problem inherent therein. Characteristically, the wisdom of one's decisions can be enhanced by advanced consideration of options that might be used in dealing with issues such as those we shall treat. Though the issues examined here appear most salient to me at this time, they will undoubtedly be replaced in the future with other equally significant evaluation issues. In an emerging field such as educational evaluation, professionals will have to be particularly attentive to the identification of current concerns, in such sources as journal articles and papers presented before professional societies. Expanding fields, although exciting, carry with them the possibility of hasty stagnation if one relaxes one's efforts to keep abreast of recent developments.

Standards for Educational Evaluation

Educational evaluation of the formal sort was born in the mid to late 1960s. For at least a decade or so following the 1967 introduction of analyses by writers such as Michael Scriven and Robert Stake, there was a substantial increase of interest in the field of educational evaluation. Myriad educational evaluations, often required by funding agencies, were carried out. Myriad educational evaluation papers were presented or published. Myriad men and women, previously trained in other fields, moved merrily into the role of educational evaluator. Clearly, myriads were myriad.

And so was diversity. As more and more players took part in the educational evaluation game, a wide variety of evaluation approaches and practices were seen. Some, rather conventional in nature, tended to resemble formal educational research. Others were far more *avant garde*, representing clear attempts to break away from the traditional scientific paradigm. I recall attending a professional meeting during the early 1970s where would-be educational evaluators were desperately

searching for new "metaphors" upon which they could base a novel approach to educational evaluation. Some of these presenters focused on a judicial metaphor in
which an attempt was made to mold educational evaluation along the lines of court-
room practice. Others touted a journalistic metaphor in which the evaluator was to
function chiefly as a reporter. Still others pushed for an anthropological metaphor in
which educational evaluators would employ procedures and orientations similar to
those used by anthropologists. Evaluators, it seemed, wanted to do educational evaluations their own way. An apt metaphor for the evaluation-metaphor movement
might have been "dealer's choice."

Although I have portrayed the quest for evaluative diversity a mite excessively,
it was certainly true that educational evaluators, for the most part, possessed *carte
blanche* with regard to the conduct of an evaluation. Most evaluations were sensible.
Some were downright silly. There were no accepted criteria by which to judge the
quality of educational evaluations. Those who attempted to judge the virtues of a
given evaluation study were obliged to rely on their own standards of quality.

Thoughtful leaders in the educational evaluation community recognized, during the mid-1970s, that the quality of evaluation practice might be enhanced if a set
of consensually derived standards could be established for the conduct of such evaluations. Accordingly, as an offshoot of a committee charged with revising the 1974
Standards for Educational and Psychological Tests,[1] a separate planning committee
was established by the American Educational Research Association, the American
Psychological Association, and the National Council on Measurement in Education
to explore the possibility of devising a set of standards for the field of educational
evaluation. Stimulated at the outset by George F. Madaus, who had been successful
in separating evaluation-in-general standards from the purview of the test-standards
committee, a committee representing the three professional organizations commenced exploratory work in 1975. The three original organizations were later
joined by representatives from nine other organizations in establishing a Joint Committee of 17 members chaired by Daniel L. Stufflebeam.

Six years later, in 1981, the committee's efforts were published as the *Standards for Evaluation of Educational Programs, Projects, and Materials.*[2] Stufflebeam and his Joint Committee colleagues, employing a developmental process in
which frequent and far-ranging communication with the field was central, identified
30 separate standards organized under four attributes of an educational evaluation,
namely, *utility, feasibility, propriety*, and *accuracy.* Each standard was described
and then followed by (1) a conceptual overview, (2) procedural guidelines for satisfying the standard, (3) a list of pitfalls that tend to preclude the standard's being
satisfied, (4) caveats, or errors arising from overly zealous application of the standards, and (5) a fictional case illustrating how the standard might be applied.

The 30 standards can serve as a first-rate "things to think about" when one
carries out an educational evaluation. Each standard is presented below[3] in the original language of Stufflebeam and his colleagues. If you wish to delve further into one
or more of the standards, for some are eminently deserving of a further delve, be
sure to consult the joint committee's full report. The *Evaluation Standards* are orga-

nized according to (A) utility, (B) feasibility, (C) propriety, and (D) accuracy.

The Evaluation Standards

A *Utility Standards*
  The Utility Standards are intended to ensure that an evaluation will serve the practical information needs of given audiences. These standards are:
  A1 *Audience Identification*
    Audiences involved in or affected by the evaluation should be identified, so that their needs can be addressed.
  A2 *Evaluator Credibility*
    The persons conducting the evaluation should be both trustworthy and competent to perform the evaluation, so that their findings achieve maximum credibility and acceptance.
  A3 *Information Scope and Selection*
    Information collected should be of such scope and selected in such ways as to address pertinent questions about the object of the evaluation and be responsive to the needs and interests of specified audiences.
  A4 *Valuational Interpretation*
    The perspectives, procedures, and rationale used to interpret the findings should be carefully described, so that the bases for value judgments are clear.
  A5 *Report Clarity*
    The evaluation report should describe the object being evaluated and its context, and the purposes, procedures, and findings of the evaluation, so that the audiences will readily understand what was done, why it was done, what information was obtained, what conclusions were drawn, and what recommendations were made.
  A6 *Report Dissemination*
    Evaluation findings should be disseminated to clients and other right-to-know audiences, so that they can assess and use the findings.
  A7 *Report Timeliness*
    Release of reports should be timely, so that audience can best use the reported information.
  A8 *Evaluation Impact*
    Evaluations should be planned and conducted in ways that encourage follow-through by members of the audiences.
B *Feasibility Standards*
  The Feasibility Standards are intended to ensure that an evaluation will be realistic, prudent, diplomatic, and frugal; they are:
  B1 *Practical Procedures*
    The evaluation procedures should be practical, so that disruption is kept to a minimum, and that needed information can be obtained.
  B2 *Political Viability*
    The evaluation should be planned and conducted with anticipation of the different positions of various interest groups, so that their cooperation may be obtained, and so that possible attempts by any of these groups to curtail evaluation operations or to bias or misapply the results can be averted or counteracted.

Source: Joint Committee on Standards for Educational Evaluation, *Standards for Evaluation of Educational Programs, Projects and Materials.* © 1980. Reprinted with permission of McGraw-Hill, Inc.

B3 *Cost Effectiveness*

The evaluation should produce information of sufficient value to justify the resources expended.

C *Propriety Standards*

The Propriety Standards are intended to ensure that an evaluation will be conducted legally, ethically, and with due regard for the welfare of those involved in the evaluation, as well as those affected by its results. These standards are:

C1 *Formal Obligation*

Obligations of the formal parties to an evaluation (what is to be done, how, by whom, when) should be agreed to in writing, so that these parties are obligated to adhere to all conditions of the agreement or formally to renegotiate it.

C2 *Conflict of Interest*

Conflict of interest, frequently unavoidable, should be dealt with openly and honestly, so that it does not compromise the evaluation processes and results.

C3 *Full and Frank Disclosure*

Oral and written evaluation reports should be open, direct, and honest in their disclosure of pertinent findings, including the limitations of the evaluation.

C4 *Public's Right to Know*

The formal parties to an evaluation should respect and assure the public's right to know, within the limits of other related principles and statutes, such as those dealing with public safety and the right to privacy.

C5 *Rights of Human Subjects*

Evaluations should be designed and conducted so that the rights and welfare of the human subjects are respected and protected.

C6 *Human Interactions*

Evaluators should respect human dignity and worth in their interactions with other persons associated with an evaluation.

C7 *Balanced Reporting*

The evaluation should be complete and fair in its presentation of strengths and weaknesses of the object under investigation, so that strengths can be built upon and problem areas addressed.

C8 *Fiscal Responsibility*

The evaluator's allocation and expenditure of resources should reflect sound accountability procedures and otherwise be prudent and ethically responsible.

D *Accuracy Standards*

The Accuracy Standards are intended to ensure that an evaluation will reveal and convey technically adequate information about the features of the object being studied that determine its worth or merit. These standards are:

D1 *Object Identification*

The object of the evaluation (program, project, material) should be sufficiently examined, so that the form(s) of the object being considered in the evaluation can be clearly identified.

D2 *Context Analysis*

The context in which the program, project, or material exists should be examined in enough detail, so that its likely influences on the object can be identified.

D3 *Described Purposes and Procedures*

The purposes and procedures of the evaluation should be monitored and described in enough detail, so that they can be identified and assessed.

D4 *Defensible Information Sources*
The sources of information should be described in enough detail so that the adequacy of the information can be assessed.

D5 *Valid Measurement*
The information-gathering instruments and procedures should be chosen or developed and then implemented in ways that will assure that the interpretation arrived at is valid for the given use.

D6 *Reliable Measurement*
The information-gathering instruments and procedures should be chosen or developed and then implemented in ways that will assure that the information obtained is sufficiently reliable for the intended use.

D7 *Systematic Data Control*
The data collected, processed, and reported in an evaluation should be reviewed and corrected, so that the results of the evaluation will not be flawed.

D8 *Analysis of Quantitative Information*
Quantitative information in an evaluation should be appropriately and systematically analyzed to ensure supportable interpretations.

D9 *Analysis of Qualitative Information*
Qualitative information in an evaluation should be appropriately and systematically analyzed to ensure supportable interpretations.

D10 *Justified Conclusions*
The conclusions reached in an evaluation should be explicitly justified, so that the audiences can assess them.

D11 *Objective Reporting*
The evaluation procedures should provide safeguards to protect the evaluation findings and reports against distortion by the personal feelings and biases of any party to the evaluation.

Compatibility with Naturalistic Evaluation

Some writers[4] have pointed out that the Joint Committee's *Evaluation Standards* may not be compatible with qualitative approaches to educational evaluation because such naturalistic forms of inquiry, with their heavy reliance on describing inner processes through the use of participant informers, may require departure from the more conventionally rooted *Evaluation Standards*. Williams[5] reports, however, that when the Joint Committee's *Standards* are stacked up against a set of criteria reflective of the canons of naturalistic inquiry, only a trivial percentage of the two sets of standards are incompatible. For example, the naturalistic evaluator's emphasis on the virtues of "thick," contextually detailed descriptions may tend to be in conflict with the *Evaluation Standards'* advocacy (Standards A6 and A7) of timely reports to be used by appropriate audiences. In other words, as the evaluation report becomes thicker and richer, it also becomes longer and thereby less apt to be used.

Similarly, whereas most naturalistic educational evaluators would subscribe to the notion that the investigator requires a "prolonged engagement" in order to discover the nature of what is truly going on in a situation, that requirement for extended data-gathering excursions may be in conflict with the *Evaluation Standards'* advocacy of timely reporting (Standard A7).

On the whole, however, it seems that the *Evaluation Standards*, even for more naturalistically oriented evaluators, proffer a pile of sensible practices. In contrast to the overall compatability between the *Evaluation Standards* and the criteria adhered to by naturalistic evaluators, fundamental differences are few.

Impact of the Evaluation Standards

The extent to which the *Evaluation Standards* will have a meaningful impact on the practice of educational evaluation remains to be seen. In the case of the *Standards for Educational and Psychological Testing*,[6] we see standards that, because they are relied on heavily by the courts, appear to be having a substantial impact on practice in the educational and psychological assessment arenas.

At the moment, the *Evaluation Standards* must rely on their own inherent virtues to attract adherence from practicing educational evaluators. If educational evaluators wish to see the *Evaluation Standards* truly influence the conduct of evaluations, it appears that there must be a concerted effort to promote their use. No court cases have yet been conducted in which the *Evaluation Standards* have been called into play. Thus it appears that, in the absence of legal pressures, use of the *Evaluation Standards* will hinge heavily on the vigor with which leaders in the educational evaluation community advocate adherence to the *Standards*.

In a recent analysis, Stufflebeam expressed guarded optimism regarding the impact of the Standards: "But, while I am pleased that the standard-setting work did not fail, that it went rather well, and that it is ongoing and viable, I am not entirely satisfied with the experience. Dissemination of the standards has not been spectacular, and the sponsory organizations, while generally supportive, have not initiated effective efforts to get their members to use the standards."[7]

The future will tell whether Stufflebeam and his Joint Committee colleagues have labored in a no-yield vineyard or whether they have sown the seeds that spawned substantial improvements in the field of educational evaluation.

Educational Evaluation in a Political Context

People can deal with problems more effectively if they can anticipate the nature of those problems. For the fledgling educational evaluator, therefore, it is imperative to point out that most educational evaluations will be carried out in a thoroughly practical milieu in which an evaluation's results will constitute additional playing cards that people will be dealing from patently political decks.

Throughout the book we have been stressing the decision orientation of educational evaluators. The evaluator should be striving to improve the quality of educational decisions so that those being educated will benefit. Such a stance seems praiseworthy. Educational evaluators should undoubtedly feel fulfilled if they have been able to enhance the quality of the educational endeavors to which they direct their attention. But because they are advised to adopt this almost saintly posture, as an "illuminator of educational decisions," many fledgling evaluators assume that the educational world is out there, feverishly awaiting such illumination. Prepare for a surprise.

Decisions involve choices. Most often, the choices aren't cast in terms of alternatives that are 100 percent good versus others that are 100 percent bad. Some alternatives, if not approved, will have adverse consequences for many of the individuals concerned. Some alternatives, if approved, will fail to have the positive consequences some people would have experienced had another alternative been approved. Education is a major-league game, where decisions can involve huge sums of money and huge numbers of people (quite apart from the learners involved).

Just to illustrate, suppose that a harshly negative evaluation of an innovative program in university-level instruction for minority students would result in the abolition of the program and, thereby, at least for the time being, the elimination of the university's most visible effort to assist minority students. In addition, the abolition of the program would result in the dismissal of 15 to 20 staff members, most of whom are minorities themselves. Now any evaluator who expects the decision makers instantaneously to adopt the "shut-it-down" recommendation inherent in the adverse evaluation report is an evaluator in need of some seasoning.

There are vested interests involved in most situations involving educational evaluations. The intensity of these interests will substantially influence the manner in which the evaluator's reports is received. In our present example, the university's president may be loath to eliminate that institution's most visible minority group program, believing that the negative repercussions from such an action (even if other replacement programs were subsequently proposed) would be harmful to the college's overall mission, and even to the college's overall efforts to provide meaningful education for minority students. Then we have the problem of the 15 to 20 staff members who would lose their jobs if the evaluator's advice were heeded. Suppose the staff organizes itself and presents an ultimatum to the university president, threatening an extensive demonstration which, they assure the president, will be supported by hundreds of students from campus minority organizations. The president is particularly anxious to avoid such demonstrations, because the university's governing board of regents has only recently been more supportive of the institution as a result of its ability to "control campus unrest." Add to this salad the pressures that certain academic departments have been bringing on the president to reduce the magnitude of the minority education program because it appears to be draining faculty resources they would rather receive, and you begin to see some of the political realities present in such settings. Do you really suppose the president will make a decision solely on the basis of the evaluation report? If you do, both you (and the president) had best contemplate other careers.

Additional Examples

Let's briefly consider a few other examples to provide an idea of the realities of the abrasive political world that awaits the educational evaluator. Although not exhausting, or even denting, the range of political realities lingering in the educational world, they may provide a bit of flavor of the political context we are considering.

There was a case on the East Coast in which a school district's teachers' organization went to court seeking an injunction to prevent the district's evaluation office from administering affective measuring devices. The affective measures were to be used to secure an estimate of the school district's success in promoting positive attitudes toward education. Although numerous observations were offered by the attorney for the teachers' organization, such as "invasion of the student's privacy," officials of the group privately conceded that their members believed the schools would appear ineffectual with respect to this affective criterion, and that such adverse publicity would work to their organization's disadvantage in subsequent salary negotiations with the school board.

In a midwestern state an evaluation firm was called in to evaluate a reading-improvement parent-aide program used mostly in the inner-city schools of a large metropolitan school district. The principals of the schools involved, prior to the initiation of the evaluation, demanded a meeting with the evaluation firm to assert that, no matter whether the evaluation showed that pupil's reading performance was helped or harmed by the program, the principals were going to retain it. The principals viewed the program's chief benefits as public relations in nature, believing that it was a potent force in promoting citizens' acceptance of the educational program. Evaluation evidence was viewed as irrelevant.

In Chapter Fifteen we considered teacher evaluation. There are dozens of recent incidents in which teachers' associations have bucked negative evaluations of

any of their members, even the manifestly incompetent, feeling that the dismissal of one teacher might trigger the future dismissal of many. A number of local teachers' organizations in various states have initiated court actions to contest certain ingredients in district teacher evaluation programs. Many of these contests have been, as admitted by all participants, less concerned with the actual evaluation plan than with the political power regarding who controls teacher dismissals.

There is little doubt that the interests of teachers, as represented by increasingly militant teachers' organizations, will have to be considered carefully as the evaluator surveys the political forces operative in a given setting.

Teachers aren't the only ones who are organizing. The emergence of citizen advisory groups is a factor to be considered by the evaluator. Many of these citizens' groups have become highly politicized, having discovered how to influence the school board's elected representatives. Such citizen groups are often comprised of serious, evidence-conscious people and are thus highly responsive to the results of educational evaluation studies. Other groups may be less inclined to attend to evidence and more inclined to push through their own views of what the schools should be about. A polarized advisory group, with equal factions of two opposing groups, often reflects a situation in which an educational evaluator is bound to lose—at least with half of the group.

Political Preparedness

The scout's motto, "Be prepared!" should be adhered to by all astute evaluators. The foregoing illustrations only begin to suggest the political tangle into which the evaluator's work will often be injected. Vested interests are everywhere. Vested interests are powerful. Vested interests have to be identified in advance by the evaluator—not to do so would be foolish.

Well, what can be done about the political world we have been illustrating? Should the evaluator merely go through the motions of conducting a study and reporting its results, fully expecting its impact to be squashed by political factors beyond the evaluator's control? Of course not. Who would be satisfied to engage in ritualistic evaluations that are destined to make no difference?

There are two main ways of coping with the political realities evaluators will find influencing their activities. The first of these is to *anticipate that quality appraisals alone will not be the only factors involved in educational decisions*. Steeled against such an eventuality, and it is almost a certainty, the evaluators will not be (1) as disappointed or (2) as likely to pick up their evaluation tools and go home. Recognize that the results of an evaluation study will often be little more than, as we alleged earlier, one card dealt from a political deck in a purely political poker game. But sometimes one card can make the difference. If two players hold a pair of jacks, the one who has an ace wins. If evaluators can influence even a few educational decisions so that they turn out well, then this is surely better than nothing. But prospective evaluators who harbor an image of themselves riding in like an Arthurian knight, to an evaluation situation where the docile decision makers will meekly follow the evaluator's admonitions, should recognize that theirs is a fairy-tale view of the world.

Besides the anticipation of political reality, there is a second ploy the astute evaluator can adopt. This involves detecting *and describing* the nature of the vested interests involved. If the evaluator can detect the chief partisan forces in the educational milieu, and can isolate their reasons for partisanship, then the mere act of publicizing their motives can sometimes (not always) have a defusing effect. Partisans, when their motives are made visible, are often less bellicose. If a teachers' union is pegged in advance (as part of the evaluation report) as being interested in its members' job security, then union leaders may be a bit less inclined to engage in majestic oratory that exclusively treats potential dangers to "the precious children under our tutelage." If a school board is identified in advance as being supported by a largely conservative electorate, than its resistance to sex education courses may be easier to decipher, hence its repudiation of such courses may be a bit less polemic. Not that this tactic will always work, because some vested interest groups will champion their cause with equal fervor whether their motives are exposed or not. But for many politicized participants among those influencing the decision makers, public notice of their reasons for partisanship may dilute the intensity of that partisanship. Ralph Tyler has recently opined that for an educational evaluator "to distribute a biased evaluation report is a real 'white-collar' crime, whether or not it is so defined by law."[8]

Ethics and the Evaluator

Next we turn to a particularly important but largely unstudied problem of *ethics* as they pertain to the work of the educational evaluator. From the previous discussion of the political context in which educational evaluations are carried out, it should have been clear that there will be all sorts of sticky decisions to be made by the evaluator. Some of these will unquestionably involve moral choices. Evaluators who imagine that they can sail through educational waters on a ship named *Amorality* will soon discover that such is not the case. Let's consider some examples of the kinds of ethical choices that will vex the evaluator.

Some of the moral implications of the decision alternatives to be encounted will be so obvious that any person would know the difference between right and wrong. For instance, is it appropriate to distort data deliberately so that the wrong program appears to be the most effective? Obviously not. Is it proper to take money from a publisher's representative in exchange for a positive recommendation to a textbook adoption committee in favor of that publisher's texts? Clearly not. Is it correct to suppress the results of a negative evaluation study because a superintendent (who would perhaps be discharged as a consequence) offers you the free summer use of a beach cottage on Kauai? Well, considering the author's awareness of that island's advantages, you should think it over carefully before deciding.

However, whereas the foregoing examples are all clear-cut (even the last one), and a moral person would reach a quick negative decision on each, some options will involve ethical choices that are not so transparent. For instance, in Chapter Seven we discussed the ethics of surreptitiously gathering measurements on people. Some persons consider the invasion of privacy to be so intrinsically reprehensible that it is ethically repugnant under any circumstances. Some persons believe that the end (improvement of the quality of education) justifies the means (surreptitious observation). Other people don't think there is anything basically evil about collecting measurements surreptitiously. These are the more common positions of individuals on the invasion of privacy issue, but there are many other somewhat varied stances on this ethical issue. Now what is the educational evaluator to do with respect to such an issue? It certainly can influence the nature of that evaluator's activities.

Ideally, with such debatable ethical questions, the educational evaluator could consult documents in which the pros and cons of various positions have been examined by individuals well versed in the moral implications of such choices. It is hoped that in the future we will see the appearance of such compilations. But for now, at least, evaluators are pretty much on their own in the ethical arena except for the guidance supplied in the *Evaluation Standards*. The best idea, at least for the present, would be to have the evaluator engage in a fair amount of personal analysis of the moral suitability of various stances, then solicit the reactions of colleagues regarding such issues. By deliberately trying to think through the ethical considerations involved, alone and in consultation, the educational evaluator will probably come up with a more defensible ethical position than would have been adopted under immediate pressures for action.

The Evaluator's Mission

Many of the particular positions that will emerge with respect to ethical issues will stem directly from the evaluator's overall estimation of what it is that constitutes the mission of educational evaluation. To some extent this is reflected in the several evaluation models examined in Chapter Two, but let's consider a slightly contrived fictitious example for illustrative purposes. Suppose we encountered an extreme representative of the decision-facilitation school of evaluation, someone who perceived the evaluator's role to be exclusively one of helping someone else make decisions. If such an evaluator, and there are some of them around, encountered programs or program goals that were (in the evaluator's estimate) immoral, the evaluator would view personal intervention or personal judgments regarding those goals as inconsistent with a decision-facilitation evaluator's role. Such a view of the educational evaluator's basic mission would obviously affect the kinds of ethical decisions to be reached by any evaluator.

Scriven opines that, among other rules, evaluators should consider themselves as "enlightened surrogate consumers."[9] In other words, not only should the educational evaluator be responsible for appraising the worth of particular instructional programs as they affect learners involved, but the evaluator should also be attentive to the ultimate impact of the program on the society at large. Clearly, such a view of the evaluator's mission would influence such choices as those involving the evaluator's responsiveness to a program staff versus responsiveness to the larger society.

For example, if evaluators conceived of their mission as servicing program directors and having no responsibility to the larger public, then they might react indifferently to the program director's suppression of a negative report. As representatives of the public, on the other hand, evaluators might be reluctant to tolerate the director's reluctance to release negative findings.

Unbias the Contingency Structure

The alert evaluator who is interested in avoiding unethical behavior will, at the outset of an evaluation endeavor, try to detect any contingencies that are likely to lead to biased behavior. For instance, if a person who is to evaluate a project is subject to dismissal by the project's director, then it takes considerable courage to come up with a negative evaluation of the project. As some evaluators have wisely observed, it is difficult if not impossible for educational evaluators to retain their popularity and their integrity simultaneously.

Well, if there are any organizational or other arrangements such that it is *in the evaluator's interest* to reach certain conclusions, then those arrangements must be modified (if possible). Objectivity, particularly in the case of summative evaluators, is indispensable. The evaluator must be sure that there are no contingencies, positive or negative, that will reduce that objectivity.

Until such time as educational evaluators adopt a well-considered code of ethics, and one hopes that this time is not too far in the future, the evaluator of educational phenomena will have to be most circumspect in matters that involve ethical considerations. The ultimate benefactors of the evaluator's efforts, namely, learners, are too important for one to engage in fast and loose ethical behavior. When in doubt, evaluators should err in the direction of scrupulously high ethical standards.

Evaluation as a Profession

To what extent is educational evaluation a sufficiently distinctive specialization that it should be regarded as a profession? In a 1985 essay addressing this question, Merwin and Wiener[10] conclude that a bona fide profession of educational evaluation is "at best on the horizon." They argue that the past two decades have seen developments which, in time, may lead to a full-blown evaluation profession, one in which there are formal governmental sanctions to limit the title of educational evaluator only to those persons who have met specified requirements. Merwin and Wiener believe, for instance, that the adoption of the 1981 *Evaluation Standards* by a number of diverse groups augers well for the future of educational evaluation as a profession. They point out, however, that it is not yet clear whether movement toward a profession will follow the more specific focus of *educational* program evaluator or the more general focus of program evaluator.

Stake is far less optimistic about the lasting duration of a profession of educational evaluation. In a personal account,[11] he recalls how his father's 50-year professional life as a registered pharmacist had coincided with the epoch of "the drugstore," now transformed into supermarkets, pharmacies, and ice cream shops. Stake speculates regarding his own professional life as an educational evaluator, wondering whether it too will coincide with a limited epoch of the "educational evaluator." In a thoughtful 1985 analysis, Stake concludes that while it is evident that there will always be a need for analytic problem solving and evaluative judgment, "it is not clear that Education needs specialists who call themselves program evaluators."

The choice before us is apparent. It is certain that decision makers in education will continue to need assistance in making better choices. Is that assistance to be proffered by people who have been specifically and *dominantly* trained in educational evaluation, or should the substance of educational evaluation be mastered by all educators, not just specialists? In other words, should we be striving to infuse a modest degree of evaluative expertise into the preparation programs of all educators rather than attempting to provide a small number of specialists with abundant training? Or should we do both?

As was indicated way back in Chapter One, the technical content needed by evaluators is generally conceded these days to be far less distinctive than was thought in the first blush of evaluation euphoria. We have not created an evaluation armamentarium so peculiar to educational evaluation that it can be said educational evaluators are, by and large, employing their own methodology. On the contrary, the bulk of evaluation methodology has been gleefully spirited away from other disciplines. It remains to be seen whether the resulting amalgam of evaluative techniques is ever regarded as the substance from which an evaluation profession is born.

The Training of Educational Evaluators

The absence of a large body of distinctively evaluative methodology, of course, impinges on the way the training of educational evaluators occurs. A personal reflection may illustrate the point.

In the late 1960s I attempted, with several of my colleagues at UCLA, chiefly Marvin C. Alkin, to organize a doctoral-level preparation program for educational evaluators. We worked out a program consisting of three distinctive courses in evaluation as well as a practicum or two in which would-be educational evaluators were obliged to putter around in the real world under the tutelage of a practicing evaluator. It didn't seem like a bad beginning. I thought that, as time twirled by, we would be adding more courses, or at least beefing up the content of those we had already established, so that a distinctive doctoral preparation program would be created.

As the years passed, however, we added little to our course content that was peculiarly related to educational evaluation. Even the courses that we had originally installed contained, upon closer scrutiny, a solid bundle of borrowed content. Increasingly, I found myself encouraging doctoral advisees to load up on the standard methodological courses such as measurement, statistics, and research design. In recent years I have also counseled them to take additional coursework dealing with the instructional process. The proportion of our doctoral program that is *distinctively* evaluation in nature, however, remains remarkably small.

Frankly, I used to be apologetic for such a state of affairs. After all, one would prefer to be purveying a potent and *special* body of content to graduate students. Yet, I now realize that there isn't all that much content that is distinctively evaluational in nature. The skillful educational evaluator is the person who can adroitly borrow tools and concepts from pertinent specializations, then blend those borrowed elements into a meaningful repertoire that can benefit an educational decision-making community.

One of the joys of educational evaluation is that it is so terribly particularistic. Each new program evaluation assignment brings with it a special set of problems. Each set of decision makers is different. Their priorities, values, and predispositions typically oblige the evaluator to devise a distinctively new game plan for each project. Educational evaluations are puzzles to be solved. The best puzzle solvers, of course, are those who can determine what sorts of solution tactics to employ for what sorts of puzzles. Thus, accomplished educational evaluators will be able to bring analytic, puzzle-solving skills to a given evaluation task so that selections can be made regarding appropriate technical tools, such as data-gathering designs or measuring instruments. The tools selected, of course, must yield information of perceived importance to those involved in the rendering of decisions.

Because of the particularistic nature of educational evaluation, a good many leaders in the field recommend that the formal training include a solid dose of practicum-like assignments whereby evaluators-in-training can observe experienced evaluators in action. Such apprenticeship approaches to evaluator training should be employed, for maximum profit, only after the trainee acquires solid technical skills.

A number of innovative approaches to evaluator training have been proposed in recent years. For example, Caulley and Dowdy have suggested that a meaningful segment of the evaluator's training could be fashioned in a Socratic manner along the lines of legal training, with analyses of evalution cases constituting a prominent preparation vehicle.[12]

Eash has observed that in the preparation of evaluation specialists there should be sufficient requirements dealing with curriculum, policy research, and the *politics of evaluation*.[13] He believes that graduate students in evaluation tend to be enamored of the technical and, in particular, infatuated with the computer. Eash argues that students of evaluation are no different than experienced evaluators in their inclination to run after computer-manipulable numbers instead of staying close to field-based data. Like many other trainers of evaluators, Eash contends that an essential in the training of doctoral students "comes from first-hand engagement with field problems as members of evaluation teams."

Evaluator-Client Relationships

Some educational evaluators will be employed by major educational systems, such as large city or county school districts, state education departments, or agencies of the federal government. Some educational evaluators will, as we have just seen, work for evaluation firms whose services are available on a contractual basis. Some will operate as private consultants. Indeed, the organizational settings in which educational evaluators function are quite diverse.

In most of these settings it is possible to conceive of the evaluator as interacting with a client. Sometimes the client will be identified in that manner, as when a private evaluation consultant or an evaluation firm is hired by a school district administrator. The administrator is clearly the client, typically having entered into a contract to pay the evaluator a certain amount of money to do a specified job. Sometimes the client is a bit tougher to spot. For example, if a school district evaluator is assigned to evaluate formatively a special music enrichment program, then the staff of the new project might be thought of as the evaluator's clients.

Now the reason for splitting out this evaluator-client distinction is that educational evaluators should give more thought to how they should most appropriately relate to their clients. We can illustrate this point with a few examples.

The Internal/External Option

One of the most important decisions to be reached between an evaluator and the client is the location of the evaluator in relationship to the project being evaluated. Will the evaluator function as an *internal* evaluator whose chief responsibilities are to the persons directing the project? Will the evaluator function as an *external* evaluator, answering to decision makers outside the project who, typically, are ultimately responsible for determining whether the project exists or not? To what extent does the evaluator's chief role, that is, formative or summative, interact with the internal/external nature of the assignment? How much autonomy (e.g., the right to release evaluation reports directly without prior approval from a superior) does the evaluator really have?

The evaluator should carefully consider these kinds of questions before agreeing to take on a particular assignment. This is an instance where such trappings as organizational charts are not superfluous. In fact, one of the first things evaluators ought to do, prior to agreeing to work on a particular project, is to verify the organizational relationships within a project's staff and to discern whether the evaluator's status in the administrative mix is tenable. Of course, it sometimes won't be possible to detect the real power structure in an agency or program staff merely from an organizational chart. Sometimes a particularly powerful person's influence is masked by such formal depictions of staff-line responsibilities. Nonetheless, the educational evaluator should make a reasonable effort to determine what the decision-making structure really is within an organization, then see whether the contemplated status of the evaluator within that hierarchy offers a viable position from which to operate.

The Point-of-Entry Problem

Another illustration of the necessity for understanding and clarifying the functional relationship between evaluators and their clients arises in connection with the point at which an evaluator is called upon to evaluate a project. Often, to the evaluator's distress, the call for evaluation assistance is issued belatedly. Sometimes this tardiness merely reflects an understandable oversight on the part of the client. Sometimes a belated call for evaluation stems from the client's wish to secure a bit of evaluation window-dressing for a project in which the decisions have actually been made already.

To decide whether the role they have been proffered is reasonable, evaluators will have to determine exactly what the decision chain is in the project, then identify the last *yet-reversible decision* they might influence. Sometimes this decision point will be much earlier than the client realizes. It is crucial, however, to reach *agreement* between evaluator and client with respect to the earliest decision that is still reversible; then it will be the evaluator's choice as to whether that point is early enough to warrant acceptance of the evaluation assignment. For example, if the choice point involving selection of instructional treatments has already been passed, and the evaluator is aware of markedly superior treatments to those being evaluated, then the assignment might be declined. Or suppose the project goals themselves were designated as irreversible yet the evaluator considered them unacceptable; again, a decision to decline the assignment might be reached.

There is a sense in which the private evaluator is freer to decline an assignment than is a member of an evaluation staff in an educational agency such as a school district. Yet, even here, evaluators can try to sort out the relationships between themselves and their superiors, particularly the degrees of freedom they have in deciding which specific assignments can be avoided.

Skill and Style

The emphasis of this entire book has been on the educational evaluator's acquisition of technical skills, because without mastery of such skills the evaluator is less apt to function successfully. Yet, as anyone who has worked around many evaluators can attest, evaluators who are bristling with technical skills can be dismal failures if they fail to display the basic attributes of sensitive and sensible human beings. The point to be registered is simple, yet significant. If an evaluator's style of interacting with people is discordant, then all the technical wizardry in the world will prove insufficient. An insensitive boor, camouflaged in technical regalia, is still an insensitive boor.

Educational evaluators must realize that their expertise is no substitute for tactful interactions with those around them. Evaluators who walk into an educational setting and expect deferential treatment, merely because they know that a *t* test is not a process used by the Lipton Company, are in for a surprise.

Ideally, a training program for educational evaluators would feature a healthy amount of sensitivity training, tact inducement, and common-sense strengthening. One suspects that these virtues may be difficult to promote, even in an intensive two-day institute. The general point at issue hinges on the attitude of evaluators toward their work. In order to function effectively, they will still be obliged to behave with all the social sensitivities displayed by international diplomats, television heroes, and prospective saints. Technical expertise is a necessary but far from sufficient condition for the educational evaluator's success.

The Human Impact of Educational Evaluation

The number of educational evaluation issues that might be considered in a concluding chapter such as this is almost unlimited. However, in view of the reader's patience, the author's exhaustion, and the prospects of a paper shortage, we shall conclude by considering a final and important issue to be confronted by evaluators of educational phenomena.

Again and again this book has been littered with assertions regarding the evaluator's pivotal role in educational *decisions*. These decisions, of course, will influence the lives of enormous numbers of students. We all recognize that. But let's not forget that there are also many other human beings who are substantially influenced by the actions of the educational evaluator. These nonstudent recipients of the evaluator's impact, though less numerous, are no less important.

Indeed, although we all hope that, as a consequence of the evaluator's intervention, the quality of our educational programs will be enhanced, we realize that even without formal evaluation, those programs would still stumble along somehow. Some of the evaluator's effects on nonstudent folks are less easy to overlook. For instance, if members of a project staff lose their jobs because of a negative evaluation of their efforts, a whole series of paychecks instantly stop. Families of these wage earners are affected significantly. A parent's self-esteem, not to mention the self-esteem of the children of that parent, can be dramatically influenced because of a job dismissal. In fact, for most major decisions in which an educational evaluator takes part, there will be a literal galaxy of nonstudent lives affected.

When one couples the evaluator's potential impact on student well-being with this potential influence on nonstudent lifestyles, the stakes in the educational evaluation game become enormously high. Anyone who enters this specialization with less-than-complete commitment, technical skill, social sensitivity, and awareness of the evaluator's potential impact on humanity should reconsider the appropriateness of a personal career as (1) a tiller of the soil, (2) a hewer of wood, or (3) both of the above.

Discussion Questions

1. Some educational evaluators have quite literally thrown up their hands in disgust at the highly political contexts in which they find themselves working. If you found yourself in similar situations, how would you try to cope with the political realities of the educational setting, yet carry on your work effectively?

2. If you were chairing a committee whose responsibility it was to draft an initial version of a Code of Ethics for Educational Evaluators, what kinds of guidelines do you think your committee would consider?

3. What is your own judgment regarding the likely impact of the 1981 *Evaluation Standards* on the actual practice of educational evaluation? In other words, do you think educational evaluators will be influenced in their day-to-day behaviors by the *Standards*? Why?

4. In contemplating the professional relationship that you, an educational evaluator, might have with one of your clients, what would be the major

points you would consider? How would these considerations be different, if at all, if you were functioning as a private evaluation consultant versus an evaluator in a state education department?

5. How could a beginning educational evaluator best prepare to be effective in the person-to-person realm so impor-

tant to an evaluator's success?

6. Suppose you were asked by a Parent-Teacher Association to present a speech on the following topic: *The Educational Evaluator's Influence.* Where would the main points of your presentation be?

Practice Exercise

As this concluding chapter focused on the raising of issues rather than providing any technical evaluation skills, it would be difficult to present meaningful practice exercises. Yet, for those readers who feel deprived of their customary postchapter merriment, perhaps a comprehensive prac-

tice exercise might be to reread the entire book (good practice for bad readers), then summarize it aloud for a friend or enemy. depending upon your own evaluation of the volume. You are, by now, supposed to be rather good at that sort of thing.

Notes

1. American Psychological Association, *Standards for Educational and Psychological Tests* (rev. ed.) (Washington, DC: APA, 1974).

2. Joint Committee on Standards for Educational Evaluation, *Standards for Evaluation of Educational Programs, Projects, and Materials* (New York: McGraw-Hill, 1981).

3. With permission of the publisher, McGraw-Hill.

4. For example, D. Williams, "Naturalistic Evaluation: Potential Conflicts Between Evaluation Standards and Criteria for Conducting Naturalistic Inquiry," *Educational Evaluation and Policy Analysis,* 8:1 (1986), 87–99; and H. F. Wolcott, "Mirrors, Models, and Monitors: Educator Adaptations of the Ethnographic Innovation," in G. Spinella (Ed.), *Doing the Ethnography of Schooling: Educational Anthropology in Action* (New York: Holt, Rinehart and Winston, 1982).

5. Williams, "Naturalistic Evaluation."

6. American Psychological Associa-

tion, *Standards for Educational and Psychological Testing* (Washington, DC: APA, 1985).

7. Daniel L. Stufflebeam, "Professional Standards and Ethics for Evaluators," in *Evaluation and Education: At Quarter Century,* ed. M. W. McLaughlin and D. C. Phillips (Chicago: University of Chicago Press, 1991), pp. 249–82.

8. Ralph W. Tyler, "General Statement on Program Evaluation," in *Evaluation and Education: At Quarter Century,* ed. M. W. McLaughlin and D. C. Phillips (Chicago: University of Chicago Press, 1991), pp. 3–17.

9. Michael Scriven, *Evaluator Skills,* American Educational Research Association Training Tape, Washington, DC.

10. J. C. Merwin and Paul H. Wiener, "Evaluation: A Profession?" *Educational Evaluation and Policy Analysis,* 7:3 (1985), 253–59.

11. R. E. Stake, "A Personal Interpretation," *Educational Evaluation and Policy Analysis,* 7:3 (1985), 243, 244.

12. D. N. Caulley and I. Dowdy, "Legal Education as a Model for the Education of Evaluators," *Educational Evaluation and Policy Analysis*, 8:1 (1986), 63–75.

13. M. J. Eash, "A Reformulation of the Role of the Evaluator," *Educational Evaluation and Policy Analysis*, 7:3 (1985), 249–52.

Selected References

Alkin, Marvin C., and Associates. *A Guide for Evaluation Decision Makers*. Beverly Hills, CA: Sage, 1985.

Alkin, Marvin C. *Debates on Evaluation*. Newbury Park, CA: Sage, 1990.

American Psychological Association. *Ethical Principles in the Conduct of Research with Human Subjects*. Washington, DC: American Psychological Association, 1973.

———. *Standards for Educational and Psychological Testing*. Washington, DC: American Psychological Association, 1985.

Berk, Richard A., and Peter H. Rossi. *Thinking About Program Evaluation*. Newbury Park, CA: Sage, 1990.

Caulley, D. N., and I. Dowdy, "Legal Education as a Model for the Education of Evaluators." *Educational Evaluation and Policy Analysis*, 8:1 (1986): 63–75.

Cousins, J. B. and Leithwood, K. A. "Current Empirical Research on Evaluation Utilization." *Review of Educational Research*, 56 (1986): 331–64.

ERS Standards Committee. "Evaluation Research Society Standards for Program Evaluation." *New Directions for Program Evaluation*, 15 (1982): 7–20.

Forst, Martin; Melinda Moore; and Michael Jang. "Issues in the Evaluation of AIDS Education Programs: The Case of California," *Evaluation and the Health Professions*, 13 (1990): 147–67.

House, Ernest R. "Evaluation and Social Justice: Where Are We?" In M. W. McLaughlin and D. C. Phillips (Eds.), *Evaluation and Education: At Quarter Century*. Chicago: University of Chicago Press, 1991, pp. 233–47.

Merwin, J. C., and Paul H. Wiener. "Evaluation: A Profession?" *Educational Evaluation and Policy Analysis*, 7:3 (1985): 253–59.

Rossi, Peter H., and Howard E. Freeman. "The Social Context of Evaluation." *Evaluation: A Systematic Approach* (4th ed.). Newbury Park, CA: Sage, 1989, pp. 417–68.

Scheerens, J. "A Systems Approach to the Analysis and Management of Large-Scale Evaluations." *Studies in Educational Evaluation*, 11:1 (1985): 83–93.

Stake, R. E. "A Personal Interpretation." *Educational Evaluation and Policy Analysis*, 7:3 (1985): 243, 244.

Thurston, Paul W., John C. Ory, Paul W. Mayberry, and Larry A. Braskamp. "Legal and Professional Standards in Program Evaluation." *Educational Evaluation and Policy Analysis*, 6:1 (Spring 1984): 15–26.

Turpin, Robin S., and James M. Sinacore (Eds.). *Multisite Evaluations*. San Francisco: Jossey-Bass, 1991.

Weiss, C. H. (Ed.). *Using Social Research in Public Policy Making*. Lexington, MA: Lexington Books, 1977.

Worthen, Blaine R., and James R. Sanders. "Dealing with Political, Ethical, and Interpersonal Aspects of Evaluation." *Educational Evaluation: Alternative Approaches and Guidelines*. White Plains, NY: Longman, 1987, pp. 281–97.

Worthen, Blaine R., and James R. Sanders.

"Evaluating Evaluations." *Educational Evaluation: Alternative Approaches and Guidelines*. White Plains, NY: Longman, 1987, 369–401.

Index